The Teacher, the School and

the Task of Management

By the same author

THE ACTIVE TEACHER
THE ENVIRONMENT OF LEARNING
GROUP STUDY FOR TEACHERS

The Teacher, the School and the Task of Management

by

ELIZABETH RICHARDSON

Reader in Education, University of Bristol

HEINEMANN

LONDON

Heinemann Educational Books Ltd
LONDON EDINBURGH MELBOURNE AUCKLAND TORONTO
HONG KONG SINGAPORE KUALA LUMPUR
IBADAN NAIROBI JOHANNESBURG
LUSAKA NEW DELHI

ISBN 0 435 80755 2

Published by
Heinemann Educational Books Ltd
48 Charles Street, London W1X 8AH
Printed in Great Britain by
Morrison & Gibb Ltd, London and Edinburgh

Contents

v

List of Figures

ACKNOWLEDGEMENTS

I am indebted to many people for help and support in the work that led to the writing of this book and in the task of revising the manuscript for publication.

I am grateful to the Schools Council for a grant of £3,675 to cover the costs of the project, to Education Services for a supplementary grant of £500 which covered additional costs entailed during the final stages as it extended into the autumn term of the fourth year, and to the Bristol University School of Education for releasing me from almost all teaching commitments so that I could put more and more time into the developing relationship with the school in which the project was carried out.

The nature of this relationship is in itself part of what the book is about. Here I wish only to acknowledge my own personal gratitude to the many members of the Nailsea School staff who have contributed to its writing, both directly and indirectly, through the help they gave me in clarifying my arguments and in shaping and reshaping the plan of the book. I have been particularly indebted to the headmaster, Mr D. W. John, who spent many hours with me discussing the problems of presenting this material to teachers and administrators who would not have shared the experiences on which it was based. He was incredibly generous with his time, from the first exploratory meeting in March 1968 (before either of us was committed to anything) to the winter of 1971 when my work on the final revision of the manuscript was nearing completion. The influence of his critical judgement has been invaluable to me in carrying out this task. The five members of his standing committee, namely Mrs J. A. Bradbury, Mr M. W. Burnham, Mr J. A. Harbinson, Mr W. R. Thomas and Mr C. Vanloo, both individually and in committee with Mr John, also gave me valuable constructive criticism when the manuscript was still in draft form and never grudged their time and their energy when I needed to discuss sections of the book with them, no matter how hard pressed they were with the immediate tasks of managing the affairs of the school.

The fact that agreement was reached at an early stage of the work that the school would be named in anything I might eventually publish about it, and the fact that the staff themselves urged me, in the final stages of preparing the manuscript, to refer to persons also by name, are indications of the support I have been given in the task of dissemination. I have been fortunate to work with a headmaster who was prepared to risk this kind of exposure and a group of staff members who were prepared personally to share this exposure alongside him, and who, when it came to the crunch, rejected any kind of retreat into code initials, which they themselves had found a barrier to their understanding in reading the draft, or into fictitious names, which might have reduced the real experience to the semblance of a charade. As one member of the staff put it: 'Once the school is named, we are all named.' I should like to record here also my gratitude to the governors of the school who, having decided to authorize me to embark on the project, took a responsible part in reading and discussing with me the two early unpublished drafts, thus supporting me in the final work of revision. In particular, I should like to thank the chairman of the governors, Prebendary A. S. Cran, with whom I had valuable discussions about the manuscript and about the project itself on two occasions.

Mr W. Sheridan, as my project officer during his period of service in the Schools Council, was the first person outside Nailsea School to whom I talked about the specific problems I was facing in the project itself. I should like to express my gratitude to him for managing, both personally in relation to me and on behalf of the Schools Council, to give me the support I needed without urging me to publicize prematurely the nature of the experiences within the school. The necessity to maintain confidentiality during the first two years of the project was indeed one of the strains involved, and I have been grateful to successive Joint Secretaries of the Schools Council, in particular Mr G. K. Caston and Mr G. A. Rogers, for freeing me to pursue the task in my own way without pressure to give progress reports that I was not ready to give.

In the later stages of the work, when it became possible to release copies of the earlier drafts to people outside Nailsea School, I received helpful comments from Mr J. B. Annand, Mr P. Fordham, Professor A. V. Judges, Dr E. J. Miller, Professor B. S. Morris, Mr J. G. Owen, Mr G. A. Rogers, Mr W. Sheridan, Dr T. R. Sizer and Professor R. C. Wilson.

Finally, I wish to record my deep indebtedness to Dr P. M. Turquet and the late Dr A. K. Rice who, during the eight years that led up to the school-based project described in these pages, taught me so much about the problems of studying inter-personal and inter-group problems in conference and institutional settings. Although Dr Rice never saw a line of this book or of the earlier drafts that preceded it, the inspiration of his leadership in this field of study was immeasurably important to me, both at the time when I was embarking on the project, when his personal encouragement strengthened me to undertake it, and during every phase of the work that developed from it. I can only continue to lament that he did not live long enough to give me the benefit of his critical comments on the manuscript.

In acknowledging all the sources upon which I have drawn, I must nevertheless accept responsibility for what I have written. If the actual publication of the book raises doubts about the wisdom of revealing the identity of the school and of the persons who are mentioned in it, I am answerable for the decision I have made to do this. My reason for taking this risk is that anonymity could at best have been only partial. Having rejected the apparent protection of anonymity, the school staff and I could not escape from the necessity to work through successive drafts of the material. I did not find, in the process of doing this, that I ever had to compromise with anything important that I wanted to say; but I did have to check my fantasies against the known facts, and I did have to ensure that my arguments were comprehensible to any persons or groups involved in the descriptive material. In the process my own thoughts often became clearer. The staff have worked with me to ensure that any facts I have recorded are as accurate as possible; I in my turn have tried to make clear the distinction between statements about verifiable facts and statements about my perception of a situation or about someone else's perception of a situation.

I cannot close this preface without acknowledging gratefully the patience, understanding and skill with which two successive secretaries have worked with me, the first, Mrs Yvonne Odjidja, during the first two years of the project, when the typing and editing of the raw material had to be kept going alongside the laborious preparation of the early drafts, and the second, Mrs Rosemary Ashley, who took over from her in the very early stages of the preparation of this book.

J. E. R.

June 1973

Prologue

The title of this book implies an ambiguity. Is it to be a book about schools in general, or a portrait of one particular school? If it is the former, we run the risk of falling into a swamp of generalizations, which will offer teachers little in the way of recognizable human experience to stir the imagination; if the latter, we run the risk of intrusion into a private world, inhabited by a relatively small number of teachers, who have been building up within their own institution an increasingly sophisticated pattern of working relationships during this time of transition and uncertainty. Ironically, the safe, generalized account might be accepted by other teachers as relevant to their concerns, while leaving them untouched in their feelings and therefore unlikely to be stirred to the point of wishing to change any of their assumptions. Equally ironically, a more provocative, personalized account of actual situations might arouse more interest, yet be easily dismissed by teachers as an idio-syncratic description of one isolated school with which they could be expected to feel no real kinship. The essential problem has been to find a way of moving back and forth between the particular and the general so that each illuminates the other. Thus the episodes and sequences of events take their place both as illustrative material for use in clarifying concepts and as evidence upon which attempts to form new concepts must be based.

When we look at problems in a generalized way we can do so, on the whole, without much emotional investment and therefore without much real dis-comfort or, for that matter, much real exhilaration. When we look at specific problems with which we are personally involved in our daily lives the situation is very different: our feelings as well as our thoughts come into play, whether or not we are prepared to admit that this is so. Alistair Cooke once expressed this essential difference between knowing about something and really experiencing it in a broadcast that has remained vivid for me over the years. He described what it felt like to move rapidly from one part of the United States to another, experiencing extremes of temperature and extraordinary variations of scenery and terrain, yet finding everywhere the same recognizably American culture; and then he added: 'All this you know in your head; but it's nothing until you've lived it!'

When, in the autumn of 1968, I embarked on this project with the head-master and staff of Nailsea School, they and I knew that we would be exploring problems of change and innovation—problems that would be recognizable to teachers in other schools; for here was a school coping with rapid expansion, not only in its numbers but also in the range of ability in its pupils and in the range of skills and interests in its staff, and a staff group already well accustomed to processes of consultation, struggling to find ways of keeping channels of communication open, in the face of a growing complexity in its structure and organization. We knew also that the staff would have to allow me, the visitor, to see a good deal of what was going on inside the staff group if we were to gain any deeper understanding of the kind of history this particular school was making. We were aware that this had to be a joint task and would in the first stages, at least by me, be regarded as private, but also that if the undertaking came to be felt as an experience worth communicating to teachers elsewhere it would eventually have to be reported in some kind of written form acceptable both to them and to me.

All this we knew 'in our heads'. But as we 'lived' it, in our feelings as well as in our heads, we were assailed by difficulties of communication and understanding that often cast doubts on the validity of what we were doing. Nevertheless the work has persisted for three years and is still going on as this book is being completed for publication.

We are concerned, then, with a school seen through the eyes of someone who worked with its staff for three years yet remained technically a visitor throughout that period, a visitor who never observed a lesson, scarcely ever spoke with any of the pupils and never directly encountered any of the parents as parents. The particular phase of the school's history that is recorded here responds to many overtones from the school's own recorded past and hints about its unrecorded future—a future that will have become the present by the time this sentence is printed. Indeed the story—taken simply as a story about a school—was already out of date by the time the last chapter was being written. But the story can also be taken as a kind of allegory, since the enthusiasms and frustrations, the bonds and tensions, the discoveries and uncertainties experienced by the teachers in this particular school may be recognizable to many of those who teach in other schools in the changing educational scene of the 1970s.

The purpose of this prologue is to define in advance what the general pattern of the book is to be, and to warn the reader that he will be required to move backwards and forwards on the time scale as separate strands of the argument are taken up in different chapters. A straightforward narrative might have been easier to read; but it would have ignored the central problem that faces any working group that is simultaneously expanding in size, re-defining its overall task and becoming differentiated in relation to its sub-tasks—the problem of what we really mean by 'management' in the context of schooling. What kind of map can I provide at this stage to prepare the reader for the journey he will take?

The book is divided into two main parts. Part One, entitled 'Theme and Research Method', provides three interconnected frameworks within which the much longer Part Two can be studied. The first of the three frameworks serves to place the work in its broader educational setting by drawing attention to some of the crucial problems with which teachers are faced in the changing secondary schools of today. The second offers a set of conceptual tools with which such problems can be studied and perhaps better understood in terms of the experiences teachers actually have as they work, sometimes in isolation, sometimes in quite intimate small groups, sometimes in dauntingly large groups where the individual can feel and seem depersonalized. The third framework provides information about the specific school in which the study was carried out and about the role I myself assumed in the school in order to use and test the conceptual ideas described in Chapter II and in order to explore the educational problems described in Chapter I. The content of the first chapter then is recognizably educational; the second draws upon the broader field of the social sciences; the third may be regarded as verging on the clinical. Or, to compare these three preliminary chapters in another way, the first outlines the problems that give rise to the research, the second describes the theoretical background against which the research was carried out and the third sketches in what the reader needs to know about the particular situation that was studied.

The structure of the second main part of the book is more difficult to describe. Here we are concerned with the particular experiences of Nailsea as a school in its own right, a school with a strong identity, manned by a staff with which I became intimately involved as consultant. Yet, as has already been indicated, a straight narrative of events would have been inadequate for the purposes of this book, even if such a narrative could have been condensed into 300 pages. Each chapter therefore contains *pieces* of narrative, glimpses into the life of the Nailsea staffroom and into the conferences which took place in the headmaster's room and in other parts of the school. But because each chapter takes up a particular strand of the general argument on which the book is based, the reader has to move backwards and forwards in time, sometimes penetrating more deeply into the life of this particular school, sometimes being drawn outwards again so that these glimpses into the life of one institution can illuminate the general problems being experienced in many others.

Part Two, with its overall title 'Secondary School in Transition', may be held more easily together in the mind if it is perceived as a kind of three-phase operation. In the first phase, covered in Chapters IV and V, the reader is asked to examine the inevitable duality of the teacher's role, and the consequent splitting apart, both in the teacher himself and in the institution in which he serves, of the two sides of his educational commitment: his concern for children and young people as persons (often described as 'pastoral care') and his concern for the development of his subject and for the understanding of its place in the general pattern of the school's work (often described as 'curricular responsibility'). The questions that emerge from these two chapters bring into focus the central problems of this book. How can teachers—whether young or old, whether new to the job or experienced in it—be helped towards a deeper understanding of the relationship between leadership and consultation so that the feelings arising both from sympathetic partnership and from sharp opposition can be used responsibly in relation to the task upon which all are engaged? How can staff together ensure that the fights are, as Dr A. K. Rice used to say, 'between the right people and about the right things', so that the conflicts as well as the mutual supports can be open and therefore potentially creative rather than secret and therefore potentially erosive?

It is these problems that are explored in the middle and longest section of Part Two, in Chapters VI, VII, VIII, IX and X. Here even more than in Chapters IV and V, the reader will be brought into contact with so much of the traditionally 'private life' of a staff group that he may find himself almost embarrassed to be reading about it in print. Yet the struggle which the headmaster and his colleagues in this particular school lived through, in coping with successive systems of consultation within the staff group as described in these pages, was itself so much a part of the learning process that it has to be at least partially shared with readers from other institutions if they are to study in any genuinely critical way the generalizations that accompany the narrative. The earlier experiences of the *ad hoc* study groups and representative committees, the emergence of a standing committee or top-management group, the gradual clarification of the responsibilities of those in middle-management roles and the effects of all these changes on role relationships in the staff group as a whole, form the groundwork of these five chapters. Woven through all of them are the various strands of 'headship', both in terms of the particular man who is head of this particular school and in terms of the role that he takes along with headmasters and head-mistresses throughout the country.

In the final section of Part Two the reader is asked to consider the potentialities of a staff group as a kind of in-service college of education. The role of the headmaster as an educator in relation to his staff group and the importance of this side of his management task is now brought more sharply into focus. In the course of the eleventh and twelfth chapters making up this final phase, the internal affairs of the staff group are seen as, after all, inseparable from the problems of handling relationships with pupils, with students in training (and those who supervise them), with parents and with governors. For the struggle to understand the nature of the head's authority is itself the precursor to a deeper understanding, for every individual teacher, of the nature of his own authority, not only in his classroom, whether as tutor or as subject teacher, but also in his contacts with the parents on whose behalf he must act, and in his contacts with the school governors who may find themselves having to speak for him in the outside world.

It is significant that as I write this prologue members of the Nailsea staff are considering how they should, in the coming months, work with parents to prepare them for the appearance in print of episodes from the hitherto private inner world of the professional group responsible for the education of their children. It is important that all those who read this book, whether intimately connected with the school or not, whether members of the teaching profession or not, should perceive the events recorded in it as part of a continuous process, a process that will have gone on for at least another whole academic year by the time it reaches publication. For the book is not just about expansion and change. It is primarily about growth and development in face of expansion and change.

PART ONE

Theme and Research Method

Current Problems in Secondary Schools

Public expectations and private hopes and fears

In this opening chapter I draw attention to some of the issues that need urgently to be examined in educational circles both inside and outside the schools. We have to recognize that the present conflicts about the purposes of secondary schooling are deep and bitter. They are deep because they must ultimately be resolved within the individual himself, whether he be a pupil, a teacher, a school governor, a parent, an employer or an apparently disinterested child or adult living in the vicinity of this or that school. They are bitter because persons and groups and even at times whole institutions find themselves called upon to make a stand on one or other side of an argument, thus being forced into extreme views for or against a proposal or trend, when the real problem is to try to understand why such polarized attitudes appear so inevitable.

It is important, however, not to lose sight of the other side of the picture. There are many people whose hopes for an improved system of education are high. There is evidence of creative thinking in the schools, some of it as yet unformulated, some of it already making its impact on the practices of teachers. And whereas in the earlier part of this century such new thinking was to be found mainly in the privately endowed 'progressive' schools, we look for it now as much, if not more, in the maintained schools that serve all sectors of the population.

The conflicts are by no means simply conflicts between generations; nor are the bolder experimental ventures being risked only by the younger members of the teaching profession. The schools of today, and the secondary schools in particular, are the target, on the one hand, of new hopes for children who, under the tripartite system were labelled far too early in their lives as 'good or bad academic material' and therefore supposedly as responsive or unresponsive to educational opportunities. On the other hand schools are targets for powerful hostility, both from that section of the consumer group that regards them as too 'permissive', 'lax' and 'undisciplined', and from that section that regards them as lamentably out of touch with the real needs of children, as 'repressive', even at times Dickensian and as hostile to the real purposes of education. The press in its various forms, both through the printed word and through visual and auditory signals emitted daily on TV channels in nearly every home in Britain, is not slow to capitalize on foolish and destructive actions by certain heads of schools and by some of those who administer the schools. It is much more difficult for the general public to become aware of the constructive things that teachers are trying to do, chiefly because the more positive information, including usefully provocative dialogues between those who are, as purveyors and as consumers, concerned in it, tend to go out mainly through 'educational broadcasts' or newspaper 'articles', whereas the outrageous things that some teachers appear to do to the young, or that some heads, governing bodies and local authorities appear to do to teachers, tend to go out, through television channels and newspapers, as 'news'.

Variations in pattern of primary and secondary education

As if it were not enough to be caught between two contrary streams of opinion about how the adult world should be educating its young people, teachers are in a constant state of uncertainty about the very structure within which they work. Riddles abound. At what point does a 'comprehensive' school become truly comprehensive? How do teachers from hitherto separated grammar and secondary modern schools cope with the task of amalgamation, particularly if the new combined school is still to be housed in the old buildings? If a school has grown up in relatively purpose-built premises, what happens when the assumptions upon which the design of its buildings was based no longer seem to be the right assumptions on which to base the sub-groupings within the developing institution? How will an established secondary school catering for the whole of the eleven-to-eighteen age range fare if the Plowden Committee's recommendations about the age of transfer from primary to secondary school are implemented in its area? Is the continued embodiment of the old 'sixth form' in the secondary school still appropriate in this latter part of the twentieth century when young people are developing physically so much earlier, even though the process of emotional maturing is being prolonged (and sometimes retarded) by the very means we set up to facilitate it? How can the hitherto more traditionally run schools adapt their policies to take account of the fact that a growing number of their pupils over the age of sixteen are being attracted towards the idea of continuing their education in some kind of junior college where they may hope to be treated more like the young adults they feel themselves to be?

Although these questions are familiar the answers to them are far from simple. And it may be that before we seek the answers we should be exploring the questions themselves more deeply. Perhaps also we need to be less fearful of acknowledging that change in one part of the school's work is bound to cause stresses and anxieties not only in that area but in the institution as a whole. Much of this stress, as we shall see, has to do with uncertainty about the boundaries that mark off areas of responsibility within the school, and therefore with difficulties over the exercise of authority by people in leadership roles, from the most junior tutor in the staff group to the headmaster himself. Much of it has to do with uncertainties about how the school relates itself to the local or regional environment which it serves, and to the national pattern as this changes and develops.

Behind the various systems of organization that exist in different schools, there is one inevitable chain of events—the sequence of a pupil's growth from the day when he enters the school as a child or young adolescent to the day when he leaves it for an adult world, where work, love and the founding of a family are the all-important issues. Society, by fixing the (pre-1973) school leaving age at fifteen and fixing the age at which GCE O-levels or CSE papers are normally taken as sixteen, has built into the secondary-school system an ambiguity about where the main breaks in the process ought to be. In the larger schools it is common to regard the first year or the first two years as a kind of transition period—a 'lower school' in which the youngest pupils may begin to accustom themselves to the change from the primary-school culture in which one teacher covers a broad area of the child's work, to the multiplicity of teacher contacts that is characteristic of the day's work for a secondary-school child. Thus the first major break within the secondary school itself is likely to be the move from a lower division into a middle or upper division. Traditionally the 'sixth form' has been perceived as the privileged 'top' of the grammar school into which, formerly, were admitted only those pupils who had successfully surmounted the fifth-year examination hurdles and were committed to some form of 'higher' education. Because of the survival of this notion the end of the fifth year has marked in the past and still marks in the present a second major break in the progress of pupils through the system.

Now the lower school is particularly concerned with helping the youngest pupils (and their parents) to cope with the problems of joining a new institution, whereas the upper school or sixth form is particularly concerned with helping the oldest pupils to cope with the problem of ending childhood and of leaving an institution which, for six, seven or eight years, has been a very important part of that childhood. I believe that the need to keep these two phases separated from each other by creating a kind of no-man's-land in the middle works against an equally powerful need to maintain some sense of an organic unity for the school as a whole and particularly, perhaps, for its teachers, who both want and fear a breakdown into smaller working groups. The result of this tension between two opposing needs may be an organizational structure that looks more logical and coherent than it really is—a system that has more to do with the separation out of the two ends, perhaps, than with the natural transition points within it.

In a school that takes in the whole of the eleven-to-eighteen age range, the lower school can become identified with the attractiveness of small pupils, whose boisterousness can be perceived as lively and co-operative rather than threatening to the maintenance of order; correspondingly the upper school, if it still has the aura of the traditional grammar school clinging to it, can be identified with the scholarliness—or at least with the expected scholarliness—of near adult students, on whose successes the good name of the school will partly depend. Meanwhile the middle section of the age range, whether or not it is regarded as contained in a separately bounded middle school, can imperceptibly become a kind of repository for behaviour problems and learning difficulties. And because it is during this phase of his progress through the school that a pupil has to make decisions (or accept decisions made for him) about choice of courses leading, perhaps, to the choice of a career, the middle school tends to become the focus also for problems about assessment.

Increasingly the task of devising valid ways of communicating information about a child's progress—to the child himself, to his parents, to members of staff who will teach him in subsequent years, to any school to which he may have to be transferred, to his future employers—all this becomes somehow confused with the problem of coping with the negative aspects of his behaviour. And so the process of assessment, which should be closely related to the process of defining and redefining educational objectives, becomes separated off from the more creative aspects of the teaching role. Because assessment is essentially concerned with the measurement of what pupils achieve, it is by implication concerned also with what their teachers achieve. If teachers are unwilling to interpret such 'results' in terms of their own task as well as in terms of the tasks of pupils, the process of assessment may become a block to progressive thinking rather than a spur to it. It is the meaning of such results rather than the mere facts about them that can be the real stimulus to educational growth within the system.

Uncertainties about roles, competences and vested interests of teachers

Much of the concern about assessment and about the communication of 'results' to parents is related to anxieties about streaming, banding and setting and—where selection has been abandoned—about the difficulties of teaching mixed-ability groups.

It has to be acknowledged that teachers who have been accustomed to classes that have, by whatever dubious routes, become identified as A, B or C streams, have to learn to modify both their materials and their techniques in quite a fundamental way when their pupils are no longer so grouped. Indeed those who approach the task of implementing this kind of change in an unthinking state of euphoria are just as misguided as those who approach it in a spirit of cynical defeatism. The trend away from premature labelling of children will do nothing for their education if it is not accompanied by radical rethinking about the whole nature of the curriculum. It is the uneasy awareness of the need for such rethinking that is making teachers justifiably anxious. For rethinking often demands the relinquishing of once easily held assumptions and the abandonment of vested interests.

At the same time it is easy for teachers to underestimate the value—as they face these challenges—of the experience they have already had, inevitably, in handling discrepancies between levels of understanding in a particular field of knowledge or skill. Which of us has ever taught a class in which all the students showed equal mastery of the ideas we were trying to explore with them? It may seem bizarre to suggest that there is really no such thing as a group in which abilities are not, to some extent, mixed. Yet this is so even at university level. Whatever we take to be the general level of ability in a teaching group, it is to that restricted band of ability that we will, as we imagine, be directing our demands. But because, unwittingly, we are aiming our thoughts at a very restricted section *within* that ability band, our very demands will produce a spread of 'ability' that will probably be wider than the 'ability band' we thought we perceived when we began. In other words there is no teacher, however new to the profession, who has no experience of being—as a child or as a student—a member of a mixed-ability group; and there is no experienced teacher who does not know in some measure, what it means to teach such a group.

I recall a student who, some years ago, accepted a teaching post in a school where mixed-ability groups were about to be introduced. He asked me, with a worried concern, whether I had had any experience of teaching such classes. My reply—as I searched my memory—was that I supposed I must have been teaching such groups just before the war but that I had never thought of them at that time as 'mixed-ability groups'. He seemed startled by this answer and commented that teachers perhaps exaggerated the difficulties of this supposedly new situation, even that they perhaps affected the way children could function by prematurely labelling groups as 'bright', 'average', 'dull' or 'mixed'.

Much of this anxiety has to do with the tension between interest in working with a subject—the reason many young people give for taking up teaching in the first place—and interest in working with children which often develops later. Secondary-school teachers, to a far greater extent than their colleagues in primary schools, come into the system with a strong vested interest in a subject, and therefore with some expectation that they will be competent in teaching certain kinds of course and with some wish to commit themselves to the work of identifiable subject departments. But what happens to the boundaries of the old familiar subjects when new 'integrated' courses begin to creep into the curriculum? How does a young teacher whose education course has prepared him to teach general subjects rather than one special subject cope with the uncertainty of not really belonging to any one department if the school he joins is still organized as though its staff were distributed between special subject departments? Conversely, how does the teacher who has devoted years to the building up of such a department handle the inevitable feeling of being suddenly undervalued when his subject is withdrawn from the curriculum as far as certain groups of children (perhaps whole year groups) are concerned, to be replaced by a new course with some such title as 'Discovery' or 'Humanities' or 'Man and Society'? What, after all, *is* a department once such changes come into a school's curriculum?

All these interrelated questions about the consequences of unstreaming, of thinning out the boundaries between subjects and of making new demands on teachers with very different backgrounds of training and experience, stem from the slow but insistent trend towards bigger schools with a bigger range of abilities and interests in the pupil intake. But this trend is still being strongly resisted in some areas of the country; small grammar schools still exist, along with small secondary modern schools. And so, for those who experience change as a disturbing upheaval of known values and standards, there is an awareness of a survival of havens elsewhere to which the hard-pressed teacher may be able to retreat if the change becomes intolerable. Conversely, those who find the experience of change, despite the anxieties it promotes, to be stimulating and conducive to the development of new skills, may be looking, not for havens of retreat, but for schools that will offer new challenges. For the richness and complexity of the secondary scene has within it new kinds of opportunity for teachers to emerge from the narrow confines of a single school subject and to take on responsibilities in sections of large schools—responsibilities that would not have been available in the smaller schools they have superseded.

Yet the old differentiation between the selective and non-selective secondary schools dies hard; and so feelings between 'ex-grammar-school' and 'ex-secondary-modern-school' teachers, though dormant most of the time, can sometimes break out in unexpected ways, often through the words or attitudes or actions of older members of staff who, because of the roles they have in the comprehensive schools of the 1970s, are also perceived as legacies from the formerly separated schools of the 1940s or the early 1950s. The role of 'senior mistress', often still described as 'second mistress', even when the incumbent of the role is the most senior woman teacher on the staff of a mixed school, carries overtones from the girls' grammar school, where the most senior woman below the headmistress could more appropriately be named 'second mistress'. The head of a remedial or E.S.N. department can as readily be perceived as someone who, but for the reorganization of secondary schools, might still have been teaching in a secondary modern school, and might not have had access professionally to children of high ability or to colleagues who, in the old system, would have been teaching in grammar schools. How easily do the younger members of a comprehensive-school staff assume, or at least suspect, that their ex-grammar-school colleagues, while capable of meeting the needs of the ablest pupils, will show little expertise in handling the least able or even those of merely average ability? How easily do they assume that their ex-secondary-modern-school colleagues, while showing more skill in the latter field, may be inadequate in the former? To what extent, indeed, do the experienced staff from the two fields secretly deplore one another's incapacity? How far are such mutual suspicions still being brought into the schools by new entrants to the profession coming, as they do, from university departments on the one side and from colleges of education on the other?

Concern over sex, drug-taking, violence and intimidation among young people

Fears about inadequacy are increasingly being experienced also in the whole complex area of behaviour, secret and overt, of young people towards one another. Teachers are facing, simultaneously, the problems of handling the full range of mental ability in the same institution, often with an outdated and inappropriate curriculum, and of responding to young people whose value system, regardless of their academic abilities or even of their social-class background, appears to be quite alien to that of their parents. We hear more and more about the gap between the generations. We are less and less sure what we mean by pornography, or at what point 'supporting the young' becomes 'corrupting the young'. Sex and violence are not in themselves new phenomena in the schools. What is perhaps new is that much of what used to be furtive is now open and apparently guilt-free, with the result that the adult world can no longer take refuge in ignorance or delude itself that it is guiltless. Teachers, perhaps more than any other section of society, find themselves under great pressure either to come out on the side of the over-protective or punitive approach to the young, or on the side of non-critical identification with the young, particularly in their dealings with non-conforming or delinquent pupils.

The alarming increase of drug taking has added a new dimension to these fears. For young people are now at risk, not only from openly hostile members of their own generation but also from other young people who profess to be offering them help. It is becoming more and more difficult to disentangle the idealism of the hippies from the ruthlessness of the drug pedlars, or to determine who precisely are to be the victims of the skinheads or Hell's angels.

The escalation of these problems has given rise to a new 'subject' on the school time-table and to a new role in the staff group. Attempts to introduce regular discussion groups under the heading, 'Personal Relationships' or 'Human Relationships' have been quite widespread, sometimes developed within whole counties rather than within individual schools only. And, at the same time, the introduction of a school counsellor into the staff group has been hailed as a way of providing, for at least one teacher, the time and leisure needed to work with individual pupils known to be facing emotional difficulties or to be in trouble with the authorities in home, school and neighbourhood. These moves towards, if not actually into, the field of psychotherapy are fraught with difficulties. For they can, in unexpected ways, threaten the existing organization instead of supporting and strengthening it as they are intended to do. 'P.R.' or 'H.R.' can be seen as interfering both with tutorial work and with much that specialists in English, drama and religious education see as their contribution to the curriculum. The school counsellor, whether supported by 'P.R.' or 'H.R.' work or not, may become a kind of walking example in the school of everybody's hopes and anxieties about handling disturbed or delinquent children, just as the much more familiar remedial teacher can become a symbol for everybody's hopes and anxieties about handling children who seem unable to cope with school work.

Crisis of authority and the generation gap

While the conditions of teaching are becoming more and more demanding, young people themselves are finding a new corporate voice through which to air their complaints. 'Student Power' is no longer a phenomenon exclusive to the universities; it is now appearing in sixth forms. Before long schoolboys and schoolgirls may have their own kind of trade union. Meanwhile they grow more vociferous and teachers turn a deaf ear at their peril.

Workers' power; student power; black power; and now—sixth form power. What kind of response can teachers make to this new challenge so as to turn what could be a destructive confrontation into a mutually enriching dialogue between the generations? This mounting crisis of authority leaves many teachers uneasily wondering at what point 'liberalism' turns into 'abdication' and sympathy with rebellious adolescents into indifference to their real needs. Conversely of course, there is the problem of recognizing the point where the right kind of authority is turning imperceptibly into tyranny. How can the sixth-form manifesto be used to advantage in the schools so that the forces of healthy rebellion can be yoked to the forces of mature dependence, thus promoting real growth on both sides of the divide? How can teachers guard against the polarization of opinions within the staff group—a polarization that will inevitably force some to over-identify with the young and others to express only hostility to the young and will therefore be destructive of any concerted effort on the part of adults to bridge the gap between the generations?

Ironically, this mobilization of senior pupils as 'action groups' coincides with the mounting frustration among teachers who feel that they lack any real voice in the processes of decision-making. Headmasters are often perceived as tyrannical and even if they consult their staffs are suspected of paying only lip service to the notion of consultation so that they can play the democratic game while keeping the reins of government firmly in their own hands. The crisis of authority is clearly not something that is located only between pupils and staff. The roots of it must be sought within the staff group itself, in a network of roles and relationships that has grown by accretion, leaving people unsure what responsibilities they really have in the system as a whole.

The key to the problem of communication between pupils and teachers may therefore be found in the kind of work the staff are prepared to do within their own working groups, through open exploration of their own internal conflicts and through their own struggle to discover which are the real and important divergences between them, and which are spurious. Yet the increasing size of the schools makes this task more and more difficult, even while it is becoming more and more necessary if the problems that are arising between staff and pupils are to be understood.

Loss of personal identity in large staff groups

As secondary schools have grown larger we have become accustomed to hearing teachers express concern about the effects of this growth on children. It is rather readily assumed that pupils will feel lost and confused when they are transferred from a primary school (or indeed from a grammar or secondary modern school) of about four to five hundred to a large comprehensive school of twelve, fifteen or even eighteen hundred. Much less is said about the problems of teachers who, accustomed to membership of staff groups of twenty to thirty (about the size of a school class) have to learn to become members of staff groups of fifty, seventy or even a hundred or more. Adults, it seems, are not expected to acknowledge that adjustments to these large staff groups can make formidable demands upon them. It is noticeable that educational broadcasts and television programmes rarely devote time to consider problems of staff relationships, except as these are perceived at the formal level. To be sure, it is now far more widely recognized that schools, no less than factories, must be regarded as institutions with problems of management. But the study of the management structures in the expanding schools of today takes little account of the extent to which unrecognized and largely unconscious feelings that teachers have about each other and about their pupils may be hindering the conscious, rational efforts being made by those same teachers, as professional persons, to implement desirable changes in their system.

The difficulty in tackling the problem of exploring these hidden feelings springs partly from the desire to keep up the fiction that feelings have no place in work relationships, or not, at least, where adults are concerned. Thus the expression of feeling about a shared situation can be reserved for those moments when friends are together. Feelings may occasionally erupt more publicly, of course, when anger breaks loose unexpectedly. But by and large staff meetings can usually be preserved as occasions when politeness is maintained and argument is purely rational, or believed to be so.

To some extent psychologists and sociologists have tried to draw the attention of teachers to the dangers of ignoring the network of relationships that underlies the work organization of the staff group. We are warned, in other words, that it is not enough to be aware of departmental groupings that owe their existence to the demands of consciously accepted institutional tasks—the official groupings that bring people together because they happen to have been appointed to undertake, jointly, a particular part of the total task. We must also recognize those unofficial groupings that may have little to do with the task—that depend on natural affinities and shared interests outside as well as inside the school and that often cut across the official work groupings; and we must take account of the effect these will be having on the work of the total group and not assume that they may affect only the leisure-time pursuits of certain individual members of that group.

The warning is necessary. But the effect of it upon teachers has often been to create a false dichotomy between structures and relationships that are recognized as 'informal' and those that are recognized to be 'formal'. The informal system of relationships, about which most members of the total staff are likely to have conscious knowledge can, it is true, both help and hinder task performance. But, in considering these co-existing sets of relationships, we have to guard against the danger of setting up a completely unreal division, not only between 'informal' and 'formal' groupings but also between 'informal' and 'formal' discussions and meetings. It is often implied that groups of staff drawn together through natural affinities may be so conflict-free, so liberated from the tensions that bedevil most formally organized groups, that they may safely contain and, hopefully, solve the problems of the institution. How often have we heard such remarks as: 'Oh, we discuss these matters informally over tea or coffee', or: 'Staff meetings are too formal for any real work to be done; we don't have them any more'. Thus, by hiving problems off into those intimate sub-groups within the staff, where disturbing tensions are supposedly non-existent, the institution succeeds in by-passing rather than facing its real problems, with the result that solutions are implicitly accepted by the staff as a group even though individuals within the group are aware that the 'solutions' are being made without regard to the needs of certain persons or of certain groups. To accept an apparent solution is easier than to embark on the difficult task of probing more deeply into the problem.

Needless to say, the extent to which members of a staff group feel able to risk exposing the real problems will depend upon the quality of the leadership given by the head. For the head stands, not, as many will say, at the top of the staff group, nor at its centre, but between the staff group and the community which that staff group serves. The head, if he is doing his job properly, will be conferring with his colleagues about the education of pupils rather than teaching pupils himself. He will inescapably, therefore, be closer in personal terms to staff than he can possibly be to the pupils of the school.

This is a truth that many heads find difficult to accept, largely because their appointment to their posts has probably followed successful teaching of children and was assumed to have depended chiefly on evidence about that kind of success. Yet, once a head is appointed, it will become more and more apparent that the skills that will be needed will be skills in working with groups of staff inside the school boundary and with representatives of the community outside the boundary. On these skills will, in great part, depend the degree to which his staff are trusted by the community to act on its behalf as educators of its children, and the skill and confidence with which they in their turn carry out their tasks.

As long as schools remained reasonably small, some headmasters managed to maintain a fantasy that they knew most of what went on inside their schools and that they 'knew' all their pupils. Part of the threat of the increasing size of the institutions, for such headmasters, has been the fear that they might lose control if they could no longer make this claim. In fact, the realistic headmaster, even in a very small school, has always recognised that he cannot possibly know more than a fraction of what goes on and that he must therefore delegate to every member of his staff full responsibility for whatever task that member has been appointed to fulfil. This in its turn involves, for the headmaster, the acceptance of responsibility for the judgements he has to make when he appoints staff.

In exercising his leadership role in the school, a head performs, essentially, an enabling function. For he has to discover ways of freeing teachers to use and develop their skills, just as his staff have to find ways of freeing pupils to use and develop their skills.

Traditionally in English schools, and far more, I suspect, than many teachers admit, every teacher has had a great deal of freedom inside his own classroom to teach his subject or subjects in the way he himself thinks best. But freedom implies responsibility; and the individual teacher in his classroom or laboratory or workshop or on the sports field has a responsibility to his colleagues, since the quality of his relationships with them will imperceptibly have its effect upon the way he and they relate themselves to their pupils. It is not too extravagant to claim, indeed, that the quality of the educational experience children have in a school may depend as much on the relationships in the staff group as on those between themselves and individual teachers. Similarly, the tutorial system in any school, large or small, depends on the capacity of every individual to accept responsibility for the way he handles his business, as a tutor, with colleagues in the system of which his own tutorial group is a part. Moreover any one teacher, as tutor, will have to communicate about the children for whom he is responsible with the subject teachers who are concerned with those children. At the same time, in his role as a subject teacher, he will have to confer with the tutors of those whom he teaches. Often such conferences require him to make judgements about whether he will take over from a colleague or hand over to a colleague responsibility for coping with some particular problem in relation to a particular pupil or group of pupils. This means that leadership carries with it both the authority to act independently and responsibly in a particular region and also the obligation to communicate effectively with those who work alongside oneself.

Differentiation of tasks in the school institution

I have just been referring separately to the 'teaching' function and the 'tutorial' function of a staff member. In doing this I am really drawing attention to a kind of duality that has had a profound effect upon the way in which the internal organization of schools has developed over the last twenty years or so. No teacher would deny that he must be concerned both with the child's learning as reflected in the various aspects of the curriculum and with the child's personal growth and development. These are essentially two sides of a unified process. But society—in all kinds of ways—forces a division between them, so much so that it is almost impossible for me now to write these sentences without using the very dichotomy I am protesting against. Thus 'teaching' is forced into the category of what—it is implied—only 'teachers' do, as 'caring' is forced into the category of what only mothers or nurses or social workers do. But in fact we all know that it is not only 'teachers', in the narrow sense of this term as 'people who earn their living by teaching in schools', who have to function as educators. Every parent, every ward sister, matron or doctor, every charge hand, foreman, factory manager or director, every curate, vicar or bishop, every administrator who is organizing an institution in which people are learning to take special roles and responsibilities, is, at least for some of the time, involved in the process of educating those who will eventually overtake or supplant him. Being an educator—in the broadest sense of the term—involves both making demands on and caring about the person. Yet in groups drawn from education, medicine, industry, commerce, social work and the church, we find repeatedly that those from the social services are described as members of the 'caring professions', with the implication that others, who also have responsibility for people, are not called upon to show care or concern for those people. Narrow the focus to a group containing only teachers and social workers, and suddenly the social workers are the 'carers' and the teachers find themselves labelled almost as 'non-carers', as mere drivers of unwilling children, as disciplinarians in rigidly organized classrooms. Narrow the focus still more so that the spotlight is on the teachers only, perhaps on the teachers in one particular school, and what do we find? Again, we find that the need to separate out the caring side from the non-caring, or result-seeking, side shows itself, this time in the form of distinguishing between the pastoral functions and the curricular functions of the teacher by splitting off 'pastoral care' and 'curricular provision' and creating an organizational structure that implies some kind of dichotomy between the two. Heads of large schools will assert that it is useful to separate the two functions and allocate 'caring' to one staff organizational structure and 'demanding' to another, thus—as it appears—using to the best advantage the different talents of staff members. Only a more searching scrutiny reveals how such a divided system may be polarizing attitudes in the staff group, and thus frustrating teachers, whose intuitions (and indeed the roles they carry in both systems) about the complexity of their task would lead them to oppose such a division of functions. There are, in fact, teachers who refuse, on these grounds, to accept a function that is described as specifically 'pastoral'.

Thus, as secondary schools become larger and more comprehensive in their intake of pupils from the primary schools, they find themselves torn between two apparently quite different kinds of organization: on the one hand, a system of house and tutorial groupings, usually perceived as 'vertical', and identified with the need to provide care for pupils through their progress from entry into the school to the time of leaving it; on the other hand, a system of year-group organization, with perhaps a two-tiered or three-tiered division into lower and upper schools, or into lower, middle and upper schools, usually perceived as 'horizontal', and identified with curricular problems and the provision of appropriate sequences of courses for pre-adolescent, adolescent and near-adult pupils. In fact, because teaching below the sixth form is done almost entirely in year groups, many schools have tried to combine both systems, some putting more emphasis on the pastoral side, others more on the curricular side. The debate going on among architects, teachers and administrators about the relative merits of the house-based system and the subject-based system, in terms of buildings and educational objectives, is really about the tension between these two sides of the educational enterprise.

Conclusion

If, in this opening chapter, I have appeared to be interested only in conflicts, uncertainties and inconsistencies, this is because it is the failure even to perceive the presence of some of these, let alone to understand them, that blocks real progress in the rethinking of educational objectives. The rethinking must take place in the schools themselves. But such rethinking will not happen until teachers can sharpen their perceptions of the roles they are taking—sometimes knowingly, sometimes unknowingly—in their own staff groups, and until they can look more critically at the management structure within which they are trying to operate. In the next chapter I will be offering a set of conceptual ideas which can assist teachers and those who work alongside them in carrying out such a study.

CHAPTER II

A Conceptual Framework for the Study of Leadership and Staff Relationships

This chapter will be focused on institutions in general rather than on schools in particular. Yet we will need to move freely in and out of the educational scene in order to establish, in general terms, the relevance of the concepts that will be presented.

It is not my purpose to offer any kind of survey of existing theories of management. Such a survey would not necessarily provide a helpful introduction to the events that will be described in the later chapters or to the generalizations that can be drawn from those events. What is necessary at this stage is some understanding of the particular theoretical approach that formed the background to the research. It is an approach that can, in my view, help people to gain new insights into the problems they are facing daily in their institutions, whether those institutions be factories, hospitals, social service agencies, churches, universities or schools. The conceptual framework I am presenting has, as it were, three dimensions: it has to do with the institution and its task, with the roles that individuals and groups have to take in order that the work of the institution can be organized, and with the way in which the members of the institution relate to one another as persons. It draws on two sources: the psycho-analytic study of human behaviour on the one side and the study of institutions as open systems on the other.

Central to the framework is the concept of boundary, which is an important concept because it helps us to examine independence and interdependence. Whether we are looking at the person, who can live as a human being only in so far as he is able to relate his own inner world to his outer environment, at the group, which exists by virtue of some kind of membrane that separates it out from other groups, or at the institution, which exists in the community or the society by virtue of what it has been created and set apart to do, we must be concerned with defining boundaries. Although it might seem more logical to start this exploration with the person, it is more appropriate—since this is primarily to be a book about schools—to start with the institution. I shall therefore begin by looking at the theory of institutional management that was developed by the late Dr A. K. Rice during the 1950s and 60s, latterly in collaboration with Dr E. J. Miller; I shall take up later in this chapter the theory of inter-personal behaviour developed by Dr W. R. Bion in the 1940s and early 50s and relate it to some of his more recent work on the nature of thinking; and I shall be looking at some problems that arise for the individual member of a large group as illuminated in a more recent paper by Dr P. M. Turquet and in the Miller–Rice formulation of the problem of representation in social institutions. In outlining this conceptual framework I shall also inevitably be communicating something about my own values.

The institution, its task and its management system

Basically Rice viewed the institution as an open system that could survive as an organism only by exchanging materials with its environment. Institutions, which are devised by human beings so that members of societies can take definable roles in them, can exist only if they take in raw materials, convert these into useful products and export the products back into society, while finding ways of using or disposing of their waste products. Even small and simple institutions perform multiple tasks, which are often contradictory in their purpose and seldom easy to disentangle and define. Rice postulated that, despite such variation and distribution of tasks, every enterprise or part-enterprise had at any given time a 'primary task—the task that it must perform to survive'.[1] Later, Miller and Rice described this concept as 'essentially a heuristic concept, which allows us to explore the ordering of multiple activities (and of constituent systems of activity where these exist)'.[2] The primary task of an institution, then, at any given time, is the import-conversion-export process to which its efforts are directed. In defining what this task is, we find ourselves having to identify the boundary through which raw materials are imported at one end and finished products are exported at the other.

The primary task of a factory may be to manufacture steel, or textiles or plastics, or specific articles made out of these materials, or combinations of these materials. The primary task of a shop is to buy in manufactured goods or selected foods, or both, and sell them to the public. The primary task of a hospital is to take in sick people and cure them, that of a school to take in children and turn them into educated adults, that of a college of art, music or education to take in young adults as students and to turn them into artists, musicians or teachers.

Put crudely like that, of course, the formulation sounds offensive because it suggests that people acquire health, personal maturity, artistic skills and professional expertise merely by having things done to them by others. It appears at first sight to offend against the notion that children have to do their own learning, that the patient must cure himself, that teachers, like artists are 'born, not made', that persons are self-determining. It seems harsh

---

[1] Rice, A. K. (1963), *The Enterprise and its Environment*, Tavistock, p. 13.
[2] Miller, E. J. & Rice, A. K. (1967), *Systems of Organization*, Tavistock, p. 25.

because it forces us to recognize that schools and universities and hospitals export people who drop out early, fail their examinations, remain sick or even die, just as factories export waste products as well as useful ones. Yet if we regard the formulation as a model applicable to a wide variety of institutional tasks, it can help us to face more honestly the problems we all have, as managers of whole or part institutions—in defining our roles as educators, for example, in relation to the pupils who pass through our schools and for whose development, one way or another, we are answerable to society. It is easier, perhaps, to accept the idea that a factory takes in 'raw materials', puts them through a 'conversion' process and exports its 'finished or waste' products, than to view human beings (whether children or adults, whether sick or healthy, whether limited or talented, whether stupid or clever) as people to be processed through a system. Teachers in particular are often reluctant to acknowledge that they are trying to bring about changes in persons. Yet if this were not so they could not justify drawing their salaries. For to create situations in which children or young adults or experienced professional persons can learn is, in fact, to be concerned with bringing about change.

If, then, we accept this basic model of the 'import-conversion-export' system, we can acknowledge that a school can survive only if it fulfils its primary task of taking in children, providing an educational programme that, hopefully, will enable these children to grow and learn, and sending them out after a number of years as more mature persons than they were when they came in. In its simplest and crudest terms the educational process involves these phases, as in Figure 1. But, having stated that, we are left with the uneasy feeling that we have been brought face to face with baffling questions

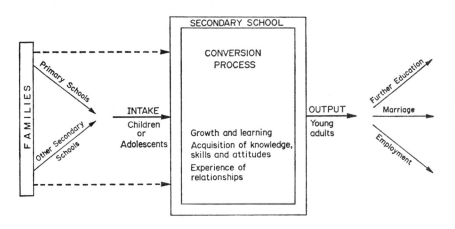

FIG. 1. The secondary school as an open system.

about how to recognize the evidence that 'growth' and 'learning' are or are not taking place, and how we as 'teachers' and children as 'learners' recognize a maturing process when we see it or experience it. We are, in fact, brought face to face with our own uncertainties about how the primary task of a school should appropriately be defined, particularly if there is uncertainty in society itself about what schools should really be doing.

The contract that teachers have to make with society concerning the education of its children is in fact very problematic. For the school is not the child's only educational milieu. He is being educated in all kinds of ways by other institutions, including, of course, his own and other people's families. Nor are children, like the goods that come out of a factory, just material products. They are human beings. As human beings they cannot be merely moulded or fashioned or manufactured by those who operate the school. Even the 'wastage' cannot be simply thrown out, as the waste materials from factories and mines were once thrown out, without fear of consequences. The 'failures', like the 'successes', take their partial success and their partial failure out with them when they leave the school, with consequent effects on their successors. Moreover pupils—unlike factory materials—are continually interacting with teachers and with one another, and their own views about what constitutes a good education and their own ways of comparing what goes on inside the school with what goes on outside it are continually affecting, both positively and negatively, what their teachers, through their contract with society, are trying to achieve.

In a complex institution the primary task has to be broken down into its constituent parts, each part appearing as a separate sub-system within the whole. Thus, in addition to the 'first-order management system', which regulates what happens on the outer boundary of the institution, there will be a second-order system providing for the management of the main sub-systems, each of which may have its own third-order system, and so on. In other words, in a complex enterprise, there will be discontinuities where one sub-system ends and another begins; and wherever there is a discontinuity a new management function becomes necessary to regulate relations between the parts so that the task of the whole can be profitably pursued.

We can illustrate this, in terms of a familiar school situation, by taking the traditional small grammar school as our example, where the headmaster or headmistress is located on the outer boundary of the whole school, possibly with a deputy, and the various subject departments are seen as the sub-systems, requiring 'second-order management', as in Figure 2(a). The problem with this model is immediately obvious. The boundaries of the sub-systems of activity do not coincide with groups of children, since all children in such a school are likely, at least for the first three years, to be taught all subjects. Nor does the leadership relate directly to staff, since some will be concerned with more than one subject. If, however, we take a school in which three sub-sections have been set up, each catering for a different age group of pupils,

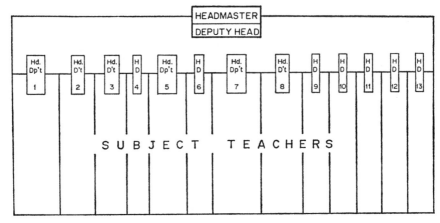

(a) SUBJECT-BASED SUB-SYSTEMS

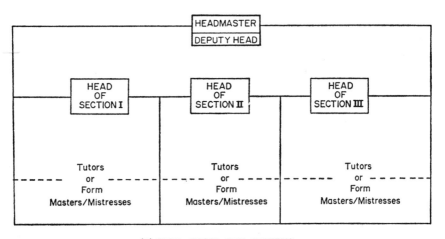

(b) PUPIL-BASED SUB-SYSTEMS

FIG. 2. Leadership as a boundary function.

the management structure may be drawn diagrammatically as in Figure 2(b). But this model takes no account of the management of curricular responsibilities.

So, already, the attempt to identify the sub-tasks within the overall primary task of the school as an institution has highlighted a possible conflict of interests within the teacher himself: that between his interest in providing leadership within a structure based on pupil groupings and his interest in providing leadership within a structure based on subject groupings. Much of this book will be found to be concerned with the problem of bringing these two things into a closer relationship by discovering a management system that is more closely consistent with the educational task than are most of those in use at the present time.

The nature of the problem is well illustrated in a relatively early paper by Miller,[1] in which he identifies three kinds of differentiation into second-order management systems: that based on territory, that based on time and that based on technology. In the world of industry, the first has to do with the physical location of processes (in separate factories or in different areas of one large plant); the second has to do with work shifts (day and night shifts for example); the third has to do with technical processes and the special skills required for them. Miller points out that an institution may be divided along one, two or all three of these dimensions.

We can fairly easily translate these into terms that can be related more obviously to the school institution. Territory comes into play through form-room or house bases, through curricular areas and through sixth-form blocks. Time comes into play in every time-tabled day, through differentiation between 'in-school' and 'out-of-school' activities, through transfer of groups of children from teacher to teacher between the summer term that ends one academic year and the autumn term that begins the next, and also through temporary transfer of groups to students in training or to stand-in staff during the illness of a regular teacher. Technology comes into play through the different specialisms (both subject-wise and method-wise) of different members of the staff group. For secondary-school pupils the confusion between these three dimensions of their relationship with the staff group and with the overall task of coping with a unified educational process must be considerable. For it is not only in moving from school to school within the boundary of the total system of schooling and further education that they have to cope with major discontinuities in the process of becoming educated; they also have to face discontinuities within each part of the total system, perhaps most of all within the secondary phase. Now the term 'discontinuity' —although it has a negative implication—need not be regarded as referring to something bad or undesirable. Discontinuities in experience are part of the reality of living. The real educational problem is not to eliminate the discontinuities but to decide where the major ones occur and to manage them in such a way that pupils can be helped to cope with them. As we have seen, it is never easy to be sure where they are even in one particular school structure because the nature of the tensions between different objectives is not fully understood, or because the existence of these tensions is being denied (see Figure 3).

Thus, when we come to consider how the overall task of the school should be subdivided into sub-tasks, different people will give different answers. For some, the main sub-systems (or second-order systems) will be seen to correspond to different age bands within the pupil population. To others it

[1] Miller, E. J. (1959), 'Technology, Territory and Time, the Internal Differentiation of Complex Production Systems' in *Human Relations* XII: 3: 243–72.

may appear that the school should be identifying sub-systems based, not on differences in pupils' ages, but rather on differences in their ability, as indeed the tri-partite system in the secondary sector as a whole was set up to do by the 1944 Education Act. By others, the overall task of the school may be perceived as falling into two differentiated sub-systems, the one concerned with the organization of pastoral care, the other with the organization of the curriculum. In the great majority of secondary schools there is considerable tension between these three ways of perceiving the task breakdown, all teachers being to some extent separated from or linked with one another on all three criteria.

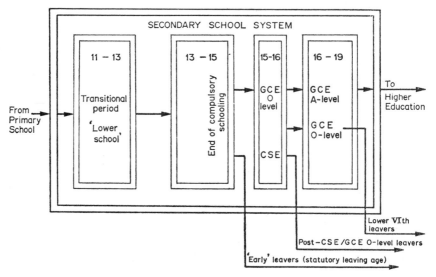

FIG. 3. Discontinuities within the secondary school.
(Note: applicable before the raising of the school leaving age to sixteen)

Task performance and personal satisfactions in the working group

Because of this kind of confusion about where people belong in the various sub-parts of the system, there is likely to be a search for some area of the school's life where personal relationships can be felt to have some warmth and permanence. For some this area may be linked to territory, as in a house system; for others it will be linked to the development of a new course taught by a cross-disciplinary team (as in a lower-school humanities course or a sixth-form general studies course), or to an emerging special-subject department such as drama or economics or technical education. Or it may be sought in voluntary working parties or discovered, perhaps unexpectedly, in special committees.

And so, alongside the task system of the institution there is what Rice and Miller have called the 'sentient system', from which the persons who man the enterprise draw much of their strength through a mutual commitment to one another and to something that can be shared as a valued object. This concept needs some explanation. Let us examine it, as we have examined the concepts of the primary task, boundary control and discontinuity, in the context of the educational enterprise, embodied in the school as an institution.

Every member of a school—whether pupil or teacher—needs to feel that he belongs to at least one sentient group. It is from the sentient group that we draw the emotional strength that enables us to do our jobs. If there were no satisfaction in belonging to such groups we should be personally weakened and therefore less effective in our roles. Sentient groups are not necessarily related to tasks. But in a healthy institution they ought to be. Indeed, one aspect of the task of leadership is to ensure that the sentience within the system can be harnessed to the task. Part of this sentience, where the sentient group is task-related, comes from the satisfactions of working with people for whom one has liking and respect, part of it from the shared commitment to a task that all the members feel to be important. Problems arise, however, when people begin, imperceptibly, to make the protection of the sentient system the primary task instead of using the sentient system to further the real work of the institution. This is liable to happen when a working group within the institution develops such strong personal bonds that its members harden their resistance to any kind of change (organizational, technological or methodological) that might cause the break-up of the group. In other words the group may seek to preserve itself, because of the value attached to a friendship structure that had its roots in shared work, by defending a system that is really obsolete.

A sentient group may be derived from activities that take place outside the institution itself, yet be related to the task being tackled inside it. Thus a teacher of English may have a sentient group outside the school in an association of teachers of English from whom he draws some of his strength and skill to do his job inside the school. A scientist who is working with Nuffield materials or in a Schools Council project may feel that he belongs to a strong sentient group that includes scientists in other schools working in the same way. Heads of schools need to feel that they are valued members of associations of heads and that they can recharge their batteries, as it were, by occasional meetings and discussions with their colleagues in other schools about the problems of headship. CSE subject panels may have a strong sentience for their members, as may committees and working parties brought together from different schools to study specific educational problems.

To look for membership of a sentient group—whether within or beyond the school boundary—does not however imply that one expects no disagreements or tensions to arise between its members. Indeed the real strength of the sentient group in the organization can be its capacity to face its own internal conflicts in the interest of the tasks it has to perform. But because conflict is usually uncomfortable, if not actually painful, there is likely to be a strong pressure on members to deny its presence even to themselves, or to avoid examination of it if it is too obvious to suppress altogether.

We are now moving into the area of personal relationships, and as we search below the visible and tangible work-group structures that are set up to deal with the shared task, we find ourselves having to take account of the unconscious as well as the conscious behaviour of persons towards each other and towards the various groups inside and outside the boundary of the school. For, along with the constraints on task performance that are brought about by agencies outside the school—such as the architects who plan school buildings, the central and local authorities who finance building operations and pay salaries, the parents and employers who put pressure on teachers to behave in certain prescribed ways—there are constraints brought about by forces inside the school; and these include unconscious mechanisms used by groups to obstruct rather than further real learning and thus to defeat the declared intentions of many individual members of those same groups.

Conscious and unconscious mechanisms in the handling of personal relationships

It can hardly be disputed that any institution, whatever its primary task, must allocate people to roles as members of working teams. In other words we are all quite familiar with the idea that in accepting a job in a factory, a shop, a government department, a school or a hospital, we agree to take on a specific role in that institution. Yet teachers are sometimes surprised, even outraged, by the idea that they have to 'take a role' in a school. There is a wish—often asserted with great vehemence—that the teacher should not be so confined as this term seems to suggest. There is suspicion that to acknowledge that one 'takes a role' is to admit to 'acting a part' like someone in a play rather than simply 'being oneself' as a person. But the resistance seems to go beyond the mere confusion between the sociologist's and the actor's use of the term 'role'. For the wish not to acknowledge that the teacher has a role—indeed several different roles—inside and outside the school seems to be allied to a wish, often asserted with great vehemence, that the acceptance of any kind of role constraint will be damaging to the relationship between pupil and teacher. Part of the problem in coming to terms with the role of teacher is that the way one functions in the role is inevitably a demonstration, not only of the degree of professional skill one brings to the role, but also of the person one is in managing that role.

Inevitably, then, in examining role relationships in an institution, we are also examining personal relationships. This involves the struggle to distinguish between the conscious allocation and acceptance of roles that have to do with the needs of the institution and the unconscious allocation and acceptance of roles that have to do with the needs of persons. This is where we can be helped by the psycho-analytic approach to the study of inter-personal and inter-group relationships within the institution, in particular by the object-relations theory based on Melanie Klein's study of infant behaviour and by the theory of small group behaviour formulated by Dr W. R. Bion.

What we need to examine more closely are the elusive unconscious mechanisms that we all use in face of difficulty, whether we are taking part in a 'formally' organized meeting or talking with our friends or bickering with our enemies in 'informal' social groups. In other words, all groups, however they may be composed or whatever the purpose that draws them together, are a prey to emotional forces that are very elusive and difficult to understand, because people unconsciously become vehicles for them. The unconscious mechanisms that we use as members of groups and of institu-tions are more powerful than we realize, enabling us to get rid of unwanted parts of ourselves, often at some cost to others. Yet the need to deny that these things are happening gives rise to the hope that the group can live in a kind of illusory belief that it is always 'harmonious', so that the inevitable conflicts that exist both within and between individuals, and both within and between groups and institutions, can be ignored. Thus harmoniousness in the staff group, if accepted as a goal in itself, comes to be used as a means of masking conflicts that could, if acknowledged and understood, strengthen rather than impede the work of a group in carrying out its joint task.

When Bion embarked on his pioneer work with small groups at the Tavistock Clinic and at the Tavistock Institute of Human Relations after the second world war, he did so with the express aim of seeking new insights into the way people behaved towards each other in small groups of about eight to twelve members.[1] His experiences led him to believe that in any group of such a size members would be engaged in a continuous struggle between the wish to learn by experience, which was conscious, rational and sophisticated, and the wish to take refuge in basic assumptions—a wish that was unconscious, irrational and naive. As members of the 'work' group, people were concerned with the testing of fantasies and the pursuit of truth; but as members of the 'basic assumption' group the same people colluded with one another in order to perpetuate fantasies and to escape from truth.

In his role as consultant to these groups Bion found evidence of three different kinds of basic assumption activity, namely 'dependence', 'fight-flight' and 'pairing'. The dependent group behaved as if it had met to be sustained and nourished by a leader, the fight-flight group as if it had met to fight or run away from someone or something, the pairing group as if it had met to pair off and reproduce itself. A characteristic of the work group (or the group behaving in a sophisticated way) was that it could mobilize one of these three basic assumptions in order to suppress the

---

[1] Bion, W. R. (1961), *Experiences in Groups*, Tavistock.

emotions associated with the other two. Thus, if courage and daring were needed, the fight-flight basic assumption would be mobilized by the group in order to suppress the helplessness and the rivalries associated with dependence and the tolerant hopefulness associated with pairing; but if faith in the skills and expertise of one particular person was needed to further the task, then dependence would be mobilized so that the destructive fear and hostility associated with fight-flight and the easy-going over-optimism associated with pairing could be suppressed.

Rice, building on these ideas, held that one of the functions of leadership in the working group was to mobilize the basic assumption that was appropriate to the task at any given time so that it could be used in a sophisticated way to promote rather than to obstruct the learning of the group members.[1] He noted also his own belief that pairing and dependence were, like fight-flight, 'opposite poles of the same assumption', adding: 'The dependent group has met to obtain security from an individual who can never satisfy the demands made on him; the pairing group in the hope of producing the new magical dependent leader, a hope that is always vain.'[2] Another way of looking at this, perhaps, is to perceive dependence and pairing as duals of one another in a basically optimistic and supportive culture, and fight and flight, or fear and hatred, as duals of one another in a basically pessimistic and hostile culture.

How, then, can we know whether these basic assumptions are being used in a task-directed (or 'work-group') way or as the means of destroying real learning? The essential difference between sophisticated (or work-group) dependence and basic-assumption dependence is that the former does not feed on delusions about a leader's omniscience, whereas the latter promotes a situation that does—the leader being required to collude with those who want to maintain him as 'infallible', so that he will not make demands on his followers to struggle with the process of learning. The essential difference between sophisticated pairing and basic-assumption pairing is that the former recognizes that even a fruitful pairing will produce only an imperfect human being, or an idea that will have to be tested and retested for its validity, or a plan that can never be without flaws, whereas the latter operates in a naïve belief that the pairing can be effortless and that one day the Messiah—the infallible leader of the future—will surely be born. The essential difference between sophisticated fight-flight and basic-assumption fight-flight is that the former offers no illusions that victory or successful retreat can be bought without cost whereas the latter seeks to maintain the fantasy that a leader can be found who will be invincible in attack and uncatchable in retreat.

Teachers may be able to recognize, in this necessarily brief and encapsulated description of an elaborate and difficult theory of group behaviour, at least some aspects of their own behaviour in staff groups and of the

[1] Rice, A. K. (1965), *Learning for Leadership*, Tavistock, p. 13 and p. 74.
[2] Rice, A. K., *Learning for Leadership*, p. 12, footnote.

behaviour of children and young people in the groups they teach. They may recognize the conflict between the naïve hope that the headmaster, being infallible, will provide people with magic solutions for intractable problems, and the reality—perfectly understood at the level of thinking though so often denied at the level of feeling—that he is no more infallible than anyone else on the staff. They may recognize the tendency of staff groups and of classroom groups to set up fight-flight leaders who, when they fail to lead the group to victory or rescue them in defeat, can be disowned and cast aside. They may recognize the ease with which they and their colleagues (or the children in their classes) will sit back while two members keep up a dialogue in the name of work, thereby ensuring that real work can be deferred while unreal hope is kept alive.

Here again—as in the presentation of Rice's theory of institutional management—we are up against the difficulty of over-compression. For no-one, least of all Eion himself, would claim that these modes of behaviour are easily identifiable. Even in a very small group there are always a great many things going on at the same time. Even when dependency seems to be fairly obviously in the ascendant, no two members of the group, as persons, are going to be affected by the events in the same way. Even in one person there are many complex and often conflicting emotions and thoughts to be handled. And the behaviour of the group as a whole is, like a kaleidoscope, constantly shifting and changing so that no two members' perspectives of it can ever for a moment be the same.

The important thing is that persons in the group are liable to be used by the group to contain and perhaps also to express aspects of other persons. This process of projection and introjection can be either helpful to growth and to the work of the group or inimical to it. What we are looking at here is, according to Melanie Klein and others who have built on her ideas, a very primitive mechanism that begins in infancy and continues throughout our lives—the mechanism that enables us to handle conflict within ourselves by splitting off our good and bad feelings and putting them out, as fantasied 'good objects' and 'bad objects', into other people. And because in earliest infancy there is for the baby no such thing as a whole person, or even a whole breast, but only a good breast that is warm, soft, comforting and always present, and a bad breast that is cold, hard, withdrawing and always absent, so the internal world of the baby, in symbolic terms, is filled with bad objects that are hostile and destructive and with good objects that are vulnerable to attack by those bad objects. Hence the need to expel his bad objects by symbolically projecting them into the mother. Examples of the adult use of these unconscious mechanisms are not hard to find. As teachers, we have all made use of them. If, for example, the ultra-conservative aspects of ourselves can be pushed out into parents, or employers, or local administrators, or the government, or perhaps into certain well-established members of the school staff itself, most of us can avoid looking at our own fears of change and deny our own wish to keep things comfortably as they are; if we can push our own ultra-liberalism out into those who train young teachers, or those who carry out educational research, or perhaps into an innovating group of experimenters within the staff group, we can avoid looking at our own rebelliousness and deny our own impatience with the establishment. In recovering these projected parts of ourselves, we have to come to terms with the reality that our good, loved objects have bad aspects, and that our bad, hated objects have good aspects. This re-integration of the whole object (or person) and the need to accept its imperfection leads to depression, which itself is part of the maturing process. Thus ˙the adult—like the baby—in coping with growth and learning, is swinging continually between the paranoid-schizoid position, which leads to the splitting apart of his good and bad objects, and the depressive position, which follows the reincorporation of his loved objects with gradual acceptance of the reality that love and hate, goodness and badness, reside in the same person, object or part-object, and also in himself.

In his more recent writings Bion has explored the relevance of these concepts for the evolution of thinking.[1] He sees as central to this the mechanism of projective identification which enables the baby, if he has good enough mothering, to use the mother as a temporary receptacle for those parts of himself and his internal world that he cannot manage. If the mother is able to show that the baby's anger and hatred do not destroy her and that she can contain his bad objects and yet still feel, and be experienced as, loving, then the baby becomes able to receive his projected feelings back into himself and thus to acquire the first elements of thinking, as distinct from the primitive and often violent feelings that cannot be understood or used constructively. If we carry this idea into the educational field it becomes possible to perceive the teacher in relation to pupils and the head (and other senior staff members) in relation to staff as having a 'holding' or 'containing' function that enables the individual, in time, to take back his own violent and potentially overwhelming feelings and work at the problem of understanding them. If members of staff experience this positive use of projective identification and work through the contingent worry and anxiety, they are likely to find themselves better able to contain the projections from their pupils. If, on the other hand, they experience only the negative and destructive aspects of projective identification, in the sense that they become unwilling containers of other people's anger, fear or contempt, they are unlikely to be sensitive to the way in which pupils stereotype one another and use one another as spokesmen, scapegoats, butts and outsiders. For if they themselves become overwhelmed by what others put into them, they cannot help children to retain their hold on reality.

In looking at these phenomena of projection, introjection and projective

---

[1] Bion, W. R. (1962), *Learning from Experience*, Pitman; (1970) *Attention and Interpretation*, Tavistock.

identification, we are concerned again with questions about the control of boundaries, not this time in the institution or group but in the person himself. For the process of learning to relate to one's environment is in essence a process of regulating what happens on the boundary between the inner and outer worlds of the person. It is the sense of preserving this boundary without making it impermeable that gives some assurance of a personal identity. Why, then, do most people fear a greater threat to their identity in large groups, where they can more easily remain anonymous, than in small groups where they can hardly avoid being exposed?

In large schools the most common defence against the practice of holding regular full staff meetings is to protest that they are boring and time-wasting because the sheer size of the group prevents people from speaking effectively in such meetings. Is this retreat into boredom and ineffectiveness really a cover for what should more accurately be described as fear of chaos? And instead of saying 'the large group is too big to work in', ought we not to be saying 'we need to know more about what may be happening in the large group that prevents us from working effectively in it'?

A recently published paper by Dr P. M. Turquet[1], formulating a theory of large-group behaviour that builds on the earlier theories outlined in this chapter, offers some helpful leads in exploring this question. The title of this paper, 'Threats to identity in the large group', indicates where its argument is centred. By 'large group' is meant a group that is too large for members to feel they are in a face-to-face group; too large to be 'taken in at a glance'; too large for members to be sure how to locate and identify its membership. This loss of a firm and unmistakable boundary round the group as a whole is accompanied by unexpected uncertainties about the identity of known sub-groups within it. Most baffling of all, the individual, even if he is known to other members of the group, lacks any real sense of being recognized by them or of being understood by them when he speaks.

In describing the nature of these phenomena Turquet uses the term 'singleton' to indicate the individual member who is struggling to escape from his isolation and become an 'I' with an established or rediscovered identity. Figuratively speaking, he must establish for himself a 'boundary skin'; and he can do this only by seeking relations with someone else in the group, thus becoming aware of the 'boundary skin' of his neighbour and winning reassurance that he himself has a skin that separates him out as an entity. But in order to interact with the group in the present, the 'I' must separate itself from its past—its background of earlier existence. Thus the 'I' becomes involved in two conflicting activities: on the one hand there is the urge to seek entry into the group and move towards others and make relations with them; on the other hand there is the urge to flee from the group outwards, backwards, and to search past experience for models on

[1] Turquet, P. M., 'Threats to Identity in the Large Group', in Miller, E. J. (ed.), *Task and Organization* (in press).

which to base behaviour in the new, bewildering, unfamiliar present. Thus the individual finds himself caught between two powerful forces: the centrifugal force urging him to flee from the centre of activities, and the centripetal force urging him to seek the centre. Hence the highly ambivalent feelings we must all have experienced in many large-group situations—the almost insoluble conflict between wanting to get into the 'central' group of those who do the talking, and wanting to keep outside this ring and remain silent, anonymous and, to all intents and purposes, without any coherent thoughts. Hence also, the feeling of panic, the loss of any sense of 'knowing' either the people who talk or the people who remain silent, the experience of hearing one's own words repeated in a distorted form and the fear of having lost parts of oneself into the group. The alternative to risking this kind of interaction with the group is to go through successive phases of retreat. The individual may first seek relief through a process of 'alienation' by detaching himself from the group and so protecting his identity from its potential destructiveness. Following this he may suffer an increasing sense of disintegration—what Turquet describes as 'desarroy', the sense of having lost his wits, of being filled up with panic and discomfort and uncertainty, of being no longer able to recognize the contents of his own mind. The third phase in this withdrawal is to escape into bizarre behaviour, by acting out some defiant form of 'being different', while staying physically in the group. The problem for the group, and for the work leaders in the group, is how to bring about a situation in which the individual member who has become the receptacle for so much of everyone's bewilderment, anger and despair can be allowed to be himself again; and this can happen only if other members of the group take back the discarded parts of themselves, or in other words acknowledge their own responsibility for the ineffectiveness, the chaos and the potential violence in the group.

How can we relate all this to the problems of management in the large institution? The head of such an organization, along with those who share with him the major tasks of leadership, has clearly a heavy responsibility, not only for devising appropriate structures of management so that the various work roles in the institution correspond to real and manageable tasks, but also to be alert to the kind of unconscious processes that will inevitably be going on within and between these structures. The difficulty is that the structures we set up are often devised to provide a defence against the anxieties of the large group rather than to make the large group more effective as a working unit. Thus, for example, staff meetings, instead of being focused on a specific and identifiable task with the aim of promoting discussion of fundamental problems, are commonly protected from the anxieties of such discussion by the packed agenda that will ensure that there is no time to study any problem in depth. It is very difficult for people to recognize that the caring and enabling function of management implies, not that the members of the institution should be protected from anxiety but rather that they should be provided with the opportunity to examine and learn about the anxiety so that the efficiency of the institution can be improved.

Relations between groups and problems of representation

It must now be apparent that an institution has to provide for the growth and development of its members. And in a school this means teachers as well as pupils, as in a hospital it means doctors and nurses as well as patients. This raises the question whether the training of teachers in a school, or of doctors and nurses in a hospital, has to be perceived as a constraint on the primary task of educating children or of curing patients, or whether it should be perceived as a built-in part of the primary task. It also raises the related question about what may be the effects of good or bad staff development procedures within a school upon the well-being of the pupils in that school.

The term 'career structure' is linked more often with salary and wage scales than with increasing skills and satisfactions. Yet when we speak of an institution as one in which morale is high, we are really indicating that the staff of the institution—including senior and junior staff, old and young, 'management' and 'workers'—feel that they have a stake in the running of the organization and that the organization offers them opportunities for self-betterment.

In a school the 'enabling' aspect of the role of head is inextricably bound up with processes of consultation in the staff group. And because the members of the institution—both pupils and teachers—belong both to the task system of the school as a whole and to different sub-systems with discrete or over-lapping tasks, the head will find himself continually having to mediate between people holding different views about what the primary task of the school, or of a part of the school, should be at any given time. Interlocked with this problem of managing task boundaries in the system is, of course, the problem of managing the sentient boundaries. At times both head and staff will find themselves experiencing painful conflict between the need to be loyal to the task and the need to be loyal to persons. It is therefore an important part of headship (and of all leadership roles within the system) to regulate the relations between the task and sentient systems so that each can strengthen and draw strength from the other.

Because authority, to be effective, has to be sanctioned from below as well as exercised from above, we are also looking at problems about the relation-ship between consultative and executive powers, or to use different words, between participation and decision-making. Any staff group that begins to look critically at its own management structure inevitably finds itself having to consider very seriously whether the boundaries that separate out the different parts of the institution have been drawn in the right places. If they have not, some of the people who officially hold leadership roles may in fact be trapped in false roles, with no real authority to control any boundary. In a time of rapid expansion such as the present, when both the size and the task of an institution may be changing, leadership roles that have once had meaning may become precarious and new leadership functions that cannot as yet be consciously identified may be emerging. One sign of maturity in such an institution is the capacity of its members to examine these anomalies. Given the willingness to undertake such self-scrutiny it becomes possible for the headmaster, in consultation with the staff, to seek ways of changing the structure so that it may reflect more of the rationality and less of the irrationality of the institution it exists to serve.

Unfortunately the line between rationality and irrationality is rarely as clear as we should like to believe. And when questions of selection among

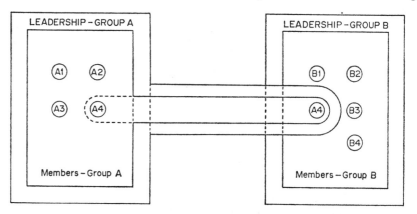

FIG. 4. The role of a representative in an inter-group situation.
Slightly adapted from E. J. Miller and A. K. Rice, *Systems of Organization* (1967),
Tavistock, p. 23.

colleagues have to be faced, as in the setting up of a representative committee, there is likely to be a strong pressure to hurry the process so that uncomfortable comparisons may be avoided. The representative may thus find himself serving on a committee or taking a role on behalf of a group without having any clear idea why he was sent and what kind of mandate he has been given.

Being a representative is essentially a lonely and potentially isolating experience for it requires one to work for colleagues or employers who are not present and by whom one may, on returning, be disowned. The representative has to embody the leadership role of the group; yet he does not necessarily have a leadership role in the situation to which he goes.

In examining this concept of representation we can be helped by looking again at Rice's theoretical formulations. Figure 4 presents the basic model. The bounded region on the right of the figure is the group to which the representative from Group A has to go. As the person who is representing (and perhaps taking some kind of initiative on behalf of) Group A, the person identified as 'A4' in this diagram has to be Group A's voice in Group B. The boundary of Group A has to stretch out, as it were, and break through the boundary of Group B, so that the representative can penetrate it sufficiently deeply to work effectively in it without losing membership of his own group. But he also takes into the other group himself as a person; and his own leadership function must be the instrument through which he manages his representative role. Because Group B has a group life of its own, it may be difficult for 'A4' to keep in touch with his own permanent group and for the members of that group not to feel that they have 'lost' him, as it were, to Group B. The boundary of Group A may then close behind him. Moreover, the members of the group he represents may unconsciously be using him as someone who merely carries their burdens for them, so that he feels abandoned by them and incarcerated within the other group to which he goes. If he and they forget that it is the leadership function of the represented group that he embodies he can no longer depend on them to support him in his actions, nor can they any longer depend on him to recognize that he is not acting only for himself as a free individual but for them also.

If Group B is a committee or working party in which the members serve as representatives of a number of different groups, every member of it is in the same situation as 'A4'. In accepting delegated responsibility from a group, a committee member must extend his view so that he can relate the group interest that he represents to those represented by other members of the committee. In entering the inter-group situation of the committee room, he may therefore be having to control an astonishingly large number of boundaries.[1] For in fact, in crossing the boundary of the group from which he comes and in penetrating into the representatives' group through its boundary he is taking with him not only the consciously formulated beliefs of his own group but also all kinds of indications, through his own behaviour, about the mood and life style of that group. Thus he has to control both the outer boundary that encloses the rational leadership of the group and the inner boundary that encloses its internal world of good and bad objects, its irrational, primitive, 'basic-assumption' experiences as well as its rationality. Similarly, when he returns from the representatives' group to his own group, he carries back more than verbal messages, for he will convey, often in ways of which he himself is unaware, information about that other group's mood and life-style. Thus it is never easy to disentangle the different strands of the messages that are carried in and out of both groups.

These notions have an obvious bearing on many areas of school management. The dynamic interplay between departmental meetings, consultative committee meetings and full staff meetings is immensely complicated even in a relatively small school. The concepts also have a bearing on the complex interplay that is going on all the time, day in and day out, year in and year

[1] Rice, A. K. (1969), 'Individual, Group and Intergroup Processes' in *Human Relations*, 22: 6: 565–84.

out, between teachers, pupils and parents. For the school must also, in a very real sense, educate the parents of its pupils and must allow itself to be educated by them. What does this really mean? To say that the school must be an educative institution not only for the children but also for the adults who operate it, or on whose behalf it is operated, is not to say that teachers have to dictate to parents, or parents to teachers. It is rather to say that parents and teachers have to strive to see one another as they really are. And 'strive' is not too highly charged a word to use, for the cards often appear to be heavily stacked against this mutual understanding.

It is not that parents and teachers lack the incentive, through their shared concern for the child, to achieve such understanding; indeed the incentive is very strong. But there is always likely to be ambivalence in the parent-teacher relationship, since each may unconsciously project into the other both good and bad parts of himself. Parents can symbolize for the teacher the loving aspects of his own relationships with pupils; but they also provide a ready receptacle for those parts of himself that the teacher would like to disown, such as reactionariness, inability to absorb new ideas, hostility to learning, and so on. Similarly, teachers can symbolize or contain for the parent his own lost opportunities, his forgotten book learning, his unused cleverness; but they can also provide a ready receptacle for the parent's unacknowledged hostility to children, his unexpressed envy of the young, his ignorance of the wider world beyond his own immediate circle. Thus each sees aspects of himself in the other, so that a meeting between a teacher and a parent, especially when it occurs in a school, is far more than a meeting between two persons.

It is not only the school, then, that must be regarded as an open, though bounded, system. Every family that is represented in the school must also be seen as an open, though bounded, system. Thus every interview between a parent and a teacher requires, first, the protection of the boundaries round the family on the one hand and round the school on the other, secondly, the crossing of those boundaries in order that one may enter into the region of the other (or in order that both may meet on neutral ground) and thirdly, the recognition of a new boundary that must include both the parent and the teacher if the interview is to be a fruitful one. In addition to all this, each person has the problem of deciding how much of himself he can bring into this encounter without threatening his own personal integrity. The complexity of this situation is illustrated in Figure 5.

A mother, as she enters the school and goes into the headmaster's room, is not only going through a series of doors, nor is she only taking through those doors herself—Mrs Smith or Mrs Jones. She comes in also as a representative of her whole family, and is thus bringing in, for the duration of the interview, the leadership function of that family. But she also brings with her unconsciously her own built-in attitudes to schools, to men or women in authority, to people who are better or less well educated than herself, to all those who, at the moment, are being represented for her by this particular headmaster. In other words, she brings her own internal world of good and bad objects—of loved and hated teachers—into that room with her, as indeed does the headmaster, and much of what happens between them will be affected in unrecognized ways by the interplay between these two internal worlds of persons as well as by the known factors in the inter-group situation between the school and one of its related families.

At the same time the mother brings with her certain expectations of the headmaster that stem partly from what she knows him to be like, partly

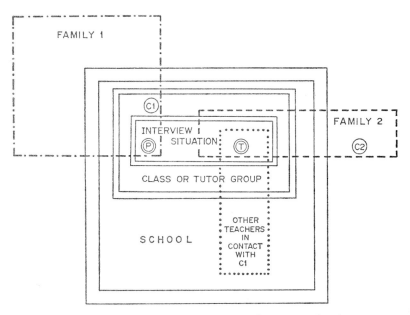

FIG. 5. The parent-teacher interview as an inter-group situation.

from what she imagines a headmaster should be able to do, and partly from her sense of dependence on him as the man ultimately responsible for the kind of schooling her child gets. Even if there are 1200 pupils in the school, she may be expecting the headmaster, magically, to have first-hand and intimate knowledge of *her* child, regardless of the fact that there are 1199 others, many with parents who look to him for the same kind of omniscience. If he colludes with this he will try to perpetuate her fantasy, but will inevitably expose his own lack of at least some of the knowledge that is being demanded of him. If he is more concerned that the parents should face reality than that they should preserve an unreal image of himself, he will refuse to pretend that he is omniscient, but will see that this mother is put in touch with the member of staff who does have first-hand knowledge of her child and is the most appropriate person for her to talk with. In other words the head will be demonstrating something about the structure of relationships within the boundary of the staff group, and acknowledging that he delegates some of his authority to individual members of that staff group and trusts them to use that authority responsibly. He also implies his acceptance of the reality that—because he is headmaster—he can no longer be as close to pupils as he was perhaps five or ten years ago. His job now is to know how to give leadership to his colleagues, and thus to free them to give leadership to their pupils. But even this is far too simple an explanation. His colleagues must also be freed to give leadership to one another. For a social organization as complex as a school has, as we have seen, many sub-parts, most of which overlap, and each of these sub-parts, whether large or small, has its own need for leadership and its own internal system of relationships which help or hinder the execution of the sub-task for which it is responsible.

Leadership as a boundary function

It may now be becoming clearer what is really meant by the concept of leadership as a boundary function. Control of a boundary, whether we are speaking of the person, the group or the institution, involves the exercise both of enabling and of inhibiting powers, since the task will demand the promotion of some activities and the suppression of others. Moreover the boundary of which we are speaking is always a double boundary, or pair of boundaries. This pair of boundaries defines a boundary region, in which the discriminating powers of leadership can operate, thus regulating the way in which the internal world of the person, the group or the institution is related to its environment and thus to other persons, other groups and other institutions. To quote Miller and Rice: 'An individual has, therefore, no meaning except in relationship with others with whom he interacts. He uses them and they use him to express views, take action and play roles. The individual is a creature of the group, the group of the individual.'[1] An essential part of leadership is therefore to seek understanding of the interplay between rational and irrational forces and, through that growing understanding, to use the authority that has been invested in the leadership role to help those to whom one owes leadership. It is not the designated leader only who has to exercise authority. All responsible persons must do so. To use authority responsibly is inherent in the problem of being human.

The theories I have been outlining have been developed in two kinds of work setting: in the setting of the group-relations training conferences, where groups have only a temporary existence, and in working institutions such as factories and hospitals, where groups are more permanent, even if fluctuating, in their membership. In both the temporary and permanent group situations, however, the role of consultant has been a constant factor. The consultant—whether to a person, a group (small or large) or an institution

[1] Miller, E. J. & Rice, A. K., op. cit., p. 17.

—accepts a leadership role, not in the sense that he takes over the direction of a conference or a hospital or a school or a factory, but in the sense that he acknowledges his responsibility to take leadership in the task. The task may be to study the inter-personal behaviour in a small group, or inter-group behaviour in a conference, or management-worker relations in a factory, or doctor-patient relations in a clinic, or teacher-pupil relations in a school. However small or large the group or institution served by the consultant, his task is to use his own role as best he can to throw light on the problem being studied, and thus to help those who have admitted him into the situation to learn through the experience they share with him. The slogan 'No research without therapy' that became associated with the work of the Tavistock Institute of Human Relations after the war implied essentially that no research role could be justified unless there was at least an intention of trying to help the members of the institution concerned to learn, and therefore to benefit, from the experience. The people with whom the consultant works must never be mere objects of study, but always partners in study. His job is to allow them to take over from him the leadership he has been exercising.

In the next chapter I will describe the consultant role that I took during the three-year period of study at Nailsea School, and sketch in the background to the collaborative research project that will be described in the second part of this book.

CHAPTER III

The Nature of Collaborative Research
and the Role of Consultant

The School in relation to the sponsoring institutions

There must by now be a great number of schools all over the country that are involved in research projects sponsored and financed by such organizations as the National Foundation of Educational Research, the Nuffield Foundation and the Schools Council, and by the DES itself. Many of these indicate an increasing acceptance of the idea that educational research, if it is to have any real effects upon practice and indeed any real validity in its own right, must include projects in which teachers in the field collaborate actively with workers from the universities and research institutes instead of merely offering themselves as 'research subjects' and their schools as 'research material'. In projects of this kind the school and the research worker (or team) must be jointly committed to an agreed task. It follows that they must also, for a limited time, acknowledge some commitment to one another, not in the sense that either accepts blindly what the other is doing, but in the sense that people on both sides are prepared to follow the work through wherever it takes them, with all the mutual questioning and testing out that is involved in such a process. The fact that the Schools Council saw the need to organize a four-day conference in the summer of 1969, at which a number of project directors and heads of schools explored together problems arising out of these developments, is one indication both of the complexity and of the potential fruitfulness of this kind of interaction.

The role I have chosen to adopt in this project must therefore be understood not only against the background of the particular history of Nailsea School but also in the total context of relationships between the school and the sponsoring institutions. In this case the sponsoring institutions were the University of Bristol, which continued to pay my salary during the period concerned while relieving me of most of my teaching obligations, and the Schools Council, which provided the financial resources to pay the costs involved and gave the work the authority of a national institution set up to promote new educational thinking, which, it is hoped, may in time influence local and central policies. Nailsea School provided the field in which the project was undertaken.

In general terms we are looking at a process flow that involves the control of resources, ideas, testing procedures, feed-back and dissemination. The writing of a Schools Council working paper based on the contents of this book will be the first stage in the formal process of feed-back to the sponsoring institutions as, in the winter of 1969–70, the writing of a long report to the Nailsea staff was the first stage in the real testing out of the basic ideas that I as project director was using. If this book becomes, in fact, the basis of a working paper and the subject of discussion and further testing out in

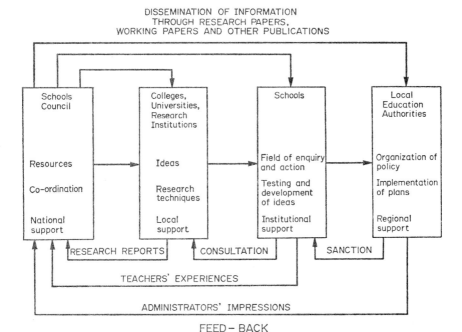

FIG. 6. Process flow and control systems for an educational project.

other schools and in colleges of education, then the process of dissemination will have begun.

The nature of the process flow can be shown diagrammatically as in Figure 6. The dilemma of the project director working in comparative isolation (that is, without a research team) is illustrated in Figure 7. At times he can feel that the work he is doing has the kind of momentum that may enable it to reach the final stage of dissemination. At other times he may feel immobilized between the institutions to which, in different ways, he is committed and which, at different times, he represents. Especially at the stage of preparing something for publication, the project director has to find ways of resolving the conflict between the pull of the consultancy work with the school itself, which is really the teaching side of the project, and the pull of the writing task, which is the reflective side of the project, involving a certain degree of withdrawal from the school and a movement towards other schools. This dilemma must be one that is shared by all teachers, within the schools, who embark on innovative work that requires both a protective boundary within which they can be left to persevere with the work and a means of crossing the boundary in due course so that they do not become isolated within their staff groups.

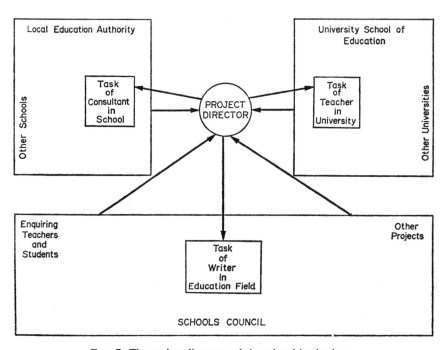

FIG. 7. The project director and the related institutions.

Expansion and the regional pattern of development

Before attempting to spell out what kind of role I took in the collaborative project with Nailsea School, I must first establish for the reader the identity of the school itself. The secondary school today, as I indicated in the last chapter, is probably in a situation of greater change than ever before in its history. Nailsea School has within it at the present time a complicated web of history. It opened in September 1959 as a three-form entry grammar school with a first-year intake of 89 children and a starting staff of four. It was destined at that time to become a large grammar school of about 800, serving a fairly scattered country area. By September 1969 it had over 1100 children on the roll and a staff of 70, of whom 58 were full-time. By the autumn of 1971 it was becoming a fully comprehensive school, serving the small but expanding dormitory town (about ten miles from Bristol) in which its buildings are located.

The school took its first comprehensive intake in the autumn of 1966. From that year new comprehensive schools were gradually opening in what had formerly been the school's catchment area, thus gradually reducing the pockets of grammar-school recruitment and increasing the proportion of the comprehensive intake. Children were still being admitted from areas served by their own new comprehensive schools as 'preference cases', if they had brothers or sisters already attending Nailsea School and if the parents concerned expressed a preference to send all their children to the same secondary school. Thus Nailsea's progress towards its new identity as a local comprehensive school was part of a regional pattern of change as Somerset gradually implemented its plan for a comprehensive system. It could also be seen as a process that was being modified by the willingness of the local authority to allow parents to maintain family unity through a gradual phasing out of the new regulations governing the allocation of children to schools. A further complicating factor was the amount of movement of families into and out of the area, and the consequent phenomenon of 'immigration' of pupils into the school from other areas and loss of pupils to other areas at all stages of the through-put system.

Because Nailsea and its neighbouring villages are in commuter country and because a fairly large proportion of the parents are business and professional people, the school is generally regarded as being in a middle-class area. Such a school, even when it faces the necessity to change from the grammar school of its origin to the comprehensive school it is destined to become, is generally perceived as an institution in an easy, trouble-free situation. When someone remarks that the 'best' comprehensive schools are usually to be found in middle-class areas, he appears to be implying that there is a simple cause-and-effect relationship between the degree of social privilege enjoyed by pupils outside the school and the degree of effectiveness of the educational provision being offered to them by teachers inside the school. The speaker seems to be saying: 'If School X is a good school, it is so mainly by virtue of the fact that it serves a middle-class community; if School Y is a bad school, it is so mainly because it has 'to function in a working-class community'. This kind of argument, by playing up sociological factors and playing down psychological ones, enables teachers to avoid some of the important educational questions by putting the conflicts outside themselves and by blaming the parents, the employers, the universities or 'society' for their problems. It also enables those outside the school to underestimate the difficulties experienced by teachers who work in what looks like a rather privileged and 'safe' sector of the secondary-school system.

It is true that a comprehensive school in a middle-class area has the advantage of a parent population in which education is, on the whole, valued. But it also has to cope with powerful pressures from parents who still measure success in terms of examination results and who fear that their children, in this increasingly egalitarian age, will be losing the securities of an élitist education. Moreover we must remember that teachers in a school like Nailsea, who are trying to cater for a far broader band of the population than that within which most of them were themselves educated, are also parents. Many of them have children for whom they may want, perhaps openly, perhaps secretly, an élitist education and a life of privilege. Some of them have children of their own actually in the school as pupils. It is here, perhaps, within the person who is both teacher and parent, that the most painful conflict is to be found, since the very changes that one wants to introduce as a teacher may be felt as militating against the interests of one's own children.

Nailsea School may be considered by some people to have had an 'easy' route to comprehensiveness—through a gradual expansion rather than a sudden amalgamation. This too has a partial truth but can have misleading implications. Nailsea has not had to cope with the discomfort of a so-called 'fusion' between an existing grammar school and one or more existing secondary modern schools, with all the built-in inter-group conflicts from which such 'fusion' usually suffers. But I believe that the conflicts between the grammar-school culture and the secondary-modern-school culture, between the value systems of the past and the emerging value systems of the present, between the demands of the intellectual life and the demands of the emotional life, have been taking other, more elusive forms in this school. I believe also that because there is within the school a tradition of consultation and shared policy-making, there is within the staff group a powerful urge to identify and understand these elusive processes.

The spoken and unspoken communications between old and new staff, between older and younger pupils and between pupils and staff are inevitably influenced by the fact that successive intakes of children are known to be going through programmes and systems that are themselves undergoing transformation. To use the language of industrial technology, the 1971 intake will not be 'processed' through the coming years in the same way that the 1966 intake was processed through the previous five years. There are therefore reverberations throughout the system, echoing up and down the year groups, of a question: 'What is going to happen to me?' or: 'What would have happened to me if the school had been like this five years ago?' Strangely enough, such a school, however much it may appear to be changing to those who have known it over the years, may present to someone viewing it from a different perspective a 'school image' that is very little different from the one he has known throughout his life.

Figure 8, which plots the progress of successive year groups through the school, gives some idea of the rapidity of its expansion during the ten years following its opening in 1959. The bounded section of this chart defines the

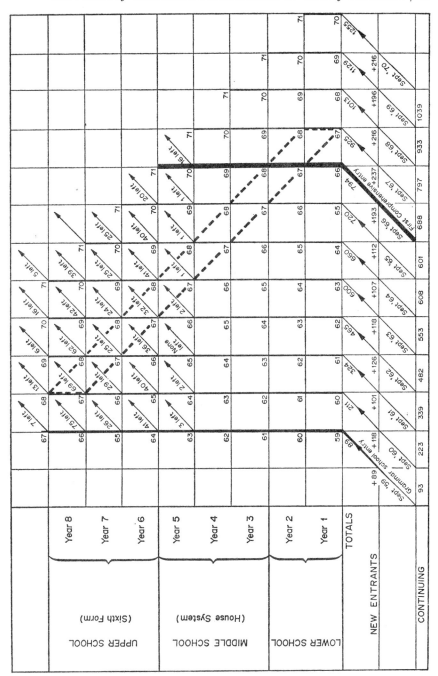

Fig. 8. The flow of pupils through a school: 1959–71.

stage this had reached by the 1967–8 academic year, during which the preliminary negotiations between myself and the school were carried out. Figure 9[1] shows the flow of staff through the school during the same period and indicates the rate of turn-over in staff appointments and departures. It records also the important facts that the school has had the same head-master and the same school secretary (now 'bursar') throughout its history, and that the deputy headmaster of 1968–71 was one of the original three assistant staff, returning as deputy head in January 1968 after a four-year period of service in another school—as head of the lower school in a near-by comprehensive school, originally secondary modern, that took its first comprehensive intake in 1964, two years before Nailsea. His return to Nailsea, in this new role, almost coincided with the beginning of my relationship with the school as a consultant to the staff group and as the director of the research project located there. For although the project did not officially start until the autumn of 1968, the work really began six months earlier, when I opened negotiations with the headmaster.

Preliminary consultations and decisions about commitment

It is important to note that the staff were brought in on these negotiations at a very early stage, both through their own consultations with the head-master and by means of a full staff meeting on 20 March 1968 which I attended, so that my first draft of a memorandum that was finally distributed in June could be discussed. At the beginning of July, after two further meetings with the headmaster, I attended a meeting of the school governors so that they, like the staff, could explore with me their reactions to my proposals. Looking back, this was probably the biggest hurdle I had to take before finally winning sanction to go ahead. Yet I remember saying at that meeting that I recognized and appreciated that the governors ought not to give their consent too easily—that it was likely to be better in the long run for doubts and misgivings to be explored at that stage, even if they could not be resolved, than for an easy, unthinking agreement to be given then without any real commitment or support. In fact the governors, I believe, accepted in principle, as did the headmaster and the staff, that they as well as I would have to be prepared to take some risk in allowing the project to go ahead.

During all these preliminary negotiations, I was aware many times of being under a subtle kind of pressure to give assurances about scientific objectivity, about protective anonymity, and about tangible results in the shape of solutions to problems, pressures which I found it by no means easy to resist. Yet I felt it was important to begin as I meant to go on. Firstly, I did not attempt to deny that my approach would inevitably contain a large element of subjectivity, since I would be coming into the situation as

[1] See fold-out at the end of the book.

the person I was, with previous experiences that would affect my view of events. I had to acknowledge that the kind of interpretations I should be trying to make of unconscious as well as conscious feelings, beliefs and attitudes within the staff group, being largely intuitive, would by their very nature be incapable of the kind of 'proof' that scientists normally looked for in their work. At best, I should be seeking for evidence, through people's words, actions and interactions, that might confirm or refute my assessment of situations. Secondly, I made it clear right at the beginning that if, as I hoped, the work culminated in a published report or book, I should want the school to be named, since 'anonymity' in research projects of this kind could never in any event be total. Moreover, my view of 'anonymity', which I expressed then and still adhere to now, is that it can too easily be used as a protective device—a device that in fact endangers the school while it protects the research worker; for, in maintaining the apparent 'anonymity' of the institution he works with, the researcher may emerge as a betrayer of confidence, having avoided the painful process of working through with the teachers who have collaborated with him the material he wants to publish about them. Once it is agreed that the school is to be named, everyone who is at any time during the project involved in recorded events has a responsibility to accept or reject what is being said about the institution. And in working together at the disagreement, teacher and researcher may arrive at a more accurate and illuminating view of the situation being described. Thirdly, I tried to emphasize at this early stage that I could not give any guarantee that any solutions to emerging problems would be found; all I could hope was that I might, by working on the boundary of the school, be able to help the staff themselves to clarify the nature of those problems, the better to arrive at their own measures for tackling them.

As a result of all these preliminary deliberations, the headmaster felt able, with the support of his governors and with the approval of the Somerset Education Committee and of the teachers' unions, to make the decision that the project should get under way at the beginning of the 1968–9 academic year. It is impossible to say exactly how many hours I have spent working directly with groups and with individuals in the school since that date. It is, however, possible to be quite precise about the sequence of these meetings and interviews and to attempt a very approximate estimate of the proportions of time spent in different kinds of meetings and interviews.

Contacts with staff group and methods of recording

Between September 1968 and July 1970 I attended in all 19 full staff meetings and 104 sectional meetings, of which 42 were meetings of the headmaster's standing committee which was formed in September 1969. I had discussions with the headmaster on at least 51 occasions and over a hundred with individual members of the staff, including at least one with every senior staff member who had responsibility for a section or department. There were eighteen occasions on which I talked with two or three staff members at the same time, thirteen of these involving the headmaster, the deputy head and the senior mistress or any two of these three. At a very rough estimate this must have added up to about 200 hours spent in staff meetings (full and sectional), about 75 hours spent with the headmaster and about 125 hours with individual members of the staff—a total of about 400 hours. The actual sequence of these events, up to the summer of 1970 but not including sub-sequent meetings during the 1970–1 session, is plotted in Figure 10[1] by means of a flow diagram.

Recording of data has been, I have to admit, highly personal, because there was at the centre of the whole enterprise a developing relationship between myself and the staff, as there is in any teaching-learning situation and in any research project involving a consultancy service offered by an individual or a research team to an institution. I did not make notes during staff meetings, apart from the occasional jotting on an agenda-sheet indicating the times at which this item or that was reached in the discussion. In interviews with individual staff members I confined my note-taking to recording such purely factual information as the numbers and identities of people within a department or section and the dates when particular roles were taken up in the school or particular appointments made. During the second phase of the project, however, by which time such interviews were always by the request of the staff member concerned and were linked with questions they wished to raise with me about my work in the school, I found myself increasingly using sheets of paper to improvise new diagrams or to redraw those I had already used in my written report to the staff, in order to clarify both my thinking and theirs about the problems we discussed.

Although the staff rarely saw me taking notes, I never made a secret of the fact that I did keep records of my experiences, by writing down or tape-recording my impressions and memories of meetings, as soon as possible after they had taken place and in as much detail as I was able to recall. These records, which are the raw material of this book, now amount to over a thousand pages of typescript. In making judgements about how to select from this wealth of material I have had to weigh up the need to maintain confidentiality against the need to demonstrate the evidence upon which I have based my conclusions. I have to bear in mind that I am not addressing this report to known teachers with whom I have now worked for some months but to unknown teachers in other schools. Readers may or may not see parallels between my perception of the problems facing Nailsea and their own perceptions of problems they are facing in those other schools in which *they* teach. The experiences that I have shared with the Nailsea staff must therefore be organized into a conceptual framework that will be valid for a

[1] See fold-out at the end of the book.

variety of school systems in different parts of the country, in cities and heavily populated areas as well as in small towns or quiet country districts.

First I have to fill in some details about the pattern of activities plotted in sequential form in Figure 10 and indicate why the sequence developed in the way it did. From the very first week of the autumn term of 1968, the headmaster made it clear, both to me and to his staff, that he wanted me to attend all those staff meetings, including meetings of sub-sections of the staff group, in which he, as head of the school, took the leadership or chairmanship role. But it was not only through attendance at the regular scheduled meetings that I gained entry into the life of the school. In September 1968 there were in existence three important 'study groups' or 'working parties'. The first, looking at the whole business of school reports, was in fact completing its work and met only once after my arrival in the school at the beginning of that term, though its chairman reported on the work of the group in the September and October staff meetings. The second working party was also nearing the end of its work by the time I entered the scene, and during that autumn term held its last two meetings, both of which I attended. This was a committee that had been set up under the chairmanship of the headmaster, with representatives from various subject areas. Its task was to construct, with the help of the recently-appointed director of intermediate studies (later head of the middle school), a new fourth and fifth-year curriculum design to meet the future requirements of the first comprehensive intake of pupils—then in their third year in the school.

At the first full staff meeting at the very beginning of that autumn term, a new working party or study group came into existence. This was a group on which people volunteered to serve, with one proviso requested by the headmaster: that its membership should not include any members of the disbanding Reports Group. The new working party was set up initially to examine approaches to learning, and—as I learned much later—was to some extent a direct outcome of the Reports Group, which had drawn the attention of colleagues to problems about communicating knowledge of children's progress to the parents. At its first meeting it was given terms of reference by the headmaster under the heading 'Organization and Assessment', with the result that it became known as 'The Organization and Assessment Group' —abbreviated commonly to 'the O & A Group'. This group met regularly during the autumn and spring terms of that academic year. After its second meeting I was invited by its elected chairman to work with the group—the other members having agreed that I should be so invited.

The third group that was already in existence when I began my work with the school contained members from all levels of the school staff, from the headmaster downwards, and had a rather different kind of task. This group was known as the 'Human Relationships Staff Study Group', commonly abbreviated to 'the H.R. Study Group'. For some years, the members of this group had been studying the problem of how to work with children, in the area of personal relationships, through the medium of discussion based on the actual experiences of children and young people as they coped with the business of growing up and coming to terms with the adult world. Because the central problem in this work was to come to terms with their own anxieties about using discussion approaches that were regarded as 'non-directive', the staff had, for some years, been enlisting the help of the Marriage Guidance Council in conducting their own internal discussions and planning how to build the new activity into the time-table. The headmaster, although he felt himself to be a member of this study group in the same sort of position as his colleagues, was clearly regarded as its leader and indeed often took this role. It was, therefore, through him that I was invited to work with this group also, as I did with the full staff meetings, the section heads' meetings and the subject department heads' meetings.

The pattern of all these meetings itself highlights the existence of the kind of organizational split between curricular and pastoral functions to which I have already referred, in general terms, in Chapter I. Much of my work with the headmaster and staff in the first year of the study was concerned with the growing recognition of the difficulties created by the structural splitting of these tasks, with the subject department heads' meetings representing the curricular side, and the section heads' meetings representing the pastoral side at the formal level. A brief explanation about the actual membership of these two senior groups now seems necessary.

The department heads' meeting was a fairly large gathering, attended by the heads of all nineteen subject departments, and also by the head of the lower school, the director of intermediate studies (later redesignated 'head of the middle school'), and the master in charge of sixth-form studies (later redesignated 'head of the upper school'), the senior mistress and the deputy headmaster, and also occasionally, for all or part of the meeting, by the four house heads. These meetings were held once a month in the sixth-form common-room, a room that also functioned as a classroom.

The sections heads' meetings, also monthly, were attended only by the deputy head and the senior mistress, the heads of the lower, middle and upper schools, and the heads of the four houses who, between them, were responsible for the third, fourth and fifth-year groups in the school. These section heads' meetings were held in the headmaster's room. It seemed inescapable that the section heads, if only because their group was smaller and more intimate and because their meetings were never augmented by the department heads, as the department heads' meetings were augmented by some or all of them, were perceived in some ways as belonging to a somewhat more privileged group. There were many in the staff group who denied quite strenuously that such a feeling existed between section and department heads. But if—as I believe—it did exist, it must have been fed by the knowledge that the section heads had a greater allocation of free time than had subject department heads. Yet the ambiguity about the relative status was also inescapable, since senior staff on both sides of the curricular and pastoral divide were distributed between B and E Grades on the salary scale, in accordance with variations in the amount of responsibility carried, and the facts about these gradings, though not formally published, were doubtless known.

As the first year of my work with the staff went on, I had a growing impression that the O & A group, at some unconscious level of operation, was representing the curricular side of the school's relationship with me, while the H.R. Study Group was similarly representing the pastoral side of the school's relationship with me. I came to believe also that there was growing uncertainty about how teachers ought to be fulfilling their responsibilities for the 'pastoral care' of pupils in the face of a rapidly changing kind of pupil intake, and that this uncertainty was being reflected in the two very different roles taken by the headmaster, on the one hand in the H.R. Study Group just referred to, and on the other hand in the committee referred to earlier that formulated, on behalf of the staff group, the new curricular pattern of studies for the first comprehensive intake of pupils as they approached the fourth year of their secondary schooling.

This second, temporary committee was clearly directed and chaired by himself, and always met—as did the section heads—in his room. In the H.R. Study Group, on the other hand, which like the department heads met in the sixth-form common-room, his role was much more ambiguous. In the presence of the marriage guidance counsellors, who came to meetings to lead discussions, offer material or suggest activities, it was clear that the headmaster wished to be regarded just as an ordinary member of the group. Yet he often found himself in the position of taking a leadership role by starting a meeting off, by making notes in the course of it, or by feeding back the content of these notes at the end. And he usually took the initiative over arranging times of subsequent meetings.

It is perhaps already becoming apparent that I will in the course of this book be using the word 'consultation' in two different contexts. At times I will be using it in the context of my own work with the headmaster and with individual staff members or groups of staff during the period of my association with the school; and since my consultations with them nearly always involved attempts on my side and increasingly on theirs to interpret the meanings of the events we took part in, the consultant role that I took in the school is contained in this use of the term 'consultation'. But I will also be using the word in the context of the headmaster's leadership role in the school and of the measures he took to enable his colleagues to participate in the processes of decision-making. The degree to which 'interpretative' comments were made by the head and others, as well as by myself as consultant, in the area of staff consultation in the school may be an indication of the long-term, as distinct from the short-term, effects of the project.

I must now indicate how I tried in this school to use consistently my own
T.S.T.M.—3

role as consultant to individuals and to groups, not in order to take over the leadership of these groups, or of the school itself, but in order to throw light on the problems of exercising such leadership. It may appear that in examining my own role in this way, I am unnecessarily drawing attention to the difficulties involved for myself. The justification for doing so, as I see it, is that these very difficulties often seemed to be reflecting aspects of the leadership role, not only of the headmaster himself but also of heads of sections and departments within his school, in various ways, of which they and I might otherwise have remained unaware.

Private discussion, public debate and the nature of interpretation

I had to make it clear from the very beginning that my consultancy role was to be seen always in relation to the overall task of the staff group in the institution, and to the separate sub-tasks for which individuals and groups were responsible. Therefore, in conducting interviews or discussions with individual members of staff, I had to resist attempts that were sometimes made to draw me out of role by involving me in discussion about matters unrelated to the staff member's own role in the school, on which my attention and his or hers had to be focused. Nevertheless, I was inevitably relating myself to persons and not merely to faceless roles in all these interviews. And it was scarcely possible for any member of staff, in examining his or her role within the school, to do so without referring to other persons in the staff group, with whom he or she had to work. It was, therefore, inevitable that in the course of all these months, I should find myself taking up with individual staff members various problems of role relationships and personal relationships and that I should become filled up more and more with knowledge about various events and about persons in the institution— knowledge which I had no sanction to refer to in public meetings.

Much of the problem of communication and of effective and open exploration of important issues in meetings, therefore, was concerned with the extent to which people were prepared to say in public things that they might formerly have hesitated to say, except to their own personal friends. In writing a book like this, I have at my disposal a great deal of material, some of which has emerged in full staff meetings, some in sectional staff meetings, some in special groups of staff, some in consultations between myself and individual persons. In making judgements about what is usable and what is not usable in a published document I have always to be considering degrees of privacy in terms of persons, of groups within the institution, and of the institution as a whole. But this is not a problem that has arisen suddenly at the point of writing this book. It was present every time I took part in a meeting of the whole staff group, or of any section of it, and every time I had a personal consultation with any member of the staff. I was very often aware in one situation of knowledge gained from another situation, which I could not feel justified in using or sharing. Staff members, and the headmaster most of all, were also faced with these problems, and were also continually having to make judgements about how and where to use knowledge. I have little doubt that the testing of my capacity to respect boundaries and the experience of following through the consequences, for me and for them, when I failed to do so, enabled members of the staff group to consider realistically how to examine in public tensions and difficulties which, as long as they were kept private and inaccessible, were impeding the work that people were really striving to do together. It was never easy, of course, to determine where the line between private and public ought to be drawn. But in so far as people were able in their roles as staff members to preserve their personal identities and their relations with each other outside the boundary of the school as a working institution, and yet avoid over-protecting one another by concealing problems of *role* relationships inside that boundary, they were demonstrating insight into the problems of professionalism in the management of a complex organization.

The management of personal relationships in the working group

What is implied here is that the staff of the school were inevitably conscious at times of feeling divided between their loyalty to the primary task of the institution and their loyalty to persons on the staff of the institution. And so the very bonds that could strengthen people in their work because of the satisfactions they provided could be sources of difficulty when the demands of the role conflicted with the demands of friendship.

Because there were six people on the staff who had already worked with me outside the school before the project started, my own role in the school was both strengthened by existing links in the institution and subject to the risk that those links might unconsciously be used, by them or by me, to evade rather than pursue the difficult task upon which we were all engaged.

I have already referred to one of the six known to me, in connection with the working party on organization and assessment that was set up during the staff meeting of September 1968, the day before the opening of the autumn term in which I began my work with the school. The man who was subsequently made chairman of that working party—a relatively young and recently appointed member of the English department—had taken his post-graduate training year in the Bristol University Department of Education. He had been quite closely associated with me during that year through membership of a voluntary study group to which I had been consultant, through a school practice period under my supervision, and through a certain amount of consultation with me over a long method essay which he had written during the summer term as part of the required work for the Certificate in Education. He had also attended, as a member, a course in the study of group relationships for teachers and social workers which I had organized a year after he had taken up his present post in the school. Because I was used regularly as consultant to the O & A Group at Nailsea, it happened that the pattern of my relationships with the staff group during the first term of my work in the school showed something like an oscillation between attendance at the meetings chaired by the headmaster, nearly always followed by personal consultations with him, and meetings chaired by this former student, followed similarly by personal consultations with *him.*

But he was not the only member of staff with whom I had previously worked professionally in a tutor/student relationship; nor was he the only one who knew from experience the kinds of methods I would employ as a consultant. There were, in fact, three other people on the staff who had, as students, been taught or tutored by me—two of them about fifteen years before this project began, one much more recently. Two others had taken part in a course in group relationships which I had directed at Bristol University, and one of them had been a member of a small group to which I had been consultant in that course. Between them, these six members covered all levels of responsibility in the staff group, since they included the senior mistress, the master in charge of sixth-form studies (later retitled 'head of upper school'), the head of music, one of the four house heads and two fairly junior members of the English department.

It was important, I believe, for the work that I was doing with the staff group, that the facts about these pre-existing relationships between myself and certain members of the staff were never kept secret. Both for those who had been most closely related to me as students earlier in their careers, and for those who had been members of my courses on group relationships, there were always twin dangers: on the one hand the danger of a mutual seduction between them and myself stemming from the wish to preserve what had been valued in the earlier relationship, and on the other hand the danger that the previous experience, which had probably involved some painful learning on both sides, could have been used defensively or even destructively in this new working relationship. In fact I believe that all these six people used their former knowledge of me as a base from which to further the work they were now engaged in, and were thus helpful agents in freeing other people to examine the problems of staying in role and, if necessary, making personal inclinations (such as the wish to turn a professional relationship into a private friendship) secondary to, though not necessarily incompatible with, the furtherance of the task of the institution.

The testing out by their colleagues that must have been going on, whether consciously or unconsciously, of the capacity of these six people (and of myself) to use pairing relationships in terms of the task may in itself have been playing some part in the various ways in which staff members perceived my relationship with the headmaster, with whom I had frequent consultations— sometimes during school hours, but more often after the end of full or sectional staff meetings, between about 5.45 and 7.15 p.m. I have little means of knowing how differently staff members perceived these consultations between their headmaster and myself; nor could any of them know what took place between us. Yet all staff had some evidence about the extent to which each of us maintained confidentiality, from the way we behaved in staff meetings; and about half the staff had additional evidence about the kind of role I took in my consultations with them, and were perhaps able to deduce from this something about the nature of my discussions with the headmaster.

What I am really saying is that the problems the staff had to face in entering into a relationship with me as a consultant are not really new problems. Because I was not a member of the staff, but came in from outside, and because I did—though still a visitor—become personally involved with the task of the school and, therefore, with its members, their feelings about me as the outsider who was gaining knowledge about them could be used as a kind of mirror in which their trust or distrust of one another, and their trust or distrust of authority, as embodied in the headmaster in particular, could be more closely examined.

As consultant to the headmaster and staff, I conceived my task to be to help them study, in terms of their own institution, the problems involved in the management of change. In order to do this I had to interpret any evidence I thought I could perceive in the immediate situation of staff meetings, committee meetings and individual interviews or consultations. The task had therefore both a research element and a teaching element. If the staff could learn nothing from the experience of having a consultant in the school, then the research could provide no new insights that might help other staff groups in other schools, with or without the help of consultants, in the task of managing educational change. The notion of attempting to publish some account of the learning we went through was both threatening to the people who had shared it and vitally necessary to them if the experience was to have any reality in the wider context of secondary education.

The experience, exposure and evaluation of a learning process

It is becoming clear that what we were all involved in throughout these two years was a gradual building up of trust. But there could never be a time, however long such a partnership persisted, when this trust would not have to be tested and retested. This was a lesson I had to learn and relearn, sometimes with considerable distress. Because I was always (rightly) seen as an outsider who was gaining inside knowledge of the school, anxieties about how I would use this knowledge were inevitably intensified whenever I was known to be making or planning to make some kind of communication to people outside the boundary of the institution, particularly if this communication had tangible existence as a typed report or outline of a report yet to be written.

It is not surprising, on reflection, that the two occasions when my own anxiety about my relationship with the school was at its highest were both occasions when such a report was already in circulation or known to exist in outline. It is also significant, I think, that the first of these two crises, coming near the end of the first year of the project, was centred in a sharp reaction from the school secretarial staff group, with whom I had had no direct contact, whereas the second, coming near the end of the second year of the project, was centred in the headmaster's standing committee consisting of his most senior staff members, with whom I had worked a great deal. In each case the explosion was sparked off by what must have seemed like an alarming intrusion into my apparently private relationship with the school, namely the intrusion (known at one level to be inevitable but felt at another level as threatening to that relationship) of my commitment to the Schools Council.

On the earlier occasion I had been asked to send to the Schools Council a brief interim report on my project for distribution, along with other reports, to the forty or so heads of schools and project directors (including the Nailsea headmaster and myself) who had been invited to attend the four-day conference to which I had already referred. Mistakenly, as I now think, I had agreed to send such a report, written it under considerable pressure, sent it off to the Schools Council in a rough typescript, and only subsequently had it duplicated and distributed to the Nailsea staff. In other words, although I did not conceal from the staff that I had already sent this report off a few days earlier, I did things in the wrong order.

The storm broke ostensibly because of one particular comment I had made in the report about relationships between teaching and clerical staff in the school. But I now believe that the real point at issue was my failure to respect the integrity of the boundary round the school by first securing sanction from within that boundary to take the report outside; for I had made an undertaking, in the memorandum prepared and distributed in the summer of 1968, that I should not publish anything about the school without first seeking sanction to do so, particularly when any individuals or sub-groups might be recognizable. If I had handled the problem in this way it would have been possible, at an earlier stage, for the Nailsea staff to face the reality that the work being done with me could have no real validity if it was to remain for ever private, since its validity would ultimately depend on the extent to which the staff and I were able to take responsibility for that work within the wider boundary that contained the Schools Council and the network of schools, research institutions and training institutions in whose interests it had been set up.

Between that event and the second crisis I have mentioned, I wrote a long and detailed report—not this time for the Schools Council but for the Nailsea staff—a report which was the subject of intensive consultation at all levels while still in draft, was distributed at the end of December 1969 to all the staff, and was discussed at a special staff meeting and at a governors' meeting during the following term, early in 1970. Only after that did I seek and gain sanction to release that report to a dozen people outside the school, including three in the Schools Council, three in the Bristol University School of Education, three in the Tavistock Institute of Human Relations, and three other influential people in the educational world whose views on the work I needed.

The second 'opening of the door' to a group of people outside the school, unlike the earlier one, did not give rise to any explosive reactions, mainly because the staff received the document first and because sanction was sought, and given, for its distribution to the few people indicated, all of whom were directly or indirectly connected with the institutions that gave support to the project. It may be also that the sharing of detailed knowledge about the actual events of that first year with educators other than heads of schools was felt to be less disturbing than the sharing of the vague and general conjectures about possible emerging issues with twenty or so heads of other schools had been six months earlier.

Despite all this, and despite the fact that my work with the headmaster and his senior standing committee became more intensive during the following months, I had to face another unexpected crisis in July 1970, this time not in the non-teaching part of the staff group, in which the problem had been encapsulated the year before, but in the standing committee. The fact that it took place here doubled the shock both for me and for them, yet made possible for all of us considerable gains in our understanding of the fundamental problem that it highlighted. I am saying, in fact, that it was right, in work terms, however uncomfortable in inter-personal terms, that the collision occurred there. Again it was basically a problem of boundary control that was really at issue.

The crisis was sparked off by my presentation to the headmaster of a draft outline of a working paper—a draft that he passed on to the members of the standing committee, rightly in my view, so that they could discuss it with me at their next meeting a day or two later. The working paper was at that time being confused in my own mind with a possible course of lectures that I had been asked to give in the School of Education in the autumn. Agreement had in fact been reached, after discussion at all levels in the Nailsea staff group, that I should both give the lecture course and write the working paper. But the sight of the unclothed skeleton of my first attempt at the synopsis of the six chapters of that projected paper reactivated all the earlier anxieties about how I might present this institution to the outside world; and it was those parts of the synopsis that referred to problems of boundary control that caused the greatest offence. One result of this crisis was that I decided to postpone giving the lecture course.

Are these events of merely local significance as part of a private, domestic and personalized experience that has affected only myself in relation to the

Nailsea staff, to the staff of the University School of Education and to the particular members of the Schools Council staff with whom I have been in personal contact? Is this just a kind of autobiographical novel that I am writing? Or have these events a wider significance when we consider, in more general terms, how any school builds up trust both within its own boundary and between itself and the other institutions with which it must relate itself if educators are to learn by their experience and improve their skills? I believe that the events I have described do have this wider significance. Nailsea is only one of thousands of schools that must search continually for a right balance between preserving the integrity of their own boundaries and accepting their commitment to work both with the schools and training institutions in their areas and with the national institutions that exist to promote the new thinking that may modify present practice.

Entangled with the natural suspicion about how my commitment to the Schools Council might threaten the integrity of the boundary round the school was the staff's awareness of my other role as a member of the University School of Education from which, during every spring term, a number of students came to Nailsea for their term of school practice. Two further consequences of this continuing link between Nailsea School and the University School of Education were that some of my Bristol colleagues were present in the school from time to time during the spring terms of 1969 and 1970 (as in other years) as supervisors to these students, consulting with heads of departments and with other members of the staff who had responsibility for them. Conversely, some of the Nailsea staff were taking roles in the School of Education as school-based supervisors, helping with the method (or 'subject') work during the autumn and summer terms; others were or had been students in the division of advanced studies, working towards the Advanced Certificate or M.Ed. degree, or taking part in special conferences in the University.

The consultant as a mirror for staff experience and the school as a mirror for the experiences of other schools

What I am really suggesting is that the anxiety that was so often expressed about what I might take out with me when I recrossed the Nailsea School boundary and re-entered the University School boundary was gathering up into itself the comparable anxieties that must always be present in any school, where every single member of staff is a potential carrier of information from the school into other institutions, in which they all take roles as citizens of the total community that contains the school. I often wondered whether I was expected or assumed to be immune from anxiety about reports that members of the Nailsea staff might be carrying out into other institutions about my activities in the school, and whether I was expected to have no curiosity about what impressions my own colleagues in the university might be gathering about those activities in the course of their own collaborative work with certain individual members of the Nailsea staff.

The preoccupation with these matters was reflected vividly for me in the last full staff meeting of the 1969–70 session, when the theme of discussion was 'assessment'. The choice of this was not fortuitous. It was the natural, and planned, sequel to a series of discussions in the standing committee and in the senior staff meeting that was to culminate in the headmaster's recommendation about how knowledge about a child's performance in all areas of his work should be communicated by teachers to one another, to the child himself and to the child's parents. This discussion was about something that was very central to the work of the school. Assessment was bound to be a strong preoccupation at this time in the history of the school, when staff were having to face and interpret evidence about the effects on their pupils of choices of options and of allocations to GCE and CSE courses, without being able to refer back to any previous shared experience of working with fourth-year pupils of such a wide ability range. Although I had been able to offer interpretative comments about these problems on other occasions, on this occasion I was silent, apart from one brief interjection which I could not feel was a helpful one. Curiously enough my inability to take part in this discussion did not reflect any sense of detachment or lack of identification with the problems being discussed. On the contrary I found myself painfully identified with them—so embedded in the arguments as to be unable to make any appropriate contributions. The language being used by the staff was more than usually emotive; the words 'private' and 'public' recurred, along with thoughts about 'informing people' or 'keeping people in the dark', about 'deceiving' parents or 'labelling' children, about 'trusting' or 'distrusting' parents, and about whether parents 'trusted' or 'distrusted' teachers. There was at one point an angry clash of feelings between a department head and the head of one section of the school. The department head —commenting on the problem of assessing a child's progress objectively while perceiving him as a member of a high-ability, moderate-ability or low-ability stream or set—said rather despairingly that it was almost impossible to get parents to understand what one was saying about a child's work. The section head retaliated sharply by pointing out that this man was, in effect, describing his own colleagues, nearly all of whom were parents as well as teachers, when he dismissed 'parents' as stupid and uncomprehending. At another point in the meeting a number of people expressed anxiety about having to assess children's work in relation to the whole of an age group without knowing how this school's standards compared with those of other schools.

The headmaster said to me afterwards that he had sensed in the discussion a certain cleavage between those who, as house or section heads, had to face parents when they came to school wanting truthful comments about where their children stood in relation to other children, and those who, as 'subject teachers', were more concerned about protecting their own relationships with the children than with satisfying the needs of the parents. For me the question behind all this was the question that the staff now seemed to be asking me: could I be concerned both with them as people and with the search for new insights about the way in which they were working? In other words, how did I reconcile my own feelings towards them as persons with the role I had to take in relation to them as teachers in this institution? Could I make objective assessments about the school and the professional staff inside it without losing contact with those I had come to know as persons? I no longer felt that the question being asked was whether I would or would not reveal the identity of the school in speaking or writing publicly about it. The question now seemed to be—given that I could not conceal the school's identity— whether I would be able to speak or write truthfully about it without labelling it as good, bad or indifferent and without betraying the trust that had been placed in me by its staff.

Although I had no sense in that meeting of being attacked or even of being excluded, I was aware of an increasing depression and aware also that this depression had a great deal to do with my own preoccupation with the problems of writing up my reflections about the work I was still engaged in with the school. Indeed the wish of one staff member to preserve the image of parents as stupid and non-comprehending echoed for me a remark he had made in January during the staff discussion of my December report, when he had implied that nobody reading that report who had not been a member of the Nailsea staff would be able to understand a word of it—in other words, that teachers, too, might be stupid and uncomprehending. The conflict that I was aware of—between my wish to preserve the Nailsea experiences by locking them up in a private world and the necessity of exposing them so that others, outside the school, could make constructive use of the information —seemed reflected in the conflict experienced by the staff in their relation- ships with pupils and parents: for members of staff were similarly torn between their wish to preserve their own relationships with children as some- thing private and inviolable and their obligation to keep faith with parents by passing on to them the information they needed in the hope that they could use it responsibly.

In retrospect it seems to me now that the important thing for the Nailsea staff during that summer term was not so much that they had become able to explore with me their own misgivings about what I might say or write about them in the future, as that—because of this experience—they were becoming able to explore openly with one another the real nature of the relationship between teaching and assessment and the difficulties of moving across the boundary that protected their relationships with their pupils in order to function appropriately within the wider boundary that included themselves, their pupils and the parents of those pupils.

There was, perhaps, at times a subconscious wish to see me as *either* identified with them against the Schools Council and the universities *or* identified with the Schools Council and the universities against them. But along with this there was undoubtedly a growing recognition that the only valid kind of identification for me was with a task that involved all three institutions. This, I believe, was another aspect of the struggle to bring back into a fruitful relationship the 'pastoral' and 'curricular' sides of the total enterprise in which all of us were engaged. For the work the Nailsea staff did with me always became real at those moments when I could be perceived as both caring about the school and trying to extract from my experience of working with it some ideas about secondary education in general that could be studied and tested by other teachers in different though comparable situations.

In what follows, I hope to show, with an increasing amount of detail and incident, how the staff in this school, as persons working in a complex and changing network of roles and relationships, studied the problems outlined in Chapter I, and how they and I were able to make constructive use of the theoretical ideas presented in Chapter II.

PART TWO

Secondary School in Transition

A. Teachers in Multiple Roles

Introduction

As we move inwards from the broad, impersonal field of secondary schooling in general into the relatively small definable area of one Somerset school, we bring into focus a group of sixty to seventy men and women, expanding in numbers during the three-year period of the study, and fluctuating in membership with the departure of some to new posts elsewhere and with the influx of others from other posts or fresh from education courses. Some of these men and women I have come to know personally; many have made an impact upon me through their work in various kinds of staff meeting; and to refer to them in what follows only by naming the official and unofficial roles they have taken in the school would be to deny their reality as persons who have contributed to the experiences recorded here. I shall therefore refer to people by name whenever it assists my purpose to do so, in the hope that the reader may both catch some of the flavour of the events and be enabled to put himself imaginatively into some of the situations described.

This procedure, of course, implies a certain risk, for we are faced at the outset with the difficulty that I will unavoidably be writing about persons as well as roles, and that my readers may, as a result of what I say about their role experiences, receive impressions and form images of these persons that would not in fact be recognizable to anyone who really knew them. It is surprisingly easy to misread a statement by failing to perceive an important word or phrase within it, or even by unconsciously substituting one word for another. If I say that Mr X was uncertain whether his colleagues perceived him as having the full confidence of the headmaster, I may be variously *thought* to have said that Mr X was uncertain whether the headmaster really trusted him to do his job, or that Mr X's colleagues did not trust him to do his job, or that Mr X had no confidence in his own ability to do his job, or even perhaps that the headmaster had no confidence in Mr X. If I say that Mrs Y sometimes wondered whether her role in the school had shrunk out of existence, I may be *thought* to have said that Mrs Y no longer performed any useful function in the school. If I say that three of the most senior members of the staff had more and more opportunities to exercise leadership in the staff group and that two others had fewer and fewer such opportunities, I may be *thought* to have implied that the former were 'strong' leaders and the latter 'weak' leaders. If I say that a certain person was perceived by colleagues to have skill in one area but not in another, I may be *thought* to have said that this person was hopelessly one-sided.

In offering themselves as mirrors in which other persons in comparable roles in other schools may see reflected some of the problems they may be encountering, the members of the particular school from which I draw my illustrative material are thus accepting the risk that they themselves may emerge from these pages as parodies of the persons they really are. Because their roles are duplicated in many schools, teachers elsewhere may project into the Nailsea situation the elements of the actual situations known to them in those other schools, thus trying to make two images 'fit' more

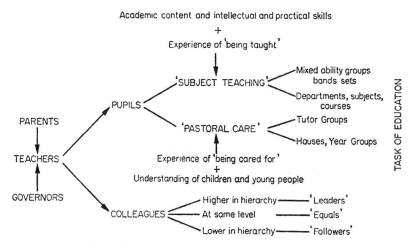

Fig. 11. The teacher, his pupils and his colleagues.

perfectly than they really do. In the same way, I myself have been suspected of bringing into the Nailsea situation my own stereotypes of the expanding secondary school and of looking for evidence that will confirm those stereotypes.

In the two chapters that follow I shall be considering some of the ways in which the Nailsea staff handled the tensions between their concern for special areas of knowledge and skill and their concern for the children they were trying to educate. In Chapter IV I shall be using the 'subject-interest' perspective, in Chapter V the 'pupil-interest' perspective; yet both strands of the problem will be present in both chapters, since it is with the merging of the two perspectives into a more fully educational view that we are all ultimately concerned (see Figure 11).

In joining a school teachers come into a ready-made structure that does not necessarily aid this process of fusion. The departmental system, based on the division of knowledge into the familiar school subjects, has long been the expected form of organization in the secondary school, and is often held by those of a revolutionary cast of mind to be the major block in the way of curricular reform. It is less often suggested that the kind of pastoral-care system that in many schools has been superimposed upon that departmental system may also be acting as a brake on curricular reform, because it implies a denial both of the caring aspects of all good teaching and of the teaching aspects of all effective caring. These two chapters will show, through the example of Nailsea's experience, how successive efforts to improve the curricular system and successive efforts to improve the pastoral system may gradually coalesce in a new kind of enquiry that is neither exclusively curricular nor exclusively pastoral in its outlook, but increasingly brings the two sides of the problem into the same focus of attention.

In order to ensure that the different events and situations can be related clearly to the important changes in the management structure that were made during the period of my work with the school, the reader is asked to bear in mind the following dates:

1. April 1969: Renaming of the director of intermediate studies as 'Head of Middle School' and of the master in charge of sixth-form studies as 'Head of Upper School'.
2. September 1969:
   (i) Formation of the Standing Committee, consisting of the headmaster, the deputy head, the senior mistress, and the heads of the lower, middle and upper schools.
   (ii) Replacement of former section and department heads' meetings by a combined monthly meeting of all senior staff.
   (iii) Addition of three new senior posts of School Counsellor, Head of Sixth-Form General Studies and full-time Librarian.
3. September 1971: Replacement of the house system by a year-group system, and of the departmental system by a modified pattern of larger subject areas, each with a head of department in charge, supported by advisors in the narrower separate subjects within each broad area.

Because we shall not be simply following an uninterrupted narrative in the remaining chapters of the book, apparent discrepancies in the terminology used must be seen as corresponding to different phases in the three-year period with which we are mainly concerned. Thus the term 'section head', if used in the context of the 1968–9 session, could refer either to a house head or to the head of the lower school or to the master in charge of sixth-form studies; but in the context of the 1969–70 session it could refer only to one of three people, namely the lower, middle or upper-school head. Similarly, the same staff member may be described by one of two titles held at successive stages of this three-year period according to the context in which he is being perceived. The effects upon individuals and upon the staff group as a whole of these changes in roles and structures of management are themselves at the centre of what this book is about.

CHAPTER IV

Curricular Innovations and the Departmental Structure

Curriculum change as a challenge to the existing organization

There are people who will say that curriculum change, in any fundamental sense, has so far scarcely begun. Yet, in an era when society itself is changing, some modification, slight or considerable, to the familiar pattern of school subjects is as inevitable as the seasonal changes in the year. Unlike the change of seasons, however, curriculum change is not a cycle. For once a new course is introduced, even if initially as a pilot scheme only, its effects cannot be wiped out. The children who have experienced it carry its consequences through into the next phase of their schooling. The planning of change must therefore take account not only of resources (human and material) and of time limitations (short-term and long-term), but also of the natural growth of a child's ability to order his own experience and to master conceptual thought. When a staff group of sixty to seventy persons embarks on this kind of process, while currently engaged in the day-to-day work of teaching and tutoring pupils the earliest efforts are bound to be tentative, the eventual route long, tortuous and elusive. It may therefore be helpful if I can make a few important signposts visible at the start, even though such signposts were not available to the Nailsea staff when they were struggling with the events themselves. They are available now because of the work they did with each other and (latterly) with me while the events were going on.

Briefly, the sequence of events bearing on curriculum change, up to the summer of 1971, was as follows. The introduction of changes began, not surprisingly, within established areas. Well before the autumn of 1968 there had been additions to the traditional pattern of subjects and courses, in the form of option courses, some starting in Year II and some in Year IV. Later the first 'integrated' course in humanities, cutting across the boundaries of four arts subjects, was introduced for first-year pupils. The first major attempt to look at the curriculum as a whole was made when the Fourth Year Curriculum group (the planning committee mentioned in Chapter III) worked together over a period of about a year during the spring, summer and autumn of 1968 to produce the new pattern of option pools for the first comprehensive intake of pupils then on its way through to the fourth year. The second attempt was through the setting up of the O & A Group in

September 1968 (also mentioned in Chapter III) to look at the whole question of organization and assessment, not in terms of any one curricular area but in the context of the whole learning task. The third attempt was centred on the study of the theoretical model proposed by P. H. Phenix[1] for redesigning a curriculum by substituting 'realms of meaning' for the traditional subject departments, a study that was initiated in the autumn of 1969 in the newly formed standing committee and then taken out into the staff group as a whole. The fourth attempt was through a long intensive series of meetings in the spring of 1970 between the standing committee and those individual colleagues who chose to accept an open invitation to come and discuss with the committee their hopes, their fears and their opinions about changes that were already going on or that might be introduced. The fifth attempt was through a new kind of staff meeting in which the major part of the available meeting time was held at first in six, then in five study groups, each group working under the leadership of a member of the standing committee, and all groups coming back into plenary session for the last half hour to work on the outcome of the sectional discussions. These meetings culminated in a major reorganization of the curricular-pastoral structure into a year-group system, along with the grouping of subject departments into large curricular areas, each year-group tutorial team and each curricular area being headed by a senior staff member.

In examining these phases in more detail, in this and subsequent chapters, we shall be engaged in tracing out a progress from the old relatively simple way of looking at the curriculum piecemeal in order to preserve the parts, towards a new and relatively complex way of examining it as a whole in order to create a total pattern that might reflect more accurately the kinds of learning it existed to promote. Inevitably we are looking at work that was neither wholly successful nor wholly unsuccessful. In fact, in evaluating this kind of process, the success/failure dimension is meaningless. The later stages could not have happened without the experiences gained through the earlier ones. My own involvement, though intense in its way, was that of a non-teaching visiting consultant, continually moving in and out of the staff group's deliberations, and therefore not committed to implementing with the pupils the results of these deliberations. Yet I found that at different times I wanted to identify myself with different parts of the staff group— sometimes with the uncertainties of those who felt that their opinions were being disregarded, sometimes with the impatience of those who wanted to push for more radical changes, sometimes with the headmaster, who had to contain within himself all the extremes of feeling and thought being expressed by the staff. Consequently I would often experience, in myself, critical, even hostile reactions to the behaviour of certain sub-sections of staff or of certain individuals, though other people's perceptions of my reactions did not necessarily correspond with my own experience of them.

[1] Phenix, P. H. (1964), *Realms of Meaning*, McGraw Hill.

For the governors, parents, teachers and indeed pupils who had a stake in Nailsea's development there was an inescapable tension between the hope that it might become a place of maximum opportunity for an increasingly diverse intake of population and the fear that it might degenerate into a place of confusion and uncertainty. As its headmaster, Denys John had both to contain his own hopes and fears about the changing situation in which he found himself and to be at the receiving end of the conflicting views about it that must have been assailing him from all sides, as others sought to enlist his support. He had commitments to parents and pupils whose expectations of the school could never be seen as simple or consistent. There was not one teacher in the school for whose appointment he had not been responsible or to whom he had not given certain undertakings over terms of appointment and conditions of work. His problem, therefore, in trying to plan for rational change, was to find a way of enlisting the support and drawing on the ideas of teachers, many of whom at the time of their appointment could not have foreseen that the small grammar school they were joining would become a large comprehensive school, any more than the first parents could have foreseen this change. Some of the teachers in the school had been committed for many years to particular ways of working with children and to particular syllabuses drawn up, revised and modified in the light of experience and of known developments in the field. Yet the fate of some of these syllabuses seemed, as time went on, to be far more in question than the staff themselves could have predicted when they drew them up—a fact about which they were bound to have mixed feelings.

During the two years on which this chapter will be mainly focused, the staff were concerned at many levels with examining two kinds of problem: first, how to provide in the lower school stable working groups in which children did not have to cope with too many teachers in the course of the two-week cycle of one-hour lesson periods; and secondly how to provide in the middle school an increasing amount of choice and variety, so that able pupils could study certain subjects in greater depth without sacrificing the benefits of a general education, while less able pupils could be provided with work that was not rooted in special subjects yet was not devoid of knowledge content.

The first of these needs had led, in the autumn of 1968, to the launching of the experimental course in humanities, perceived initially as the work of a small team of four, made possible by the pooling of time-tabled periods hitherto allocated separately to English, history, geography and religious education, and sanctioned by the heads of these four departments, one of whom, the head of religious education, was a member of the team. The second of these needs had been met by the appointment of a director of intermediate studies, who was to be the chief adviser to the staff on the design of a new curriculum that would be appropriate for a comprehensive intake of pupils.

In terms of the 'signpost' metaphor, the terrain, during the two years under review, was uncharted and the route uncertain, sometimes moving into new areas, sometimes looping back to more familiar territory. It was inevitable that confusion and uncertainty should be part of the experience of redefining objectives and of modifying the procedures for working towards the new objectives, even that such confusion and uncertainty could at times spark off anger and disillusionment and distrust. I am even saying that Denys John, caught between so many pressures, could find himself at times distrusted as headmaster even by colleagues who trusted him as a person, and that he could be opposed in staff meetings by the very colleagues who supported most strongly the educational ideas for which he stood. The problem of leadership, for him, was to provide the staff with a secure framework within which they could work to influence the decisions he would ultimately have to make. And this framework, as we shall see later in this book, involved on the one hand the use of a structure based on the principle of representation and on the other hand the use of a time perspective in which the phasing of consultations leading up to a decision could be made known in advance to the whole staff group.

Inevitably, like any other head, Denys John had his own personal convictions, even his own obstinate resolves, about the direction in which education ought to be heading. Like his colleagues, he had had his own starting point in his commitment to a special subject—namely modern languages. He once said in a senior staff meeting that one of his particular sticking points, on which he would not yield ground, would come if he were ever asked to legislate in such a way that certain children would be denied the opportunity even to try out a subject. Thus, in the particular context in which this assertion was made, he felt that all children in the school should be exposed at least to the possibility of learning French. Although he would concede that some children might appropriately be advised to opt out of French after a year's trial in order to tackle work for which they might show greater aptitude, he would not, as headmaster, accept the idea that the least able children ought not to embark on French at all, since until such children had had the chance to try it no-one could know what their response to it might be. Commenting on this declaration of principle some months later, he added that he would use the same argument concerning any subject, not only the subject which had been his own initial specialism. He was also, by 1968, known to be in favour of an extension of the teaching done in mixed-ability groups, so far used only for art, crafts, music, physical education and games; and this wish was very much linked up in the minds of colleagues (and probably in his own mind also) with his interest in breaking down subject boundaries through the development of team teaching.

A good deal of the uncertainty centred also on the deputy head (formerly head of history and religious education) Robin Thomas, who was in the peculiar position of being not only Denys John's deputy but also the only member of the teaching staff who had been one of the handful of colleagues with whom he had opened the school in 1959. Unlike other senior staff who had been present during the school's earliest years (if not as early as 1959), Robin Thomas had spent four years as head of lower school in the neighbouring comprehensive school (formerly a secondary modern school) at Portishead, where the intake of unselected pupils had begun two years earlier than at Nailsea. It was he who, with the help of the senior mistress Joan Bradbury, always prepared drafts of proposed curriculum patterns, duplicating them, usually over his own initials, for distribution to staff. He was also, as a history specialist, one of the four members of the teaching team that launched the first-year humanities course in September 1968. Thus, for some colleagues he was identified with the small grammar school they had known before the Somerset reorganization got under way; and for others he was identified with the post-reorganization era through his 'defection' to Portishead and his return to Nailsea, no longer as head of history and R.E. but as deputy to a head who was known to be committed to changes that many did not want.

The other senior staff member who came into the staff group with experience of a changing comprehensive school was the director of intermediate studies, Clive Vanloo, who came to Nailsea from a Bristol comprehensive and, before that, one of the big London comprehensives. He did not appear to bring into the school a personal vested interest in a 'subject', since he had not been head of a department in any previous post. Although in his education course he had specialized in natural sciences, it was with the field of social studies that he was most strongly identified at Nailsea.

Looking, with hindsight, at the very different ways in which innovations were introduced, at first-year and at fourth-year levels, during the crucial years of 1968 and 1969, one begins to see a developmental pattern. It is impossible not to be struck by the fact that the lower-school innovation, in the form of the experimental humanities course, was never felt by the staff to have been the result of corporate planning to nearly the same extent as the middle-school innovation, in the form of the pattern of fourth and fifth-year options, was. The difference seems to have turned on an implied contrast, at that time, between the role of John Harbinson (head of the lower school since 1963) and the role of Clive Vanloo, subsequently head of the middle school, but appointed originally, as we have seen, with a title that linked his responsibility specifically with curricular concerns in that area. Although John Harbinson later took a teaching role in the humanities course, he never had responsibility for it in his role as head of lower school. Hence perhaps the feeling among some of the staff that the humanities course was not really backed by the authority of the staff group or even by the authority of those mainly concerned with the lower school.

Meanwhile in the sixth form a comparable change was going on, based on new thinking about the sixth-form general studies course—a change that was being worked out between the head of the upper school, Mike Burnham (formerly head of English) and one of his sixth-form tutors, who was also a colleague in the English department, namely Graham Morris, who in fact became in the autumn of 1969 the first holder of a new senior post as head of Sixth-Form General Studies. Graham Morris was the man who acted as chairman of the O & A Group during the 1968–9 session. I shall have more to say about the work of that group in a later chapter. Here, it is relevant to establish his link with Mike Burnham and his own growing interest in an integrated course that was firmly rooted in the upper school, a course that was not, so far, having the same kind of repercussions on the staff group as a whole that the curricular developments in the lower and middle schools were having. It seemed that the staff group, while regarding the sixth-form general studies as an almost private area for which Mike Burnham and Graham Morris were responsible, was projecting its major anxieties about curricular innovations into the humanities course in the lower school and its major hopes about curricular change into the new pattern of options in the middle school.

Alignments and divisions between departments over banding and setting

I shall return later in this chapter to the humanities course and the conflicts that became associated with it. But, because its fortunes were so closely bound up with the related problem of de-streaming as it affected different subject departments, I will first examine the system of banding and setting that existed in the school at the beginning of the 1968–9 session.

It was in fact partly through the banding and setting arrangements that certain alignments and polarizations had come into existence. Yet, seen in the perspective of teaching objectives rather than in that of time-tabling problems, some of the resulting partnerships seemed unreal. The English department had natural links with art, music and physical education—three of the four areas in which the teaching had always been linked to mixed-ability groups. But up till the summer of 1970 English was linked, for time-tabling purposes, with history and geography, the three departments agreeing to have the same setting arrangements within two broad ability bands. Mathematics was similarly linked with science in setting within similar bands determined on achievements in this combined area. Which department in each of the two groupings really played the major part in the decisions about these arrangements?

If there were disagreements or difficult concessions these were never reported or referred to in staff meetings. The mathematicians and scientists in particular were loudly insistent that they experienced no difficulty in reaching agreement. Yet one piece of evidence came to light in the early part of the 1969–70 session that suggested that it had really been the scientists who had called the tune. Because the science department was involved in the Nuffield 'Science for the Young School Leaver' course, which required small sets of not more than eighteen, the sets at the top of the ability scale had to be correspondingly large. In the senior staff meeting of October 1969 Robin Grist, the head of mathematics, drew attention to the difficulties for the mathematicians of having these large O-level sets in the fourth year, some of which could contain as many as 37 or 38 pupils. He related this, not to the reality that the mathematicians were having to accommodate themselves to the needs of the Nuffield science course for the lower-ability groups, but to his own feeling that this imbalance in the size of the groupings could legitimately be used as a means of persuading the county to increase the school's staff quota and thus enable it to move from a seven-form to an eight-form entry. Denys John, in order to correct this error, had to point out that the problem of the imbalance for these two subjects, because of an option that was 'expensive' in use of staff, was illustrative of the over-all problems of staff deployment in a system that provided crafts and practical subjects that had to be taught in half sets and options that were 'expensive' because relatively few pupils chose them.

If it is hard to credit that the agreements reached by the mathematicians and scientists were not accompanied by concessions on one side or the other, it is equally hard to imagine that the three arts departments of English, history and geography necessarily wanted to use the same criteria in arriving at their agreements. And as English was the only one of these three subjects that had been able to retain a proportion of its teaching time when the humanities course was introduced into the first-year curriculum, the historians and geographers must have felt they were at a considerable disadvantage when the negotiations over the second-year sets took place. In fact the historians and geographers were repeatedly expressing anxieties about assessment in the second and third years, and, although these were nearly always voiced in the context of discussion about humanities, they may well have been related to questions about which sets children were placed in after the first year and about the effects on the later work of these decisions. It appeared that the system of division into sets within two broad bands of ability (excluding two 'general subjects' groups, each of about twenty remedial and 'fringe-remedial' children, in the first and second years) had given rise to a fairly widespread belief that whereas science and mathematics demanded fine setting, the three arts subjects did not. In fact this belief was without foundation, for, although the two setting patterns were different, there was no evidence, according to Robin Thomas, that those for English, history and geography were any less rigidly based on estimated attainments than were those for mathematics and science. Indeed, he expressed the view— perhaps speaking more as a historian than as deputy head—that the history and geography departments had been forced by the system (or by English?) into a finer setting system than they really wanted. Yet my impression had been that the scientists and mathematicians were continually putting themselves in the role of 'requiring' fine sets because of the demands of their subjects, whereas the specialists on the arts side seemed to be implying that fine setting was not required for their work.

Nevertheless, the existence of these two different banding and setting arrangements had made it possible for pupils who could excel, either in the arts field or in the science-mathematics field but not in both, to be allocated to a higher set in one area and a lower one in the other. It thus reduced, to a considerable extent, the 'streaming' element in the banding system, because it allowed for some differentiation of skills and special abilities and provided some assurance to parents that a child would not be given a kind of blanket grade that denied these differences.

During the 1968–70 period the amount of setting was gradually decreased in proportion as the amount of work done in the mixed-ability tutor groups was increased. It was this process itself that awakened the standing committee during the autumn of 1969, to the disturbing idea that the banding system— although certainly a departure from the old streaming system as practised in many grammar, secondary-modern and multi-lateral schools of the past— had really been perpetuating, in a modified and therefore disguised form, the tri-partite system of which the original 'Nailsea Grammar School' had been a part. The three-sevenths of the total intake that was broadly defined as the 'upper band' and the four-sevenths (excluding the 'remedial', 'fringe-remedial' or 'general subjects' groups) that was broadly defined as the 'lower band' had, after all, been roughly equivalent to the old grammar-school/ secondary-modern-school division, in areas where the grammar-school provision was exceptionally generous, giving places to roughly 43 per cent of the population.

My own initial difficulties in grasping the details of the banding and setting system during the first year of my work with the school, and my continuing unawareness until well into 1970 of the fact that the arts and sciences used different bands as well as different sets, seem to have been reflecting the ambivalence of the staff group towards this whole problem of grouping. And no doubt it also reflected the conflicting wishes of parents, who might find themselves favouring one kind of arrangement for one member of a family and a quite different arrangement for another.

In the autumn of 1969 the old banding system was abolished for the first-year pupils. For time-tabling convenience only, and without respect to ability differences, tutor groups, in which the humanities course was being taught for the first time, were now arranged in two sub-groups, and it was therefore across the whole ability range in each sub-group, including the remedial children, that the sets for mathematics and science were arranged. For French, as before, children were in sets that were organized according to two criteria. First, all in-coming pupils had to be sub-divided into those who had learned French in their primary schools and those who had not; and then the resulting 'experienced' group was further sub-divided according to what was known about the progress the children had made.

The transition to the new system in September 1969 brought into sharp focus the extent to which movement from the lower band to the upper band (or vice-versa), despite formal assurances to parents about its possibility, had been obstructed in the past. This had been so partly because the very existence of the banding system had made it imperative that any child entering the school from another area having gained a grammar-school place there had to be given a place in the upper bands at Nailsea. Hence the loss of flexibility and the problem of over-crowding in some of the top sets. The recognition of this problem, during the term in which—for the incoming year-group—it was ceasing to exist, came to the standing committee with a sense of shock. As Joan Bradbury put it: 'We can no longer hide from the evidence'.

There was another shock to come also. For in the senior staff meeting of October 1969 John Harbinson divulged that he, as head of lower school, had arranged the setting for the current first-year mathematics and science groups himself, and that, contrary to the general belief, the setting was not fine at all but very coarse. This announcement followed soon after the head of physics had said that the setting across the total ability range, which they had feared might not be fine enough, was proving 'quite all right'. John Harbinson's revelation seemed to fall into the midst of the meeting like an unexploded bomb. Although the implications of it were not discussed directly at all, there was a curious kind of flight into talk about the need to let the present year run through before any decisions were made about continuing the new system into the second year. It seemed that the discovery that the 'unstreaming' had gone even further than many people had realized was considerably unnerving, perhaps because it was forcing people to ask themselves what they might have been doing to children in previous years by assuming that they could be accurately divided into sets. Perhaps also there was an uncomfortable sense that the words 'fine' and 'coarse', as applied to methods of grading children, contained a faint echo suggesting that it might be the children themselves who had been perceived as 'fine-grained' or 'coarse-grained'. And behind all this anxiety about what they had been doing in the past was the growing recognition that a further extension of 'mixed-ability teaching' might necessitate reappraisal not only of grouping methods but also of teaching methods.

Humanities as a spear-head of change and as a receptacle for fears about change

Once the problem of looking critically at teaching methods is faced, teachers find themselves having to embark on the painful process of reassessing their own skills, perhaps after years of successful teaching, or teaching that has seemed successful in terms of the criteria used in the past. Such questioning must start within the relatively secure framework of a known field of study;

for it is from these explorations within the known subject areas that teachers gain confidence to move outwards into new territory, and perhaps to question the validity of the partitioning of knowledge as accepted traditionally by the schools.

Humanities, beginning as a sort of packaging together of four of these known subjects, was the first clear break with that tradition. But the humanities course, taught experimentally to all the first-year pupils during the 1968–9 session and extended later into the second year, was not the first addition to the curriculum. The departments of history, geography and science had already produced off-shoots in the form of courses in citizenship and the British Constitution (both rooted in history), in geology (rooted in geography) and in human biology and rural studies (both rooted in science). These were taught, concurrently with Latin and with German or Russian, as the 'second-year options' and were regarded as 'enrichment' courses, allowing for choice and variation beyond the normal, familiar secondary-school diet. They catered for the ablest pupils who wanted a second language or a third science, and they provided alternative new studies for pupils who had not showed promise as linguists or scientists but could not for that reason be presumed to have no promise in any area of study. In other words, this introduction of a range of new studies was an advance on the old notion that children who could not take Latin or a second modern language should be occupied during those periods with 'extra English'. Along with these optional courses for all pupils, two additional courses in local studies and practical drawing (provided by the departments of geography and technical education respectively) were taught concurrently with French for the children who had failed to make any progress with French during their first year in the school.

The humanities course differed from the (by then) familiar second-year options, and from the comparable fourth-year options that had followed in 1967, in two important respects. First, it was provided not just for one group of children but for an entire age group, thus falling into the category of what universities commonly describe as 'required courses'; and secondly, it was not offered by a single department but was evolved as the result of consultation between the four arts departments, as a result of which it was agreed that the team should consist of four volunteers, one from each of the four subject areas. History and religious education were represented by Robin Thomas and Graeme Osborn respectively, geography and English by two relatively junior staff, Bob Jarratt for geography and Pam Thackeray for English. It should be noted here that Bob Jarratt was also assistant in the remedial department. During that trial year, the humanities course was being taught, not in the mixed-ability tutor groups, but in the banded groups hitherto used in teaching the contributing subjects—that is, in sets within either the upper band (or top three-sevenths of the total intake) or within the lower band (or remaining four-sevenths, which included the remedial or 'general subjects' group) of the total intake. Yet discussions about the future of humanities became inextricably intertwined with the feelings of the staff about the whole controversial problem of unstreaming.

The earlier additions to the curriculum provided by the departments of history, geography, science and technical subjects had not been regarded as intrusions into the time-table but rather as enrichments. But the humanities course, which replaced the first-year history, geography and R.E. courses and used one-third of the time hitherto allocated to English, became the focus of a good deal of the growing uncertainty about the once familiar boundaries round subjects and, indeed, round definable phases of growth. It was easier to perceive the 'new' methods and the 'integrated' courses as being appropriate for first-year children who came into the school still trailing the experience of their primary schools than to entertain the idea that the separation of knowledge into subjects, as defined in most secondary schools, might not be the most appropriate basis for planning learning situations for adolescent pupils as they moved through the school towards the once protected scholarly area of the sixth form. If 'humanities' in particular and 'integrated courses' in general could be partitioned off as something suitable only for the relatively young or for the relatively backward, and perhaps also for sixth-formers as a sort of 'cultural' adjunct to pre-university studies, then the familiar pattern of subjects could remain undisturbed as far as the abler children in the middle school were concerned. The trouble was that teachers who had taken these first steps and as a result were experiencing a new kind of teaching-learning relationship with their pupils were daring to suggest that the new approach might be more effective with the older and the abler children also. They were not the first to reach this conclusion, for Reg Clarke, the head of remedial education, had suggested some years earlier that methods that were proving beneficial to children of low ability might also be beneficial for those of near average ability.

Yet who is to say that the fears about embarking on this unfamiliar way of teaching were groundless? None of us can presume that the first attempts to break down the old subject barriers will not be accompanied by anxieties and even by panic—a feeling that I experienced vividly through a process of identification, when I sat in on a group of staff as they struggled with the task of preparing the new second-year course for the autumn of 1970. The other part of the dilemma—the concern about future examination requirements—was equally real; for the examination system, particularly as far as GCE was concerned, still operated on the old subject basis and could always be presented as an immovable constraint on new educational thinking.

I had no doubt that many of the staff were painfully divided within themselves about these matters. A decision to abandon O-level courses in favour of CSE Mode III for all the pupils taking a particular subject, regardless of their comparative abilities, would have been an act of faith that would have brought with it a compelling obligation to convince the parents concerned that such a decision on a teacher's part would not penalize any child who might, with a different teacher, have been entered for GCE. And who, after all, could be certain that it would not do so?

When the future of the humanities course came up for discussion at a department heads' meeting in January 1969, strong feelings against its continuation into the second year were expressed, first by Allen White, the head of geography, and then by Joy Sollars, the head of history. On that occasion it was these two who were left to carry the hostile feelings, almost, it seemed, condemning humanities as a lunatic fringe that was endangering the curriculum rather than as a new growth that might in time strengthen it. The difficulty in accepting the new course was inextricably interwoven with the difficulty of devising methods of assessing it that would both be valid in terms of the course itself and would give relevant information to those who would, as it were, inherit the pupils who had taken the course. There was as yet no past experience upon which any member of staff, whether involved in the teaching of the course or not, could predict what concepts or skills the children concerned would carry from it to later courses in history, geography, English or religious education.

The strength of the doubts expressed by the heads of history and geography and the absence of any firm recommendation from the other department heads concerned prompted Denys John, between that January meeting and the end of the spring term, to call two special meetings of the staff most directly involved in the problem to discuss further the pros and cons of extending the course into Year II in the following academic year. At the second of these special meetings, to which I was invited, it became evident that Allen White and Joy Sollars were not the only people who had doubts about the wisdom of such a step. The heads of English and music—Lewis Smith and Tony Frost—also raised questions about it. For the historians the trouble was that the children taking such a course might not acquire in time the ability to master facts, with the result that assessment of their attainments in history in the third year would lack any real basis. For the geographers the trouble was that the over-all five-year syllabus was threatened, since subject matter hitherto covered in the second year would not necessarily find any place in a course in which geography was only one of several ingredients. For the English department the trouble was that the course seemed too heavily weighted with fact finding, with the result that the education of the imagination and emotions might be neglected. And for at least one member of staff outside this network—a musician—the trouble was that a course on humanities, while claiming to be focused on the human condition and the activities of the human race, included no scientist in its team of teachers.

Religious education, it seemed, was the one untroubled voice. Yet the kind of dilemma revealed in the continuing argument about the strengths and weaknesses of the humanities course was illustrated most clearly of all in the splitting apart of two aspects of religious education. Both Graeme

Osborn, the earlier head of R.E. and David Sellick, who succeeded him in the autumn of 1969, saw a need to differentiate between 'R.E.' (religious *education*) as taught in the lower and middle schools and 'R.K.' (religious *knowledge*) as taught to GCE candidates in the fifth and sixth forms. Thus the dilemma for R.E. teachers in general appeared to exemplify the same kind of difficulty that faced any subject specialist who was having to temper his educational ideas about later learning to the realities of the examination system, yet was still striving with younger children to modify the existing educational practices.

These special meetings revealed the need for a new kind of dialogue between those who were teaching in the humanities course and those who, though affected by it, remained outside it. They also revealed the difficulty of conducting such a dialogue. Yet the dialogue did begin. Two of the four members of the 1968–9 humanities team were not able to attend the meeting. The other two—Robin Thomas and Bob Jarratt—both spoke at some length about the unexpected responses they were having from children who in the more conventional kind of history or geography lesson might have shown little interest, ability or talent. Now these two were really speaking as teachers of children rather than as teachers of history or geography. But, to those who were listening to them it was probably their specialisms and their roles and statuses that mattered most. Robin Thomas was, without doubt, being heard by some of his colleagues as an experienced history teacher and by others as the deputy head who supported the ideas the head was anxious to promote in the school; Bob Jarratt was probably being heard by some as a geographer and by others as the remedial teacher who, like Reg Clarke, was now bringing to the notice of his colleagues evidence about the beneficial effects for all children, and not only for the less able among them, of the thinning out of boundaries between subjects. And so the opinions of these two—based not on hearsay but on their own personal experience of the new approach—had now to be placed alongside the reservations expressed about it by the heads of English, history and geography, none of whom was actually teaching in the course.

The problem of communication between those who were and those who were not taking part in the experimental work of trying to launch such a course had therefore to be faced. How could the humanities teachers, in their detachment from the 'parent' departments, make their own experiences known to their colleagues while these experiences were actually happening to them? How could they make their colleagues hear and listen? It was the attempts made by Robin Thomas and Bob Jarratt to start this process that released John Harbinson to make available to the others present at that meeting the experiences he himself had had some years earlier, when, as a young P.E. teacher, he had found himself having to respond to radical changes in the whole field of physical education. Listening to him I recalled how Bob Miller, his successor as head of P.E., had spoken to me of similar experiences some months before when I was having individual sessions with all department heads, and how I had wondered then whether such experiences (parallelled by those described to me by Tom Purvis, head of art) could be brought into staff meetings to illuminate what was currently happening, here as in many other schools, in the academic field.

As yet it was easier, it seemed, for staff to share past experiences than to expose their present uncertainties about where the new ideas might be taking them. Nevertheless, these experiences, particularly those of the art and P.E. teachers who had lived through revolutionary changes themselves, provided helpful indications that those involved in the present revolution might also have the capacity to survive and ultimately even to welcome creative change.

It was not, perhaps, surprising that in this developing situation I more than once received the impression that those who were committed to planning and teaching a humanities course felt that they were being abandoned by the subject specialists, particularly by the department heads, whose strengths they needed. The course was constantly beset by two apparently incompatible needs: the first, to discover for the work a new basis that was independent of the contributing subjects and thus to escape from the necessity of living on borrowed time; the second, to placate and reassure the heads of those contributing subjects, so that the borrowed time—or moratorium—could last a little longer. It seemed at times that those who taught it found themselves wondering whether the department heads were placing them in a fool's paradise—almost, perhaps, tempting them to play with a new 'subject', for a year, or two years, while half threatening them with extinction if their work raised any questions about the balance of the middle-school curriculum or the content of existing syllabuses.

At the time when the humanities course was being introduced, there was what Joy Sollars later described to me as a phasing problem. Because the pre-1966 grammar-school intake was still working its way up the school, the pressure on the few specialist teachers in the history and geography departments to fulfil their obligations to the pupils in the examination forms was heavy, the more particularly because the new pattern of appointments, catering for the changing needs of the lower part of the school, had left two unfilled gaps when a historian and a geographer left the school in the summer of 1969.

These difficulties were undoubtedly genuine. In the 1969–70 session the specialists in history and geography appeared to have no real choice. Yet the ambivalence towards the humanities course was evident too, and indeed openly expressed on various occasions—Allen White acknowledging more than once that children seemed to be approaching the humanities work with energy and commitment, yet still maintaining his doubts about its place in the curriculum. It appeared that he and Joy Sollars both wanted and did not want to be actively involved in the venture. And when, in the summer of 1970, Joy Sollars did agree to be a member of the second-year humanities team for the following year, circumstances in the end prevented her from joining it, even though she had taken part already in planning meetings, because of the unexpected loss of a history specialist who was to have freed her from the examination form that she did, after all, have to teach. As for Robin Thomas, who had taught in the first pilot course, he was evidently regarded as a renegade by her, for she told him publicly on one occasion, with a somewhat stinging humour, that he was now 'only a guest artist', thus expressing in one short phrase both her conscious regret that a gifted history teacher should be so much less available than she, as his own successor in the role of head of history, would have liked, and her unconscious anger with him for being available to teach humanities and therefore less available to teach pure history.

The ambivalence felt by many colleagues towards the work of the humanities team (or teams) was particularly evident in the English department, which contributed to the twelve humanities periods only two out of its total allocation of six, in contrast to the other three departments concerned, which relinquished all their available periods. The effect of this was two-fold. To those outside, English was at least partially 'opting out' of humanities. Inside the department the effect of this partial commitment (or partial non-commitment) must have been to make English seem fragmented—unsure what parts of itself were still being conserved in the 'English' lessons and what parts of itself were becoming merged with the subject matter of the humanities course.

The immediate result of these enquiries about the future of the humanities course was that its status in the curriculum was left somewhat undefined. As far as the 1969–70 session was concerned, it was—as an official part of the curriculum for all children—still confined to Year I. Thus, if the staff, as they separated for the summer holidays of 1969, were having to question some of their old assumptions about the autonomy of department heads, they also took away with them some evidence that Denys John too recognized the limits of his autonomy, since they had been able to prevent, or at least to postpone, the extension of the humanities course into Year II. He had scarcely concealed his own desire to see the course continued for the children who were moving into the second year in the autumn; nevertheless he had bowed to the doubts of those who were opposing this by agreeing that further thought be given to the matter before any decision was made. On the other hand, he did have his way over the extension of the teaching to be done in mixed-ability groups for the second year children; for English, history, geography and religious education, along with art, crafts, music and physical education, were now to be taught in tutor groups. This meant also that the 'general subjects' or remedial groups ceased to exist as teaching groups. Henceforth, children in need of such help were to be extracted from their tutor groups at arranged times, the first-year children for work with Reg Clarke and the second-year children for work with Bob Jarratt. At the same time, humanities gained a toe-hold on the second year: for Graeme Osborn and Bob Jarratt, with the backing of Reg Clarke, had been able to persuade the heads of the departments concerned to allow them to teach with their own two second-year groups a further course in place of the separate courses in English, history, geography and religious education. It seemed that, within this area of the curriculum, there had been a kind of unconscious bargaining going on.

All this raises the question: who decides which curriculum changes should be allowed and which should be suppressed? Where is the line drawn between policy change and spontaneous change brought about by individual teachers acting more or less in isolation? How in fact—in this instance—did Denys John use his powers as head to encourage one and inhibit another? Was he really bowing to the opinions of his colleagues, and, if so, to which? Or was he just biding his time? Did he in fact force his own decisions through?

It is a significant comment on the nature of the change that came later, with the modifications to the existing management structure, that despite all the talking that I had done with him and all the staff discussions I had attended and indeed taken part in, I was not really clear in the autumn of 1969 just how the compromises about the curriculum in the lower school had been arrived at, or how Denys John (who never pretended, either to me or to any of his colleagues, that he did not regard the final decision about such matters to be his responsibility) would have answered questions about how these particular decisions had been influenced by staff opinions. He himself, looking back on that time from the autumn of 1971, was in no doubt about the basis of those earlier decisions, since his guiding principle, then as later, was that without a strong body of support among the staff who would have to implement any particular change of policy, a decision by a headmaster to introduce such a change would be doomed to failure. In the summer of 1969 he had felt that there was enough support to carry the extension of mixed-ability teaching into the area of the general arts subjects, but not enough support to carry an extension of the humanities course into Year II. The experimental extension of that course, for two tutor groups only, fell into the category of innovation proposed by an individual or sub-group (in this case a pair); and where this kind of development was concerned, he was prepared to endorse it, provided those involved had sought and won the consent of any heads of departments or sections who would be affected. All this was clear to him at the time, but may have been very unclear to some of his colleagues, as indeed it was unclear to me. Yet where *later* decisions were concerned, I was very consciously aware of the ways in which opinions had been invited, explored and weighed and of the extent to which Denys John had worked towards joint decisions with his standing committee, to the point where they were not, as on past occasions, decisions made in isolation after staff discussions, but decisions made in the presence of the committee and felt to be shared by the committee. In the earlier

T.S.T.M.—4

negotiations described in this chapter, because the machinery for such consultations did not yet exist, the processes by which he arrived at his decisions were still blurred and often appeared to be only tenuously related to the discussions in the staff meetings.[1]

Developments in subject teaching and the concept of pastoral care

By the autumn of 1969 it could hardly be denied, despite the ambiguity of its status in Year II, that 'humanities' was a new arrival in the time-table whose identity had to be acknowledged. But the nature of this identity, and perhaps the extent of its stability, were still hung round with questions. Was it an 'integrated course' or a new subject? A new constellation, brought into existence simply because certain people were perceiving new relationships between pieces of learning that they had always known about, or a new star made of different material altogether? If it turned out to be a new subject and not just an unfamiliar amalgam of old subjects would it—eventually—become a new department, with its own department head?

Meanwhile another subject was beginning to claim a new identity: drama. In the autumn of 1969 there was not as yet anyone with the title either of 'director of the humanities course' or of 'head of humanities'. But there was already a drama specialist on the staff; and he had been there for four years. Yet drama did not really exist in the time-table as a subject in its own right, but only as a kind of mini-option, offered as an adjunct to the 'B' second-year options, sharing with geology B, human biology, rural studies and woodwork the option time available for the four groups of pupils taking these courses at the same time as the abler pupils were taking Latin, German or Russian, geology A or citizenship. The specified distinction between geology B in the former list and geology A in the latter list symbolized the distinction between the two lists taken as option groups, since the A courses were linked with GCE O-level courses in the fourth and fifth years, whereas the B courses were linked with CSE courses in the later years. Thus, by implication, drama was a subject that only the less able children took, along with the chosen one of the four subjects linked to it in the B options.

Now by 1969 citizenship, geology and rural science were all being included —along with history, geography, and biology—in the official departmental responsibility of Joy Sollars, Allen White and Gwen London respectively. In other words, the idea of an area of knowledge, in which the management of related 'subject areas' could be exercised by the same person, was already in people's minds and indeed already in the management structure. At the same time, staff members other than heads of departments were being given delegated responsibility for some of the special options, almost regarded as separate 'subjects': notably, a historian and a biologist (both women)

[1] Figure 12 relates the events described above to the subsequent extension of the Humanities course into Year 2.

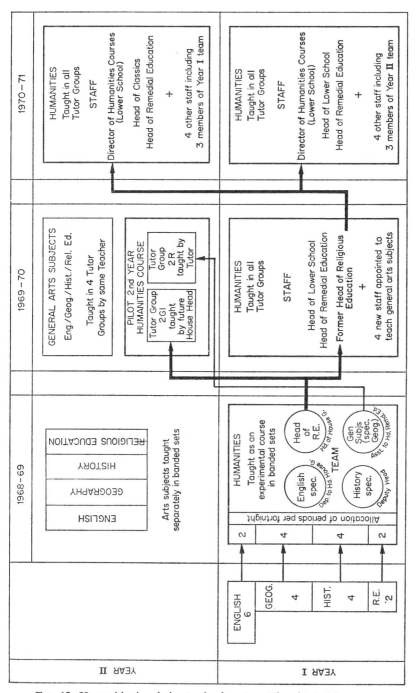

FIG. 12. Humanities in relation to the departmental and tutorial systems.

who were held responsible for the courses in British Constitution and Rural Studies respectively. There seemed to be evidence, therefore, that two rather different processes were going on: the process of allowing 'departments' to grow by accretion, and the process of hiving off special courses and allowing them to develop as 'subjects' in their own right. The problem for drama—as an offshoot of English—was whether it was to remain part of the existing department of English or to aspire to independent status as a subject—and therefore perhaps a department—in its own right.

In September 1969 David Williams, the man in charge of drama, began to raise with Denys John, in personal discussions, questions that were taking shape in his mind about the status of drama in the curriculum. And so the wave of special meetings held in the spring to consider the future of humanities was succeeded in the autumn by a second wave of meetings, attended by some of the same people, to consider the future of drama. It was these meetings, all held in September, that probably precipitated the later series of meetings in the following term, to which individual members of staff from all levels in the hierarchy came, at their own request, following a general invitation from Denys John, to talk with the standing committee about specific aspects of curriculum development.

The meetings about drama were held in the head's room and were attended by the deputy head and the senior mistress, the heads of the lower and middle schools, the heads of English and remedial education, the drama specialist himself, and—after the first meeting—the heads of art, music and physical education. They were held as the result of a specific request from David Williams that the place and 'status' of drama should be reviewed. This was the first open sign that the questions about the future of 'integrated courses' were bringing in their wake a number of related questions about the emergence of new embryo 'departments'.

In presenting his case to his colleagues, David Williams was at pains to point out that it was for the intellectual status of his *subject* rather than for his *own* status in the staff group that he was pleading. Yet the fact was that he had been appointed, four years earlier, without head-of-department status and that his scale allowance (and therefore his level in the hierarchy) depended not on his expertise as a drama specialist but on his role as deputy to one of the house heads; and for this role he had been selected, not as a drama teacher but as a person. It was also a fact that he had not been eligible to attend either the section heads' or the department heads' meetings up to the summer of 1969, and that he had not yet been named as a member of the senior staff meeting that now embraced both those earlier categories. Although he now headed a drama team of six, he had no room of his own in which to hold meetings. Yet he seemed to be anxious to conceal any hint that these matters also might be important to him.

In putting forward the claims of drama as a subject in its own right, he pointed out that it could be perceived in two ways: first as a study that made intellectual demands on pupils, and secondly as a way of exploring human experience, a way that was available to teachers of various other subjects also, including English, religious education, history, modern languages and classics. He implied that, despite the school's generous provision of material aids to the development of drama as a subject, the curricular pattern itself acted as a constraint on those developments. Because it did not appear in the curriculum for the first year, and only as an option thereafter, children had no experience of drama on which they might base a decision to choose it later on. He also pointed out that he was, in the year just starting, further hampered in his efforts to raise the status of drama by the fact that the teaching was now being spread among a relatively large number of the staff, with the result that he was, as he felt, less able to control the methods being used.

It was these discussions about drama that began to reveal that the notion of an 'integrated' course contained within it the plight of the 'disintegrated' or 'disintegrating' subject. In a similar kind of way, I was beginning during those weeks to hear lurking behind the word 'enrichment'—originally used of new courses developed within existing fields of study—the unspoken word 'impoverishment', perhaps because 'enrichment' was coming to be used more and more with reference to courses that only the less able children would be free to take. Ironically, it seemed, drama itself might be able to develop as a subject in its own right only if it robbed English and physical education of the very things that had in the past ten years given *them* new vitality. Was drama, as the new child in the curriculum—somewhat uncertain of its parentage—to find itself flourishing only at the expense of English and P.E.? Or was it to become suspended uneasily between them, as geography appeared sometimes to be suspended between the arts and the sciences?

At one stage in the third of these special meetings the existence of this kind of tension between the drama, English and P.E. interests was demonstrated rather dramatically. The group had been discussing the idea that drama might be built into the first-year curriculum as an additional ingredient of the humanities course. Suddenly David Williams put directly to Lewis Smith a question that seemed on the face of it conciliatory, even deferential, coming to a head of department from a member of that department: did Lewis consider, he wondered, that it would be presumptuous of drama, originally an offshoot of English, to enter the humanities programme independently—as it were on an equal footing with English? But Lewis Smith never answered this curiously provocative question, because John Harbinson intervened with a comment, and then, a few minutes later, urged David Williams to justify the existence of drama as a separate subject in the curriculum by spelling out its educational objectives, which, he presumed, 'somebody' had worked out. He almost seemed to be saying 'Well, go on: do what we in the physical-education field had to do some years ago when we were struggling to get our subject recognized as something more than gym.

and games!' But David Williams in his turn was prevented from giving any direct answer to this question. This time it was Denys John who intervened, perhaps needing to justify his own action four years earlier in appointing a drama specialist at all. He said that at that time someone had certainly known what the objectives of drama in school might be, but it did not follow that everyone present at this meeting knew what they were now. Having offered this comment, he looked across the table as though hoping that John Harbinson's challenge could now be met. But by now David Williams had relapsed into silence; and it was difficult to know whether he had somehow been immobilized by his colleagues or whether he was resisting what he felt to be an unreasonable expectation that he would offer a further justification for his own presence in the school.

In so far as he had already attempted to justify his subject, he had done so mainly by stressing its claims to be.regarded as an intellectual discipline. But drama could also be perceived as an activity that could have a certain therapeutic appeal both for teachers and for pupils. To put this in another way, drama, as an activity through which problems of human relationships could be explored, had links with the school's responsibility for the pastoral care of its pupils. It was thus allied not only with its parent subject, English, but also with religious education and possibly with certain aspects of humanities, art and physical education, in so far as these subjects opened up for children areas of thought and action that touched on their own concern with the business of discovering themselves and learning to understand the complexities of their own feelings towards others. David Williams was very much concerned with these matters in his other role, as deputy to one of the house heads. Moreover, both in this capacity and as the man responsible for the drama teaching, he had to relate his work to that of the newly appointed school counsellor, Margaret Fisher, who was one of the five women now assisting him in the drama work. As it turned out, her views about how drama should be approached in schools were somewhat different from his.

At the time of these special meetings about the future of drama in the curriculum, David Williams was already holding meetings with the other five drama teachers to discuss teaching approaches and difficulties being encountered in the actual work of the classroom. Having no room of his own in which to hold these meetings, he had accepted Margaret Fisher's invitation to use hers, thus unconsciously drawing attention to his own lower status in the staff group. In the second of these meetings, which I attended at his invitation, he seemed to be putting himself under the same sort of pressure to justify the place of drama in a school curriculum as John Harbinson was to put him under in the headmaster's room a week later.

The meeting began with a monologue from himself, emphasizing the intellectual aims of drama teaching, as he perceived them. After a pause, there was a fairly prolonged dialogue between himself and Margaret Fisher on the relative importance of performance, which he had been stressing, and of self-discovery, which she perceived as more important. Towards the end of the meeting all six became involved in a discussion about the anxieties inherent in this area of teaching, where criticism of a child's performance could very easily be experienced as destructive of a child's personality.

More and more as this discussion went on, it seemed that David Williams, who had come into teaching from work in the theatre, was in some danger of equating intellectual respectability with 'performance' and thus of being split off from his team and from Margaret Fisher in particular, leaving them to carry the 'caring' side of the work. Moreover, because he was the only man in the group, there was also, it appeared, considerable risk that the intellectual or 'thinking' side might come to be equated, for the pupils as well as for the teachers, with masculinity, and the expressive or 'feeling' side with femininity. At the time of these meetings he was seriously contemplating a move to a teaching post in a theatre school; but in fact, six months later, he accepted the post of head of the lower division of another comprehensive school. It seems clear that he was experiencing during that last year at Nailsea a fairly painful tension between the part of himself that wanted to be an actor and the part of himself that wanted to be a teacher, and that this tension was revealed in the conflict between his concern about the 'theatrical' component of school drama and his concern about children's growth and development— as demonstrated in his work as a deputy house head. It is probable also that the group of staff (most of them relatively young) who were teaching drama had been feeling this tension quite strongly in their relations with him, with their classes, and perhaps also with other subject specialists with whom they had to work.

Identification and leadership of new courses

If David Williams had felt, up till the summer of 1969, that he was a leader without an acknowledged department, the problem for those involved in the teaching of the humanities course during the following year was that they were becoming a department without an acknowledged leader. Yet in the 1968–9 academic year the four people concerned had strenuously denied that any of them was the 'leader' or even that they felt the need of a formally designated leader. In those months, when the team had included Robin Thomas, the staff had tacitly assumed that because he was the deputy head of the school, he was the one who spoke for the team in staff meetings and who negotiated with department and section heads about matters arising from the course itself. Although he accepted this role in practice, he denied it in theory, and stated this denial in public once at a full staff meeting, adding, 'We don't have a leader'. On that occasion the bubble was pricked by Mike Burnham, who said laughingly: 'Yes; but when we want to know anything about humanities we just nobble Robin!' Later Robin Thomas himself came to realize that they had all been evading this important issue of leadership, and that he had colluded with everyone in this evasion by accepting a kind of unofficial leadership role that really had more to do with his position as deputy head than with his membership of the humanities team.

The next attempt to solve this problem, when the humanities team was about to become considerably larger, seemed more rational. Reg Clarke— on the ground that he was already in charge of 'general-subjects' work with the remedial and 'fringe-remedial' children in the lower school—was named also as leader or director of the humanities course. But this raised problems for him, because, not having taught in the course in the 1968–9 pilot stage, he did not feel that he had any real authority to negotiate with department heads about it, either in terms of agreeing on the syllabus or in terms of bargaining for material resources. In fact, although he held a meeting at his home during the summer of 1969, he really delegated the task of organizing the 1969–70 course to Graeme Osborn. The formal request to Reg Clarke to take on this leadership role had been, it seemed, a compensatory kind of move, intended to give him higher status; but in the event it made him feel down-graded, because it coincided with his loss of the remedial group, for which he *had* had real responsibility and over which he *had* had real authority by virtue of a real expertise. Moreover the change in status meant that, whereas he had formerly included mathematics in his area of teaching, he now had to lose this, except in relation to the backward children who were drawn out of lessons for special work with him.

The third move was to explore the possibility of finding a department to 'adopt' the humanities course, and Lewis Smith was first tentatively asked whether English could take it on. But this proved an abortive move, since he felt that English was already being fully stretched. Further tentative moves were made in the direction of the department of religious education—moves which, as we shall see later in this chapter, had somewhat painful consequences for David Sellick, the new head of R.E. In the event, it was Graeme Osborn who was asked to accept the responsibility, on the ground that he had the necessary expertise to discharge it and thus the necessary authority with the department heads to negotiate with them on behalf of all those who were to teach the course.

As the 1969–70 session went on it became clear that drama and the humanities had been useful receptacles for all kinds of uncertainties about educational objectives, uncertainties that must have been just as acute in other areas of the curriculum, especially perhaps in the middle school, where untried methods of combining subjects in 'integrated courses' were knocking at the doors and shaking the equilibrium of the old grammar-school curriculum in which people had been able to believe that they felt reasonably secure.

The struggle going on in the arts field between the concern for 'knowledge' in its narrower sense and 'education' in its broader sense must have had its counterpart in the science field. But the arts teachers were compelled, because of their lack of a containing boundary, to expose their conflicts in public, whereas the scientists, who belonged to a tightly organized sub-group of the staff, were able to maintain a fairly united front in public. But there was one topic that produced a division of opinion between the biologists on the one side and the chemists and physicists on the other: namely, the topic of setting as opposed to mixed-ability grouping. Gwen London always maintained that she was prepared to accept a wide range of ability in the biology teaching groups, whereas the chemists and physicists maintained that they required fine setting because of the demands of the examination syllabuses. Where did the scientists stand on the related questions about integrated courses?

The only science-based equivalent to the first-year humanities course was the Schools Council sponsored 'Science for the Young School Leaver', a course for the less able pupils in the third, fourth and fifth years. This, like the humanities course, was supported by funds from outside the normal school budget; but—unlike the humanities course—it allowed teachers to remain anchored in their own subjects. It was an 'integrated' course only in the sense that themes were handled sequentially by biologists, chemists and physicists. Different specialists therefore had to confer with each other over the management of these sequences, the content in each subject area being largely determined by the Nuffield syllabuses the school had agreed to implement. They did not—like their arts colleagues in the humanities course —have to work out a combined cross-disciplinary syllabus in which, at any one time, a specialist in one area might be committed to giving a lead lesson to a whole year group on behalf of the teaching team and in the presence of other subject specialists who would have to follow it up later with the separate teaching groups. The scientists, as practitioners in classroom and laboratory, were thus less exposed to one another than were the arts teachers, who—in varying degrees—were mutually involved in the processes of developing the integrated courses, at first in the lower school and later in the middle school also.

Some of the unease experienced by the arts teachers during this phase must be attributed to the strains of this increasing amount of mutual exposure. Equally, perhaps, we have to ask ourselves how far the scientists, because of the protectiveness of their containing boundary, were becoming an isolated group within the staff group as a whole. For alongside the strains imposed by greater mutual exposure in a work situation there is likely to be an increase in the amount of mutual support that becomes available for the members of such a working group.

Despite the uncertainties and tensions I have described, the tenacity of the departmental system is considerable. Yet what is a department? It is certainly not, in the average secondary school, an identifiable group of pupils. It is not even a group of teachers, for this would imply that every member of staff belonged only to one department. It may involve more than a twelfth part of the total staff group or consist of one lone teacher. It may justify only one responsibility allowance; or it may include three or four. It may have an umbrella function, acting as protector of homeless courses and activities; or it may, in the academic sense, be linked still with a 'pure' subject. Its function may be almost indistinguishable from the activity usually described as 'pastoral care'; or it may be strongly academic in its ethos; or it may be largely recreational. It may be sex-linked, in the sense that both pupils and staff engaged in its programme are either boys or girls but not both. The possibilities of splitting and projection within a 'system' of such departments are enormous.

Images of subject departments

During the era of the O & A Group and the divided senior staff meeting, my own image of the departmental system was based partly on my knowledge of certain facts about the member patterns within the different departments and partly on the roles taken by different department heads during discussion on curricular matters. It is probable, therefore, that I was seeing the departments far more in terms of their fantasies about each other than in terms of the realities about the way they operated as units. For this very reason it may be important that I include in this report, as I did in my report to the staff in December 1969, my received impressions of these fantasies, along with the known facts about the structure and functioning of particular departments, since they may be necessary to an understanding of the situation in which Denys John and his standing committee worked from September 1969.

Two of the most persistent images that I carried over from the 1968–9 session into the following one concerned the modern languages and science departments on the one side and the geography and history departments on the other. The former I saw as the 'giant' departments which seemed able to make their own conditions regardless of changes elsewhere in the system—almost, at times, to be holding the staff up to ransom. In contrast to my impression of power and independence in these areas, the departments of geography and history seemed to me to be suffering more than any others (except perhaps classics) from the problems of encroachment, erosion and loss of wholeness. How much substance was there behind these images?

The science department (see Figure 13) was indisputably large; and it contained within it the three separate departments, each with its own head, of biology, chemistry and physics. In the 1968–9 session the management structure of the science department looked strangely similar to that of the school as a whole. The group, consisting of Phillip Armitage, his three senior colleagues and the group of technical staff who were responsible to him through the head technician for the services they provided, looked almost like a mirror image of the top management group—namely, Denys John, his two senior colleagues and the group of clerical staff who were responsible to him through the bursar.

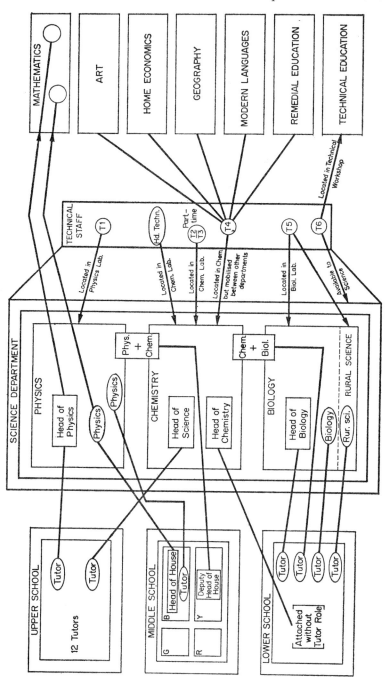

Fig. 13. The science department as a bounded region.

But if the science department seemed to be mirroring the top management group, the modern languages department (see Figure 14) appeared almost to have absorbed it. The staff could hardly have been totally devoid of feelings about the fact that Denys John, his wife Ada John (a part-time teacher) and Joan Bradbury all taught languages and were therefore members of the modern languages department. Furthermore we have to probe only a few months back into history to discover that Robin Thomas's predecessor as deputy head, who had occupied this role during the four years leading up to the summer of 1968, had been a German specialist. There was no evidence to suggest that this extraordinary concentration of top management in the special area of modern languages presented any problems to the other members or to the head of the department. Yet we have to ask ourselves how the rest of the staff coped with the uncertainties about its implications. Were the modern linguists perceived as being fortunate in their close links with the headmaster? Or were they seen as being particularly vulnerable because of these links—less rather than more likely to have their own way if disputes arose between themselves and other departments? How was the crowding of the department with top management—or conversely the crowding of top management with modern linguists—perceived in relation to the other observable facts: that the department had no internal department headships despite the fact that it handled four different languages, and that it had to rely rather heavily on part-time staff?

By a strange quirk of fate, the heads of these two departments—namely Phillip Armitage and Peter Atkinson—were the only members of the staff with doctorates and theirs were the first two names in the alphabetical list of staff members. Were their departments allies, rivals, or equally powerful independent forces in the school? Both were staffed almost entirely by specialist teachers; neither did any appreciable sharing of personnel with other departments; both insisted, or appeared to insist, on finer setting by ability throughout the school than any other departments did; both were concerned with the development of new methods of teaching that involved the purchase, control and maintenance of expensive technical equipment.

On one occasion—in the department heads' meeting of February 1969—the two giants clashed. The meeting was concerned with the dates of fifth-form examinations and with the whole question of assessment in the lower school. Phillip Armitage announced that his department would want an examination of an hour and a half for all the first-year pupils. The announcement was greeted with a deathly hush; but the nearest anyone came to objecting, at that point in the meeting, was Tony Frost, who asked mildly whether this examination could not be given in two parts. Phillip Armitage was left to carry the burden of the refusal to consider this modification, his colleagues in the science department remaining silent. When the outburst came, it came rather unexpectedly from Peter Atkinson. He directed his attack, not on Phillip Armitage, but on Gwen London, who had in fact been

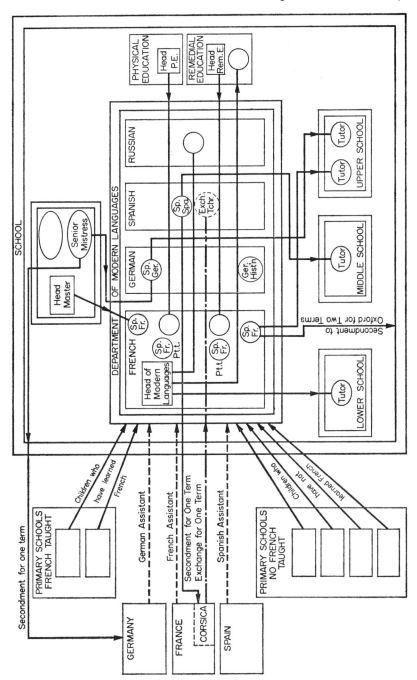

Fig. 14. Department of modern languages in relation to the school and the outside world.

expressing some disquiet herself about the way in which the year was being broken up by examinations at various times. Peter Atkinson asked her sharply why the scientists were prepared to take time from other people to ensure that their examination for the first year should be time-tabled. Though momentarily taken aback, she stoutly nailed her colours to the mast and explained that the scientists really did need this amount of time because of the difficulties of organizing laboratory work.

Later in this same meeting the discussion turned to the problem of making predictions based on examinations, particularly in relation to setting and banding arrangements. Very near the end of the meeting there was a sudden explosion when Allen White suggested despairingly that perhaps the real need, since the disappearance of the eleven plus examination, was for a big testing procedure at the end of the first year. Immediately, three of his colleagues—Joan Bradbury, John Harbinson and Reg Clarke—all of whom were associated with the arts side rather than with science, turned to him with expressions of shocked surprise. With varying degrees of concern, persuasion and outright anger they tried to convince him that his proposal was unthinkable. But was it? Why did Allen White, who had spoken personally rather than departmentally, bring down on his head so many shocked reproofs, when in the same meeting, Phillip Armitage, speaking on behalf of science, had been able to carry his request for just such an examination procedure? It seemed that the staff group could find several spokesmen to express its collective disapproval of Allen White's *words* but that only the head of modern languages dared suggest that Phillip Armitage's *actions*—or rather the actions of his department—ought perhaps to be questioned. And in doing so, Peter Atkinson was left very much out on a limb. Ideas, it seemed, might invite censure, whereas actions could go almost unchallenged. The act might be seen as having respectability; the thoughts behind it could not.

It was after this meeting that I began to think of geography as a department that was trapped—or perhaps suspended—between the arts and the sciences, having allegiances to both sides and a visible link with both sides through geology, but fearing encroachment from the arts side because of the uncertainty about where its subject was rooted (see Figure 15). In the recurring discussions about the humanities course, geography was always linked (uneasily perhaps) with history, as mathematics seemed, in the recurring discussions about mixed-ability grouping, to be uneasily linked with science.

If I saw geography as an area that was either being crushed between opposing forces or being stretched in opposite directions, I saw history as an area that felt itself to be shrinking (see Figure 16). The encroachments on its territory from humanities in the lower school, from social studies in the middle school, from general studies in the upper school, and perhaps also to a lesser extent from ancient history through classics, had to do partly with the loss of recently acquired subject matter, even of new approaches first

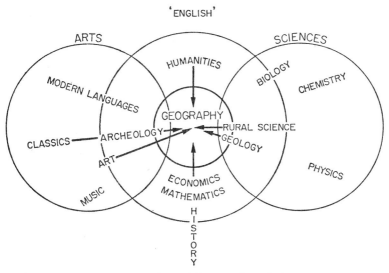

FIG. 15. Geography and the arts-science dichotomy.

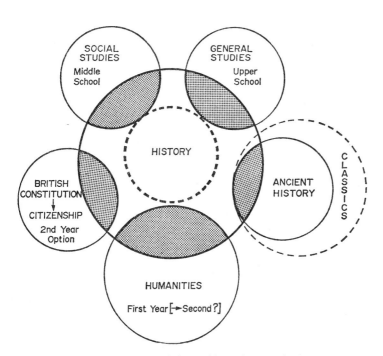

FIG. 16. History and the problem of encroachment.

worked out in terms of history, and partly with the loss of contact with younger children.

The department of English, like those of modern languages and science, was large in the sense that a large number of staff took part in its teaching. Unlike modern languages and science, however, it was not fully staffed by specialists in its own field of study, only four out of its eleven members in the 1968–9 session being graduates in English. Moreover, if modern languages had absorbed two-thirds of the top management group or 'triumvirate', English had absorbed the whole of what might in that year have been called the 'middle management group', namely the heads of the lower, middle and upper schools. The English department, viewed as a teaching unit, also included the head of classics, the head of the remedial department and his assistant, the drama specialist and the deputies to two of the house heads. Small wonder that Lewis Smith referred more than once in staff meetings to the difficulties he always had in arranging departmental meetings in face of the diversity of functions in which the English staff were engaged.

To some extent the department of mathematics shared these problems (see Figure 17). Out of its ten staff, only three were mathematics graduates; one of these was a house head, and another was deputy to the head of lower school. The rest included two young college-trained teachers (who had made mathematics their main study and were in their first post), the head of physics and another member of the physics department who was a house head, the head of the remedial department and his assistant, and the head of the lower school. Thus mathematics, like English, was staffed by people with heavy responsibilities elsewhere in the system. The heads of these two departments, and probably also the special honours graduates in the two subjects, must increasingly have had to ask themselves whether the teaching strength within these two areas was being 'diluted' or 'enriched' by the incoming non-graduates and by the specialists in other subjects on whom they relied to share the teaching load, for there was always the possibility (and indeed the hope) that the college-trained English or mathematics teacher, or the teacher lent by another special area, might compensate for a lack of specialist knowledge by a richer and more varied experience in other fields of study. Part of the fear of 'dilution', therefore, may have been the possibility that the hitherto prized degree might turn out to be a less valuable part of a teacher's equipment than it had formerly seemed to be.

Between the science and arts blocks the mathematics department occupied a position rather like that of a buffer state. Robin Grist seemed to perceive his own teaching interests as allied with science rather than with the arts. Yet he was to discover personally through his experience of contributing to the general studies course in the upper school in the 1969–70 session that 'curriculum development', as distinct from the modification of existing syllabuses anchored in subjects, was not a mere slogan but a reality that would have to be faced if the needs of the pupils already working their way

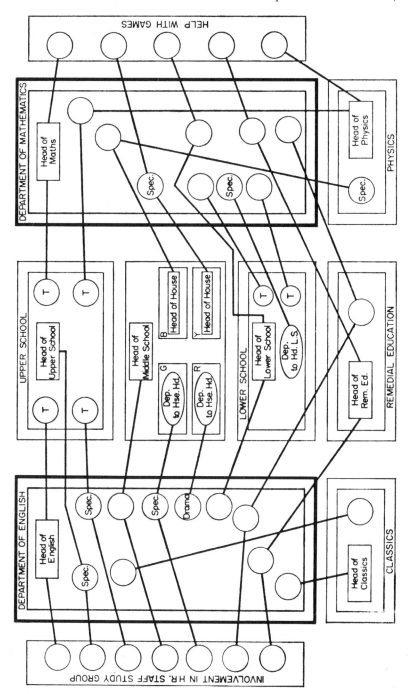

Fig. 17. Enrichment or dilution in the departments of English and mathematics.

through the school were to be honestly met. For him, the conflict between the concern for knowledge and the concern for education became explicit and recognizable during a meeting of the upper-school tutors in the summer of 1970, when the case of one particularly difficult upper-school pupil was being discussed. As a mathematician, he found himself condemning this boy as a time-waster who was unlikely to achieve his A-level in mathematics—a pupil whom he was inclined to write off. But, as someone now teaching in the sixth-form general studies course, he had also to acknowledge that he had seen the same boy in quite a different light, making useful contributions in this other area of work and showing considerable commitment to it. It was the problem of this boy's ambivalent attitudes towards his schooling that drew from Robin Grist the troubled observation that the school was not yet providing appropriate courses for the range of pupils already entering the sixth form; and he seemed to be acknowledging his own recognition that behaviour problems among upper-school pupils might have to be related to this failure on the part of staff, rather than viewed as the sole responsibility of the pupils themselves as persons.

No department had a more acute survival problem than classics. The head of classics, Cyril Routley, was one of the surviving nucleus of eight whose appointments dated back to the early years (1959–63), when the staff group had still been small and the school had not yet acquired a sixth form. By 1968 he was having to face the problem of being head of a diminishing curricular area, which brought him as a specialist teacher, and the colleague who spent part of her time teaching Latin, into contact with fewer and fewer Latin scholars. Classics, more perhaps than any other subject, had a stake, therefore, in the future of integrated courses, since its links with ancient history, local studies and archaeology were its natural life-lines. It was ironical, in view of this, that Cyril Routley had missed a possible chance of taking part in the first humanities course because of uncertainty about whether he might be jeopardizing what was left of his classics work if he committed himself to this new area—an uncertainty which made him hesitate until the fourth and last place in the humanities team had been taken up.

The one-teacher department of commerce had an entry problem that was in some respects similar to the survival problem of classics. In the 1968–9 session, the head of this department had contacts only with sixth-form pupils. Although most of her colleagues assumed that the teaching of a subject called 'commerce' was synonymous with teaching shorthand, typing and other office skills, to her it was more closely linked with economics, social history and human geography and—like classics—had natural links with courses in humanities and social studies. It seemed that if classics suffered from being the once academically respected, now diminishing subject from the old grammar-school curriculum, commerce suffered from being the technically useful but not yet academically respectable subject from the old secondary-modern-school (and present technical-college) curriculum. My sense of her as a lone operator on the staff, neither part of the office staff whose technical skills she shared nor fully part of the academic staff whose teaching task she shared, was emphasized by the homelessness of her subject, which she had to teach sometimes in the near-by Further Education block (on the periphery of the school campus) or in the geography room or in one of the house blocks.

We are left with four subjects (distributed between five departments) that have already been mentioned in this chapter as the group of subjects that were, by 1968, being taught, up to and including the fifth year, in mixed-ability tutor groups: namely, art, crafts (including home economics and boys' crafts), music, physical education and games. Now the five departments included here were those that, even in selective grammar schools, would generally be headed by non-graduates from colleges of art, music, home economics, technology and physical education, although in this school it happened that the heads of art and music were both graduates. It seemed that this 'non-academic' area of the curriculum, because of its associations with recreation, creativity and home-making, was being required to act on behalf of the curricular system as a whole by preserving the link, below the sixth form, with the tutorial system that had been set up to provide continuous pastoral care for all pupils, thus relieving the more obviously academic subjects, up until the autumn of 1970, from taking their share in the task of strengthening these links between the pastoral and curricular functions of all staff members.

Two of these departments carried, more than any other department in the school, the problem of sex-based stereotyping that was present to some extent, as we have seen, within the drama teaching group: namely, the departments of home economics, traditionally concerned only with girls, and of technical subjects, traditionally concerned only with boys. The heads of these two departments were beginning to breach this separation, by exchanging groups, so that girls could learn jewellery in the metal workshop and boys could learn cookery in the home economics wing. But the groups themselves remained segregated, not because either department was opposed to teaching mixed groups but because the most administratively convenient way of sub-dividing tutor groups to produce the smaller sets was by sex: by this means the time-tabling of the craft work for boys and girls could be linked with the time-tabling of physical education and games, for which boys and girls had to be kept in separate groups so that sports hall and field could be used by one group while gymnasium and hall were being used by the other.

Thus home-making, which is essentially based on heterosexual pairing relationships, and physical recreation which is, for most people, essentially social, were here, as no doubt in the great majority of our secondary schools, deprived of an important dimension, despite the fact that in all other departments but these three work was being done in mixed classes. Again it seemed that the concern for personal growth and the concern for knowledge and skill had to be forced apart, masculinity being incarcerated in the workshops and femininity being incarcerated in the kitchen and sewing room. The problem with such enforced separation, as we all know, is that true masculinity does not thrive without the presence of women, and that true femininity does not thrive without the presence of men. How far, we must ask, are the constraints of the traditional time-table, despite the provision of well-equipped school flats, workshops and sports halls, turning them into traps for both teachers and pupils rather than areas where all-round growth and development can be stimulated?

It was probably in the department of religious education that this conflict between concern for persons and concern for knowledge was most evident. We shall see in the next chapter how this had affected Graeme Osborn, the earlier head of R.E. But it was David Sellick who experienced it more acutely in the 1969–70 period, because his arrival in the staff coincided with two innovations—on the one hand, the creation of the new post of school counsellor and on the other the inclusion in the time-table of the new activity called 'H.R.' or human relationships. Both of these could have been, and undoubtedly were at times, perceived as encroachments on that area of religious education that had to do with helping children and young people to understand themselves in relation to others. The nature of the dilemma in which David Sellick eventually found himself as head of R.E. cannot be properly understood without some exploration of the problems that surrounded this adjacent area of H.R.

'Human relationships' and its impact upon curricular developments, tutorial work and counselling

This was an area that could not be felt as 'curricular' in its old, narrow sense, and yet demanded great teaching skill. It overlapped in its content with several other subjects in addition to religious education, notably with English, drama and humanities (see Fig. 18). Up till the summer of 1969 a dozen or so members of staff had persisted with the work of the H.R. staff study group and two others had attended courses outside the school.

The idea of 'human relationships' as a focus of study had always, it seems, been both attractive and frightening to those who committed themselves to the task of developing it as an integral part of a pupil's school work. It was attractive because it enabled teachers to be personally engaged with their pupils in a way that seemed less possible in classwork that was syllabus-bound. As one member of the H.R. study group once expressed it: 'I can be myself when I am working this way with children'. Yet it was also frightening because it had no textbooks, indeed no definable subject matter, and because it called for the use of discussion techniques rather than for didactic teaching and could not easily make use of practical activity with materials and equipment as could art, science, home economics or technical education. From the early days the Marriage Guidance Council had been seen as an outside resource for those who wanted to increase their own confidence in this more open-ended way of teaching. Denys John himself had a double reason for looking in this direction for such help: first, because he himself was chairman of the local branch of the Marriage Guidance Council and therefore had easy access to personnel; and secondly because his own brother was head of the training department in the National Marriage Guidance Council in London and made himself available to work with the staff in occasional long afternoon and evening sessions. Because of these links with marriage guidance coun-

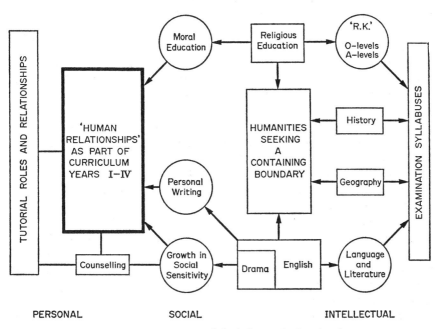

FIG. 18. Human relationships and the balance of educational concerns.

sellors, and because H.R. was, generally among teachers, inextricably linked with earlier debates about sex education, it was associated in people's minds with something vaguely perceived as therapeutic work or counselling. Here, as with humanities, there was for a long time a barely recognized problem about leadership.

I have described already how Denys John found himself accepting the internal leadership role in the study-group sessions, despite his conscious wish to be regarded as 'just an ordinary member' of the working group, committed like his colleagues to the exploration of discussion methods in 'unstructured' teaching situations that were as unfamiliar to him as to anyone else in the group. Indeed, it seems that he was in a similar position in relation to this staff study group as Robin Thomas was in relation to the humanities teaching group: both for the headmaster and for his deputy, senior rank in the hierarchy made a self-imposed reduction to non-senior status in the working group well-nigh impossible.

What, then, was the position of Joan Bradbury, the 'Number Three' in the triumvirate, with regard to H.R. work in general? In one way her role, as it was actually experienced by other members of the group, was very central. She was the only woman to persist with the study until the end of that year; and on any occasion when Denys John was absent from a meeting, she took over his leadership role in no uncertain fashion, and appeared to be accepted in that role by her colleagues, this despite the fact that in almost any other kind of meeting it would have been Robin Thomas who deputized for the head. She was a natural claimant for the leadership role in this area, partly because she had been involved in it from the beginning, and partly because the role of senior mistress, which she had been given in September 1963, had grown out of an earlier role she had held since 1961, as 'mistress in charge of girls' welfare'.

In another way, however, her position was ambiguous, in that she never appeared to be given or to be able to take the authority to organize and direct the work at the point where it was taken into the tutorial groups. In so far as she shared with Robin Thomas the responsibility for constructing the time-table, she was jointly responsible for the way in which H.R. work was administratively organized for the autumn of 1969. Yet the real leadership role still eluded her. For in that term the school was provided with funds to pay for occasional help from outside in examining the experiences that the H.R. tutors were having with their groups. And so again Denys John—and indeed Joan Bradbury herself—looked outwards to the Marriage Guidance Council for this help, and two counsellors were brought in to take two groups of staff who were involved with the work at the teaching level.

At this point the boundary round the H.R. study group—or the team that had been preparing itself for this work for at least a year—became blurred in three ways. It was joined by several other colleagues who had not been members of the earlier study group, including some new members of staff, and also, at the request of the local education authority that was supplying the money, by three teachers from another school who were involved in a similar venture; and it had to adjust itself to the leadership of two marriage guidance counsellors who had not previously worked with the school and so could have known little about the thinking and exploration that had been going on in the previous year, except through reports from Joan Bradbury, who acted as an intermediary in this transition phase.

Once the 1969–70 session got under way, I myself completely lost sight of the H.R. field of work. Yet in the earlier year I had felt that it was in this group of staff that I had been most closely in touch with new thinking. It was as though once H.R. was actually being 'taught' in the school, the group of people involved in it became as much a closed department as were the subject departments, which, apart from single invitations from drama, English and R.E., the first of which I was able to accept, never invited me to any departmental meetings. Because the marriage guidance counsellors were uneasy about the prospect of my presence in the discussion sessions as a consultant, and because the staff themselves were uncertain how they wanted to use me or even whether they wanted to continue to use me in this area, I attended no more H.R. meetings after the summer of 1969, and experienced considerable difficulty in coming to terms with the loss of the role I had previously taken in relation to this study group. I later had to ask myself to what extent my own envy of the marriage guidance counsellors and my resentment against them for being in touch with a part of the staff group with which I had formerly worked must have been reflecting the feelings of Joan Bradbury. For she, also, found herself unable to take any responsibility for offering leadership to her own colleagues in this area, even though they might have needed it from someone within the school rather than from an outsider who could not know enough about the tutorial situation into which the new work was being inserted. Moreover my own frustration about not knowing anything about the work of these new H.R. groups or about the experience of those who were taking them must have paralleled very closely the mystification of colleagues in the staff group who were outside the circle of 'H.R. tutors'.

Joan Bradbury maintained later that she had always believed that pastoral care—or to use the earlier terminology, 'welfare'—must be rooted in a work relationship. Thus, in her view, H.R. could have no future except in relation to curricular development. For Denys John, it seemed, H.R. was linked more with ideas associated with social work, hence perhaps his reliance on the Marriage Guidance Council for help in tackling it.

Months later, in the autumn of 1970, I learned at a meeting of the standing committee that the H.R. study-group members had really been divided on the question of how the H.R. work ought to be built into the time-table: there were those who considered that it should be separate from the curriculum and, by implication, handled only by those staff members who felt a real affinity with this way of working with children; and there were those who feared the development of a mystique in connection with this work, not to say the formation of an *élite* in the staff group, and felt that it must be part of every teacher's work, to be integrated with whatever 'subject' one taught, since it was really implicit in the relationship between teachers and their pupils and between the pupils themselves and must be handled in that context. My own view was that it must in the long run become an integral part of tutorial work, or in other words that the tutorial function should embrace the kind of leadership in exploration of human relationships that was associated with H.R. work wherever it was located. But I never thought that this could be accomplished quickly, or that it could even be attempted without built-in leadership for the tutors themselves, any more than the humanities work as it expanded could have developed in the continued absence of a clearly defined leadership role.

During the 1969–70 session, H.R. was built into the time-table in the following way: every tutor group up to and including the fourth year was divided into two sub-groups and once a month a period of an hour was devoted to H.R. work, each half tutor group being taken by one of those staff members who had declared themselves willing to tackle this kind of discussion work. In some groups the tutor himself or herself took one of the H.R. discussions; in others the tutor was not involved.

When the 1970–1 session began, H.R. as a named activity on the time-table ceased to exist. It was now assumed to be there in essence as part of tutorial work as handled by all tutors. But because no clear understanding had been reached about where the tutorship to the tutors ought to be located, Denys John was left feeling that the purpose of H.R., as a nucleus of staff had been working to define it, had really disappeared, leaving tutorial work more or less as it had always been.

Joan Bradbury's role in the H.R. work was now even more ambiguous. At the beginning of the previous year, when discussions about curriculum development were moving well beyond the boundaries of separate, once insulated, departments, she had been enthusiastically contemplating the possibility of organizing another quite different kind of study group, not to examine H.R. as a basically pastoral activity best located in the tutorial groups, but to re-examine it as a basically curricular activity, best located in the subjects that overlapped with it in content and method. In other words, what she wanted to do at that time, with the help of a carefully selected group of colleagues, was to explore ways of building H.R. into the bones and sinews of the curriculum itself. There had been some evidence during the previous year's discussions that H.R.—rightly conceived—was very much a part of the teaching of English, religious education and drama, and that it could find a place in history, art, human geography, home economics and some aspects of science. But Joan Bradbury's study group never materialized.

In this continuing debate about where H.R. belonged in the whole curricular-pastoral organization, the department of religious education was particularly vulnerable because, in its content and in its aims, it fell between 'humanities' which was perceived as 'curricular' and 'H.R.' which was perceived as 'pastoral'. H.R. work, being concerned with relationships and problems of living, was inevitably focused a good deal of the time on questions about morality in the broadest sense.

David Sellick, although he attended the meetings with the marriage guidance counsellors during the 1969–70 session, did not himself act as an H.R. tutor. He told me in the following year that he had felt it to be important that religious education should not be the only curricular area in which boys and girls had opportunities to discuss problems of morality, in the broadest sense of the term, with the help of staff members. But the real problem became more painful for him in the 1970–1 session, when H.R. was no longer a time-tabled activity. He was therefore left wondering whether the moral education that he had, in a sense, parted with in the 1969–70 session, was being picked up elsewhere, perhaps in tutorial work, perhaps through English, drama or humanities. Throughout those two years he must therefore have been very unsure whether his own subject was being split down the middle, with the 'curricular' part going into the humanities course and the 'pastoral' part going into the H.R. tutoring, or whether R.E. itself must take the leadership role in ensuring that these matters were being handled some-where in the curriculum.

The apparent failure to make any lasting use of all the thinking that had been going on in the H.R. study group must be seen also as part of a gradual move away from the idea that consultation about change could go on best in small, self-selected or representative study groups and working parties. For it was in the autumn of 1969 that Denys John himself was moving towards the idea of working out more carefully how discussions in the standing committee, the senior staff meeting and the full staff meeting should be handled in relation to each other and how the issues that seemed most important at any one time could be discussed at all these levels so that final decisions could be based on all the available evidence about staff feelings and opinions. It may be, therefore, that 'H.R.' as a special area in the time-table, achieved with considerable triumph, even euphoria, for the 1969–70 session, had not so much 'fallen into the ground' a year later as begun, at least here and there, to penetrate more deeply into the teaching role itself. The problem for Denys John was that he simply did not know. H.R., by the winter of 1970–1, it seemed, was as closed to him as any department in which he had never carried a teaching role. Had the whole venture been silently abandoned? Or was it still alive, at least in some areas of the school?

Dichotomies within the curricular system

In this chapter I have been looking at the departmental system as it is inherited from the traditional school organization of the past. In doing so I have tried to examine the kind of dichotomies that appear, between the sciences and the arts, within the arts field and within the science field. Even when we try to narrow our focus so that we can concentrate on 'purely curricular' matters within the system, it seems that we find a strong pressure to split off the 'caring' and 'demanding' sides of the educational task and to put them into different departments and therefore inevitably into the different persons who carry responsibility for the work of those departments. What happens to teachers who become identified with subjects that are (in the public mind) concerned mainly, if not entirely, with 'facts' and 'skills'? It seems they may come to be perceived, and may indeed come to perceive themselves, as people who accept the domination of external examinations, who use rigidly 'objective' methods of assessment, who expect pupils to be highly competitive with one another and correspondingly docile towards staff. And what of those teachers who become identified with subjects that are considered to be at least partly if not mainly concerned with personal growth and development? For them too there is a danger of being stereotyped. For others may perceive them, and they may come to perceive themselves, as people who reject external examinations without question, who use only 'subjective' methods of assessment, who expect pupils to be over-protective towards one another and correspondingly rebellious towards staff. Thus, it may be very difficult for a scientist to demonstrate that he has interest in anything but 'hard facts' and equally difficult for an English specialist to demonstrate that he has any respect for facts at all. Similarly, it may be difficult for an English specialist to demonstrate that he does make demands on pupils, and equally difficult for a scientist to demonstrate that he does have sympathy with pupils. The English specialist may therefore be labelled as one who over-indulges his pupils, the scientist as one who drives them ruthlessly.

In a time of expansion, as new management skills become needed in the schools, teachers have to face decisions about what they relinquish and what they retain as they seek promotion in the system. It seems that in a system that forces teachers to make a choice between the area of 'pastoral responsibility' for children and the area of 'curricular responsibility' for a subject or subject area, scientists feel that they have more to lose by moving into the pastoral area, whereas arts teachers, in moving in that direction, feel that they are extending interests and skills that have always been important to them in their teaching function. P.E. specialists, whose careers in the field of physical education are inevitably age-linked, as careers in home economics and technical education tend to be sex-linked, seem to move naturally and easily into the area of pastoral care, perhaps because their work can bring them into closer relationships with children through the informal situations of the games field and the changing room, perhaps because these very situations make them especially alert to phenomena of growth and development, both physical and emotional, that may be less apparent in the classroom or laboratory. To the scientist—perhaps indeed to any graduate—the P.E. specialist who gains promotion by moving into the pastoral side of the system may be seen as having bettered himself, whereas the scientist may be perceived as having cut himself off from more desirable promotion in his own field by making such a decision.

In the next chapter I will take up the other strand of this general argument and examine the relations between the curricular and pastoral sides of the school's work from the perspective of the pastoral-care system.

CHAPTER V

Pastoral Care and the Problem of Boundary Control

Identification of pastoral care with a house-tutorial system

The departmental system can be said to have been inherited from the past. But the pastoral system has been acquired to meet the perceived needs of a changing present. Superficially it may seem that the curriculum is concerned only with organization of subjects, the pastoral system only with care of children. But, to leave such a bald statement without modification would be to invite indignant criticism for oversimplifying what even the least experienced teacher in a school recognizes to be a much more complex, not to say baffling, matter.

The term 'pastoral care' is relatively new in the language of teachers. Yet the kind of responsibility evoked by the term, with its suggestion of the 'good shepherd', is not new in the work that teachers have always done. The function of today's 'tutor' is not, after all, so very different from the function of yesterday's 'form master' or 'form mistress'. But once children are grouped not just into forms or tutor groups but also into larger units that are named 'lower schools' or 'houses', each with its own sub-head, the institution is consciously setting up a system in order to ensure that what was perceived as the caring part of the head's role in the small school will not be left to chance in the large school.

When a headmaster had only about 500 pupils, he could regard each form teacher as a kind of extension of himself into each class of thirty or so children. Generally speaking, it was the head himself who stood behind each form teacher to give support whenever it was needed: he was expected to be available when praise 'from the top' was required for a child who had made special efforts or reached special distinction, when conflicts arose that could not be resolved between pupil and form teacher without recourse to a higher authority, or when it was considered that punishment or reproof must be administered by that same higher authority. The pastoral role of the head thus had in it the ingredients not only of the good shepherd but also of the approving or disapproving parent and at times of the priest who had to receive confessions and demand penance or offer absolution.

When it is known that a community of 500 is to swell to one of 1000 or 1500 it seems destined to become far more than twice or three times as big as the known, manageable community it has hitherto been. One man cannot pretend that he will be able to contain this enormous flock. 'Pastoral care' must be delegated to senior colleagues who, it may be supposed, will become like 'mini-headmasters' in relation to the pupils and to those who tutor the pupils in their sections of the school. In fact, of course, the delegation of pastoral responsibility turns out to be a more complex matter than the notion of the mini-headmaster or even of the mini-school, created in duplicate or triplicate as it were, suggests. For the head does not simply place copies of himself at various strategic points in the community in order to create miniature schools within it and so to subdivide himself symbolically. He entrusts new roles, having first defined them in relation to different groups of pupils and staff, to a number of persons, each of whom must interpret in his own way how he uses the authority vested in him both by the head who appoints him and by the colleagues who agree to work in his section of the school. It will be surprising if there are not aspects of headship, even of the head himself as a person, to be discerned in each of these delegated roles as they are performed by the persons who undertake them; but this is not the same thing as saying that each is essentially a kind of carbon copy of the headmaster, operating in a smaller region.

The evolution of the pastoral system, as many teachers know it, seems to have been accompanied by a notion that the tutorial or 'caring' function should be as free as possible from work associations. The strange institution of 'moral tutors' in certain universities rests on this same belief: that the pupil (young or old) can be 'known' as a person and therefore helped as a person more effectively if the caring adult does not also have to teach him mathematics or science or French or English or any other subject. This seems to be a questionable assumption.

The different feelings about the two kinds of responsibility—curricular on the one hand and pastoral on the other—seem to have something to do with the balance between a public policy that is decided through group discussion and a private philosophy that is demonstrated by the individual acting on his own initiative and judgement. The problem of curriculum change—even in its very limited sense of change within a particular area of the curriculum—nearly always calls for some kind of team, or working party or committee. But pastoral care—though handled by sub-groups of staff—seems to be regarded much more as an individual matter, once the institutional framework for it has been accepted. The teaching of subjects is organized in departments and acknowledges the constraints of agreed syllabuses; it therefore involves groups of teachers, or individual teachers who are seen almost as embryo groups, as in a one-man department. But caring for children is felt to be, in the last resort, something that an individual teacher does in relation to individual children and groups of children. Hence, for example, the importance attached by house heads to their own obligation to be available at any time to 'chat' with any child about any trouble or problem, in contrast, perhaps, to the subject teacher's preoccupation with the problem of communicating with and controlling large classes. Paternalism in the house-tutorial system can also extend to the tutors in a section, the tutors in a house perceiving themselves as a close-knit family group that carries on most of its real business, in face-to-face meetings, mainly in pairs, within the physical boundary of the house block, at risk of becoming somewhat insulated from the institution as a whole.

In the first chapter I referred in general terms to the problem that schools have often had in coping with the conflicting attractions of the kind of system that is designed to satisfy the security needs of children and the kind of system that is designed to satisfy the academic needs of the curriculum. How were the security needs of the rising numbers of children at Nailsea catered for and how did the system set up for this purpose interlock with the curricular system examined in the last chapter?

The first stage in the process of delegation in this area was the appointment of Joan Bradbury as 'mistress in charge of girls' welfare' in 1961, when the 1959 intake was moving into the third year. This appointment reflected the traditional idea that the headmaster of a mixed school must allocate the caring part of his role, as far as the girls in his school are concerned, to the senior woman on the staff. This idea seems to rest on the assumption that 'welfare' (in a way the precursor to 'pastoral care' in the terminology of schools) is essentially something handled in sexually segregated groups. Since the corresponding role of 'master in charge of boys' welfare' is rarely if ever found, it may be seen as implying also that boys need less 'care' than girls—or that the care of boys can be left to chance, whereas that of girls must be specifically catered for. In practice Joan Bradbury included in her role the medical care of the boys, and it was to her that any cases of children of either sex needing first aid or aspirin or an escort home would be sent. The welfare role thus has embodied in it the imagery of the family, headed by a father who is seen to be supported by a wife and mother, as perhaps in a girls' school the family may be felt to be headed by a mother, supported by someone who has to take the role of the surrogate husband and father. The linking of 'welfare' functions (sometimes restricted to girls) with the role of the senior woman on the staff of a mixed school has had profound effects upon the role of the senior mistress throughout the secondary-school system. I shall be taking up this point again in a later chapter.

The second stage in this process of differentiation and delegation, reached in 1963, was the decision to give John Harbinson (appointed in 1960 as head of physical education) the task of organizing the first and second-year children as a lower school. And so, by the time the first partially compre-hensive intake arrived in September 1966, this section was well established as a unit, numbering, in that year, 297 pupils, organized in six first-year tutor groups and four second-year tutor groups, involving a tutorial staff of ten.

By 1970 it had risen to 414 pupils, distributed between fourteen tutor groups.

The third stage came in 1964 with the arrival in the sixth form of pupils from the first grammar-school intake, when Mike Burnham, the head of English (appointed in 1962), was asked to take over responsibility for organizing their courses, with the title of 'master in charge of sixth form studies', a title that he retained until the spring of 1969, when, as we have seen, it was changed to 'head of upper school'. By 1965 there were 171 sixth-formers, organized in twelve tutor groups; by 1967 the number had risen to 207, and it remained at that figure for three years, rising to 224 in 1970.

Meanwhile the area that lay between the lower school and the sixth form —which in the earlier grammar-school years had been left without any determinate kind of boundary—had been reorganized into a house system, planned in the spring and summer of 1966 with the appointment of four house heads (two men and two women) and four deputies, each of the appointed house heads choosing a deputy of the other sex in the course of the summer term from among those colleagues who were not in posts of special responsibility. Three of the house heads were appointed from among internal staff—namely, Peter Chapman (head of physics), Graeme Osborn (head of religious education) and Catherine Walker (a mathematician). The fourth was appointed from outside—namely, Pat Chapman, who came from Portishead School, where she had been head of girls' P.E. and a tutor in the lower school headed by Robin Thomas.

Ultimately the new house system was to embrace the third, fourth and fifth years. But in 1966 the new buildings were only half completed and temporary arrangements had to be made, with pairs of houses sharing territory and one house also sharing territory with the sixth form. These arrangements left one year-group out on a limb—namely the group of 114 pupils from the 1962 entry who, at the time of the reorganization in September 1966, were entering their fifth year in the school. These boys and girls had a unique experience of the problem of transition, since they found themselves in a no-man's-land, belonging neither to the new house system nor to the sixth form into which they could not yet be admitted. They were thus too old to be in one sub-system of the school and too young to be in another. The overall responsibility for this year group was given to Cyril Routley, who had applied unsuccessfully (in competition with two older colleagues) for one of the house headships, knowing that as these posts were sex-linked, only two of the four would go to men. Thus, the members of a somewhat stranded year-group of pupils and a somewhat disappointed staff member were jointly given some assurance that the system had not abandoned them. Nevertheless the temporariness of their status as a unit in the system, accommodated in huts while the house groups occupied new buildings along with the sixth form, must have been only too apparent to them.

Once the house-tutorial system was set up the groups formed in Year I remained intact, apart from annual losses and gains of pupils through family movements out of or into the area, until the end of Year V. Those who went on into the sixth form became members of completely new tutor groups. In these they might or might not find members of their earlier groups, since the formation of tutor groups in the sixth form was not, as in the rest of the school, based on the criterion of heterogeneity, but depended largely on the exigencies of the time-table and thus on the matching of staff and pupils who happened to have free periods at the same time. Hence there was within the upper-school groupings an appearance of special subject allocation—a kind of faculty flavour—although there had been no conscious intention to assemble specialists in any one subject in the same group with a tutor who specialized in that subject. By the summer of 1970 discussions were beginning to expose a good deal of uncertainty on the part of the staff concerned about whether these new sixth-form tutor groups had very much meaning either for them or for the pupils, because it proved extremely difficult in practice for any one group to have regular tutorial meetings which all its members could attend.

About fifteen months before this, in the early spring of 1969, the sixth-form tutors had been expressing their disquiet in a somewhat different way: not in terms of doubts about their own internal tutorial organization, but in terms of anxiety about the 'under-achievement' of sixth-formers, a situation they seemed inclined at that time to attribute to a house system which they perceived to be focused more on leisure pursuits than on work. Now the upper sixth in that year (1968–9) had in fact been part of the displaced fifth-year group in 1966–7; and the lower sixth had been among those who, at the point of entry into their fourth year, had been split between the four new houses, presumably with some loss of their identity as a year group, at the very time when they were having to face a considerable amount of change in the focus and organization of their academic work.

We must now look more closely at the nature of the change that was introduced into what we may call the school's socio-academic system in that important year. What was the emotional impact of the new situation in the middle part of the school upon those who were involved in it and upon those who remained outside it?

The inauguration of the new house system in September 1966 brought with it the demise of the old grammar-school 'houses' which, like the new ones, had been four in number. The membership of those earlier houses had been drawn more or less equally from each form; their identity had been based almost entirely on competitive games and merit awards and they had therefore owed whatever loyalty they commanded to an 'us-versus-the-rest' kind of motivation. Appropriately, or perhaps ironically, they had been named after birds of prey—eagles, falcons, hawks and kestrels. With the launching of the new house system, which was to be linked with territory and with mixed-ability tutor groups, these names disappeared and with them, it was assumed, the inherently competitive nature of the old 'houses'.

At the time of the transition the school council (which had representatives from all year groups) was consulted about whether the new 'tutor groups'—which, like the old 'forms', were to be mixed-ability groups—should be based, in the first place, on the existing house groups or on the existing form groups. The vote went overwhelmingly in favour of preserving the forms and letting the house groupings disappear. It seemed that there had been little sentience in those earlier houses, as far as the pupils were concerned, in comparison with the strong sentience in the form groups. And so the forms—hitherto named with the initial of the form teacher's surname—came into the new houses, intact but renamed as tutor groups and, apart from one, whose form mistress was to be deputy to one of the house heads, with new tutors.

The old houses had been associated with the four primary colours—blue, green, red and yellow—and it was decided that these should be retained in the new system for use in identifying the house-linked tutor groups so that they could keep the same letter symbol all the way through the school from the first to the fifth years. But how were the houses themselves to be named?

In fact it was the four colours that led, in the end, to the choice of the names. For those chosen—Pegasus, Dolphin, Pelican and Lion—were linked, through various literary and mythological associations, with the symbolism of those four primary colours. Pegasus, the winged horse, as the symbol of poetic inspiration, was associated with the blue of the sky or heavens from which inspiration is supposed to come; Dolphin, as the symbol of youthful hope and promise, was associated with the green of springtime, with its promise of rebirth and its hope of immortality; Pelican, as the symbol of self-sacrifice, was associated with the blood shed for others; and Lion, as the symbol of authority and power, was associated with the yellow (or gold) of the sun and hence in religious imagery with courage and strength.

I have just outlined the thoughts of certain members of the staff in the spring of 1966 when these names were chosen, as they were described to me by Denys John in the summer of 1971 at the very time when the houses, as pastoral units, were being given up in favour of a year-group organization. But when the symbolism—as perceived in 1966—is followed up, we find that the idealistic interpretations of those names contain their own contradictory elements: for if red (or the female pelican who was believed to feed her young with her own blood) symbolizes self-sacrifice, it also symbolizes violent attack, since red stands for war and useless slaughter, and the legend about the pelican presents the male pelican as having murdered his rebellious offspring. Similarly, yellow has its associations with jealousy and hatred, as the lion has its suggestion of cruelty and oppression. Pegasus was the bearer of Zeus's thunderbolts as well as the bearer of inspiration, and the hope of the dolphin (or of the dauphin prince) is rarely realized.

Looking back to the autumn of 1968, when I began to form my own earliest impressions of the house groups, and reflecting on my present interest in the processes by which the naming of the houses and their associated tutor groups was determined, I have been surprised to realize how unaware of all the mythological symbolism I was at that time. In fact, throughout the 1968-71 period, I continued to have difficulty in remembering which house name or which tutor-group letter I ought to be linking with each particular house head. I was also, I understand, remarkably deaf to Denys John's occasional attempts to explain to me just how the transition from one kind of house system to another had been made. And I remained blind to the visual descriptions of the four sets of symbols which were displayed just inside the doors of the houses, although I always found myself glancing appreciatively at the pictorial signposts outside those doors. It seems probable that the children too—and indeed many members of staff—remained fairly oblivious of the intended significance of the house names.

The staff, who were involved in these decisions, by emphasizing the good aspects of their selected symbols and suppressing their bad aspects, had hoped to infuse into the house groups corresponding ideals by which the children and their tutors might guide their behaviour, ideals of nobility and altruism and courage that would, it was hoped, suppress selfishness and greed and fear. But the ghosts of the birds of prey were, it seemed, not so easily to be laid as the new system took root. Among the staff the capacity for denial was strong. For some months they continued to express disbelief when I tried to draw attention to the interpersonal and intergroup rivalries and antagonisms that I was perceiving. If there was competitiveness in the new system, they maintained, it was being created by the children and did not exist among the staff. But I found myself wondering frequently, in those early months, how much of this conflict was being projected into the children unconsciously by the staff.

To me, in that first year, it was the accidents and manoeuvrings of the 1966-8 period rather than the ideals embodied in the house names that were of absorbing interest. For however deaf and blind I may have been to some things, I found myself building up very strong impressions about relationships between house heads, about attitudes towards the middle school revealed by staff who were concerned mainly with lower-school or upper-school affairs, and about the tensions between the section and department heads.

The real imagery that suffused the life of the house groups, as I perceived it in the 1968-9 session, was the image of the family. And the four families, it seemed, like those in many neighbourhoods, were continually oscillating between their need to cooperate with one another in order to survive as a combined unit within the school, and their need to compete with one another in order to preserve their separate identities.

It would be easy now to present the reader with a set of rather meaningless facts and figures, showing the rate of expansion in the various sections, the fluctuations and variations in the size of tutor groups and the corresponding movements of tutors into or out of sections as demand or inclination changed

T.S.T.M.—5

from year to year. But these facts are useful only in so far as they can throw light on the inner world of the Nailsea staff group during the years when I was working with them. I therefore propose to select those facts which seem to me now to be important for the central task of this book. And in this chapter we are concerned mainly with the problem of the divided system—a system that, in my view, forced the middle-school houses into a mutually competitive situation in which the sentient system within each house had to be protected and in which pastoral care, introduced to support the educational task, seemed at times to be at variance with that task.

In order to understand the complexity of the relationships both between the three main sections of the school and within the house system, it is important to be clear at this stage how the actual constitution of the various tutorial teams was affected both by the kind of freedom people had to choose their destination in the system and by the constraints upon that freedom. Freedom operated—relatively speaking—in two ways. Individual tutors had the opportunity to express a preference for placement in one or other section, even of movement from one section to another; and heads of sections had the right to bid for particular persons as deputies and supporting tutors in their own sections. But there were two kinds of constraint on these choices, stemming from two basic principles which Denys John observed in making appointments and in confirming allocations to sections or groups: first, the principle of sex balance, ensured through the rule that every section head must have a deputy of the opposite sex, and that, within the house system, there should be two housemasters and two housemistresses; and secondly, the principle of the spreading of responsibilities, ensured through the rule that no-one who already held office as a department head should be appointed as a deputy to a section head. The second rule contained a built-in contradiction. For of the six section heads operating at the beginning of the 1966–8 session, only two were free from leadership roles in the curricular structure: namely, the two housemistresses, Catherine Walker and Pat Chapman. The four men, who between them headed the departments of English, physical education, physics and religious education, all continued in these roles for at least one term, because the appointment of successors had to be delayed for varying lengths of time until the school was large enough to carry the four additional posts of special responsibility that were needed before they could be relieved of these tasks. The first to hand over his department was Peter Chapman in January 1967; John Harbinson handed over the P.E. department and Mike Burnham the English department in September 1967; Graeme Osborn continued to take responsibility for religious education until the summer of 1969, and was thus the only remaining section head to be carrying major leadership roles on both sides of the curricular-pastoral divide in the year when I began my work with the school.

Because the first house tutors to join the house heads as deputies had to be relatively junior members of the staff, it was inevitable that the department heads already established in the school should find themselves tutoring either in the lower school or in the upper school by the time new middle-school tutors were needed. The effect of this initial steering away of senior people, other than the house heads, from the house-tutorial teams was that by 1968 there was a marked concentration of heads of departments in the lower and upper schools with an equally marked absence of senior academic staff in the houses. Bob Miller, arriving in the school as head of physical education in September 1967, and Eva Tucker joining him a year later as head of girls' P.E. and as his assistant in running the department, were the only senior staff members acting as tutors in the middle school.

I myself first became curious about this distribution of staff between the three main sections when, in the spring of 1969, at Mike Burnham's invitation, I attended the meetings that he had begun to hold with the sixth-form tutors, and was struck by the high concentration of heads of academic departments in this particular group of tutors. Further scrutiny revealed that, with the exception of Bob Miller, all the other department heads were based in the lower school. Moreover, with the exception of modern languages and biology, it was the heads of those subjects usually described as 'non-academic', namely art, music, technical education and physical education, who were found in the lower school. The other surprising fact was that, apart from the head of chemistry who did not actually have a tutor group but was loosely attached to the lower school, all the scientists were biologists, Gwen London being accompanied by the whole of her department in the lower-school tutorial team during that particular session. The facts about this distribution are shown diagrammatically in Figures 19, 20 and 21. It was hardly surprising that the unconscious segregation of staff that had been going on during these years following the reorganization of the middle school was having its effects upon the relationships between this section and the lower and upper schools between which it fell.

A group such as a house staff group or a sixth-form tutors' group may be perceived in fantasy by those outside it as either torn with internal conflict or free from conflict to the extent of appearing monolithic and undivided. But it soon becomes apparent that no system is either wholly one or wholly the other. At the same time it is difficult to acknowledge that other systems may have both good and bad parts since this would involve acknowledging the badness as well as the goodness in one's own system. Thus an image of a middle-school house system united in its search for social unity, if necessary at the price of intellectual achievement, may give way to separate images in which each house is perceived with exaggerated and unreal simplicity as either 'authoritarian' or 'democratic', as either 'governed on a tight rein' or 'organized in accordance with liberal educational principles', as either 'happy' or 'discontented', as either 'controlled' or 'undisciplined', as either 'serious' or 'trivial'.

Doubtless all the Nailsea staff were aware during the years of rumours and

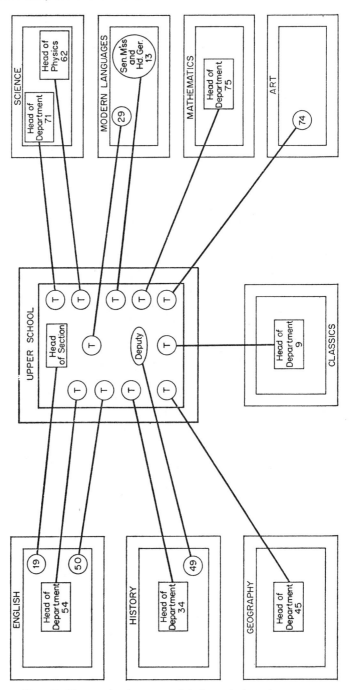

FIG. 19. Upper-school tutors and their curricular roles: 1968–9.

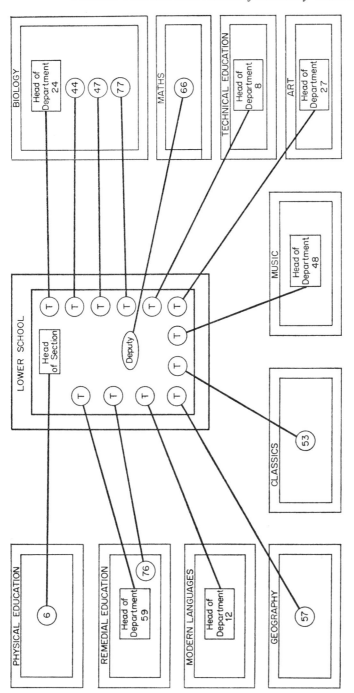

Fig. 20. Lower-school tutors and their curricular roles: 1968–9.

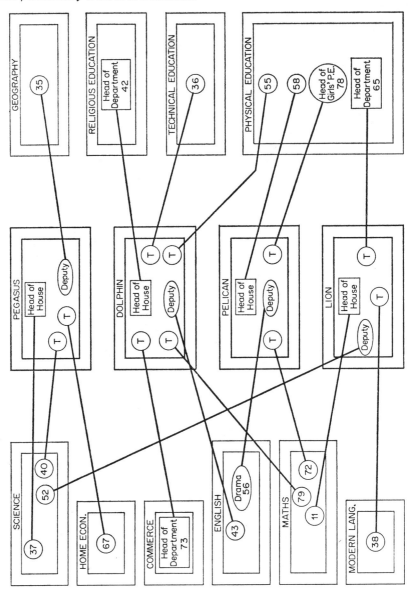

Fig. 21. Middle-school house tutors and their curricular roles: 1968–9.

beliefs about the different ways in which the four house heads carried out their leadership tasks and how they interpreted their pastoral functions both in relation to the tutors in their houses and in relation to the children. History entered into these myths and fantasies and must also have been affecting the realities in those four bounded house groups. Catherine Walker, whose appointment to the school staff dated back to its second year, had come to the present comprehensive-school house system from an earlier role as a house mistress in the original grammar school. How might she have been influenced by this earlier experience of a house system based far more on competitive inter-house rivalry than on the building up of a real intra-house life? There was a good deal of evidence that her colleagues put pressure on her to be the spokesman in defending the rights of the houses and in claiming that it was through their house and tutor-group membership that children and perhaps staff also could find their security. How important was it that Pat Chapman had come into her role as house head from an earlier experience as a tutor in the lower part of another comprehensive school, one that had originally been a secondary modern school? To what extent did her work as a P.E. teacher, accustomed to handling children in the open, socially un-inhibited, sometimes explosive situations of the gymnasium and the games field influence both the way she perceived her role as house head and the way her colleagues outside her house perceived her in that role? How was the relationship between Peter Chapman and Graeme Osborn, both of whom entered the school in the same year, being affected by the knowledge that the former had relinquished his post as head of physics to take on the role of a house head, whereas the latter, right up to the autumn of 1969, continued to be head of R.E. as well as head of his house? To what extent were the two Chapmans—unrelated, but happening to share the same surname—who, in the first year of the house system shared one set of premises, seen as the pair who could co-operate while Graeme Osborn and Catherine Walker, who had originally shared the other available premises, found themselves to be the two who quite often became sparring partners in staff meetings?

Curiously enough my own observations of the roles taken by the four house heads in section heads' meetings during the 1968-9 school year did not always fit the images they appeared to have in the eyes of their colleagues. Peter Chapman, who was generally considered to have a 'liberal' approach, once complained bitterly that colleagues in the other houses were not making sufficiently strict demands on pupils over dress and hair styles; and on another occasion Graeme Osborn, who was considered to be a 'strict' disciplinarian, spoke of activities that implied an almost over-liberal interpretation of the functions of the tutorial period. Yet the power of these images seemed to be very strong. I recall a full staff discussion focused on the current uneasiness over litter, unmannerliness, smoking and related problems in which John Phillips, who was deputy head of a house generally seen as being tightly controlled was forced by the meeting more and more into a position where comments on the extent to which even staff could be guilty of these 'offences' were being turned into comments about lack of standards among pupils. I recall a rather similar situation in a combined meeting of the lower and middle-school tutors held towards the end of the summer of 1970 to consider whether links between the lower-school tutor groups and the houses for which they were destined were real or imaginary, and if real whether they were essential to the work of the school. This meeting was chaired by Robin Thomas and attended by John Harbinson and Clive Vanloo. Afterwards these three members of the standing committee all said they had been struck by the fact that those middle-school tutors who had felt free in that meeting, the first of its kind, to question openly in the presence of their house head the assumptions upon which the house system was based were all members of one of the houses that was considered to be most liberal in its outlook. It is difficult to know how far these differences in behaviour between the members of different houses stemmed from *real* differences between the attitudes and beliefs of the persons concerned and how far the total staff group, acting collectively on assumptions about the house communities to which those people belonged, was unconsciously putting pressure on them as representatives of their house communities rather than as individual persons to behave as they did.

The meeting to which I have just referred was remarkable for the sophisticated level at which the discussion was conducted, despite the discomfort involved in examining so critically the system to which people had developed such strong personal loyalties. In striking contrast were my own recorded impressions of the first section heads' meeting that I had attended about eighteen months earlier, in October 1968. At that earlier meeting the dominant feeling being expressed had been of competition and rivalry. At one point there was discussion about the 'unfairness' of the contests for house trophies; and as fast as one of the house heads pointed out how a house with two fifth-year tutor groups was in a position to score over others in sports events, so another was pointing out that a house with two third-year tutor groups was in a position to score more highly on merit awards, since staff in general in their subject teaching were less inclined to bother with the handing out of merit points in the fourth and fifth years, where the pupils themselves were becoming indifferent to such rewards, than in the third year which still retained some of the characteristics of a lower school.

Now in fact, in that particular year, Graeme Osborn had in his house two fifth-year tutor groups, one fourth-year group and two third-year groups. Numerically his house population stood at 136 with five tutors in addition to himself, as compared with 89, 85 and 102 children in the other three houses, each with three tutors in addition to the house head. How had this discrepancy in size (and correspondingly perhaps, in some people's eyes, in power) come about?

Dolphin House had in fact gone through some strange vicissitudes in the 1967–8 and 1968–9 sessions (see Figures 22 and 23). The expansion of this house had begun in the autumn of 1967, when it had acquired its second fourth-year tutor group as a result of the splitting of 3G into two smaller groups, named 4G1 and 4G2. The reason for this regrouping, as Graeme Osborn himself explained it to me in the autumn of 1971, was that the group, to which he had himself been tutor, had acquired a bad reputation in its

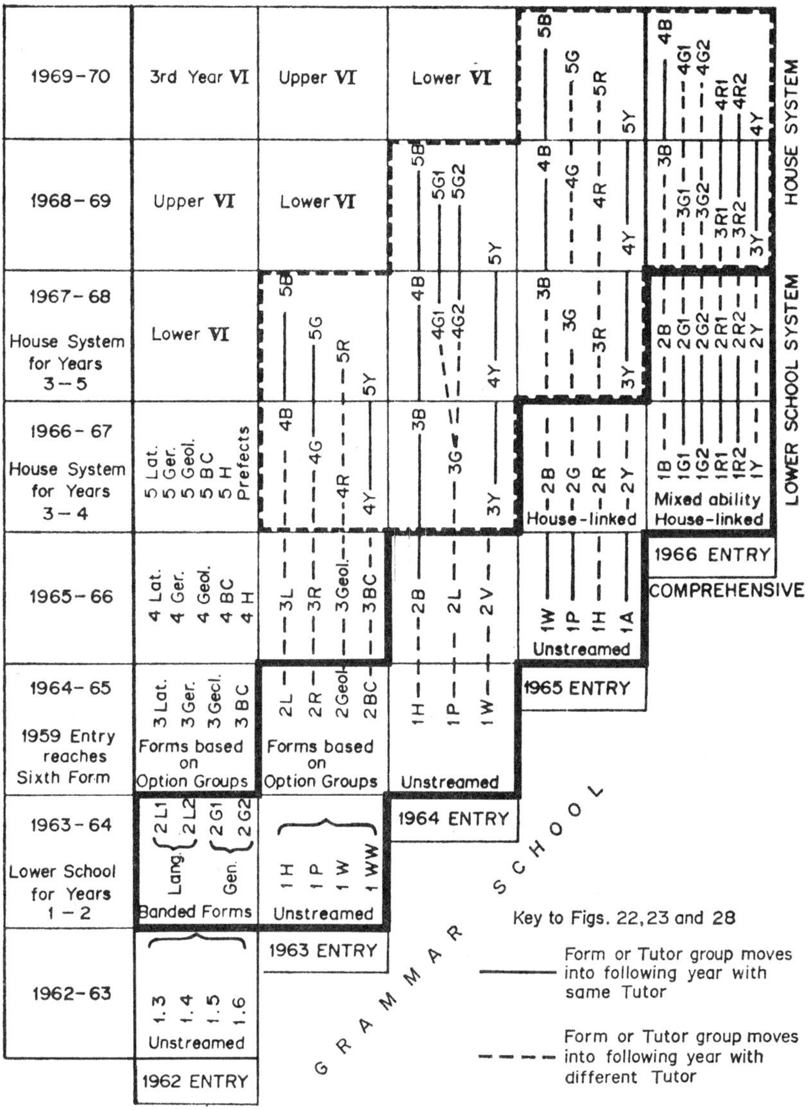

				5B	4B	
1969–70	3rd Year VI	Upper VI	Lower VI	5G / 5R / 5Y	4G1 / 4G2 / 4R1 / 4R2 / 4Y	HOUSE SYSTEM

| 1968–69 | Upper VI | Lower VI | 5B / 5G1 / 5G2 / 5Y | 4B / 4G / 4R / 4Y | 3B / 3G1 / 3G2 / 3R1 / 3R2 / 3Y | HOUSE SYSTEM |

| 1967–68 House System for Years 3–5 | Lower VI | 5B / 5G / 5R / 5Y | 4B / 4G1 / 4G2 / 4Y | 3B / 3G / 3R / 3Y | 2B / 2G1 / 2G2 / 2R1 / 2R2 / 2Y | LOWER SCHOOL SYSTEM |

| 1966–67 House System for Years 3–4 | 5 Lat. / 5 Ger. / 5 Geol. / 5 BC / 5 H / Prefects | 4B / 4G / 4R / 4Y | 3B / 3G / 3Y | 2B / 2G / 2R / 2Y House-linked | 1B / 1G1 / 1G2 / 1R1 / 1R2 / 1Y Mixed ability House-linked | 1966 ENTRY |

| 1965–66 | 4 Lat. / 4 Ger. / 4 Geol. / 4 BC / 4 H | 3L / 3R / 3Geol. / 3BC | 2B / 2L / 2V | 1W / 1P / 1H / 1A Unstreamed | COMPREHENSIVE |

| 1964–65 1959 Entry reaches Sixth Form | 3 Lat. / 3 Ger. / 3 Geol. / 3 BC Forms based on Option Groups | 2L / 2R / 2Geol. / 2BC Forms based on Option Groups | 1H / 1P / 1W Unstreamed | 1965 ENTRY |

| 1963–64 Lower School for Years 1–2 | 2L1 / 2L2 Lang. / 2G1 / 2G2 Gen. Banded Forms | 1H / 1P / 1W / 1WW Unstreamed | 1964 ENTRY |

| 1962–63 | 1.3 / 1.4 / 1.5 / 1.6 Unstreamed | 1963 ENTRY |

| | 1962 ENTRY |

GRAMMAR SCHOOL

Key to Figs. 22, 23 and 28

——— Form or Tutor group moves into following year with same Tutor

– – – Form or Tutor group moves into following year with different Tutor

FIG. 22. Progress of the 1962–6 intakes through the pastoral system.

third year, a reputation that was perhaps linked with its position as the largest tutor group among the fractionated third and fourth years dispersed between the newly constituted houses. Anxious that this bad image should not be perpetuated in the coming two years, he had proposed that the group should be broken down and reconstituted as two entities, a manoeuvre that was made possible institutionally because an additional tutor was available for the coming year. In fact the move gave this house two additional tutors rather than one, since Graeme Osborn himself, along with only one of his three fellow house heads (Pat Chapman) gave up being a tutor in the 1967–8 session. Thus he already had in that year a team of four tutors, as compared with three each in Pegasus and Lion and only two in Pelican. His numbers were further augmented by chance in the following year, 1968–9, because the year group then coming into the houses had been the 1966 six-form entry, and two tutor groups had, as it happened, been allocated to Dolphin. My own perception of Graeme Osborn's as the 'giant house'—which matched

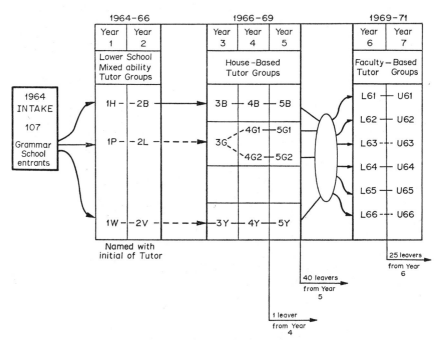

FIG. 23. Progress of 1964 entrants through the pastoral system.

my perception of science and modern languages as the giant 'departments'— was all the stronger during the 1968–9 session because I was not yet aware of all the causes that had led to its being relatively overgrown. It is conceivable that members of staff also, being unaware of all the reasons for the imbalance, may have read into these discrepancies signs that Graeme Osborn himself might be seeking some kind of power in the house system. And indeed he himself, in thinking about these manoeuvres at a later date, could not really be sure to what extent, in seizing opportunities to improve the conditions of work in his house, he had been acting on behalf of children and to what extent he had been acting on behalf of himself, for it is never easy to know where the line is drawn between professional zeal and personal ambition. I shall return later to the question of the dual responsibility he carried at that time in the school system as a whole by virtue of being both a house head and a department head.

Transition stages in the pastoral and curricular systems

It may already be apparent that we are looking at a structure that raises questions not only about where the discontinuities in the pastoral organization are, but also about where the boundary round the house system is perceived to be. Was the house system contained in the middle school, or did it overlap the lower and upper-school boundaries? My own impression, built up during the 1968–9 session and persisting through the following winter and spring, was that the lower-school tutor groups, although sometimes referred to as the 'future house bricks', had little contact with the house groups into which they would be moving in due course, and that the links between the houses and the sixth form were even more tenuous. I was told on one occasion that in the house that spilled over into the sixth-form territory the fifth-form tutor group appeared to have an unspoken agreement with the neighbouring sixth form that they should ignore one another. The culture seemed to demand that the same separation be maintained between the middle-school house system and the upper-school sixth-form system as existed between the middle school, housed in its four separated territories, and the lower school, housed as one unit in the main school building. It was therefore with considerable surprise that I learned that pupils had been considered in theory to be linked to particular houses throughout their school lives. We shall see later, however, that the discussion that took place during the summer of 1970 about whether these links existed in reality or only in fantasy, and the conflicting views expressed about this, both by tutors and by house heads, opened up some fundamental questions about the implications of this kind of organization. And in fact, following those discussions, the pupils entering the lower school in September 1970 were, for the first time since 1966, allocated to tutor groups without any guaranteed link with particular houses, and were not given the B, G, R, and Y labels. The way was thus opened for a reorganization of these children into new tutor groups at their point of entry into the middle school if this should seem, when the time came, to be in the interest of the educational programme planned for the coming phase.

If we now examine the pastoral organization and the curricular organization in parallel as it were, we begin to see how important it is to be clear about where the discontinuities in the educational process should really be. Figure 24 picks up some of the facts described above and presents them in a different way, using the import-conversion-export model described in Chapter II. This chart clearly demonstrates how in the context of the pastoral organization the discontinuities occurred at the end of Years II and V—at the time of the first move from the lower school into the houses and, at the

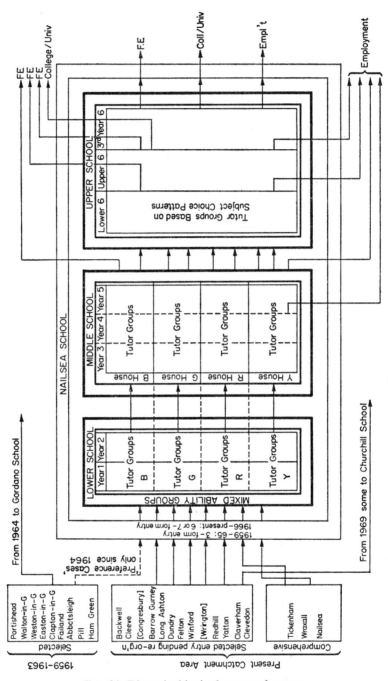

FIG. 24. Discontinuities in the pastoral system.

time of the second move, for those who stayed on at school, from the houses into the sixth form or upper school. In the lower school, despite the anticipation of house identities, the real emphasis was, I believe, on the organization into year groups, as it was in the upper school following the disbanding of the house-based tutor groups. But in the middle school the emphasis was on organization into house groups, an organization that blurred the year-group boundaries and possibly also the middle-school boundary within which it was by 1969 organizationally contained.

How does this breakdown of the pastoral system into the lower-school, middle-school and upper-school sections compare with that of the curricular

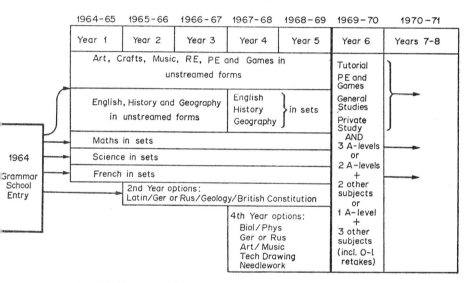

FIG. 25. Progress of 1964 entrants through the curricular system.

system? Are the major discontinuities found to coincide in the two systems or do they differ?

To contain within a comprehensible diagram the complicated curricular developments described in the last chapter is a near impossibility. Nevertheless the attempt is worth making, since a diagram, however imperfect, can highlight certain problems that might be lost in a verbal account. Figures 25, 26 and 27 show the progress of three different groups of pupils through the curricular system: namely, those who entered the school in 1964, in 1966 and in 1969. These charts show that, both before and after 1966—that is, before and after the school began to take in an unselected entry—the major discontinuities in the process appeared after Years I, III and V, more importantly after Years I and III, since the choice of options in Year IV provided its own kind of continuity between Years V and VI for those who stayed on after the fifth year and entered the upper school. This situation was

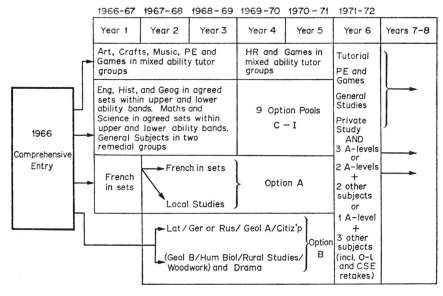

FIG. 26. Progress of 1966 entrants through the curricular system.

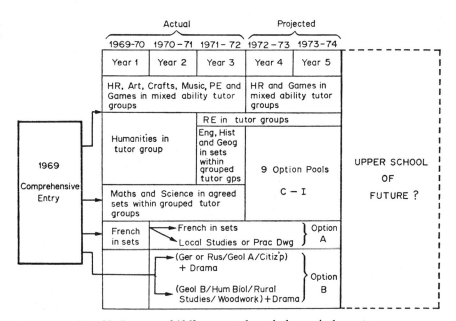

FIG. 27. Progress of 1969 entrants through the curricular system.

changed considerably in 1970 when, for the first time, children were being taught, in their mixed-ability tutor groups, a two-year humanities course the length of which coincided with the length of their stay in the lower school.

In effect, then, before 1970 children were having to cope with some form of discontinuity, over and above the break of the summer holiday, at the end of every school year apart from the fourth, either in the form of a move from one tutorial base to another, or in the form of a major change from one pattern of courses to another. Figures 25, 26 and 27, taken as a series of interrelated diagrams, show how the school was modifying its curricular provision between 1968 and 1970 to meet the demands of the changing intake of pupils: too fast perhaps for some of its members, too slowly for others. In Figure 28, which plots the progress of one particular intake (that of 1968) through both systems, the difficulty of reconciling the need for stability and the need for variety and the resulting imbalance between the two systems are more clearly revealed.

The dialogue that was going on in the staff group during these years about this problem of the reconciliation of apparently irreconcilable needs sometimes revealed lurking ambiguities in the way words were being used, with the result that discussions about one area of concern appeared at times to be masking anxieties about other areas of concern. I recall that on two quite different occasions during the autumn term of 1968 two different senior staff members (both lower-school tutors) expressed very strong indignation about the abrupt changes experienced by the younger children when they moved from the relatively unstreamed situation of the first year into the more rigid banding and setting system of the second year. Yet one of these two, Reg Clarke, while disapproving of streaming in principle, was anxious that the 'general subjects' or remedial group for which he was responsible should not be affected in any future move towards unstreaming. Now this group, as a result of his own policy some years earlier, included, along with the handful of children who really needed remedial help, as many more who were of near average ability. In other words he himself had for long advocated that 'remedial' children should not be segregated; yet he was resistant to the dispersion of these children through mixed-ability groups for teaching in subjects other than those non-academic subjects that were already being taught in tutor groups. It was difficult for him to know how much of this resistance was based on his conviction that such children needed a containing framework for all their work—a framework that was strongly 'pastoral' in its purpose—and how much it was unconsciously being affected by his own need for this semi-tutorial relationship with children who, even given that protection, were very difficult to help.

Such tensions, which are experienced by all teachers in some measure, have been so strongly institutionalized in secondary schools through the structural splitting apart of the curricular and pastoral functions, that it is easy for an individual teacher to become over-identified with one set of

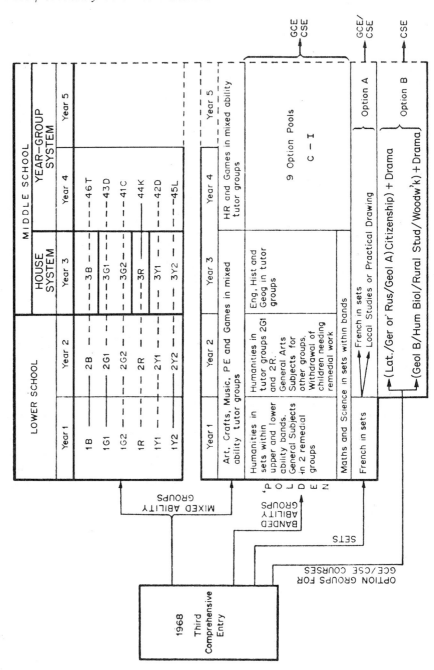

FIG. 28. Progress of one year group through the school system.

attitudes, to the point of denying the co-existence within himself of the other set of attitudes. Thus, although the education of the least able children in the school was as much a curricular as a pastoral matter, a remedial teacher was likely, in the divided system, to place more stress on the pastoral side, and so to regard containment within a secure, if somewhat isolated, group as of prior importance for retarded pupils.

But the problem of this balance was just as acute for those whose expertise was with the former grammar-school pupils and whose prestige depended, or seemed to depend, on their success with pre-university sixth-form pupils. In the past the provision of opportunity for a relatively small proportion of the pupil population in grammar schools has made it possible for highly educated specialist teachers to carry with them into their own particular fields of interest a large enough number of pupils to ensure a sense of achievement. The dispersion of these highfliers amongst a wider spectrum of the child population and the obligation to provide opportunities for all pupils, whatever their estimated level of attainment, seems to reduce these chances. And so it is hard for the specialist who has seen his goal as nurturing the future scholars in his own special subject to be sure when he is really thinking of the needs of all his pupils and when he is thinking of his own need for a sense of achievement through the successes of his brightest pupils.

We are faced, it seems, with the problem of reconciling the demands of the educational task, which requires that the *pupil* be the object of concern, with the search for professional recognition and satisfaction, which makes the *teacher* the object of concern. It is useless and hypocritical to pretend that the second is ignoble and irrelevant. Teachers just as much as their pupils need to feel valued; more importantly in terms of the task, they have contributions to make through their own developing skills as leaders in different parts of the enterprise. The evolution of the dual structure that I have been describing in terms of a system for educating children must therefore be seen also in terms of a career structure for teachers—a structure that does not make it easy for them to be clear what their own motives are in moving in one direction rather than another or what it is that attracts them to one role rather than to another. Such a system puts a premium on finding a safe and familiar vehicle for one's work as a teacher and staying in it rather than on risking new ventures that might promote new thinking about the nature of the educational enterprise itself.

The dual system as a career structure

For those who were teaching in grammar schools twenty years ago the normal route to a headship was from a university through the teaching of a special subject, via the headship of a department, and possibly a deputy headship or the post of senior mistress. For non-graduates proceeding from a college of education, transition to a grammar-school post of responsibility was relatively difficult. Even those who came into grammar schools from specialist colleges of art, music, home economics or physical education, although they might very quickly reach positions of special responsibility within their own subject areas, were unlikely to proceed to headships. The situation now is very different. An increasing number of graduates go directly to posts in secondary modern or comprehensive schools, even if they have special honours degrees, and an increasing number of non-graduates move within the comprehensive-school system to posts of greater and greater responsibility.

The range of experience represented in the staff of a school like Nailsea, as illustrated in Figures 29 and 30, is much greater than it used to be in the old type of grammar school. This general career structure indicates that the old dichotomy between graduate and non-graduate or between those with grammar-school experience and those with secondary-modern-school experience is not really evident at all. Nevertheless, these diagrams indicate that it has perhaps been replaced by another, subtler, kind of dichotomy. For it seems that in making a decision about whether to seek promotion on the pastoral side or whether to seek it on the curricular side people may feel that they have unwittingly labelled themselves as relatively strong or relatively weak in their subject specialism. Equally, the decision to go one way rather than the other seems to carry with it an implication that one is either predominantly interested in one's subject or predominantly interested in children. Yet probably all teachers would agree that good teaching demands interest in both. We must also recognize that some people are pulled one way or the other more by accident and chance opportunity than by design. Sometimes, indeed, a conscious choice to move off in one direction may be thwarted and be followed by a compensatory move in the other direction.

Cyril Routley and Graeme Osborn were walking illustrations of two sides of the dilemma that individual teachers had to cope with in the divided system. If Cyril Routley, as head of the diminishing department of classics and as the unsuccessful applicant for a house headship, exemplified the plight of the experienced staff member who felt under-employed, Graeme Osborn, who was for three years both head of religious education (a subject taken by all pupils throughout the school) and head of a house (the largest, as it happened, in the 1968–9 session) exemplified the problem of the experienced staff member who felt over-employed.

Cyril Routley received some recompense for his disappointment over the house headship and his subsequent loss of the temporary leadership of the fifth-year unit in the form of a sabbatical year in 1969–70, which enabled him to equip himself academically for a future broadening of the hitherto narrow area of classics to include the allied studies of ancient history and archaeology. As it turned out it also equipped him to accept with enthusiasm a new role in charge of resources in the reorganized system that took effect in September 1971.

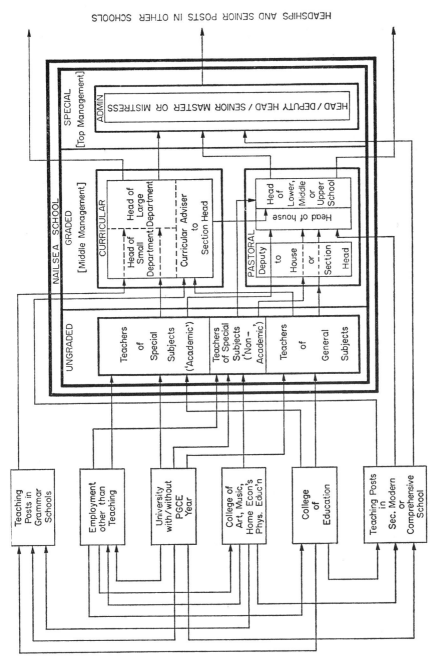

FIG. 29. General career structure in the comprehensive system.

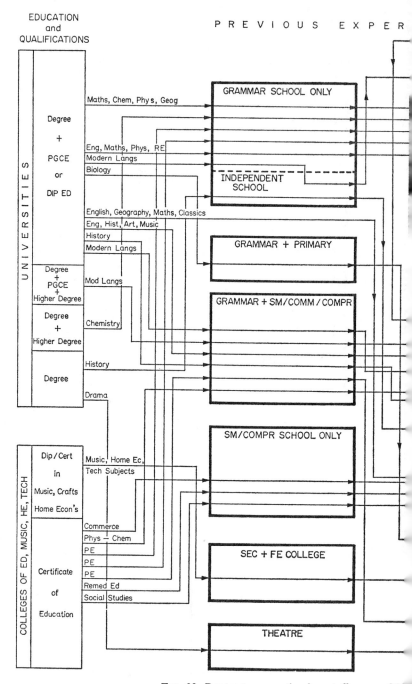

FIG. 30. Routes to promotion in a staff group of 19

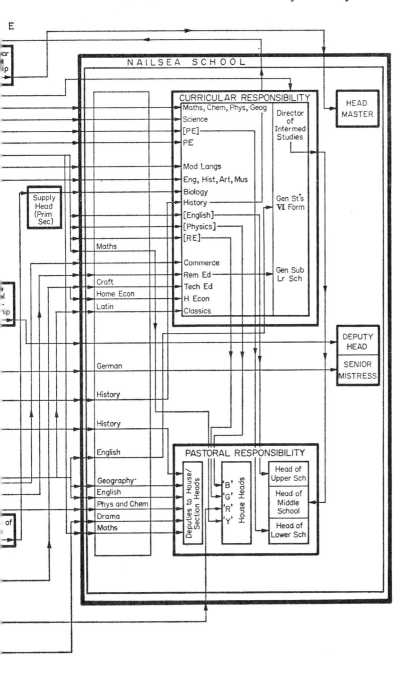

For Graeme Osborn that same 1969–70 session, in which he was relieved of his responsibility for religious education, brought a dramatic swing of interests, which I have plotted in diagrammatic form in Figure 31. In the 1968–9 session his problem, as he often described it, had been that he had to 'wear two hats'—that of a house head and that of a department head, at a time when section and department heads met separately. During that year he regarded the 'pastoral' responsibility for his house as his major priority, and recognized that there were times when he had to neglect the other priority in order to honour this one. Notably this was so when he had a fifth-form R.E. period first thing in the morning, when he would sometimes be preoccupied with house business and might find himself having to set work to occupy the class for the first part of their lesson. In the 1969–70 session, with the arrival of David Sellick, he thankfully shed this departmental burden, and with it much of the examination work, and was therefore free to devote more of his time to house matters. Apparently, then, the tension between the pastoral and curricular concerns had gone: he no longer had two conflicting areas of responsibility that were pulling him in opposite directions. But by this time the humanities course was expanding, with seven people teaching it in Year I and with a pilot course being taught to two tutor groups in Year II, one by Bob Jarratt and the other by himself, a course for which he took the major responsibility. Moreover, with the departure of Bob Jarratt to a new post elsewhere in the middle of the 1969–70 session, with Pam Thackeray away on secondment and with Robin Thomas no longer teaching humanities, Graeme Osborn was left as the sole representative of the original humanities team still teaching in the course. By the summer of 1970 it was becoming clear to him that his growing interest in humanities as a teaching medium—an interest that drew him towards the lower school and perhaps brought his interest in pastoral work into a closer relationship with his teaching interests—was gradually weaning him away from his earlier strong engagement with the task of being a housemaster. And so, by the summer of 1970, having accepted the invitation to direct the lower-school humanities course (about to expand into a two-year course involving a team of thirteen staff) he found himself once more handling major responsibilities in both the pastoral and the curricular systems. Moreover, by that time he was well aware that it was now the house headship rather than the leadership role in the new curricular area that he wanted to drop.

The management structure in the dual system

The tension between these two aspects of the job can be seen most clearly, perhaps, in the change that took place in the spring of 1969 in the titles of the present heads of the middle and upper schools.

Clive Vanloo's earlier title of 'director of intermediate studies' suggested a responsibility located clearly in the curricular area of the school's total

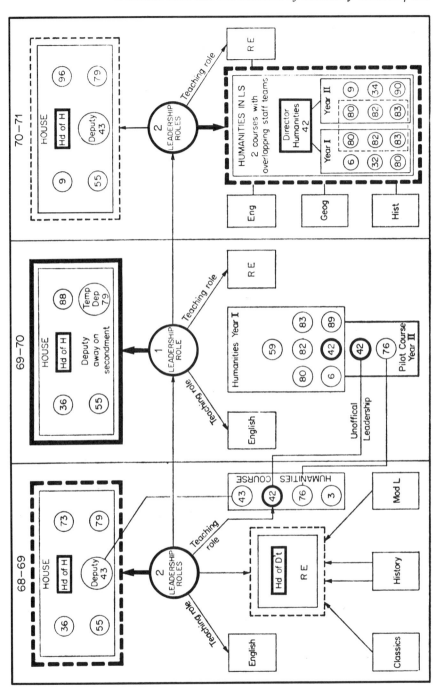

FIG. 31. Dual leadership in pastoral and curricular systems.

task. During the autumn term of 1968 he was working very closely with the headmaster and the members of the Fourth Year Curriculum study group which was planning the new programme of courses, based on nine option pools, which came into operation in the autumn of 1969, when the first comprehensive intake of pupils was moving into the fourth year. Denys John, while chairing the committee meetings as headmaster acknowledged that Clive Vanloo had been the chief architect of this plan and when it was presented for discussion at a full staff meeting in December 1968, he made this publicly clear. On that occasion Clive Vanloo sat next to him and, although he did not take over the chairmanship role, he did take a leading part in clarifying the details of the plan and in taking up queries and doubts as they were raised by his colleagues.

It was at that meeting that the ambiguity of his position, while it was still tied only to curricular matters, first became apparent. Listening to the discussion I was struck by the general concern about which teachers would get the ablest children for their courses; it seemed to me that more was being said about this than about the needs of the abler children themselves. All this prompted me, fairly late in the meeting, to ask a question about something that I thought was being concealed, namely who was to have the final say in any case where a choice pattern as advised by a head of house or tutor conflicted with a choice pattern as advised by a head of department. Now in fact this question had not been concealed. It was clearly stated in the document that it would be Clive Vanloo, as director of intermediate studies, who would have to make this decision and be the arbiter. Furthermore I had myself seen this document before the meeting and had studied it carefully. Indeed I had discussed the implications of that very clause with Clive Vanloo himself and also, I think, with Denys John. Yet in that meeting I was genuinely bewildered and was asking a question not to make a point but because I really wanted this clarification for myself. I was conscious that they both looked surprised, not to say startled, by my question. And even when I was reminded by Denys John about the clause in the document it was some moments before I found it again, recognized it, recalled that I had seen it before and became aware of my own mistake and confusion.

I refer to this because I think it throws light on the difficulty that people were experiencing at that time in acknowledging their anxieties about the implications of Clive Vanloo's developing role in the school. It was not until some time after the meeting that it occurred to me that I myself had been caught up in the general concealment, not of the decision that had been made about who should have the final say about any particular child if there was a dispute, but of the implications of that decision. In other words, when I looked back on the meeting afterwards, it struck me as surprising that nobody had mentioned this as a source of any kind of anxiety though in fact it must have been raising all sorts of questions about the autonomy, not only of the heads of departments, but also of the four house heads. Once Clive Vanloo was given authority over the curricular arrangements for the fourth year, it had to be recognized that his role included the co-ordination of house affairs and therefore placed him on the boundary that enclosed all the house boundaries. It was in recognition of that reality that he was officially redesignated 'head of middle school' in April 1969. Thenceforward the house heads and their tutorial staff had to recognize, as did other members of the staff, that his role could no longer be associated only with the curricular side of the school's work, but had to be associated also with the pastoral side.

The change in this title brought into question the appropriateness of the title hitherto held by Mike Burnham who, up till April 1969, had been known as the 'master in charge of sixth-form studies', a title that suggested something rather bookish, academic, linked more with universities and colleges than with adult life outside those institutions. Mike Burnham had joined the Nailsea staff in the fourth year after the school's opening, when the existence of a sixth form, even in grammar-school terms, was still two years away in the future. By 1968, as we have seen, his responsibilities had greatly increased and could certainly not be seen as limited to curricular matters. This reality was also recognized in April 1969 when Denys John, in announcing Clive Vanloo's change of title, added that Mike Burnham should now correspondingly be renamed 'head of upper school'. Curiously enough the school journal still used the term 'sixth form' in naming that section of the school while rewording Mike Burnham's title to 'head of upper school'. The image of the grammar-school sixth form was, as we shall see, to die hard.

I have already indicated that John Harbinson's appointment as head of lower school pre-dated those of both these other section heads. The lower school had come into existence in 1963, a few months after the initial decision that the school was to go comprehensive but three years before that decision was implemented. My impression has been that John Harbinson's post was never seen as predominantly either curricular or pastoral, but rather as a fusion between the two. Thus the lower school perhaps remained relatively free from the artificial dichotomy which I believe affected the growth of the middle and upper-school sections. One of the surprises that I experienced on first coming into the school was to find that the headmaster's room was up on the first floor and that the room near the main entrance, which had originally been the headmaster's room, was occupied by the head of the lower school. This room change took place in September 1967, the year after the first comprehensive intake of first-year pupils had entered the school. Thus the room that had hitherto symbolized headship of the whole school was handed over to the lower-school head at the time when the management of the import system of the school was suddenly acquiring a new complexity.

At that time, Denys John was facing a crucial change in his own role, from being head of the selective grammar school to which he had originally been appointed to becoming head of a comprehensive school destined to grow into a much larger institution than the original one would ever have become. He was handing over his room to John Harbinson at the very time when further acts of delegation to senior colleagues (and to one new colleague) were taking place through the developing work of the four house heads. Thus the change of room symbolized in a very tangible and visible way the process of delegation that was going on.

The setting up of the standing committee three years later, in the autumn of 1969, a few months after Clive Vanloo and Mike Burnham had been given their new titles, can now be seen as a direct, even if unexpected, sequel to the appointment of John Harbinson as head of the lower school in 1963.

During the 1968–9 session the management structure was still being perceived fundamentally as it is depicted in Figure 32, with the 'section heads' standing for the idea of pastoral responsibility and the 'department heads' standing for the idea of curricular responsibility. The drawing of the various boundaries on this chart immediately brings to light two curious anomalies: the fact that Mike Burnham, despite his (then) title of 'master in charge of sixth-form studies', appears on the pastoral side of the divide, and that Clive Vanloo, though entering the school with the impressive title of 'director of studies', had no recognizable leadership role within the existing structure. It was not these two people only who must have felt divided in this dual system but also practically every member of the school staff, since everyone —whether senior or junior, whether senior in a section-head capacity or in a department-head capacity—had to reconcile two roles: as tutors or section heads on the one hand, and as subject specialist teachers or department heads on the other.

Much of the complexity of relationships within the staff group stemmed from the fact that the senior and junior members of it owed allegiance to one another in overlapping areas of the system, so that it was never easy for anyone at any given stage of a discussion to know whether he was speaking primarily as a member of somebody's tutorial-staff team or primarily as a member of somebody's subject-department team. The dilemma was illustrated vividly on two occasions: once in a full staff meeting when Graeme Osborn challenged John Phillips to say whether he was speaking 'as a tutor or as a subject teacher', and once in a meeting of upper-school tutors, when Lewis Smith found himself impelled to remind Mike Burnham and his other colleagues that what he was paid his special allowance for was to run his department, and that being a tutor was incidental. Yet part of the reality of the role of a tutor, for the individual person who takes the role and for the children he tutors, is that he is also known to be a scientist, or a musician, or a modern linguist, or a P.E. specialist, or something other than these, perhaps also in charge of a particular subject department. And there are other difficulties: for as the school takes in children of an increasingly wide range of abilities, the staff group is augmented by teachers whose interest may spread over several territories and who may, therefore, be in great difficulty in determining which bounded regions they really belong in. One of the dangers,

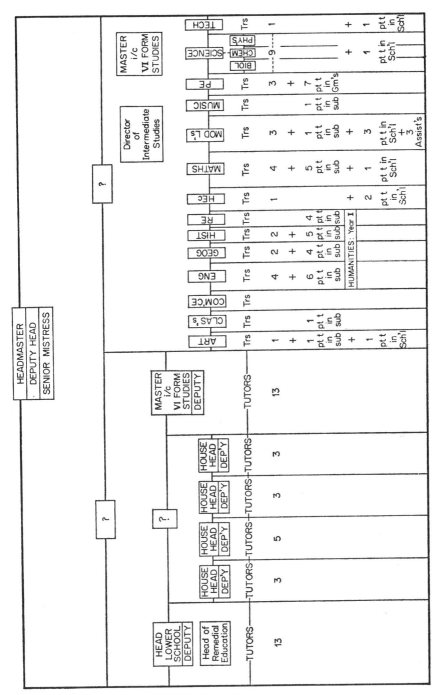

FIG. 32. The management structure: 1968–9.

then, of a system in which knowledge is organized in one sub-section and children's growth in another is that some teachers find themselves in a no-man's-land.

The service role and its relation to leadership in the two systems

When we attempt to clarify where boundaries are being drawn round areas of responsibility and therefore where different leadership roles are located, we find ourselves having to define the position of another kind of role that is very important to the management of the total institution and to the sub-parts of that institution, namely the service role.

A service role can be defined as a role that enables someone who has special skills that are supportive to the work of the institution to provide a service to colleagues in that institution. Thus it is not a leadership role in the sense that its occupant operates on the boundary of the institution or part-institution for which he provides the service, although if the service requires that he have assistants, he will have to take a leadership role on the boundary of that group of assistants. Thus a librarian may have assistant librarians, a bursar a secretarial (or office) group, a technician a team of technical staff, a counsellor a group of assistant counsellors, a remedial teacher a remedial staff, and so on. Clearly it is less easy, in the last two cases, to be sure whether we are still talking about a service role or not; but I take the view that we are, because the necessity for the provision of remedial or counselling help for children is a fluctuating one requiring the kind of relationship between staff that enables some to ask for help and others to provide it on request, each side recognizing the impossibility of forecasting the extent of the need at any given time.

Certain things have to be made clear, when we are considering the way in which a service role is to be provided: namely, the location of the boundary within which the occupant of the service role works, and the level of management to which he is responsible, and the identity of the group for which he provides the service. Thus, decisions must be made about whether a group of secretarial staff is to be regarded as providing a pooled service for the whole staff group, being responsible to the headmaster (on the outer boundary of the whole institution) through the principal secretary or bursar, or whether individual members of the secretarial staff are to be regarded as providing services for specific named sections within the staff group, with direct responsibility to the respective section heads. The same is true of technical services. The same is true of remedial services, library services and counselling services. It is often unclear whether a counsellor is regarded as operating within the school as a whole or only within a particular trouble area, such as the middle school; similarly, a remedial teacher may consider that his services are needed for older pupils as well as younger ones, yet be regarded by his colleagues as operating only within the lower-school boundary.

Where secretarial and technical staff are concerned, these questions have become even more blurred, often with unfortunate effects upon relationships both between teaching and non-teaching staff and within the senior staff group on the teaching side. As schools have expanded the tendency has been to avoid looking at the changes that have been taking place in the demands made on these service teams—and indeed at the very fact that what was once a service provided by an individual has become a complex of services provided by a group. Thus a headmaster may still be unconsciously regarding the school bursar as his personal secretary, as in the days when she was, in fact, more like a personal secretary. Yet, as bursar, she probably has control over many services in addition to secretarial ones, particularly those concerned with caretaking, cleaning and provision of meals. Similarly, the single 'lab. assistant' of the past—regarded, probably quite appropriately, as working only for the science staff and therefore responsible directly to the head of science—has for some years been turning gradually into a complex group of technicians whose services are by no means limited to the science laboratories but are increasingly needed in many departments, in particular those of modern languages, technical subjects, home economics, geography, and history, and also to any individual teacher who makes use of technical apparatus on occasion.

The service role can often give rise to uncertainty both in the person or group that provides the service and in those who receive the benefits of the service. Thus, it is by no means unusual to find that teachers in schools, colleges and university departments are very unsure how far their rights to secretarial help with correspondence, with preparation of teaching materials and with the typing of reports and memoranda can extend. The office staff on their side have to establish priorities, and because certain tasks are seen as administratively more urgent than others, they are frequently faced with decisions that appear to favour some colleagues at the expense of others. Since administrative tasks that receive high priority are usually associated with colleagues of high status, the friction that sometimes breaks out between teaching staff and secretarial staff may well have its origins in feelings between colleagues on the teaching side of the boundary.

There may also be ignorance among newcomers to a school about how free the teaching staff are to go in and out of the office, since some school offices are not accessible to any but the head whereas others are open to all staff equally. New staff members may therefore bring in from other schools assumptions about 'office rules' which they do not even think of testing, and may be surprised to learn after several weeks or even months that they have a right in the new school that was denied to them in the school from which they have come; or they may arouse resentments by assuming that the office is more 'open' to staff than it really is, because, in the school from which they have come, anyone was free to go in and out. Whichever kind of change is experienced, whether by the incoming staff member or by those who have to cope with him as a newcomer, the terms 'open' and 'accessible' will not mean precisely the same thing to any two people.

We are here faced again with the problem of boundary control, since any service department, if it is to provide those services efficiently, must protect its boundaries to ensure that neither the input of requests nor the output of accession to those requests is blocked by misunderstandings on either side of the boundary. And if one source of misunderstanding can be the refusal of those outside to acknowledge the need for the boundary, another can be the unwillingness of those inside to admit that their door must, to some extent, be guarded, however much everyone desires to preserve good and friendly relationships at the personal level.

Within the teaching group this kind of uncertainty contains the further complication that certain individual members of a teaching staff, because of the skills they possess, may find themselves having to accede to or to resist pressures from their colleagues to use those skills in a service capacity rather than in a teaching capacity. Departments of commerce, art, home economics and technical education are particularly susceptible to this kind of pressure and consequently find themselves having to make judgements about whether a request from a colleague is a reasonable request that might be balanced by similar help coming from the other side or whether it is a kind of exploitation that must be resisted.

Thus both the asking and the giving of services such as secretarial or technical or artistic or domestic help can be accompanied by guilt feelings on either side—fears that the help asked for may be unreasonable and fears that the help given may be insufficient. And guilt—and uncertainty about whether the guilt is really deserved or whether it is misplaced—can be a powerful cause of irritation and resentment. Yet anyone who points out that such difficulties may exist in the relationship is liable to be attacked from both sides and perceived as someone who is merely trying to stir up trouble in an area where harmony has hitherto existed.

Looking back now at the incident that followed my circulation of the interim report for the Schools Council in the summer of 1969, we can ask some further questions about the nature and cause of the indignation that was aroused at the time by my reference to tensions between the teaching and secretarial staff. The first evidence about the existence of this tension had been very clear in the second full staff meeting I attended in October 1968, when, in the presence of the school bursar, Ethel Hawker, the whole question of availability of secretarial help in the preparation of teaching materials and staff memoranda was raised. It was clear that this discussion was a continuation of a much earlier movement on the part of certain staff members who had been campaigning for the appointment of a 'staff secretary' —someone that is who would not be regarded as part of the office group but would be directly responsible to the staff other than the headmaster for the provision of this kind of service. Six months later, at the beginning of the summer term, the question was being raised again in a full staff meeting, at a time when money that might have been available for a staff secretary had been used to provide another kind of service in the form of ancillary staff to take over supervision of playgrounds during the lunch-hours. Between these two staff meetings (in January 1969) the problem had come up also in a section heads' meeting concerning the difficulty that sometimes arose when a house head needed to have a letter typed and sent off to a parent, but might not always be sure that it could be done in the same afternoon.

It was thus becoming evident that the tension was not only between certain teaching staff and the office, arising from the very real difficulty for any teacher in knowing where rights ended and favours began. It also seemed to be arising from the rival requirements on the administrative or caring side, located mainly in the section heads, and on the teaching side, located mainly in the department heads. But the conflict existed within the individual teacher also, since any one member of staff might find himself making incompatible demands which could have the effect of cancelling each other out. Thus, for example, a department head in his role as a tutor responsible to a section head might recognize the existence of a conflict of priorities between two different demands being made at the same time by himself on an over-worked secretarial staff group. Conversely, a section or house head in his role as a subject teacher might also have to recognize that he himself could be making two incompatible requests of this service group.

Once the problem could be examined in the context of the task system, where it was the nature of the service role that was in question, rather than in the context of the sentient system, where it was personal loyalties and personal grievances that were in question, it became possible for the staff to work on it as an institutional problem. What happened, in the course of the summer and autumn of 1969, was that Denys John himself modified his view of the working relationship between himself and Ethel Hawker, and relinquished his own earlier unwritten claim upon her as his 'private secretary'. Thus, her own role became more clearly defined as being on the boundary of the group of staff that provided, between them, secretarial services to the staff group as a whole, so that she was freed to make her own decisions about which particular member of the secretarial staff should handle any particular piece of work, and how priorities should be worked out. Denys John's requests thus ceased to have the kind of priority they had had before as 'headmaster's requests', and were subject to the same scrutiny as everyone else's before they were given their place in the queue. Thus, if one of his requests was given priority, it would be because of the urgency of the task rather than because it was his request. In fact the teaching staff had always had access to the office. But the existence of the connecting door between the office and the headmaster's room, and the earlier uncertainty about who made the decisions about priorities, had apparently made it appear at least to some staff that work needed for teaching purposes was likely always to go to the bottom of the pile. And of course, despite the 'accessibility' of the office staff, there could at times have been some foundation for this belief, though not at other times.

After the setting up of the standing committee and the combined senior staff meeting, it was noticeable to me that no further references were made in staff meetings to the need for a staff secretary. The reorganization of the office itself and the redefinition of Ethel Hawker's role must have been important factors in the disappearance of those earlier uncertainties. But the measures taken in the office staff might not have had very much effect upon the relations between secretarial and teaching staff if other work had not also been going on among the teaching staff. For it would seem that much of the pressure upon the office group had been coming from the need of the teaching staff to deny their own internal conflicts, in particular those between people who at different times were representing sectional interests on the curricular or the pastoral side. Once these were being explored more publicly, the misunderstandings between the office and the staff room noticeably decreased.

Some of this internal conflict within the teaching staff group stemmed, as I now believe, from bewilderment about how, in the divided management system, the two sides could use each other's expertise. The lack of clarity about leadership was creating a situation in which people were uncertain whether they were in leadership roles or service roles in relation to each other. The work of the Reports Group which was in its final stages in the autumn of 1968 had really been highlighting this problem: for its conscious concern with questions about how staff could more effectively communicate with parents had brought into focus a related question about how staff were communicating (or failing to communicate) with one another. In other words, it was evident that a tutor could not do his job effectively, either with pupils or with parents, unless he was provided with the information he needed by all those colleagues who taught the children in his tutor group. Conversely subject teachers and particularly department heads depended upon tutors, either directly or through their section heads, for overall information about the children they taught when they were trying to understand the implications of a child's performance in one particular area of his work in relation to his total development, both as a person and as a scholar.

The management system as it was up until the summer of 1969 really showed two yawning gaps, since the dual structure did not provide for a head of the pastoral system or for a head of the curricular system. The effect of these gaps on the roles of Robin Thomas and Joan Bradbury is something we shall have to explore later in this book. Acceptance of the dual system, given these additional roles, carried the further implication that every subject-department head, in addition to his leadership role on the curricular side, had to regard himself as carrying a service role in relation to the pastoral side, just as every section head on the pastoral side had to regard himself as carrying a service role on the curricular side. I have already indicated that Clive Vanloo, despite the fact that he assumed a leadership role during the period when the new curriculum pattern for the fourth and fifth years was being constructed, had no clear permanent leadership role up to the spring of 1969. Thus in Figure 32, as director of intermediate studies, he appears in a service role, within the boundary that includes all the subject-department heads.

Problems in the separated meetings of department heads and section heads

As long as the department heads and section heads held their meetings at different times, the possibility of examining these problems of role relationships seemed just out of reach, although the problems themselves were never far below the surface of the discussion and indeed sometimes erupted in unexpected ways. The very separateness of the two senior staff meetings must itself have been a source of considerable friction.

I have suggested in an earlier chapter that the department heads must have been very conscious of the number of senior staff having the right to attend their scheduled meetings (about twice a term) as compared with the very restricted number (nine only) who attended the section heads' meetings (also about twice a term). Of the five staff other than department heads who came to their meetings regularly, Joan Bradbury was the only one who could be said to be present partly in the role of a department head, since she was technically head of German as well as senior mistress. Graeme Osborn, although present at these meetings as head of religious education, was known to be one of that other much smaller group of section heads whose meetings were never reciprocally attended by any department head.

Throughout the 1968–9 session I was struck by the fact that both these senior staff meetings continued to be focused on a number of discrete agenda items, often amounting to four or five different topics, rather than on one currently important theme that required prolonged discussion at some depth. Yet the full staff meetings were already breaking free from the multiple agenda by November 1968. The effect of the multiple agenda on the discussions of the senior staff in the two sub-groups was that difficult areas could be by-passed and discussion on one theme avoided. I never found these meetings boring; but I often found them exasperating, because of the uncanny skill with which people would avoid the difficult items on the agenda by ensuring that the other items took up most of the time. There was evidence that the staff themselves experienced similar feelings, even while they contributed to the behaviour that made this kind of avoidance possible.

The problem for both the department heads' meeting and the section heads' meeting was that neither group could feel itself to be a team of persons responsible for a definable part of the school's work. They were merely two overlapping groups of individuals taking roles which had acquired certain labels. At times, in either kind of senior meeting, individual staff members might protest that they were losing sight of the pupils in their discussions about organization. On one occasion I felt surrounded by department heads who seemed to be wondering whether their colleagues in the roles of section heads or tutors were withholding information about pupils from them; on another occasion I felt surrounded by section heads who seemed to be wondering whether department heads were keeping information from *them*. Yet across both these groups and across the total staff group there were inter-departmental teams of staff who were having to work together all the time in their day-to-day work in order to keep the school operating.

Between October 1968 and the following May, Denys John made two attempts to get the department heads to talk about the role of a head of department. On each of those early occasions it was evident that they were most unwilling to discuss this, except in terms of the difficulty that heads of large departments experienced in arranging meetings which all their colleagues could attend. In fact they deflected the discussion into the related question about the role of the department heads' *meeting*, a manoeuvre that reflected their own dissatisfaction with the split senior staff meeting, although no-one could as yet identify what it was that was causing this dissatisfaction.

Similarly, in section heads' meetings during this period, three attempts by Denys John to focus attention on the role of the tutor met with varying degrees of failure or frustration. The section heads seemed as unwilling to discuss the problems of pastoral work and leadership as the department heads were unwilling to discuss the problems of curricular work and leadership. On the first occasion, consideration of the implications of tutorial work was totally avoided, since the entire meeting was taken up with discussion of relatively trivial items that preceded it on the agenda sheet. On the second occasion the discussion resolved itself into an almost boastful recital of things that tutors did with their tutor groups rather than exploration of the problems of being a tutor. And on the third occasion, a paper presented by Denys John about the role of the tutor was subjected to very adverse comments by section heads, who indignantly protested that their tutors were likely to be insulted by such a written statement, or brief, about duties with which they were very familiar—a feeling in which I found myself secretly concurring, even while I felt irritated by the denial that was being implied of the difficulties inherent in the tutor's role.

In fact the undercurrents that could be detected in many of these meetings were concerned, not with the isolated exploration of this kind of role or that kind of role, but far more with the problems of communication between people involved as house or section heads and people involved as subject-department heads, and therefore, by implication, with problems of communication between tutors and subject teachers. In other words, it was role relationships rather than roles as such that seemed central in the concerns of the staff during that period.

The change in the management structure as depicted in Figure 33 did not,

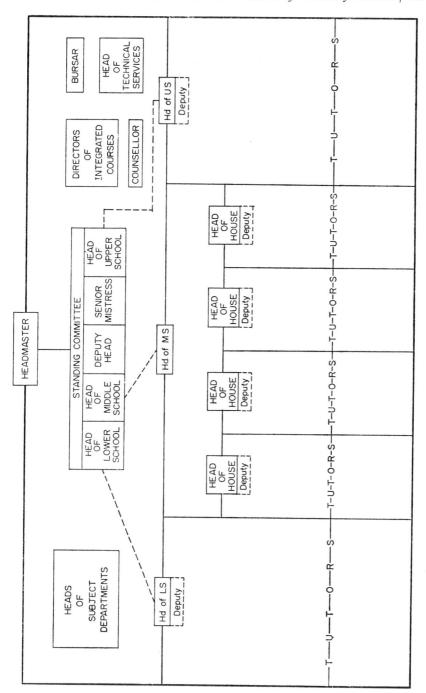

FIG. 33. The management structure: 1969–71.

of course, produce a magical easing of all these difficulties. Indeed, if anything, life became more difficult. But the redrawing of the boundaries round the phases of a developing task rather than round split-off bits of the total task seemed to make it possible for leadership to be exercised in new ways.

Denys John's decision to change the management structure was not an arbitrary decision made by him without reference to the events of the year before. Nor was it made in response to any direct suggestion from me. It arose rather from an accumulation of evidence that is difficult to organize and present because it was appearing in so many different ways and in so many different places. In the next five chapters I will try to reassemble some of this evidence by looking at three different ways in which the whole problem of staff consultation was being tackled—first, through the developing network of committees and working parties, secondly through the redefinition and clarification of top-management roles and of the relationships within the top-management group, and thirdly, through the changing functions of those in middle management. As we shall see, it was hard to know, before the reorganization of the management structure, where middle management ended and top management began. What was becoming increasingly clear was that the expansion of the school and the increasing complexity of its task necessitated an enlargement of the top-management group, with consequent effects both upon the supposed autonomy of those in middle management and upon the roles of the deputy head and the senior mistress.

What the staff were having to come to terms with during the uneasy months of 1969 was a gradual redistribution of power. Whether those who did not find themselves in the now enlarged top-management group were diminished or strengthened in their own roles by the changes is a question that cannot easily be answered. Certainly many staff members, in redefining their own leadership roles, were compelled to re-examine, at times in quite a painful way, the basis of the authority they exercised in the school.

B. The Task of Headship and the Nature of Consultation

Introduction

Current discussions about how headmasters ought to be managing their schools and how staff members ought to be participating in decision-making often demonstrate the same kind of splitting process that I have been examining in the last two chapters. We are told of a division between two kinds of approach to the problems of organization: on the one hand the 'human relations' approach which some people label as 'tender-minded', and on the other hand the 'structural' approach which some label as 'tough-minded'. I hope to show in the following chapters that this, like the question about curricular and pastoral responsibilities, like questions about 'scientific rigour' and 'artistic freedom', is not an either/or question at all.

There can be no school in existence that does not have a structure: nor can there be in existence any school in which human relations can be ignored. Yet heads of schools can very easily allow themselves to be put into categories: if they bother about human relations they may be perceived as inefficient organizers; if they bother about organizational efficiency they may be perceived as indifferent to the human side of the enterprise.

The whole problem about consultation raises fundamental questions both about the nature of leadership and authority and about the nature of autonomy. Teachers are very willing to discuss their right to participate in decision making, but remarkably unwilling to surrender what they perceive as their 'autonomy' in the classroom or in their subject departments.

Professor Eric Hoyle, in a paper to the Education Section of the British Association at its Swansea Meeting (1971), while giving 'guarded support for planned innovation', has confessed to 'misgivings' about the accompanying threat to the satisfactions that teachers derive from their freedom, within the boundary of the classroom, to develop their own skills in personal relationships with pupils and in understanding of children's learning processes. His paper emphasizes the importance of carrying the planning and implementation of change through to the stage of institutionalization; but he considers that, while some teachers are personally strengthened by the opportunity to take part in what he calls 'extended professionality', others

149

find their strength in 'restricted professionality'. He is here using the term 'restricted', not in a pejorative sense, but in the sense of being contained, appropriately, within the context of the classroom group rather than of the staff group, where innovation is studied institutionally, or of the regional or central planning group, where it is studied nationally.

It seems, from this argument, that some teachers will want to be involved in collective planning in order to develop and use their organizational skills and to explore the problems of relating theory and practice, whereas others will want to be freed from such responsibilities in order to follow their own bent within the relatively private domain of a classroom. I prefer to argue that teachers are ambivalent about these matters. It seems to me that most teachers both want to participate in long-term planning and want to deny their responsibility to do this; for if they can deny their responsibility as members of the teaching group, they can, at least in fantasy, preserve their autonomy and their right to make decisions in their own classrooms without much reference to what is happening in other classrooms. I go further, and suggest that the school as an institution, even with a headmaster who is anxious to involve all his staff in the processes leading to decision-making, is very likely to obstruct the understanding of this ambivalence by resorting to the setting up of voluntary *ad hoc* working parties and isolated teams, thus perpetuating the split between those who are 'good at administration and planning' and those who are 'good in the classroom'. In my view the real struggle should be to reduce this polarization. But the struggle will not be unaccompanied by pain; nor can it be without some cost. What we do not yet know is to what extent an individual teacher who has considered the cost too great in one school, may, in a post of greater responsibility in another school, be able to use that uncomfortable and even disturbing experience constructively in the new situation.

The willingness of a staff group to embark on the shared exploration of fundamental educational beliefs implies a willingness to make public a great deal of what has traditionally been private. It must now be acknowledged that the boundary round the classroom, which has in the past—in theory at least—been inviolable, is really a permeable zone rather than a protective wall. The assumption that what Mr Black does in his English lesson has nothing to do with Mrs Brown who teaches R.E., or that what happens in a humanities course in the first or second year (which is providing new excitements and satisfactions to a handful of innovating teachers) is having no effect upon the efficiency or self-esteem of the English or geography or history specialists who will be teaching the products of this course when they reach their third, fourth or fifth years, is no longer tenable. Moreover, it becomes more and more evident, as innovation extends into different areas of the school's work, that the tensions that have been recognizably present in the past on the boundaries between subject departments or between senior and junior staff, exist within each of these groupings—that is, within subject departments, within groups of young and inexperienced staff, within groups of experienced staff not yet in leadership roles, and within groups of highly experienced staff in key leadership roles. The testing of the fantasies about supposed similarities or differences of viewpoints within and between such groups is difficult to undertake because of the fear that to do so will be to reduce what has been a reasonably efficient organization to confusion and uncertainty and to expose it to the threat of chaos.

The merging of concerns between different specialists in the staff group has been symbolized during the past ten years or so by the tendency for more and more subjects to be given names that include the word 'education'. Thus 'P.T.' (physical training) has become 'P.E.' (physical education); 'R.I.' (religious instruction) has become 'R.E.' (religious education), with 'R.K.' (religious knowledge) reserved for courses associated with public examinations; the old woodwork and metalwork have been amalgamated with new developments in crafts and elementary engineering as 'technical education'; the *ad hoc* remedial teaching has been systematized into 'remedial education' as a separate department of work; and now the term 'moral education', even occasionally abbreviated to 'M.E.', is finding its way into the language of the curriculum. If we link all this with the change from 'training colleges' to 'colleges of education', and from 'technical colleges' to 'colleges of further education', we find ourselves looking at a fundamental change in the concept of education itself, since what we have to recognize in the pattern of staff concerns is that what used to be regarded as encroachments upon or exclusion from private territory must now be studied as interactions that take place in zones between neighbouring regions. In the language of the conceptual framework described in Chapter II, these zones are the boundary regions that mark off the discontinuities between one part of the system and another.

The problem that arises, then, is whether the management structure (and the consultative system) of the school should be perceiving the discontinuities primarily in the context of the subjects that people teach or primarily in the context of the phases of growth through which pupils pass in the course of their schooling. I hope to show in the following chapters that the first should be regarded as a constraint upon the second rather than the second as a constraint upon the first.

CHAPTER VI

Committees, Working Parties and the Concept of Representation

The use of resources in the staff group

One of my reasons for choosing to approach Nailsea in the spring of 1968 was that I knew it to be a school in which many members of staff at all levels were involved in discussions of important issues as members of study groups and working parties. Yet by the following spring I was beginning to question the validity of these very groups as vehicles for a consultative process, not because I doubted whether serious work was being done in them, but because they lacked the authority, within the management structure as a whole, to translate into action the ideas they generated through discussion or to work through thoroughly with their colleagues such action as they were able to take as a result of that discussion.

During his years as headmaster, Denys John had always sought for ways of enabling staff, however new and however inexperienced, to involve themselves in the processes leading to decision making. Yet he never denied the reality of his own responsibility when a decision had to be made about a matter that concerned the whole school. Because he consulted staff a great deal and expected matters of importance to be discussed at all levels, he could easily be accused by those colleagues who would have preferred a less demanding kind of leadership from him of failing to give them the direction, in terms of simple instructions, that they felt they needed from him. Conversely, because he insisted on his right, indeed obligation, to make ultimate decisions, even after long phases of discussion and argument, he could be accused by others of setting up a rather hollow kind of democracy.

To some, the apparently simple process of taking a vote on any controversial issue—a vote that would be binding on the headmaster—appeared to be the obvious solution in moments of conflict and disagreement. But when matters of real importance to the school were at stake, the taking of a vote did not recommend itself to him at all, since this would have inevitably left in the staff group dissatisfied, over-ruled minority groups that could hardly have been expected to work whole-heartedly to implement decisions enforced by the majority. It seemed very difficult for staff to accept the idea that the taking of a vote might really be an evasion of their own corporate responsibility to explore differences of opinion, not with a view to inhibiting possible action on the head's part but with a view to making his action more informed. In other words, even if they could not take from him the privilege, or the burden, of making important decisions over long-term policy, or of making a quick decision in an emergency, the staff had the power to influence considerably whatever decisions he did make.

Denys John's own views about the relationship between policy-making and staff consultation were set out, in the summer of 1968, in a written paper entitled 'Policy change and decision making', which he circulated to the staff in September at the pre-sessional staff meeting. In this he had included a section on the function of study groups in bringing about the kind of participation he wished to promote. In presenting this paper to the staff, he publicly acknowledged that he had felt impelled to write it during the summer because he had, as he put it, 'been under fire' in the previous academic year. Thus his decision to work collaboratively with me, following the exploratory discussions with the staff and the governors, coincided with an open challenge to the staff to test the validity of his belief in the processes of consultation, and indeed to test his own integrity as a headmaster prepared to act on that belief.

Staff meetings were obviously an important ingredient in any consultative processes, so much so that by 1968 there were few weeks in the year in which meetings of some kind were not taking place. While the staff group was expanding, the problem of how to make these meetings effective had been increasing. And the facts about rate of expansion at Nailsea, as Figure 34 shows, were dramatic. When it opened as a one-year, three-form entry grammar school in September 1959, the staff group was the size of a small family. In the following year it more than doubled itself, although still a small face-to-face group. In its fourth year it doubled itself again; even then it was considerably smaller than the average school class. Up till the end of that year it was probably possible for consultation to go on in the total staff group without any elaborate machinery for ensuring that it happened; and in fact nine members of that small staff group of 1962–3 were still in the school in the autumn of 1968. In the fifth and sixth years of the school's life, the number of teaching staff rose steeply from 34 (of whom 27 were full-time) in September 1963 to 51 (of whom 43 were full-time) in September 1965. Four years later the number was up to 68, of whom 58 were full-time. During these later years the full-time teaching staff, even without the additional part-time members, comprised a very large group.

Such rapid expansion creates for a headmaster a dilemma about how best to use the resources within his staff group in the actual process of policy formation. Some heads give up having staff meetings when size becomes 'unmanageable'; others persevere, though with growing doubts about their efficacy. What, then, is to be done?

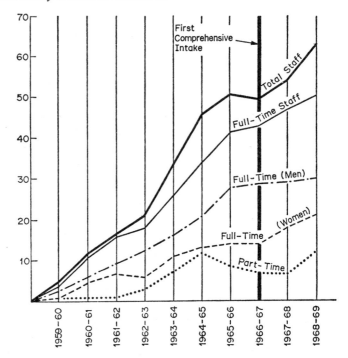

FIG. 34. Expansion of staff group: 1959–69.

The working-party approach to problems of consultation

The natural defence against the potential boredom (and the potential chaos) of discussion in the large, unwieldy staff group of over fifty is to set up working parties and study groups that are sufficiently small and intimate for every person to feel that he can get a hearing. If such groups are brought into existence to carry out limited tasks and to report back to the staff their findings, proposals or conclusions, staff meetings are provided with a kind of insurance policy: at least with a number of study groups currently working on different problems there is likely to be assured, ready-made agenda for every full staff meeting.

But an agenda-sheet compiled in this way may acquire a boomerang quality, in that the last study group named in a sequence is likely to find itself having to present a hurried report at the tail end of a meeting, perhaps after the official time has run out when staff are already trickling away. Moreover, the search for items for such an agenda-sheet may at times create a kind of smoke screen that obliterates the very problem currently being debated in the 'informal' encounters of the staff room. Thus a meeting may be cancelled because of the apparent absence of 'agenda', and an opportunity for exploration, in the presence of the head, of important current pre-occupations may consequently be lost. Unfortunately, the frustration caused by such a loss of opportunity is apt to be less evident in the staff group than is the more easily expressed relief from the strain of yet another meeting. And so everyone goes home assuming that the meeting was never really necessary anyway.

The use of voluntary or *ad hoc* study groups also implies a problem of continuity. Because Nailsea School—like all schools of this size and complexity—was continuously having to cope with the loss of established and familiar colleagues whose behaviour was to some extent predictable and with the absorption of new and unfamiliar colleagues whose behaviour was not at all predictable, no-one could ever be certain how temporary or how permanent a working relationship might turn out to be, either in a subject department or in any of the less easily defined cross-disciplinary groups in the institution. The network of study groups and working parties in operation at Nailsea for all or part of the 1968–9 session was tangled and confusing, as Figure 35 shows. The setting up of these groups had undoubtedly originated in a genuine search for ways of ensuring that all staff could participate in the processes leading up to decision making. Yet it is evident from this diagram that some staff were not participating in any of them. Moreover, in the course of the session the existence of this network was laying the headmaster open to suspicions that his consultative methods might be covering up a determination to have his own way and that the staff might find themselves living in a sham democracy.

During the 1968–9 session the organizational problem being faced by Denys John and his colleagues was how to harness the energy, experience and power of the staff group by defining the boundaries on which potential leadership skills could be most appropriately used and developed. And so there was a third problem about the use of the voluntary working party: namely the uncertainty about whether the working parties existed primarily to create sentient groups that would give staff members other than those in leadership roles the feeling that they were valued contributors to policy making, or whether they existed primarily to ensure that the real leadership within the staff group could be exercised in task-related groups that could, through their work, develop some sentience that could sustain that work.

Successive study groups must have been producing a considerable accumulation of experience in various kinds of committee work. Yet, on completion of the limited task for which any one group had been set up, or when the task itself became indefinable or unmanageable, this experience would fall back into the large staff group where it seemed submerged and lost. It took courage for a relatively junior staff member (and even perhaps for a senior staff member) to refer back in a full staff meeting to the experiences of a committee on which he or she had once served, knowing that most people would be finding it difficult to remember just which colleagues had in fact

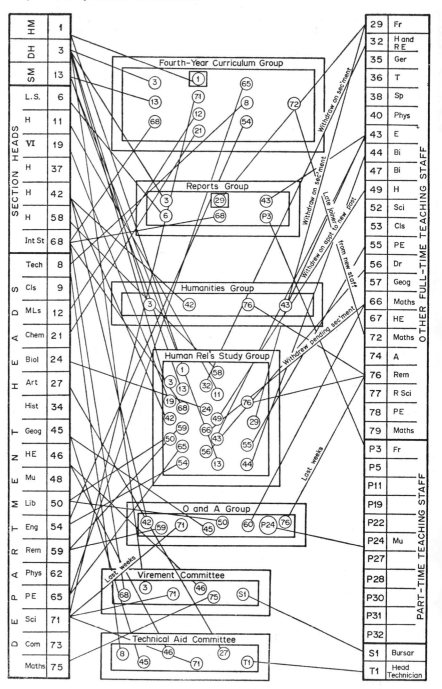

FIG. 35. Network of study groups, committees and working parties.

served on that committee and that newcomers to the staff group might not even know that the committee had ever existed. Continuity between study groups or special committees was left to chance, or in some cases deliberately avoided, with a consequent weakening of the authority vested in them (see Figure 36). Since a new committee could not be sure of having even one member with previous experience of committee work in the school, each one

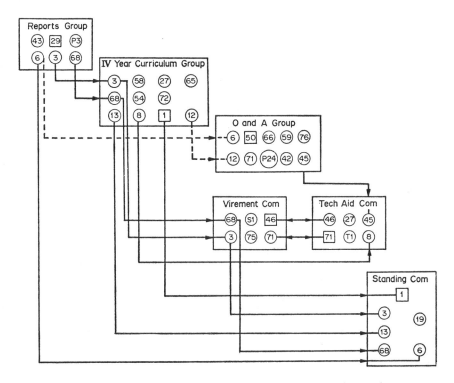

FIG. 36. Continuity and discontinuity of experience in working parties.

had to start from square one, as it were, in finding a way of working together on its task and in building up some kind of agreed structure within which that work could be done. Hence perhaps the phenomenon, recurring as it seemed in group after group, of requiring one person to combine the quite different roles of convener, chairman and recorder, and probably along with these the role of reporter in the staff meeting.

The study groups and working parties thrown up by the staff group to look at different facets of the school's task thus reflected both the long-term objectives of the standing institution and the ephemeral nature of the various sub-groups within it. The name 'standing committee', which was Denys

John's own name for the new top management group that he set up in the autumn of 1969, expressed very accurately the growing need of the staff group for some kind of permanence in its own internal structure.

Tasks, roles and relationships in three working parties

My own difficulty in discovering the underlying pattern in all the activity of the weeks before and after the Christmas of 1968 was perhaps a measure of the fragmentation that was going on in the staff group at that time. It was not only the curricular/pastoral split that divided its members, but also the varying tasks undertaken by the three study groups then in existence—namely the Fourth Year Curriculum group, the Human Relationships group and the Organization and Assessment group.

In my view the term 'study group' as it was used indiscriminately of all these three was masking essential differences between them and thus facilitating the unconscious use of them to split off different aspects of the problem of consultation. The Fourth Year Curriculum group (which I shall refer to from now on as 'the F.Y.C.' group) was really a committee set up to frame definite proposals for the year 1969–70; the H.R. group was really a teaching team, set up to consider how the study of personal relationships, hitherto offered outside the time-table only to a limited number of pupils, could be built into the time-table for all pupils up till the end of the fourth year, and how materials might be prepared for this work; the O & A group was really a working party asked to take on the task of examining current problems relating to the organization of teaching groups and to the assessment of individual pupils, and possibly in due course to make recommendations.

Denys John, as headmaster, took quite different roles in relation to these three groups. In the first he was, *ex officio*, chairman; in the second he was a fellow member, calling upon the Marriage Guidance Council to provide outside leadership; in the third he was, it seemed, a kind of father figure, usually but not always an absent one, yet unsure how much independence he really wanted the group to achieve.

Viewed in another way, these three temporary working parties can be seen as linked in function and style of operation to three kinds of working group that later emerged with more permanent roles in the management structure of the school. To understand the potentialities of the F.Y.C. group, we have to see it in relation to the later standing committee; to understand the potentialities of the H.R. study group we have to see it in relation to the later lower-school humanities team; in order to understand the potentialities of the O & A group we have to see it in relation to the later sub-division of the full staff meeting into its five small groups, each working under the leadership of a member (other than the head) of the standing committee. It is on the first and third of these temporary study groups (the F.Y.C. group and the O & A group) that I want to concentrate now, since it was the interplay between them during the 1968–9 session that laid the foundations for the later development of a more coherent management structure.

The unconscious embodiments of satisfaction and frustration in two working parties

Readers of this book may be wondering whether Denys John, in moving away from the study-group/working-party type of organization towards the management-committee type of organization, was abandoning a 'human-relations' approach in favour of a 'structural' approach, and whether persons in the staff group became more like cogs in a machine in consequence of this shift in policy. Now the fact is that there was a good deal of toughness present in the earlier looser kind of organization or, as some would say, the more 'democratic' system, and there was a good deal of tenderness in the later tighter organization or, as some would say, the more 'authoritarian' system. It is not for me to assert categorically on the basis of only one school's experience that the tighter committee system is 'good' and the voluntary working-party system is 'bad'. A school that was already working with a management committee might conceivably have moved in the other direction by setting up study groups to test the authority of that committee. I believe now that the existence of a top-management committee, provided it is under-pinned by a strong senior staff group and by regular meetings of the total staff, makes for more effective consultation between the headmaster and his colleagues. I believe this; but I cannot be sure.

Denys John's paper on policy change, distributed to the staff in the very meeting that brought the O & A group into existence, suggested that he was looking for a new working party, at the beginning of the 1968–9 session, to undertake what might have been described as the 'parish work' of preparing colleagues to receive positively the proposals of the F.Y.C. group when they were prepared for circulation later in the autumn term. It is probable that he depended on the O & A group, more strongly than either he or they realized, to fulfil this function, not only in its own meetings but also, more importantly perhaps, through 'informal' talks with colleagues in the staff room. The O & A group, knowing that its predecessor, the Reports group, had been accused of 'steam-rollering' the staff, attempted to fulfil these expectations by offering to expose its work in various ways. Its chairman made a point of talking with his colleagues—particularly with heads of departments—about the content of the group's discussions; there was a tacit agreement in the staff group that 'observers' would be welcome at meetings; and summaries of the group's discussions were duplicated for distribution at frequent intervals.

Meanwhile the F.Y.C. group, which consisted of the top management 'triumvirate', the director of intermediate studies, the heads of English, modern languages, chemistry, physical education and technical education, one house head and (in the last two meetings) a young newcomer to the staff, worked on the actual planning task. About two months after the O & A group's first meeting, the F.Y.C. group, having drawn up its proposals, disbanded, almost in a state of euphoria. In its final meeting there was a feeling that a difficult task had been accomplished. But there was no suggestion that the group, as a committee, might have to remain in existence for some months in order to work through with the staff group the problems of implementing its new proposals or of modifying them in the light of staff reactions. The O & A group thus became a convenient receptacle for some of the doubts and unease about the changes being introduced into the once familiar curricular pattern, the more so since those who had volunteered to join it back in September had probably been perceived at that time as being either 'for' or 'against' the new developments.

In retrospect it seems that at that time the staff group was unconsciously splitting off the 'feeling' side of the work on curriculum development and putting it into the O & A group, leaving the 'thinking' side in the F.Y.C. group. Certainly my own experiences in these two groups suggested that conflict was remarkably absent from the F.Y.C. group's deliberations and very often present in those of the O & A group. This splitting had the effect, later, of leaving Denys John poised uncomfortably between the department heads (who had been at least nominally represented in the F.Y.C. group) and the O & A group, which had been holding the uncertainties both of heads of department and of the 'rank and file'. To understand the mood of the staff group during the months that followed the circulation and discussion of the F.Y.C. group's proposals, we need to examine the constitution of the two groups and the nature of each one's relationship with the head on one side and with the staff group as a whole on the other.

The F.Y.C. Group

The membership of the F.Y.C. group, perceived in terms of its standing as a representative body, implied an intention that every section of the staff group that would be affected by changes in the curriculum for the fourth and fifth years should have a voice within the planning committee (see Figure 37). Along with Clive Vanloo (present in his role as director of intermediate studies) were five heads of departments, representing five subject areas, namely, modern languages, the science-mathematics area, the English-history-geography area, the area of aesthetics and technical education, and the area of physical education. Whether those who taught in the named areas perceived themselves to be represented remains to be questioned.

Only two of these areas had obvious claimants for the task of representation: namely, modern languages (represented by Peter Atkinson) and physical education (represented by Bob Miller). Gerry Lloyd, although technically head of chemistry, was acting head of science at the time of the

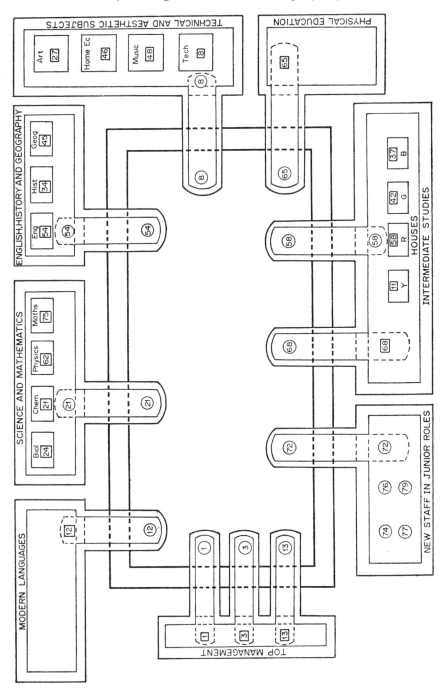

Fig. 37. Representation in a fourth-year-curriculum planning committee.

committee's inception and—pending the arrival of Phillip Armitage and Robin Grist to take up their new appointments in September 1968—was the obvious person to cover the science-mathematics area. The other two were more problematical.

Although Denys John had explained to me in some detail, before the first of the two F.Y.C. meetings I attended, that Lewis Smith was representing English, history and geography and not his own department only, and that Pip Ridgwell was representing art, music, home economics and technical education and not *his* own department only, I very soon lost sight of these facts as I listened to the discussions. Later I wondered whether I had heard Lewis Smith only as the 'voice of English' because I myself, as a former teacher of English, would have found it very difficult to speak for colleagues in history and geography, but easier to speak for linguists and musicians, or whether Lewis Smith himself had been losing sight of the interests of the historians and geographers and speaking only as the English specialist on the committee. Similarly, when I looked back afterwards I could not recall that I had actually perceived Gerry Lloyd as representing anything other than science or that I asked myself any questions at the time about how far he was really representing the mathematics department as he was supposed to be doing in theory. It was Pip Ridgwell's role, more than any other in that group, that seemed to me at the time to be illustrating most clearly the problem of representing what looked like a very diverse group of small departments; for although it quickly became evident to me that he saw his work as related closely to art and to home economics, I could not see him as representing in any way the interests of music.

I draw attention to these impressions in order to highlight the initial problem the staff must have had in setting up the committee—the problem of deciding how the boundaries round areas should be drawn. In the light of the later staff discussions—using hindsight as it were—Denys John himself began to question whether the areas he had selected at that time had necessarily been the most appropriate. But however the boundaries had been drawn the problem of choosing a representative would still have been very difficult.

Behind these questions lies a much more fundamental question about the nature of choosing. What are the criteria used in selecting colleagues to undertake a piece of curriculum planning? This earlier temporary group— in contrast to the later permanent standing committee—represented, at the level of conscious intention, knowledge about the teaching of subjects rather than knowledge about the growth needs of a particular group of pupils. It was as though the staff were saying, collectively as well as individually: 'This, this and this subject has to be taught: how can we put together the new jigsaw puzzle so that none of them gets left out?' The resulting committee was thus based on the need to maintain the *status quo*, though with some new variations, rather than on the need to rethink in fundamental terms what the curriculum was really for. The later standing committee, which also became involved with curriculum planning, consisted of people for whom the preservation of subject identities was no longer as important as the discovery of pupil potential in different phases of their growth. This is not to say, of course, that former special subject responsibilities did not reassert themselves very frequently in the deliberations of that later committee, or that individual members of the F.Y.C. group did not concern themselves with the growth patterns and needs of pupils.

There were two members of the earlier F.Y.C. group who, at the conscious level of intention, were not representing subject interests at all: namely, Pat Chapman, who was present as the representative of the house heads, and Dawn Castell, who, from September 1968, was present as a new staff member brought in to gain experience of the staff group's working methods. The presence of these two raises interesting questions about the relationship between pastoral and curricular functions, and about the relationship between sentience and task in such a committee.

The decision to ask the house heads to send a representative to the committee that was working at middle-school curricular patterns for the future is a striking example of the extent to which the pastoral function was at that time being located in the house groups and of the extent to which Clive Vanloo's role, as it was envisaged then, was being seen as purely curricular, even perhaps as likely to bring him into conflict with house heads. Moreover, if we bear in mind that the head of physical education was a member of the committee and was present to carry the interests and concerns of that department considered as part of the curricular structure, it seems rather significant that the house heads chose to send that one of their number whose teaching was being done in the area of P.E. and games. Is this another piece of evidence that pastoral care, in the middle school in particular, was being seen as linked more with games and leisure than with the pursuit of academic work?

Dawn Castell's inclusion in the committee is a little more complicated. She was one of the youngest members of the staff, fresh from a college of education, a member of the mathematics department and a tutor in Pat Chapman's house. As it happened her first attendance at a meeting of this planning group coincided with mine. I recall that Denys John opened that meeting by saying: 'There's nothing hierarchical about this group', a remark that struck me at the time as odd, since it was evident that it was very hierarchical, in all probability rightly so in view of its task, in the sense that all the members—apart from the newcomer herself—were in posts of special responsibility in the school. I found myself wondering at the same time whether the wish to make a newcomer feel at home by bringing her in on a sub-group of staff already engaged in a very difficult and complex task might be in conflict with the needs of that task, and whether Denys John's assurance about the lack of hierarchy did not have more to do with making a young and inexperienced teacher feel comfortable in a manifestly senior group of colleagues than with the problems of the committee members themselves, trying to speak not only for their own departments but also for the other department heads whom they were representing. Dawn Castell, if she represented anyone, was really representing, though not officially, the five new members of the full-time staff and might indeed have been given the task of feeding back to them information about the proceedings of the planning committee, as perhaps she did informally through friendship channels rather than in a work situation.

Nevertheless, the fact that the school was working with imperfect systems did not mean that nothing was being achieved through them. For despite all these problems about subject boundaries and representation, the F.Y.C. group did succeed, before the end of the autumn term, in drawing up a complex pattern of option pools. This scheme was to make it possible for the ablest pupils to study special subjects in greater depth without sacrificing a general coverage of the main areas of the curriculum; and it was to provide for the less able pupils a greater variety of options over that range than would have been possible in the existing grammar-school pattern of subjects. A number of integrated courses, combining two or three of the nine 'pools', were to be available in various combinations, extending into new areas of study the kind of learning already being explored in the first-year humanities course (see Figure 38).

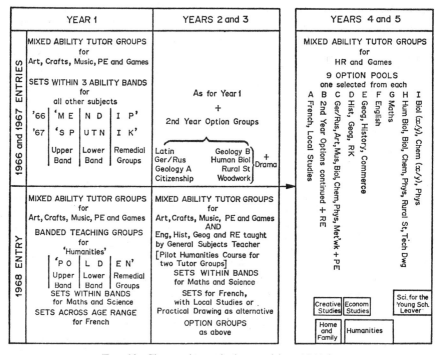

FIG. 38. Changes in curricular provision: 1966–9.

The O & A group

We saw in Chapter IV that these developments, and the accompanying move towards organization in mixed-ability groups for an increasing proportion of the work of the lower school, were having repercussions in various parts of the departmental system. It was to explore some of these problems arising from the new approaches to learning that the O & A group came into existence in September 1968. Although the phrase 'approaches to learning' was actually used in the staff meeting when the head suggested that such a group should be formed, its work, indeed its *raison d'être*, was associated from the very beginning with the current uncertainties about destreaming and about the problems of teaching in mixed-ability groups.

During the autumn and winter I was continually asking myself why the original theme had been submerged, both in the written brief given to the group by Denys John at its opening meeting and in the expectations of the staff about the content of the group's discussions. Why had 'organization and assessment' been substituted for 'approaches to learning'?

The O & A group came into existence at the time when the Reports group was making its final recommendations to the staff about the form and timing of future communications to parents about the progress of pupils. But communication to parents is only one aspect of the whole problem of assessment; it is also concerned with problems of communication between teachers. Assessment, it turned out, was to be a very dominant theme in staff discussions throughout the period of my work with the school. At one level, as was pointed out to me in the summer of 1971, this anxiety must have been particularly acute in that year, because Denys and Ada John, Tony Frost and Pat Richardson all had daughters in the school who, in the summer and autumn of 1968 were coping with the difficult transition from the third to the fourth year. At another level, also, the extent to which I might be engaged in assessing the school itself must, all this time, have been a major preoccupation.

Now the O & A group was the only study group in existence during the autumn of 1968 that did not have in its membership any representative of top management. Both the H.R. group and the F.Y.C. group had all three members of the 'triumvirate'; and one of them, Robin Thomas, had also been a member of the Reports group. Clearly, it was with the disbanding Reports group that the O & A group was most closely linked when it first came into being. It was not surprising therefore that, as the term went on, it was the former chairman of that earlier Reports group, Pat Richardson, who kept the closest watch on the proceedings of the O & A group, almost, it seemed, offering herself as the unofficial spokesman of the staff group in conveying to its members and particularly to its chairman the anxieties of her colleagues about the possible influence of their deliberations on school policy, and suggesting in writing at one stage that a member of the office staff ought to attend their meetings in order to take detailed notes about what occurred. The link was all the stronger because, at Denys John's request, the membership of the new group was not to include any staff who had just been serving on the Reports group. In fact one of them, John Harbinson, did attend the first few meetings of the O & A group and then withdrew. He was not the only influential member of staff who did this, for the heads of music and modern languages, Tony Frost and Peter Atkinson, also joined it at the beginning and then withdrew, the former having explained that either he or his part-time assistant, David Silk, but not both, would be available, the latter giving pressure of departmental responsibilities as his reason for withdrawing.

The six steady members of the group were: Graham Morris (elected as its chairman in the first meeting), Reg Clarke, Graeme Osborn, Sue Redfern (John Harbinson's deputy in the lower school and a member of the mathematics department), David Silk and Allen White. To what extent, we must now ask ourselves, did this group cover—by accident or by design—the different areas of concern in the staff group at the time when it came into existence?

Three members of the group were known to be committed to the development of new integrated courses—Graham Morris in the upper school through his involvement in sixth-form general studies, Graeme Osborn in the lower school through the first-year humanities course, and Reg Clarke, who had always worked across subject boundaries with the remedial groups in the lower school and was known formally as 'head of general subjects'. Yet two of these three also reflected the polarization in the staff group of attitudes for and against the newer kind of teaching approach. Reg Clarke was known to be strenuously defending the boundary that protected his remedial groups: indeed, at the moment of volunteering to join the O & A group he had publicly declared that he was doing so because he felt there should be somebody in this group to oppose the views he assumed most of the other members if not all would hold. He did not make it clear what views he would be opposing but seemed to be implying that he felt some kind of obligation to be in this group in order to protect the *status quo*. It is hard to say therefore what kind of label he was putting on himself at that moment. Equally, Graham Morris offered himself along with a certain kind of label, since he had just been protesting in that meeting that teachers ought to be prepared to accept responsibility for investigating the effects of changes they introduced into the system rather than leaving outside research workers to do this investigating for them. Thus at the outset, staff members probably perceived Graham Morris as someone who was joining the group to embody Denys John's belief in the necessity for rational and informed change—in other words perhaps to be the headmaster's voice in the group—and Reg Clarke as someone who would oppose new policies and commit himself to the defence of the existing system. In the light of later discussions in the full and sectional meetings it would seem that two of the other three members of the O & A group, namely Sue Redfern and Allen White, also reflected this kind of polarization in the eyes of those outside it, since Sue Redfern was more often identified with willingness to welcome change and was known to be close to Graham Morris in age and a friend of his outside the school, whereas Allen White identified himself more with resistance to some of the changes that were going on and was closer in age to Reg Clarke.

What did David Silk—the remaining one of the six steady members of the group—represent for those inside it and those outside it? Was he perceived primarily as a musician who shared Tony Frost's views about educational issues and could therefore be accepted as a substitute for him? Or was he seen primarily as a member of the part-time staff, many of whom attended staff meetings as regularly as their full-time colleagues even though they could not by definition have so much influence on long-term policy decisions? How significant was it that scientists appeared reluctant to commit themselves to the work of such a study group yet anxious enough about its activities to hover on its edge—Gwen London, attending one or two meetings in the early stages as 'an interested observer' and Phillip Armitage joining it only in time to take part in its last two meetings? Was there some difficulty about bringing into the group the known differences of opinion between the biologists and the other scientists on the subject of mixed-ability teaching, lest both this disagreement between them and their agreement about the difficulties of teaching integrated science courses might have to be examined in the presence of arts teachers?

I do not wish to suggest that the six committed members of the O & A group and those who joined it for a while at the beginning or end of its life had no reality for each other or for their colleagues outside the group as persons in their own right. What I am saying is that the group, despite the fact that it very quickly developed an internal life of its own, contained within itself not only individual persons capable of independent thought but also parts of the total staff group—its senior established part, its junior questioning part, its fringe sub-groups, its age and its youth, its masculinity and its femininity. In Figure 39 I have attempted to show how these sub-parts were, unconsciously at least, part of the internal life of the group, and therefore affecting the way those outside were perceiving it.

Within the boundary of the O & A group itself the attitudes and alignments of its members were by no means predictable from their behaviour in large staff meetings. The sharpest exchange during all the meetings that I attended occurred not between an older and a younger member but between the two most experienced teachers in the group, namely Allen White and Reg Clarke. This exchange, which occurred in a fairly early meeting, had far less to do with support of or resistance to new methods than with uneasiness about how the ex-grammar-school teacher, unaccustomed to working with children of lower ability, and the ex-secondary-modern-school teacher,

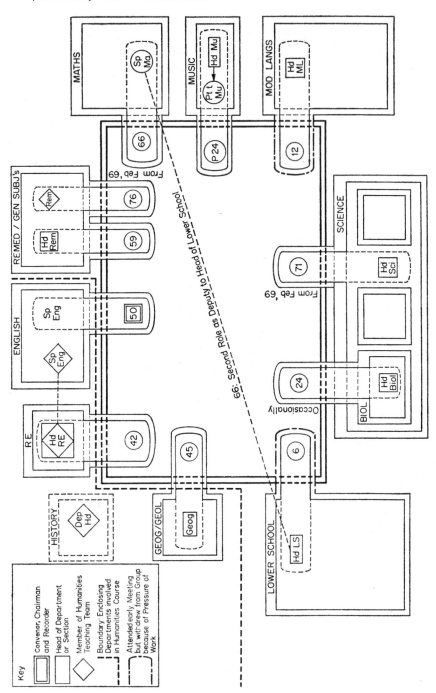

FIG. 39. Representation in a working party on organization and assessment.

unaccustomed to working with children of high ability, perceived each other's strengths and weaknesses as colleagues in a comprehensive school.

The only comparable clash of feeling between two individual members of the group that impressed itself as strongly upon my memory occurred between Phillip Armitage and David Silk very near the end of the group's working life, during a discussion on assessment, particularly as it related to decisions about allocating children to CSE or GCE courses at the end of the third year. This took the form of two fairly long thoughtful statements exposing a fundamental difference of opinion about the true nature of the problem. In a strange way it dramatized the kind of internal conflict that all teachers experience when they find themselves having to evaluate work done by pupils they have come to care for as persons. For Phillip Armitage the problem was to discover what common elements were discernible in the two examinations in any particular subjects and then to try to devise a CSE Mode 3 which would be more comparable to GCE. For David Silk the problem was to recognize, and to help pupils to recognize, that children, like teachers, varied in their talents and abilities; that just as he himself would need to accept, as he put it, his own 'ordinariness' when compared with more talented people, so children needed to learn how to accept others less or more gifted than themselves. For him the crucial question concerned the way people learned to use and develop what skills and talents they had, whether small or great. Behind the scientist's plea for intellectual rationalization and the musician's plea for emotional tolerance, behind the search for sameness and regularity on the one side and for difference and variation on the other, it seemed that these two had acted out on behalf of the rest the teacher's unending struggle to steer between the Scylla of over demandingness and the Charybdis of easy indulgence. Surprisingly Phillip Armitage, who seemed often to personify the toughness of the demanding intellectual and David Silk, who seemed to personify the gentleness of the artist, were almost changing roles: for the scientist's solution was really the more protective of personal self-esteem and the musician's plea was the more uncompromising in its demand for personal self-knowledge. Again it seemed that the false dichotomy between tough-mindedness and tender-mindedness was breaking down.

The weakness of the working-party system as revealed in the events of one winter

Although a good deal of time was devoted both in full staff meetings and in department heads' meetings to consideration of the work of the O & A group and to discussion of the reports it submitted, the morale of this group was never very high. It had a young chairman who attended the department heads' meetings not by virtue of heading a subject department but as head of library in the absence of a full-time librarian. It was a wandering group, trying out various meeting places, first in Graeme Osborn's house block, later on one occasion in the library, once during the half-term holiday, in the absence of the rest of the staff, in the staff common-room, and latterly in Reg Clarke's room near the remedial group's classroom.

From the beginning the members of the group and also Denys John realized that they would have to keep the channels of communication open between themselves and their colleagues if the work was to prove of any value. Their first attempt to do this by reporting back to the staff meeting of 3 October (by which time they had held two meetings) was somewhat abortive, because the report was the fifth item on the agenda and was not reached until very late in the meeting when the staff were beginning to leave. In this rather desperate moment the only clear part of Graham Morris's message was a request to the heads of the departments for statements about the extent to which streaming or setting was necessary for the effective teaching of their subjects. Already although I had not yet attended any of its meetings I was beginning to have an image of a group in considerable trouble.

During the next month or so they held four meetings culminating in one long one during the half-term holiday. Although during this time the group developed considerable cohesion within its own boundary, it seemed to do so at some cost. Graham Morris in particular as its chairman found himself the target of a good deal of hostility from some of the department heads, although two of them gave genuine support to the group and to him personally by sending in full and helpful statements about the work in their subject areas and about their views on setting. In one of these meetings Allen White expressed vividly his own sense of being divided in relation to the new kind of teaching approach being used in the humanities course, recognizing that children were responding well to it, yet voicing his unease about its long-term effects on specialist work in geography. More surprisingly, Graeme Osborn, who was actually teaching in this course, expressed an equally strong ambivalence. This kind of evidence that within the group its members were able to trust each other with some of their real and complex feelings about the changes that were afoot was at variance with their nervousness about how they would be able to function when they had to give an account of themselves in the November staff meeting which was to be devoted entirely to their work. They seemed to fear that their colleagues might prove so un-willing or so unable to examine real educational problems that they themselves would be incapable of taking back into the full staff meeting the experiences they had been having in their own meetings. Yet in one of the two meetings of the F.Y.C. group that I attended, Gerry Lloyd had revealed his ambiv-alence about the School's Council 'Science for the Young School Leaver' project (his approval of it as a teaching approach and his worries about it as a foundation for GCE work in physics) in much the same way as Allen White and Graeme Osborn had spoken in the O & A group about the humanities course. It was hard to know what kind of wall was being built around the O & A group to make it feel so isolated within the staff group.

The ambivalence of the staff towards this group and its activities was conveyed to Denys John on the day of the November staff meeting through a series of messages from a number of staff members who sent apologies for absence, with the result that he arrived at the meeting feeling that staff were attacking him through the O & A group by opting out of the meeting that he had put aside for discussion of its work. Graham Morris himself, because of a coach duty, was twenty minutes late for the meeting and was therefore unable to open the discussion. Afterwards he divulged to me that he had welcomed the excuse for arriving late (and had therefore made no attempt to find someone to take over his coach duty) because he had feared that he might be the sole spokesman for the group if he was there at the beginning. Throughout the meeting the emphasis was on the problem of how *teachers* could *teach* in face of the changing conditions and of the difficulties of moving away from the tried and familiar methods. Only very near the end did Graham Morris—in response to a direct invitation from Denys John—break his silence. When he did so he protested that the O & A group could not proceed very far until the staff were able to turn their attention to the problem of how *children* could best *learn*. Thus he seemed to be trying to reassert the purpose for which the group had originally been brought into existence: to study approaches and objectives.

Throughout this winter and spring of 1968-9, Graham Morris repeatedly requested heads of departments, in consultation with their staffs, to prepare written statements about their teaching objectives. His request was never really met. Towards the end of the last meeting of the heads of departments in the summer of 1969, he announced with considerable feeling that he would not mind if the O & A group ceased to exist, provided the departments tackled this task even if it took them a whole year to accomplish it. But even then, he did not really get any answer, other than a somewhat empty assurance from Denys John that the department heads now seemed committed to this —empty because there was no real evidence that such a commitment was being undertaken. The department heads themselves managed at that moment to take flight from the pain of saying either 'yes, we will' or 'no, we will not', some taking flight quite literally by getting out of the meeting between Graham Morris's asking of the question and Denys John's answer. The nearest anyone came to accepting such a commitment was Peter Atkinson who said that he would not agree to have such a statement ready by the end of September (the first date suggested by Graham Morris) but would be prepared to undertake it as a long-term task for himself and his department.

It is often difficult to distinguish between firm dependable leadership and an over-dependent paternalism, especially in an educational situation in which something new and untried is being attempted. This is well known to teachers as they perceive themselves in relation to pupils; it is much less familiar—and more difficult to acknowledge—as a problem that is inherent in their own relations with a headmaster. Denys John's search for a style of leadership that was dependable without being over-protective, and astringent without being repressive, was observable over and over again in his relationship with the O & A group. In the November staff meeting it found expression in a careful, patient and quite prolonged exposition on the problems of finding new themes for integrated courses, an exposition that had the effect of taking everybody off the hook, thus protecting the O & A group from any real exploration of its relations with the rest of the staff group and protecting the rest of the staff from the necessity of examining their ambivalent attitudes towards what the O & A group seemed to them to be representing. If the staff had any feelings about this paternalism they kept them well under cover during that meeting. Denys John's long exposition was listened to in a submissive kind of silence. Feelings about paternalism came out not against him but against Reg Clarke, in a half-expressed rumbling sort of attack on him for wanting to preserve his remedial group and his role as its 'father figure' when the rest of the lower school was having to accept a growing measure of de-streaming. Was this at least partially a displacement of anger with Denys John for wanting to keep sub-groups of staff over-dependent on him?

Yet this protectiveness was partly the result of the dependency of the staff themselves and in particular of the O & A group, who wanted cut and dried terms of reference from him as much as they wanted him to free them to work in their own way. Soon after the November staff meeting its members requested a special meeting with him to redefine and clarify their task. The meeting was held over lunch in his room. But it was not Denys John himself who suggested this location, but a member of the group—namely, Sue Redfern, to whom Graham Morris, who was recovering from 'flu, had evidently left the arrangements, since he did not arrive in the school until the meeting was due to begin, thus unconsciously re-enacting, to some extent, the reluctance to take the role of initiator that he had shown by delaying his arrival at the November staff meeting. The staff had been informed about the special meeting, which was described as open to visitors, as indeed all meetings of the O & A group were, at least in theory. And five visitors came. Much of the discussion took the form of a series of dialogues between Denys John and certain individual persons. The O & A group members, sitting in a row on the opposite side of the table to him, with visitors on either side of them, were gradually reduced to a kind of audience and when they did contribute addressed their remarks directly to Denys John. He himself refrained with some effort from opening the discussion, despite an initial uneasy silence over the meal, but waited for Graham Morris to open it; on the other hand he distributed before the meeting a new statement, referred to later as 'the head's manifesto', in which he had set out what he believed the task of the O & A group should be. Thus he re-enacted in this meeting what he had done at the beginning of the term when he had made it clear to the O & A group in its first meeting that he did not feel it would be appropriate for him to be a member of the group, yet had given it very specific terms of reference in the form of a paper containing questions about organization of teaching groups on the one hand and assessment of individual pupils on the other. My own feeling that he had given the group too little authority to work out their own approach to the task was confirmed in this special meeting, first by one of the visitors and then by a member of the O & A group. Both these declared themselves to be in complete agreement with the head's written statement, at the same time implying that it left them feeling that their own thinking was somehow inhibited by it. It was as though he had unwittingly tied their hands by deciding on behalf of everybody what all the questions ought to be.

It was only near the end of this meeting, following a long discussion about the role of examinations, that the real nature of the headmaster's dilemma became apparent, when questions were asked about the extent to which the heads of departments were 'autonomous' and therefore beyond the reach of any influence that might be brought to bear upon them. Denys John's somewhat troubled response to this question was to say that if the O & A group came up with any proposal that he could not approve of it would have wasted its time, but equally that if a department head's activities should be at odds with his own objectives as headmaster then he would want to know the reason why. This feeling of being pushed or pulled in different directions by the department heads and by the O & A group found expression later in the meeting when he tried to counter a direct question from Graham Morris about the extent to which the group could really concern itself with teaching objectives. His reply to this was that the group had the right to examine *methods* of teaching but not to examine the *content* of syllabuses. Thus at the very time when at the conscious level he was trying to offer leadership to the O & A group, he unconsciously weakened it by implying that the content and method of teaching could and must be maintained as separate domains, the first to be left entirely in the hands of the department heads, and only the second to be open to the scrutiny of the group. Graham Morris's bewilderment at that moment was clearly visible on his face. And there was no time left in the meeting to work on the nature of this bewilderment.

Why was this such a difficult and frustrating meeting, both for Denys John and for the members of the O & A group? In the first place, it was a meeting in which the boundary round the group and the boundary round the primary task of the meeting were both equally blurred. What had been requested as a meeting between the group and the headmaster became, in effect, a meeting between the headmaster and five other members of the staff about the worrying aspects of the 'new thinking' which was being identified with the O & A group. Indeed the visitors, collectively, seemed to be personifying the ambivalent attitudes of the staff towards the group, as Graham Morris was at that time experiencing those attitudes and as he was to experience them even more powerfully a few weeks later. The five visitors included three members of the earlier Reports group: John Harbinson, Ada John and Pat Richardson. The other two were Phillip Armitage and Bob Jarratt, who joined the O & A group later in the following term, only in time to attend its last two meetings (as John Harbinson, at the beginning of its life, had attended its first three meetings). Thus what was taking place in the headmaster's room during that lunch hour was really an encounter between the two study groups that had been given the task of examining problems of assessment—the earlier one as it affected teacher-parent relationships, the later one as it affected teacher-pupil relationships. My own single contribution to the discussion, made with some trepidation when time was running out, was to the effect that I had been puzzled to know what meeting I was attending, that I thought the O & A group had, in this meeting, been taken over by the headmaster and swamped by the visitors, and that the discussion had seemed to me more like a rehearsal for the department heads' meeting that was due to take place on the following day than the kind of consultation the O & A group had sought with the headmaster. This interpretation produced indignant reactions from two of the visitors—significantly enough, from Ada John and Pat Richardson—one of them reminding me sharply that the O & A group members themselves had always indicated their willingness to be visited by colleagues. Graham Morris was equally quick to dissociate himself from my remarks by denying that the group had been immobilized in the meeting; yet he went on to affirm that he did not feel any clearer as a result of this meeting about the real nature of the problems the group was supposed to be studying on behalf of the staff. As I left at the close of the meeting I had a strong impression that Denys John had been both hurt and angered by my suggestion that he had 'taken over' the group; not surprisingly since I had done so in the presence of his wife and another of his colleagues in the modern language department. Partly because of this, and partly because I could not decide whether Denys John or Graham Morris had really been in the role of leader or chairman on this occasion, I found myself unable to offer either of them the post-meeting consultative discussion that normally followed such an event.

The blurring of the boundary as a result of the influx of visitors into a meeting which the members of the O & A group had needed in order to talk directly with the headmaster about their predicament was symptomatic of the magnitude of the task the group had been given at the beginning of the term. It seemed that the staff wished to encapsulate the whole problem of defining 'education' within this small handful of colleagues who had been rash enough to volunteer for such a task; yet simultaneously there appeared to be a wish to deny these volunteers the right to protect their boundary so that they could undertake the task with some assurance that the staff were trusting them to do so. The group members themselves, of course, by declaring their willingness to 'welcome' visitors, had colluded with this. Consequently they never really knew, from one meeting to another, whether they would be observed by visitors or left severely alone. The blurring of the boundary in the special meeting in the head's room was also an indication of Denys John's uncertainty about how to handle simultaneously his relationships with three different groups of staff: first, with the F.Y.C. group, which was to hold its final meeting only two days later; secondly, with the heads of departments, who, if they chose to oppose the F.Y.C. group's emerging proposals, could nullify its work; and thirdly, with the O & A group itself.

The procedure used by Denys John for presenting the F.Y.C. group's proposals to the staff in the January staff meeting revealed both the weakness of the existing framework for staff consultation and the vulnerability of the O & A group at this particular time. Was he to 'consult' the O & A group before working out with Robin Thomas and Joan Bradbury a form in which the proposals could be presented? Or was he to make known to all the staff how far the thinking of the top-management group had gone irrespective of the O & A group's reactions to that thinking? In fact he tried to do both. In December he gave the O & A group copies of the proposed curriculum design, asking them to consider it and prepare comments to feed back to the full staff meeting in January. The group held a long meeting on the day before the school reassembled in January in order to do this. But when the spring term opened, Denys John authorized Robin Thomas to have the document duplicated and distributed to the staff before the January meeting. Graham Morris was not told about this until the morning of the meeting, just before the papers were distributed. Thus his own thinking about how to feed back to the staff the results of his group's deliberations and how to get some of the anxieties of staff members out into the open before the proposals were actually put before them in what might well look like a final form, was suddenly invalidated, since the situation was now changed from the one he had been expecting. Moreover, Robin Thomas, in distributing the document to all the staff that morning, issued along with it an agenda-sheet which relegated the comments of the O & A group members to second place; their contribution therefore *followed* general staff discussion of proposals instead of *preceding* it, and in a way introducing it, as they had expected it to do.

Although, in introducing this general discussion, Denys John emphasized that the new proposals had been formulated with reference to work that had been going on both in the F.Y.C. group and in the O & A group, there was a great deal of distrust in the air. Graham Morris indicated later that he had felt that the ground was being cut from under the feet of the O & A group. Yet he was unable to bring this out publicly in the staff meeting, fearing that he might obstruct the changes he wanted to see implemented by protesting about the way in which the change was being managed. After the meeting he found that colleagues, including department heads, who had previously been ready to talk with him about the work of his group, sometimes after preliminary skirmishing and leg-pulling, were no longer willing to do so, but avoided any discussions with him about the implications of the new proposals.

Thus it seemed that at one blow the O & A group had lost both its link with the headmaster and any sense of identification it had once had at least with certain individuals and with certain sub-sections of the staff group.

Because the O & A group came together as a number of individual persons who volunteered to devote a good deal of time and energy to the study of problems that were central preoccupations of the staff group at that time, was bound to excite speculation, even suspicion perhaps, among colleagues. Having no authority to act either on behalf of the head or on behalf of the staff group, it was always in danger of becoming an unwitting go-between and as such was liable to pick up unacknowledged fears and suspicions on both sides. Moreover, because the brief given to the O & A group, unlike that given to the F.Y.C. group, had not been limited to the fourth and fifth years where the intake of pupils was undeniably changing, but had embraced the whole age range of pupils, the F.Y.C. group had been relatively protected by the very existence of the O & A group from the full impact of the staff's reactions to its proposals. The peril of the O & A group was that colleagues might unconsciously wish to perceive it either as a group set up by the head-master to work 'informally' in support of his policies or as a kind of revolu-tionary group or people's government thrown up by those factions within the staff group that were opposed to the head's policies. In both cases its members were in danger of being perceived either as a monolithic power group or as a weak puppet group acting under orders. If they had colluded with those who wanted to elevate them as a power group they would have found themselves fighting for the head against the staff or for the staff against the head, irrespective of their own need to examine more closely—as respons-ible teachers—their own beliefs and attitudes about the policies being evolved. If they had colluded with those who wanted to reduce them to the level of a puppet group then they would in time have been discarded, as puppets always are when they no longer embody the wishes and beliefs of the puppet master. In fact the group disbanded itself when it became apparent that the work for which its members had come together could no longer be contained within its boundary. In other words the group was sufficiently task-centred to face its own ending realistically when the time came rather than attempt to maintain itself as a sentient system that no longer had any genuine task.

Staff unrest and the testing of a headmaster's integrity

Between the beginning of the spring term and the end of the 1968–9 session the staff went through a period of considerable unrest and dissatisfaction. It is difficult to describe this without presenting a picture of a staff group supposedly torn with conflict and no longer able to carry out its task. But teachers, like their pupils, are remarkably resilient; and the evidence of unrest and uncertainty in the staff room, particularly during scheduled staff meetings where some confrontation between the headmaster and the staff and between different sections of the staff group was unavoidable, is not incompatible with the probability that the day-to-day work in the various parts of the school was going on much as usual. Nevertheless, the feelings of unrest, if unexplored, must in the end have militated against that work and would certainly have militated against future developments in the school's over-all policy. In so far as staff were able to examine the nature of their dissatisfaction and even to acknowledge their doubts about Denys John's course of action, they made their own experience of the problems of relating to authority available as a model to help them to understand the increasing difficulty of exercising their own authority with children and young people whose image of authority was undergoing considerable change. I shall be considering in the final section of this book some of the evidence that the struggle to understand the ebb and flow of feelings, both warm and hostile, was having some effect upon the way in which members of the staff were redefining their own roles as tutors, subject teachers and section heads.

So far the hostility towards the headmaster, as the person who had to accept the ultimate responsibility for the changes he was trying to bring about, had been expressed only in indirect ways. There were rumours that people were looking for new posts elsewhere, that disillusionment with the processes of consultation was spreading and that the pressure of meetings was becoming intolerable. I myself was aware of a kind of rumbling discontent, which in two of the four January meetings (one full staff meeting and one section heads' meeting) took the form of an undercurrent of talk that was being carried on at intervals against the open and audible discussion—a phenomenon that had certainly not been present in earlier meetings that I had attended. More and more, during that winter and early spring, I had the feeling that the staff, despite all the evidence they had that Denys John did consult them over every change he introduced, were facing some kind of crisis both in their relationship with him as headmaster and in their internal relationships with one another. At the feeling level I was experiencing this myself—as someone closely involved in the events though in working contact with relatively few members of the staff—as a sense, in some meetings, of 'sitting on a keg of gunpowder' and in others of being 'at the centre of a collision'. What the colliding forces were I was never quite sure. At times it seemed that I might be at the centre of a conflict between the head and a particular individual or sub-group, at other times that I was caught between department heads and section heads, at yet other times between one sub-group, such as the O & A group or the humanities team, and the rest of the staff.

Now, words like 'gunpowder' and 'collision' are strongly emotive words, and were felt to be so at the time when I used them in the school. But emotive words are needed when we try to describe a situation that is loaded with people's feelings. The strength of the feelings being experienced by many staff members at that time (and, indeed, by me) was an indication that the staff group was having to contain a great deal of uncertainty and confusion during that period. It was not their own doubts only about the ultimate effects of their headmaster's educational beliefs that they were having to tolerate, but also the doubts of parents and employers about the ultimate effects of the educational policies being pursued by the local education authority. For just as I was experiencing their anxieties as though they were my own, so perhaps they were unconsciously taking into themselves some of the anxieties of people outside the school about what was going on inside it. Denys John, as headmaster in this changing situation, was always on the boundary between Nailsea School and the local environment it served, and therefore between his own staff group and the local authority *he* served. Thus his own leadership role on the boundary was essentially concerned with the management of the relationship between the internal policies of the school and the external policies of the county administration. And this ultimately was what the whole struggle to find a valid structure of management within the school was really all about.

It was in fact the local education authority that unwittingly triggered off the explosion in the staff group that led to the setting up of two more study groups or committees towards the end of the summer term of 1969. And it was the sequel to these events that in the end made possible the fundamental changes that occurred in the consultative structure and the use that was made of this new structure in the 1969–70 academic year. The event that hastened these processes was the arrival on the headmaster's desk of a letter from the chief education officer that was sent out to the heads of all the schools in the area—a letter in which the mysterious word 'virement' appeared. The proposal from County Hall was that part of the responsibility for decisions about how money was to be allocated should be taken by the schools themselves, since some priorities could probably be more accurately defined within the schools themselves than by the local authority to which they were responsible. The term 'virement' was defined as 'exchange of expenditure from one heading to another' and the letter invited heads of schools to put forward schemes, after consultation with their staffs, for such redistribution of funds within a given total allocation. Thus a head who decided that sums hitherto used for the employment of ancillary help (for play-ground supervision, technical aid or secretarial work) would be better spent on equipment, or that ancillary help had higher priority than equipment, or that one kind of ancillary help should be replaced by another, might make a proposal to the committee in accordance with this decision.

Denys John, having received the chief education officer's letter (dated 29 March 1969) just as the spring term was ending, lost little time in consulting the staff about the suggestions put forward in it; for he devoted the staff meeting of 29 April (less than a week after the opening of the summer term) entirely to discussion of its implications. He also arranged for all the staff to have copies of the letter before this meeting. There could have been little doubt in anybody's mind that this new move from County Hall, coupled with his own immediate response to it, would be linked in people's minds with the earlier unrest in the staff group over the question of secretarial and technical help. It was also bound to be linked with two events, one in a neighbouring comprehensive school, the other in Nailsea itself. The event in the other school, to which reference had been made in one full staff meeting, was the appointment of a 'staff secretary'; the event within the school was the fairly recent appointment of three women as ancillary staff for playground supervision.

Despite all this, attendance at the April staff meeting was thin—only about thirty-two being present out of the total staff group of sixty-three. Denys John's reference to this was protective; he merely announced that several people were absent 'for good reasons'. And indeed this was true since some staff were away at field courses and conferences. But it seemed to me that these events accounted only for a small proportion of the absentee group. This was the meeting which he opened with the announcement about Clive Vanloo's new role as head of middle school and about the accompanying change in Mike Burnham's title to 'head of upper school'. Having made these announcements he asked whether anyone wanted to comment, and then pressed on rather hurriedly to the main item for the meeting, namely the proposal from County Hall. It is hard to say now whether the stony silence that ensued was blanketing over the comments people had not really been given time to make about the implications of the two altered titles, Clive Vanloo's in particular, or whether it expressed unwillingness to take seriously their headmaster's wish to learn their views about the letter from County Hall. As it turned out Denys John had to work very hard to get any discussion going at all. Had I been a complete outsider with no knowledge of what had been happening in the staff group since the autumn I might have imagined that nobody present had any interest at all in having access to available funds of money. With my knowledge of the earlier events, however, I had to conclude that what the staff, including the absent staff, were really saying to the head was: 'It's all very well calling a meeting to consult us about this kind of thing; but you don't really mean it. When we do tell you what we think you take no notice.'

The real feelings began to emerge when Mike Burnham suggested that people were finding it difficult to discuss this in real terms because they did not know where they stood in relation to their colleagues; he added that he was thinking of a major economy he might make that would enable him to put a good deal into a new common pool, but that he would not be willing to do this unless he could be reasonably sure that he would benefit from whatever might be bought with the money. Tony Frost followed this up by indicating that he and his colleagues could not discuss the future use of funds without knowing how money was being allocated at present. This produced an indignant retort from Joan Bradbury, who reminded heads of departments that they had always been given information about how funds were allocated to departments and suggested that perhaps what the department heads were really implying was that they had not been in the habit of sharing this information fully with members of their departments, and that this was why in a full staff meeting like this people were confused and uncommunicative. This somewhat angry defence of the headmaster by the senior mistress enabled those present to give more rein to their own accumulated feelings of disillusionment, distrust and cynicism.

The feelings came to a head when Denys John—almost it seemed out of despair—proposed that another study group should be set up to look into the whole question. This produced a sharp reaction from Lewis Smith, who turned and asked—almost it seemed using code language—whether a particular piece of work he himself had done on behalf of the staff earlier in the year had been 'useless'. It then emerged that he was speaking at that moment, not as head of a department, but in another role as secretary of the staff common-room committee, and that he was referring to a report he had made to the head several months earlier, having taken soundings in the staff group on the question of the appointment of a staff secretary. Almost immediately Tony Frost took up the cudgels again and asked Denys John point blank why he had appointed playground supervisors—implying, though not actually saying, that the head had done this in the face of evidence that the staff wanted the money to be used for the appointment of a staff secretary.

Following this question the hostility became more open. Denys John responded to the question by giving a long and detailed reply. He reminded the staff that he had warned them in the autumn term that he did not yet know what County Hall would sanction in the way of new uses of funds, that members of the staff, despite assurances that they were willing to carry out meal supervision themselves in order to save money for the other purpose, had not shown much willingness to do playground supervision, and that in order to fulfil his obligation to ensure the safety of pupils during the lunch-hour, he had had to employ supervisory staff. While he was speaking it became increasingly difficult to hear what he was actually saying because of a mounting noise of background conversation. Eventually I myself commented on this, passing on my own impression that the staff felt that they had been lumbered with ancillary help they didn't really need, and that they now preferred not to hear about the head's reasons for appointing these women helpers. My intervention produced an indignant denial from two people, who assured me that they had been delighted to be relieved of this work of supervision.

The meeting ended somewhat stormily. Denys John continued to insist on the need for a 'Virement Committee' but refused to nominate people to serve on it, saying that the staff must themselves decide who should be on it. There was some acknowledgement that the old system of 'volunteering' might not be appropriate and that the staff might have to go through the painful process of selecting those with relevant skills as their representatives on such a committee. Yet in the end the problem about the membership of this group was shelved and it was left to the chairman of the staff common-room committee to decide which volunteers or nominees from the staff group should finally be asked to serve.

The staff common-room committee existed to handle the social side of the staff group's life rather than its work as an educational task group. Moreover the staff common-room did not technically include the headmaster, and he was always careful not to intrude on its meetings unless specifically asked to attend, even when they took place during the first fifteen minutes or so of a scheduled staff meeting. Thus the chairman of the common-room committee (Kitty King) had to prepare herself for a dilemma: for if the staff were to throw up a large number of volunteers and nominees she would have to make judgements that would have less to do with her role as elected chairman of a socially organized sentient system than with her appointment to a formally organized task system. In the latter she had dual roles as deputy to Mike Burnham in the upper school and as a specialist teacher of history responsible to Joy Sollars for the middle-school optional course known as 'British Constitution'.

Her task was further complicated by another fact: Denys John had announced in this meeting that he had already asked Phillip Armitage—who, as head of science, was nominally responsible for the work of the technical staff—to set up and head a committee to look into the whole organization of technical assistance in the school. Thus the new Virement committee was being brought into existence at the same time as yet another working party, whose task would inevitably include questions about the appointment or replacement of technical staff.

Denys John's own confusion at this time about the network of study groups and committees through which responsibilities were being dispersed expressed itself in a fairly urgent request to me after that meeting to have discussions with Kitty King and Phillip Armitage before either of them went any further with the tasks that had been delegated to them by the staff group and himself respectively. Following my interviews with these two, neither of the committees they subsequently set up invited me to attend any meetings. Furthermore my own impression, based on the reports given at the full staff meeting, when both these study groups reported on their activities, was that the staff, by accepting the two reports without comment or question, were acting out a certain unwillingness to work seriously—as a staff group—on the controversial questions which the study groups had been set up to examine. Yet both reports, in contrasted ways, contained important implications which needed to be explored by all the staff. Phillip Armitage reported that his committee had decided that the technical staff should henceforth be a separate service department under the leadership of the head technician, Bill Smith, who was to be responsible directly to Robin Thomas, and that the science department should continue to have the right to 90 per cent of the time available for the seven technicians at present employed. The report from the other group, in contrast to this, was to the effect that the task of the Virement committee was so fraught with difficulties and would take everybody on to such dangerous ground that rather than risk offending or threatening anyone they would not be attempting to do anything at all about the spending of money during the coming academic year. Neither statement produced any reaction from the staff, who seemed to have been presented with a *fait accompli* on the one hand and with a denial that anything at all could be accomplished on the other.

Again, as I believe, the staff was being faced with the fundamental problem besetting study groups or working parties that did not really have the authority to make decisions on behalf of the institution and whose members were therefore uncertain whether they even had the power to influence the headmaster in the decisions that he made. The Technical Aid committee did, it is true, make an important decision in recommending that the technicians should operate as a department and cease to be an adjunct to the science department. But the implications of this change were not really discussed publicly in the staff group. The change of title conferred on Bill Smith from the autumn of 1969, although it did give him a good deal of authority to approach heads of departments directly, did not radically alter the situation in which the science department had the prior claim to the time of technicians. Moreover the change in title brought into focus another question about the relationship between the secretarial and the technical staff. As school bursar, Ethel Hawker was officially responsible for the work of all ancillary staff in the school. Thus it was possible to argue that Bill Smith was responsible to her rather than to Robin Thomas. The membership of the Virement committee and the Technical Aid committee as shown in Figure 40 unconsciously drove a wedge between these two, Ethel Hawker being asked to serve on the former and Bill Smith being asked to serve on the latter.

Between the April and May staff meetings to which I have been referring there was a department heads' meeting which now in retrospect seems to have given Denys John the sanction he needed to close the gap between department heads and section heads by bringing them together into the new monthly 'senior staff meeting' that he inaugurated in the following September, along with the new top-management 'standing committee'. The agenda for this meeting included three items each backed by documentation: namely 'Heads of Departments' with an accompanying paper prepared by the headmaster himself, 'Courses for Groups or Individual Pupils' with an accompanying paper also prepared by him and 'Details of Allowances for 1969–70' prepared and signed by Ethel Hawker. It seemed that Denys John was feeling the necessity to demonstrate both his dependability as someone who would offer decisive leads about how tasks should be carried out and his openness as someone who shared with the staff all the available facts about material expenditure.

But the important thing at that meeting had little to do with any of these papers. For somehow his suggestion that department heads should look at their roles and functions in the light of new developments and of the work of the Virement committee in particular was taken into quite a different area of discussion—namely the role not of a head of department but of department heads' *meetings* in relation to the full staff meetings.

Again it was from Lewis Smith and Tony Frost that the real challenges to the headmaster came, as in the full staff meeting a week earlier. But they came this time not in the form of attacks, but rather in the form of an

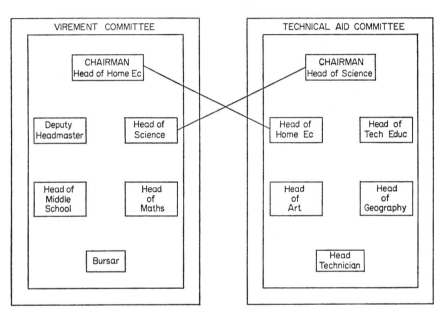

FIG. 40. Management of resources as a single task split between two committees.

exploration of the real problems of consultation. Lewis Smith was not present at the meeting; but he had asked Mike Burnham to act for him by putting to the meeting the question 'what was the difference between a department heads' meeting and the full staff meeting?' Tony Frost carried this question further by opening up the whole problem of the relationship between the department heads (assumed to have curricular responsibilities) and the section heads (assumed to have pastoral responsibilities), indicating that he could not understand how the two could be divided. Later in the meeting he put two further questions directly to Denys John, first about how he, as headmaster, saw his role in relation to the department heads' meetings, and secondly about whether he would act on a recommendation of the Virement committee without any further consultation or whether he would bring any such recommendation back to a staff meeting for discussion. The puzzled look on

Denys John's face and the even more puzzled inflection of his voice when he replied to this second question, saying that it had never occurred to him *not* to bring such recommendations back to the staff meeting, probably did a great deal more to restore belief in the genuineness of his wish to consult staff than any of his written papers in the course of the year had done. But the real testing out was still some months away.

Emergence of a new consultative structure

I have been looking at some of the problems of representation that were affecting staff members, whether or not they were serving on working parties or committees, and have been drawing attention also to some of the ways in which certain individual members of the staff were unconsciously acting on behalf of their colleagues in full and sectional staff meetings. Prominent among those who opposed the head during those months were two men who had joined the staff as department heads in the autumn of 1965, having previously been colleagues at another comprehensive school. Graham Morris, who had come to Nailsea in the same year, straight from the Certificate course in the Bristol University Department of Education, had also put challenging questions to the head from time to time, not so much opposing him as pressing him to clarify his reasons for the actions he took. It may or may not have been mere coincidence that two of these three had once been students of mine, one only a few years before in Bristol, the other many years before in another university department, and two of them taught English as I had formerly done. In the context of the school's history, it was the year of their arrival on the staff that seemed the more important of these two facts, since they had all three joined it when the school, though still a grammar school, was due to accept its first comprehensive intake in one year's time. In the context of the Schools Council project that I had started in September, however, the personal and professional links with me must also have been important factors in the behaviour of these three people. Did they feel safe in challenging Denys John because they believed that I would be able to prevent their attacking or probing questions from becoming too damaging? Or were they unconsciously seeking to weaken, perhaps even to destroy, any pairing relationship that might develop between him and me by trying to make me question the sincerity of his efforts to involve staff in the processes of policy making, or by trying to make him blame me for the disturbances that were being experienced?

There can be little doubt that both these hopes were unconsciously present in much that these and other members of staff did to Denys John and to me during those months. For a headmaster of a school, like the father of any family, must expect to be on the receiving end of powerfully ambivalent feelings. The same colleagues who seek, through some of their actions, to preserve the head as a good object, will seek, through other actions, to destroy him as a bad object. In the particular school situation I am describing, there was an additional and unusual element: the presence of myself in the school as a consultant. This, although undoubtedly a complicating factor in an already complex situation, was also available as a source of clarification, in so far as we were able to use it in this way. Since I myself, in my role as consultant, was at the receiving end of ambivalent feelings similar to those directed at Denys John, it must have been as difficult for the staff as it was for the two of us to separate out those attitudes that should have been directed at me from those that should have been directed at him. Yet the very effort to do this in itself threw light on the reasons for the existence of those attitudes. It is hard to say, even with hindsight, how far the mounting anger with Denys John during the spring of 1969 was a displacement of suspicions about my research methods, or how far the later storm over my interim report to the Schools Council in June was gathering up into itself some of the earlier suspicions about his consultative methods. Either way, the important thing to recognize is that those who were able to take the risk of challenging him in public were also expressing a growing trust in him by doing so.

The new top-management (or 'standing') committee contained within itself many of the elements that had been present, in dispersed form, in the various working parties and study groups that had preceded its inauguration. The work of the F.Y.C. group and the work of the O & A group in particular are better understood if perceived as two sides of the work subsequently accepted by the standing committee—work that included both short-term and long-term planning, both practical action and theoretical deliberation, both thoughts about change and feelings about change. The members of the F.Y.C. group worked directly with the headmaster; with one exception they were senior members of staff with identifiable responsibilities who brought with them some sanction from constituent groups within the task system to act on behalf of others; the products of their work were concrete and specific plans for future curriculum change in one particular area of the school. The members of the O & A group worked, for the most part, without the headmaster, though within the terms of reference given to them by him; they included people whose leadership roles in the system were changing, and they brought no sanction from any sections of the staff group to do anything on behalf of others; the products of their work were intangible—perhaps a heightened awareness of the conflicts in the staff group about curriculum change, and of the ambiguity of terms like 'mixed ability groups', 'integrated courses', 'enrichment' and 'assessment'. The F.Y.C. group seemed relatively protected from feelings and little troubled by internal conflict. Its work ended with a feeling of achievement and satisfaction. The O & A group experienced a good deal of internal conflict and was vulnerable to attacks from outside. Its work ended with a feeling of uncertainty and frustration.

The standing committee was able, as time went on, to combine the leadership, driving power and optimism of the F.Y.C. group with the capacity of the O & A group to pick up and interpret the feelings of staff about current planning and development. As top management, its members would have been unable to offer sensitive leadership if they had remained protected and invulnerable within the boundaries of the committee itself. Nor could they have offered effective leadership if they had allowed themselves to become a sort of collective receptacle for the fears and hopes of their colleagues. When they began their work, questions about subject boundaries, areas of know-ledge, the implications of streaming, banding and setting and the control and distribution of material and financial resources were still reverberating from the summer term. What they provided was a firm structure within which these questions could be examined. Gradually, as the new academic year got under way, it became possible to question the reality of some of the conflicts between departments and between the arts and the sciences, and to begin to detect some of the splits and divisions within single departments and to recognize the important growing points in different parts of the system.

In the struggle to offer this new kind of leadership to their colleagues, the members of the standing committee found themselves having to examine the tensions within the committee itself in order to arrive at a deeper under-standing of their own roles, not only in the committee, but also in the senior staff meeting and in the full staff meeting. The standing committee, unlike any of its predecessors, was permanent. Its members therefore had to come to terms with the fact that membership of this committee in itself changed the quality of their relationships with colleagues who were not on it. Each one had to find a way of operating back in staff meetings—a way that was consistent both with his or her beliefs as a person and with his or her commit-ment to the tasks of leadership in the staff group and of representation on the committee.

In describing the difficulties of the O & A group in the previous year I had once used the image of the lunar module facing the hazard of rejoining the parent ship. The standing committee also had this problem, but with a difference: the fact that all its members carried in the task system leadership roles that placed them near its outer boundary. It was therefore less *easy* for them to escape back into their own sentient groups outside the boundary of the committee; conversely, however, it was less *difficult* for them to follow through in the various parts of the system the work they were doing together in the committee, since they had authority to do so not only by virtue of the persons they were but also by virtue of the roles they carried.

The danger of encapsulation for the members of the O & A group had been that they might, as a group trying to carry out a task on behalf of the institution, be forgotten or ignored by their colleagues. The danger for the members of the standing committee was that they might be perceived as so walled round and inaccessible (and perhaps so united in their own internal consultations) that the views of the staff could never reach them, let alone influence them or affect in any way the decisions ultimately made by the headmaster. It was to offset this danger that the committee embarked on a long and arduous series of meetings with individual members of the staff during the spring term. Concurrently, in senior staff meetings, discussions were becoming less and less agenda-ridden and more and more focused on fundamental problems about curriculum change and staff deployment, in a system that had to take account both of its opportunities and of the constraints placed upon it by the environment of which it was a part.

By the end of the summer term of 1969, despite or perhaps because of the strains the staff had had to live through, the way was clear for a new kind of consultative structure, a system that had an inner logic because it was directly related to the leadership roles that had to be taken daily within the institution. In the next four chapters we shall be examining the evolution of the new top management group and the problems that were being explored concurrently in the complex and changing area of middle management.

CHAPTER VII

Authority and Responsibility in the Top-management Group

Difficulties in clarifying boundaries in a new structure

In the context of discussion about school organization, the term 'top management' would, until recently, have referred to the two or at most three people at the top of the hierarchy, namely, the head and the deputy head in a single-sex school, or these two plus the senior master or mistress in a mixed school. But this is changing. 'Top management' may now refer to a group comprising the six, eight, maybe even ten or twelve most senior members of the staff. Who, then, qualifies to serve on the management committee or in the 'cabinet', once the head admits into his closest councils colleagues other than the deputy head and the man or woman next in rank?

As soon as the pair or 'triumvirate' is augmented by other members of the staff, the distinction between senior and very senior colleagues—formerly blurred by such terms as 'department heads', 'section heads' and 'house heads'—has to be made much more overt. We can no longer disguise the fact that those in the top-management group have greater responsibility and are therefore nearer to the head during the process of decision-making than are the members of middle management. And as the size of the top-management group increases, so it becomes more important than ever that the boundaries on which different leadership roles are located are clearly identified by all members of the institution, so that people are not brought into the top-management committee for the wrong reasons—that is, in the interest of reassuring individuals rather than in the interest of carrying out the task of the institution.

At Nailsea the creation of the standing committee in 1969 immediately brought the heads of the lower, middle and upper schools into a real consultative relationship with the headmaster and his two most senior colleagues. Thus the fantasy that house heads and sections heads were of roughly equal status, which had persisted despite the known differences between the D Grade allowances for house heads and the E Grade allowances for section heads, could no longer be maintained. But the standing committee did not become a top-management group magically overnight. The process of becoming one was, I believe, long and arduous. Concurrently with this process, the rest of

188

the senior staff on both sides of the former curricular-pastoral divide, in the newly constituted senior staff meeting where they worked alongside the members of the standing committee, must have found themselves in a more complex but more reality-based situation than in the previous year.

The subconscious wish to keep the new boundaries slightly blurred showed itself in various ways during the months that led up to and followed the setting up of the new management structure. Often it was Denys John himself who became the unwitting instrument of these unconscious manoeuvres to prevent the new roles and the new sub-groups from disturbing the old and valued patterns of relationships. Thus, for example, the four house heads continued during the summer of 1969 to have weekly meetings alternately with him and with Robin Thomas, joined, after a few weeks, by Clive Vanloo. Yet the continuation of these meetings, just because they were still 'in the time-table', implied a denial that it was with Clive Vanloo that the house heads ought by then to have been conferring about house problems, since he had had delegated to him by April 1969 the responsibility for heading, or 'managing', the middle school. It seemed that the house heads could not bear to relinquish entirely their special privilege as the 'pastoral' leaders in the school, and that Denys John could not quite bring himself to make the house heads face the full implications of the new role of 'head of middle school' and the fear that their own status might thereby suffer reduction.

This mutual difficulty in ending a practice that was not consistent with the changes being introduced into the management structure was paralleled later in the new standing committee itself, by the continuation into the autumn term of the weekly meetings at which Denys John had hitherto consulted with Robin Thomas and Joan Bradbury about current school problems. Yet the continuation of these meetings implied a denial that the standing committee, with its additional three members, was now the top-management group.

I became aware of the difficulty the committee members were experiencing because of this built-in split between the two sub-groups when, after the second standing committee meeting, I found myself involved in a kind of post-mortem discussion, not with the headmaster alone, which would have been appropriate in terms of my role as consultant, but with the original top-management 'triumvirate', in the absence of their three colleagues. The latter part of the committee meeting had been focused on the question of the possible need for separate staff meetings for the lower, middle and upper-school tutorial staff groups, to be taken by the respective section heads, perhaps once or twice a term in place of some of the monthly full staff meetings. At the end of this session Robin Thomas and Joan Bradbury went out of the head's room with the other three; but a few minutes later there was a knock at the door and the two re-entered and walked straight over to the table, obviously returning for their scheduled meeting with Denys John.

He at that moment was talking to me about his growing fear that he might ultimately become redundant in his own school. He had just said—in a mood that I can only describe as a sort of comic depression—that if more time were thenceforth to be spent in sectional staff meetings he would begin to feel, on his rare appearances at full staff meetings, rather like the Pope being brought down and shown to the people. And so it was this problem—of how a leader comes to terms with feelings of being left out, after delegating authority to colleagues—that became the main theme of this meeting of the former top-management group, at which I was present more by accident than by design.

Robin Thomas and Joan Bradbury discussed the problem as though it were peculiar to the situation of a headmaster who might feel diminished in proportion to the amount of responsibility he gave to others to take over parts of his own former role. But these two themselves had been experiencing for some months a good deal of uncertainty about the validity of their own roles, which, in contrast to the leadership roles exercised by John Harbinson, Clive Vanloo and Mike Burnham in their sections of the school, were gradually being reduced to mere administrative functions with occasional deputizing tasks. And so there were really two ways of interpreting the fact that Denys John, having set up his new standing committee two weeks earlier, had been unable to bring himself to discontinue his weekly scheduled meetings with his two most senior colleagues. In one way the meetings could be seen as serving to protect him from his own growing sense of isolation; but they could also be seen as an unconscious device to protect the other two from the fear that it might be they, the deputy head and the senior mistress, rather than he who would become redundant. As long as these two roles existed, there was bound to be a problem for the head in determining when it was appropriate for him to consult only his deputy or only the deputy and the senior mistress, and when it would have been excluding the other three from the newly established consultative procedure to do this.

The heads of the lower, middle and upper schools, when they became officially part of the top-management group at Nailsea, had to make a difficult transition from their former position, which had kept them at some distance from the triumvirate, to a new position in which they could almost have replaced the deputy head and the senior mistress as the headmaster's closest advisers, because their own leadership roles in the three main sections of the school put them in touch with the real burning issues in the staff group. This take-over might well have happened, had not the committee from the moment of its inception held regular long weekly lunch-time meetings in which the problems inherent in these new role relationships, as well as the scheduled items for consideration of the committee, were discussed.

The work of examining these problems was linked—for the standing committee as for the earlier O & A group—with questions about the control of the group's own boundary, or, in other words, with criteria on which to base decisions about the admission or exclusion of visitors. I myself was an almost permanent visitor throughout the 1969–70 academic year, except on certain occasions when other commitments made it impossible for me to attend meetings. I always tried to make it clear that I never regarded myself as a 'member' of the committee, any more than I regarded myself as a 'member' of the staff. But I was always present with a definable role, usually as a consultant. Thus, although my role did change in the latter phase, in that at times the committee accepted a role as a consultant group to myself as the author of this book, the purpose of my presence at their meetings was, I believe, generally understood, or, if not understood, openly questioned.

On two occasions, very early in its history, the boundary was broken by visitors who had no continuing role in the group; and much later, during the spring term, there was a series of meetings at which individual members of the staff group met the standing committee to put forward views or to raise questions about curriculum developments. On all these occasions the committee experienced difficulties in varying degrees in preserving its own boundary without denying its relationship with the rest of the staff group and in admitting conflicting ideas without becoming swamped or immobilized by them. But by the time the spring meetings took place there was a growing recognition of the importance of clarifying the task of the committee in a particular meeting and the role of a visitor or visitors during that meeting.

The two earlier, isolated, instances of this kind of breaking of the committee's boundary, although related to similar kinds of innovation as were the later instances, both had elements of the 'entertaining of a visitor' that tended to obscure some of the difficulties in the role relationships that were being experienced. The first of these earlier visitors was the new school counsellor, Margaret Fisher, who was asked to attend the second meeting of the standing committee in the third week of the term, so that she could talk with the committee, following a preliminary discussion with Denys John the day before, about her role in the school and about foreseeable problems that would arise, both for herself and for her colleagues once her work with children got under way. The second visitor (in the fourth week of term) was not a member of the school staff but a Schools Council project director from London who was currently visiting a number of schools in which integrated courses in humanities were being taught, with a view to studying the effects of these innovatory practices upon the curriculum as a whole.

In neither of these meetings was the discussion entirely limited to the specific field in which the visitor's concerns were located. Thus the discussion with Margaret Fisher about counselling and the discussion with the London visitor about the humanities course overlapped with the committee's explorations of their own problems of role change in moving from this kind of meeting to the senior staff meetings or full staff meetings that sometimes followed it, and with their discussion about the advisability or otherwise of having regular meetings for the lower, middle and upper-school tutors in their separate sections.

For the London visitor there was no problem of an aftermath. But for Margaret Fisher there was, since she was one of those colleagues who later came to the standing committee, in the spring-term series of consultations, to discuss various aspects of curriculum change. On her first visit, in the middle of September, she joined the group for lunch, helped with the serving out, and enjoyed, perhaps, the illusion that she was, in effect, a 'member of the group' during that session. But on the second occasion, at the end of January, she did not join the committee at lunch, but was asked explicitly— as all other colleagues were during that term—to come after the meal. This assertion of the committee's right to hold its usual private meeting over lunch, before facing other colleagues, was evidently felt by her to be a rejection; the discovery that she was not a 'member' of this group had, for her more than any of her colleagues, a certain element of shock.

But Margaret Fisher was not by any means the only member of the staff to experience difficulty in penetrating the boundary of the standing committee. For her the difficulty was to come to terms with the fact that the boundary really existed; for others the difficulty was to come to terms with the fact that although the boundary existed it was essential that it should be broken in appropriate ways for the committee to do its job.

Curriculum development as a focus for thinking in a new top-management committee

During the autumn of 1969 the new committee had found itself increasingly preoccupied with questions about the leadership of new courses. As we saw in Chapter IV these questions were focused particularly on the lower-school humanities course, officially built into Year I and extended partially into Year II in the pilot course being taught to two of the tutor groups by Graeme Osborn and Bob Jarratt. In December, Denys John produced for the consideration of the committee a paper to which he gave the title 'Rationalization of direction of "new" courses'. This paper was based on Phenix's concept of 'realms of meaning'[1] and it attempted to relate the existing departments and the emerging courses to the categories 'personal education', 'empirics', 'synoptics', 'aesthetics' and 'symbolics'.

The paper was full of the imagery of birth, adoption, christening and rechristening. Thus the history department was seen as having already adopted courses on citizenship and the British constitution, geography as having adopted geology and local studies, art as likely to adopt the new fourth and fifth-year creative studies and R.E. as a possible contender for the adoption of humanities and H.R. work. Art, music, technical education and home economics were seen as loosely associated together under the general heading of 'aesthetic subjects', and the tiny one-teacher department of commerce as belonging partly to the general area of empirics and partly to the area of symbolics. More alarmingly, perhaps, R.E., R.K., H.R. and

[1] Phenix, P. H. (1964), *Realms of Meaning; A Philosophy of the Curriculum for General Education*, McGraw Hill.

humanities were seen as grouped, along with tutorial work, under the possible new heading 'personal education'—alarmingly, because any move in the direction of identifying a curricular area of this kind was bound to be felt as an encroachment into territory that belonged to all teachers, whatever their specialism, and could certainly not be conceded to the specialist associated with religious education in particular.

Following the discussion in the standing committee, the paper was distributed to all staff. At the beginning of the spring term it elicited a sort of counter paper from Lewis Smith, who came to the first of the consultative meetings to discuss his ideas further with the committee. Denys John then wrote and distributed a reply to this counter paper. It was partly to follow up and explore staff reactions to these three papers and partly to extend to other special areas the kind of opportunity given to David Williams to discuss the future of drama, that the standing committee opened itself up to the subsequent series of consultative meetings with colleagues. Over this matter, at the January meeting of the senior staff, Denys John did something that he very rarely did: having asked his colleagues whether they would be willing to let the standing committee handle the questions that needed to be explored, he then took a vote. This gave him sanction to use the standing committee as a base for all the subsequent consultations.

His next move was to issue a verbal invitation in the staff room during a mid-morning break, which was heard at least by some staff members as an invitation to 'sit in on' standing committee discussions. A duplicated notice was then issued to all staff, following this verbal approach, inviting colleagues to 'present views' or 'ideas' about any part of the emerging curriculum pattern or about rationalization of the new courses 'across the whole field under consideration'. The note drew attention to the existence of the papers that had already been distributed; and it requested those who wished to talk with the standing committee to complete an attached form, which was headed 'Curriculum Pattern and Direction of new Courses', and read: 'Please indicate briefly the question(s) to be raised'.

Now this written notice allowed for a wide scope of contributions, but it did put upon staff other than those on the standing committee the onus of formulating some kind of comments in advance of actually meeting the committee. If the verbal invitation that preceded the issuing of this circular did contain the phrase 'sit in on', it may have conveyed the idea that the committee was open to observers, as, in the preceding year, the O & A group had been. The typed circular, on the other hand, made it clear that anyone who responded to the invitation had to come to the committee either with some new proposals or with comments upon those already put forward. The staff were thus being asked to enter into a continuous dialogue with the headmaster and his closest colleagues about long-term policy. This implied that they had to accept responsibility for the kind of influences they brought to bear upon the head during the discussions leading up to decisions.

Between 21 January and 15 March the committee held twenty of these consultations, at which they talked with twenty-eight members of the staff. Of these, six came together as a department (the P.E. department), six came in pairs (the first pair to discuss humanities, the second to discuss human biology and rural studies, and the third to discuss classical studies) and the remaining sixteen (including eight department heads) came alone. When pairs came they acted with complete unanimity, as did the members of the P.E. department, who allowed Bob Miller to be their spokesman. It was only in the series of meetings with individuals that certain divergences of interest and belief within departments became perceptible to the committee, although not yet in a way that enabled any of its members, or even the headmaster himself, to bring them into the public arena for open exploration in full staff meetings.

As the meetings went on the committee found itself having to contain an accumulating mass of incompatible ideas. But it was not only ideas that were jostling together demanding their attention. They were, as one member of the committee put it, having to handle people's emotions. Sometimes, indeed, it was very difficult to disentangle the feelings from the thoughts, or to be sure how to account for the kind of behaviour, described wonderingly by another member of the committee as 'bizarre', that colleagues were quite unexpectedly exhibiting. Moreover, by the end of the term it was becoming clear that certain members of staff who were in different ways concerned about the curricular matters under discussion and therefore presumably had a stake in the kind of exploration of fundamental issues that the committee was trying to promote, were choosing not to present themselves at all. Among these were the following: Graham Morris, whose experience as chairman of the O & A group might have been valuable to the committee and whose current concern about general studies in the sixth form was relevant to the discussions; Phillip Armitage and Robin Grist, the recently appointed heads of science and mathematics, who had allowed themselves to be receptacles for other people's conservatism despite evidence that they themselves as persons were not opposed to all kinds of change; and Reg Clarke, who came only as someone who helped with the work of the P.E. department and not in his own right as the person responsible for remedial work, and whose role was suffering a good deal of modification about which he was known to be uneasy. It was also noticeable that none of the house heads (apart from Graeme Osborn who came on behalf of humanities and not in his role as house head) took advantage of the opportunity to be involved in these discussions with the top-management group about curriculum change.

Relations between the top-management group and the rest of the staff

For Denys John, the purpose of these meetings was, initially, to involve the staff in the process of working out some way of rationalizing the departmental structure by redefining the boundaries round areas of knowledge and skill, and by clarifying where the leadership of the new courses was to be located. It was not surprising, therefore, that colleagues who opted to take advantage of the invitation did so either to bring to the committee their doubts about the fate of their own established courses in the future pattern or to bring proposals for entirely new courses that would cut across existing subject boundaries.

The humanities course had been initiated centrally, the idea emanating from the headmaster himself, who had called a series of lunchtime meetings of the heads of the arts departments during the 1967–8 session to discuss the possibilities of a team-based approach to first-year work in this general area. But the new proposals for subject-free courses were coming from relatively young and recently appointed members of the staff, who were seeking ways of combining their own special skills with allied interests in neighbouring fields of study. The standing committee was visited by four such people, who arrived with varying degrees of confidence to sell their ideas to top management. One scientist proposed a new lower-school course in creative technology, bringing with him a collection of models to illustrate the kind of work he believed children could do in this area if their inventiveness in relation to specific tasks was given scope; a second scientist proposed a new course for the less able pupils in the fourth and fifth years, a course on man, his home and his environment, which would draw together the various bits at present located in science, home economics and social studies and would make use of elements of sociology and economics; an English specialist sought some way of devising a time-table that would allow for more collaboration between teachers of English, art, music and drama, not only pre-planned collaboration but also unforeseen and unforeseeable spontaneous developments cutting across different teaching groups; and a geographer presented ideas about changing the focus of geography teaching so that it leaned more towards the empirical sciences and deductive methods and less towards regional studies and descriptive methods.

The standing committee thus found itself having to provide an equally sympathetic hearing to those enthusiasts for new courses who seemed to be saying: 'Listen to me! Give me my head! Promote me!' and to the guardians of already established courses who seemed to be saying: 'Protect my interests! Look after what you already have! Value my long experience!' Because those who appeared in the first category were, in general, younger and more exuberant in their approach to the committee, they impressed themselves on me as people who seemed to be acting out a policy of intrusiveness in the sense that they injected into the committee with varying degrees of forcefulness demands for change and modification. Conversely, those who came into the second category seemed to be acting out a policy of protectiveness, in the sense that they were seeking to preserve what already existed rather than to make proposals about new developments. And just as young people seemed to dominate the first category, so older people seemed to dominate the second, which was hardly surprising, since the older people had much to lose and the younger people much to gain by radical change.

The problem for the committee was to know how to respond to the excitement of the new thinking and at the same time acknowledge the constraints of time, space and personnel without merely using these as blocking devices. For what they were really being presented with was a problem about shifting boundaries. Which, in future, would be the containing boundary: the course, the single subject or academic discipline, or the new multi-subject department? Would the director of a course in creative technology, for example, find himself out in a no-man's land that was neither science nor technical education nor art? Or would he be carving out for himself a new territory that would take over parts of these departments? How could the projected course on man, his home and his environment, if rooted in science, ever get under way without prejudicing the existing courses in social studies, humanities and home economics? And how would the already established course in human biology be affected by this new outcrop? It seemed that people who offered themselves as the initiators of such new studies were taking considerable risks. For they could find themselves being encouraged, only to end up as the loneliest people on the staff; or they could be seen as trying to dislodge their seniors and push their way into the seats of power by getting the headmaster on their side at the outset.

The use of the standing committee as a receptacle for apparently incompatible ideas was reminiscent of the way in which, in other kinds of meetings, certain staff members had colluded with one another to keep the play of opposites going. The effect was always to exaggerate the differences between individuals and to deny the conflicts within departments or the tensions within individuals. The unconscious collusion to keep such polarization going also diminished the areas in which staff were in fact able to share convictions. That such areas existed was demonstrated, both in November 1969 and again a year later, by the Open-Day exhibitions of children's work. From these it was evident that departments were reaching out towards one another in many ways. Thus mathematics went hand in hand with artistic design in the preparation of mathematical graphs and models; scientific findings were presented by many pupils with imagination and artistry and with a sense of personal discovery; technical education was seen to be incorporating jewellery making and wood carving, and geology to be encouraging the development of sensitivity to form and texture; the study of oil drilling and processing might be rooted in any one of a number of subjects or courses such as physics, geology or sixth-form general studies; a chemist who had discovered an interest in history and art through making a collection of brass rubbings was sharing this enthusiasm and teaching the skill to a group of pupils, whose rubbings were exhibited side by side with his own in the part of the main building that was described, appropriately enough, as the Link Block.

We have to recognize that this linking and merging of subjects, while it suggests an enrichment of experience for pupils and the possibility of far-reaching changes in the way their teachers work together, also brings into the staff group accompanying fears lest the new ideas emanating from one teacher or group of teachers or from one department or pair of departments may cancel out or in some way inhibit the growth of new ideas appearing in another area. In other words, the same teacher may be saying at the same time: 'Co-operate with me in this new venture!' and 'Keep off my territory!' We all want to share our new ideas and have them accepted; but—perversely —we also want to keep them to ourselves and defend them against possible competitors.

The immediate effect of this rich flow of ideas—because of the collusive polarization that accompanied it—was that Denys John found himself for a while almost immobilized. By presenting him with mutually destructive attitudes, the staff made it extremely difficult for him to make any decision that would not be interpreted as favouring those at one pole at the expense of those at the other pole. Yet there were elements of innovation in the old established courses that were being defended just as there must have been elements of traditionalism in the new courses that were being advocated.

There were quite startling deviations in the way different staff members approached the committee when they presented themselves in the head-master's room to attend a meeting. Those who came in the second half of the series were, on the whole, less anxious or if they were anxious were better able to make constructive use of that anxiety. To what extent this reflected the increasing skills of the committee members themselves to make use of the resources within the staff group and to what extent it indicated that it was the more anxious members who pressed for the earlier appointments it is very hard to say. But why should these people have experienced so much anxiety about presenting their opinions and ideas, or even about expressing their misgivings, to colleagues, all of whom (including the headmaster himself) were well known to them as persons who were perfectly approachable in the day-to-day context of school life?

The standing committee had credentials that no-one could question—a fact that was acknowledged very seriously by the head of physics in the first combined senior staff meeting, when he said, speaking it seemed for his colleagues as well as for himself, that he felt the setting up of this committee made a great deal of sense and that there was no doubt in his mind that the right people were serving on it. The validity of the committee's task and the appropriateness of its membership was also acknowledged later by the head of modern languages, in an individual interview with me, when he said that the setting up of the committee had freed him to get on with his real task by taking off his back the necessity to accept part of the responsibility for over-all leadership in the work of policy-making.

If the credentials of the committee were beyond question, anyone who took the risk of facing that committee, whether as an individual or as a representative of sectional interests, was liable to feel exposed to the scrutiny of the committee and bereft of the support of like-thinking colleagues. The shock for the committee was the discovery that those of their colleagues who responded to the head's invitation by attending a meeting in order to present ideas about future developments or comments on current proposals, did so almost as though they were attending some kind of interview, by implication to apply for new posts that might come into existence along with changes in the curricular pattern, or to defend their right to remain in the posts they already occupied. The shock for the committee's visitors was to discover that they *were* only visitors—that although they could join a particular meeting, they could not join the committee, but could only attempt to hold some kind of dialogue with it. Because of this sense of a mutual distancing, the sessions, while extremely fruitful of ideas, were fraught with emotional difficulties on both sides.

Denys John in particular found himself torn between his wish to put his colleagues at their ease and his wish to pursue the real task of the committee. A lunch-hour meeting would start, as in the weeks before this special series of meetings, with lunch in the headmaster's room, with no other colleagues present; two people would be scheduled to join the meeting after lunch, the first at 1.20 and the second at 1.40. But twenty minutes never gave anybody enough time to develop with the committee the theme that he or she had come to discuss: and it might not always be clear whether the 1.20 visitor knew that another was due at 1.40. And so Denys John would find himself unwittingly providing for the needs of one visitor—usually but not always the earlier one—at the expense of the other. In his anxiety to offset the nervousness people felt about coming face to face with this top-management group, and perhaps also in his own nervousness about conducting this kind of dialogue in the presence of his most senior colleagues rather than in the much easier face-to-face situation which had been the familiar situation formerly, he would go out of his way to make the visitors feel welcome by assuring them as they entered that they could sit anywhere at the table since no-one had special seats, and by avoiding any overt suggestion that they should leave when their time was up. Thus the most insistent of the visiting colleagues were able to occupy the committee for a longer period than the scheduled twenty minutes, whereas the less insistent were liable to find their interviews squeezed into less than twenty minutes, even on one occasion squeezed out altogether and postponed for ten days.

The dilemma in which Denys John was being placed had already been recognizable in the paper that he had written in December on 'Rationalization of direction of "new" courses'. Two months later, after fifteen of these consultative meetings, including eight with individual department heads, he fell back on the theoretical structure that he had incorporated into that earlier paper, and tried, with the committee, to construct a grid by means of which all the existing subjects and courses might be related to these 'realms of meaning' as described by Phenix. The list proved so long, and subjects and courses alike so intractable that the attempt was abandoned. But the struggle to wrest a pattern from all this brought home to the committee the extent to which the concept of a department had been confused with the concept of a course in the debate that had been going on. Lewis Smith, indeed, in his reply to the head's paper, had suggested that three quite different concepts had been used almost inter-changeably—the concept of a course, the concept of a subject and the concept of a department that might embrace several subjects; and he had urged that people should be clear which of these they were talking about at any given time. Denys John's own comment on his own paper had in fact been more devastating than Lewis Smith's; for he had said sadly to the committee after their first discussion on it in December: 'But this is only an aspirin!'

His own difficulty in knowing how to respond to the varying needs of the staff was not unlike that experienced by any subject teacher in wondering how to respond to the varying needs of pupils. On the one hand he would have liked, perhaps, to revolutionize the curriculum, to start from the beginning, having discarded all the old categories; on the other hand, he could not go back on agreements made with the department heads, whose graded posts and the responsibilities that went with them had to be conserved, any more than a specialist teacher could disregard the expectations of pupils and parents that he would ultimately 'get his pupils through their examinations'. The long-term problem for Denys John was how to work with the staff towards some kind of redeployment of skills, knowledge and expertise that would make a reconstruction of the field of knowledge possible without sacrificing individual teachers or penalizing individual pupils.

But there was also a short-term problem; how to ensure that those already engaged in teaching the new courses had adequate leadership. And so one thing that emerged from this struggle to match the Phenix realms of meaning to the Nailsea departments was the recognition that the top-management group had to face the painful task of choosing a person to head the humanities team, a task that necessitated the matching of a person to a role and could not really be evaded through the mechanism of finding an 'adopting' department. The reluctance of Denys John and his committee to do this earlier was understandable: for in schools, as in other institutions, promotion and recognition for one person may imply for another a lack of recognition or even a subtle kind of demotion.

The decision to ask Graeme Osborn, in view of his experience in handling this work, to take over the leadership role, was not arrived at without difficult examination of criteria on the part of the committee or without discomfort and even pain, both for them in arriving at the decision and for those colleagues who, in coming to terms with it, had to face their own feelings of disappointment, let-down or apprehension. No-one was more directly affected than the new head of R.E., David Sellick; for, less than three weeks before this decision was made, he had responded to Denys John's 'Rationalization of leadership' paper by bringing to the standing committee his proposals for a new department of 'personal education', which was to have embraced humanities. This move had exposed him to the double risk of being either elevated to a position that would have made him a threatening object to all his colleagues or of appearing to have been given considerably less responsibility than he felt capable of handling in the general management structure. It was inevitable, therefore, that he would—at least for a while—appear diminished in his own eyes, if not in the eyes of colleagues, by the appointment of Graeme Osborn as director of the humanities course, even though the position did not command any increase in salary or any official change of post, and even though he was sufficiently in sympathy with Graeme Osborn's approach to be able to work constructively with him in planning and implementing the new course. But the heads of the other 'contributing' departments may also have felt a shadow moving over their areas of responsibility. Was the naming of a director of the new course to be only the first move towards the creation of a department of humanities that would embrace the hitherto independent departments of English, history and geography? And what about the people who were raising the wind in other areas of the curriculum? Were they perceived as putting in their bids, not just for new courses, but for new subjects that might later burgeon into departments?

Perhaps all this sounds exaggerated or merely alarmist. Are colleagues really as competitive or as threatening to one another as I am suggesting? And if they are, what kind of leadership can they be having to allow such things to happen? The answer probably is that not many staff groups do experience this kind of open acknowledgement of anger, doubt and confusion. But I am suggesting that the feelings—even if unexpressed—are there in all schools, and that it was precisely because morale was high in this school that the risks of exposing conflicts could be taken. I am also suggesting that the top management was ultimately strengthened rather than weakened by its capacity to tolerate this kind of discomfort and live with a certain amount of risk.

I do not, therefore, offer these observations in order to make judgements or to imply that the discussions that were held were empty. On the contrary, I believe that there was a great deal of important and necessary testing out going on. The process enabled the committee members to test the reality of their roles as members of a new top-management group, not only in relation to colleagues in the staff group outside the committee's boundary but also in relation to one another. It enabled the staff group to test the sincerity of Denys John's consultative procedures by putting him through a considerable ordeal which exposed his own leadership skills in a more personal way than, perhaps, they had ever been exposed before. And it enabled certain individual members of the staff group to expose their own bewilderment and frustration in the face of accelerating change and others to expose their own excitement, even their missionary zeal, in a relatively safe and protected place. The committee could have misused much of what took place in those meetings, as indeed I could. In fact the committee was trusted with a great deal, as perhaps I was also.

Study of tensions and anxieties within the standing committee

It was after one of these meetings that I became aware, for the second time, of the split between the old top management and the former 'top middle management' in this committee. In this meeting—a late afternoon one— a situation had developed in which the 'visitor' (Joy Sollars) had subjected the committee to some rather sharp criticism about the way changes were being effected in the curriculum and had in turn been put under distinctly uncomfortable pressure by members of the committee to spell out then and there the teaching objectives of her department. Somehow in the end, Denys John found himself left doing all this probing and pressurizing, as though on the committee's behalf, to the point where he almost seemed to be persecuting the visitor. Angry both with him and with his colleagues (who were completely opting out of the discussion) and also with Joy Sollars, who had brought a good deal of hostility into the meeting in the first place, I found myself saying that I thought the situation was becoming cruel and that I did not know where the cruelty had started. The interview then came to a rather abrupt end. Joy Sollars left, evidently feeling rather offended by what had happened, and the second visitor (David Sellick) came in almost immediately afterwards, but not before Denys John had protested indignantly about my intervention. David Sellick had clearly come to offer new ideas rather than to defend the *status quo*. In fact this was the occasion referred to earlier, when he presented his proposals for a 'department of personal education'. An hour later he was still there, and in all that time I had been unable to say a word, although the committee members had seemed quite undisturbed about what had occurred in the earlier part of the session with the other colleague. It almost seemed that I had had to contain the conflicts so that the committee could be freed to work with the second visitor. Eventually the discussion with him came to an end and he left. As the committee was breaking up to follow I made an explosive comment to the effect that they had now been protected by the presence of a visitor from examining what had been going on earlier in the session. Mike Burnham, John Harbinson and Clive Vanloo were already on their way to the door and left hurriedly. Although I was about to follow, I found myself almost being held in the room by Denys John, Robin Thomas and Joan Bradbury who were clearly as anxious as I was that some clarification should be sought about what had happened between the head and myself, between the head and the rest of the committee and between the committee and the first visitor. In fact we talked for three-quarters of an hour. Meanwhile, as we learned several days later, the other three members of the committee—far from being well on their way home and therefore out of reach—were waiting, first in the staff room and later in the car park, wondering whether they would be asked to return.

Four days later the committee had an unexpected opportunity to look back at this incident and at the confused feelings it had left in the two halves of the group. In this meeting, quite painful uncertainties were voiced about the internal relationships in the committee itself and anxieties were expressed about how they were functioning as a group in relation to colleagues. It was in this meeting that, for the first time, I felt—suddenly and dramatically—that the standing committee had now in reality become a top-management group: a group that was prepared to think, not only about the feelings and thoughts of their colleagues but also about their own task as a management group committed to working with all sections of the staff and all the individual members of it, however divergent and contradictory and incompatible might be the ideas these different people brought in to them.

The right to be on such a committee by virtue of the leadership role a person has in the institution does not in itself include any certainty, in his eyes or in the eyes of his colleagues, that he has the competence to exercise the right effectively. If the standing committee had to accept the need of the staff to test its competence as a working group, every member of it had to realize that his or her own competence as an individual entrusted with this role was being tested all the time, since every new situation presented new challenges that could not be matched by former experience.

No-one was more exposed during this process than the headmaster himself, for the more he opened up problems for discussion in the staff group the more did he make available for study his own way of exercising leadership. On several occasions in department heads' meetings and in full staff meetings, as we have seen, this examination of his role and of the basis of his authority became quite open and explicit. And in the standing committee it came under the spotlight even more. In the early days it was his relationship with the staff outside the boundary of the committee that was discussed; in the later days the members of the committee recognized and responded to the need to examine their own relationship to him.

It was no surprise that the later discussions in this area proved to be more searching and uncomfortable than the earlier ones. It was easier to use the pronoun 'they' than the pronouns 'I' and 'we', particularly when it was disharmony and opposition rather than harmony and agreement that were under scrutiny. It was relatively easy for Mike Burnham to suggest to Denys John in October 1969 that he was a 'good headmaster' but a 'bad public relations man', that he ought to have a special staff meeting to present a statement about his policy for the school and that he might perhaps institute a 'Headmaster's seminar' for new staff members. It was much more difficult for him to say in the standing committee about six months later that it had cost him a good deal to be on this committee, that he missed the pairing relationship he had had with Denys John in previous years, when he had consulted him privately about matters arising in his section of the school, and that he found it difficult to share that consultative relationship with the other members of the committee. In acknowledging his own wish for a close personal relationship with the head, Mike Burnham was expressing in a direct, undisguised way,' what many other staff expressed less openly, sometimes as individuals, sometimes in pairs or sub-groups. Phillip Armitage, for example, had a regular weekly discussion with the head, over and above the senior staff meetings (and the earlier department heads' meetings) evidently on the grounds that he ran the largest and most complex department; and it seems probable that this privilege was associated, both for himself and for Denys John, with the fact that he was the only head of a subject department with a Grade E allowance and therefore the only senior staff member at that level who was not in the standing committee. This need for a special relationship denied to other staff was also expressed, as we have seen, in the continuations of the head's meetings with Robin Thomas and Joan Bradbury after the institution of the standing committee, and of his meetings with the four house heads, after the appointment of Clive Vanloo as head of middle school. It took a rather dramatic form about six weeks after the opening of the autumn term of 1969 when the new members of the staff, of whom there were fourteen, asked for a separate meeting with the head, in order to talk with him about their experiences as incoming staff and their reactions to the school of which they now found themselves a part.

It was in fact Denys John's own rather depressed account of that meeting given to the standing committee a few days later that prompted Mike Burnham's remark about the head as a public relations man. For the new staff had made very critical, not to say hostile, comments about the school, complaining of the 'bad manners' of pupils and even of colleagues, and saying that they were very confused about what was expected of them because of the difficulties of accepting the 'new' Nailsea School image and because the established staff varied so widely in the kinds of demands they made on children, in terms of standards of both work and behaviour. They had also expressed surprise that there was so little unanimity of opinion in the staff group concerning educational policies and implied that such conflicts of ideas had not been present in the schools from which they had come or of which they had heard or in which they had done their teaching practice as students. My own immediate reaction to this and to Denys John's resulting anxiety about whether he was giving enough leadership to his staff was to defend both him and the school from the imputations and to wonder how much suppression of conflicts had been going on in the schools from which these new staff members had come.

His colleagues in the committee seemed to be perceiving these reactions of the new staff as indications of alarm at finding that in this school feelings they were accustomed to keep under cover were being more openly exposed, including feelings that might at times be directed against authority, even the authority of the headmaster. And indeed I identified myself quite strongly with these interpretations of the situation. But as the discussion in the committee went on, I began to wonder how far the anxieties about change were being projected into this sub-group of new colleagues—a sub-group that included two with special responsibilities, the school counsellor and the new head of R.E.—so that they were unconsciously being given the task of expressing on behalf of the established staff the suspicions and discontent about the directions in which the school was moving. Were the members of the standing committee preserving their own solidarity at the expense of new colleagues who were still struggling with the problems of joining the staff group, and so denying some of their own joining problems in the committee itself?

Towards the end of that same committee meeting there was some confirmation that the difficulties of searching for the 'new' Nailsea School image could not all be safely put into the newcomers in the staff group; for the committee members suddenly began to talk almost compulsively about the problem of litter on the school premises. This sudden preoccupation I found puzzling, and even amusing, since in all my comings and goings around the school I had never been aware of litter either indoors or outdoors. Nor had I received any impression that corresponded with the allegations being made by the new staff about the 'bad manners' of the pupils: on the contrary I had always been impressed by their courtesy, whenever I found myself going in or out of the buildings at times when pupils were also moving about the school.

Increasingly it seemed that these anxieties about standards—whether they took the form of complaints about litter, or of assertions that pupils were ill-mannered, or of fears that neither pupils nor staff were sufficiently demanding of themselves in the area of study—were expressing a general uncertainty and uneasiness about shifting boundaries. For as boundaries changed, so leadership roles had to be redefined, with consequent changes in staff relationships. And the more the headmaster delegated the emerging leadership tasks to members of his staff, the less certain people were about what values he himself still regarded as important in the running of his school and what new values he might now be paying more attention to. If he could be made so anxious by the comments of his newly appointed staff as to feel that the school might really be deteriorating, then he might find himself doubting the reality of his own leadership and, by implication, the wisdom of delegating so much of it to senior colleagues. Thus the staff, through the newcomers, seemed to be trying to force him to adopt a more dictatorial approach, failing to recognize that if they had been in a school that did have a dictatorial head, they would probably have been exerting a comparable pressure to *reduce* the amount of direction from the top.

It is becoming evident that the top-management group, as constituted by the autumn of 1969, was far more than the group of six individual members of senior staff than it might at first sight have appeared to be. We are looking at a network of role relationships and personal relationships, even at a system of inter-group relationships, in which pairs and trios were continually forming and reforming as the context of discussion and consultation and action and reaction changed and developed.

On the boundary of this top-management group, partly inside it, partly outside it, Denys John himself seemed at times like a mirror in which his senior colleagues could recognize aspects of themselves, their wanted parts and their unwanted parts; at other times he would seem like something fragmented and distributed and almost lost to himself. And so, in examining the experiences of the different members of the standing committee, we find that their roles, whether we see them as expanding or as diminishing, can be understood only when viewed in the perspective of the headmaster's own response to the changing task of his school. It is this developing pattern of top-management leadership, with its emerging problems concerning the overlapping of old and new roles, that will be the theme of the next chapter.

CHAPTER VIII

Reorganization and the Interplay of Diminishing and Expanding Roles

The person and the role

When we come to examine the specific roles taken by the members of a top management group, we soon discover that they cannot be understood except in terms of their dynamic relationship to one another and to the role of the head. But a committee is not just a cluster of roles: it is also inescapably a group of persons. These persons may have known each other and worked together for a considerable number of years. They are likely to have been faced with the problem of incorporating new colleagues, and of losing old ones. Even if their experience of acting as a committee is short, their attitudes towards one another, both as persons and as professional colleagues, have been building up over a long time.

All this, as we have seen, was true of the Nailsea standing committee. Apart from Clive Vanloo, who had been in the school for only two years before its formation, the members of the committee had been colleagues for at least seven years. Denys John, in addition to being the headmaster whose leadership they accepted, was also very much a person to them—a person with whom each of them had had pairing relationships either in the primary task of the school as a whole or in sub-tasks located in its three main sections (see Figure 41).

I had had very little direct experience, before 1968, of the pattern of role relationships that was emerging at Nailsea during my first year's work with the staff. I had previously thought of 'top management', in so far as I had used this term at all, mainly in terms of a pair: that is, in terms of a head and his or her deputy. It had seemed to me probable that as schools became larger, and as the administrative tasks of leadership became heavier, a staff group might push the one further and further into a purely administrative role, leaving the more rewarding tasks of leadership to the other. Thus, if a headmaster was to be preserved as the human, approachable kind of father figure, his deputy might find himself identified more and more as the cold, rigid and somewhat distant organizer of information. Conversely it seemed possible that the deputy might be preserved as the warm, approachable leader, while the bad feelings about leadership (and indeed about administra-

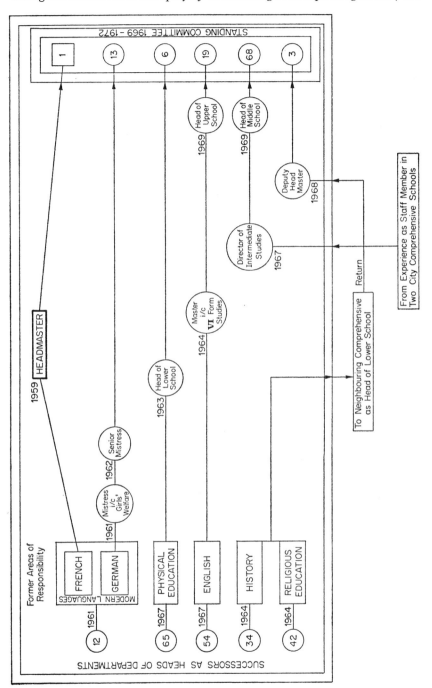

FIG. 41. Former responsibilities of the members of a top management group.

tion) were projected into the head, so that he came to be seen either as a tyrannical figure, looking only for conformity from his staff, or as a somewhat weak figurehead with no real leadership skills at all.

I had always believed that this kind of splitting and projection would be much less likely to happen in a school where there was genuine consultation going on between the head and his deputy and between them and the rest of the staff. What I saw at Nailsea was something a great deal more complex than either my most optimistic image or my most pessimistic image of the head/deputy-head partnership, for I had to begin by looking at a trio, not at a pair, and then found myself having to shift my perspective again in order to look at a small group of six.

The real problem about the increasing size of schools is not just that there are more people around. It is that leadership must be dispersed more widely —that a greater number of the experienced people in the staff group must be given more power. How does a headmaster, having delegated important tasks to colleagues who operate as leaders on the boundaries of sub-systems within the school, provide the over-all leadership that they still need from him? How does he do this without taking back the responsibilities he has delegated to them, and how do they discharge those responsibilities without denying their continuing need of him?

In considering the 'styles' of leadership as they appear to characterize different persons in comparable roles, we have to be on our guard against the danger of creating stereotypes and thus suggesting that each must inevitably remain fixed in the 'personal style' that is most natural to him. Equally we have to avoid falling into the error of perceiving a particular person's style of leadership as wholly the result of pressures exerted upon him so powerfully by those he leads that he has no choice but to act in the way they force him to act. The latter denies the responsibility of the person; the former denies the contributory responsibility of the group, and the demands of the particular institution in which the leadership is being exercised. It is perhaps more useful to speak of 'modes' of leadership rather than 'styles', since this enables us to attend both to the inner consistency of a particular person's approach to the task of giving leadership and to the reality that he will use different modes in different circumstances, without necessarily becoming untrue to what he is as a person or to what he believes as a professional in his job.

If we use Bion's theory to help us to understand how a head can use himself most effectively in the task of giving leadership to the staff group, we can recognize that where one head may be more predisposed to mobilize dependency or pairing, another may be more predisposed to mobilize fight/ flight. The danger for the dependent leader is that he may, metaphorically speaking, be discarded, betrayed or crucified by his followers for failing to be omnipotent and for subjecting them to the discomforts of mutual jealousy and envy and to the fears of abandonment or let-down. The danger for the fight/flight leader is that he will arouse so much hatred and fear that his followers will be unable to work with him and will in the end run away from the task rather than continue to work at it. The leader who—while operating mainly in the dependency/pairing culture—can also mobilize enough fight to enable his dependability to be tested and enough flight for work to go on without his continuing presence—is using his own preferred mode in such a way that his followers, while expecting him to be dependable, are not over-dependent upon him. The leader who, although operating mainly in a fight/flight culture, can also mobilize affection and trust, is using his own preferred mode in such a way that his followers, while engaging him in strenuous, even fierce argument, do not basically want to defeat him or to escape from him. And so it seems that the dependent leader longs for people to challenge and test him, lest he create over-dependent followers, or find that his strength in adversity is underestimated, whereas the fight/flight leader longs for people who will be loyal to him and to whom he can give loyalty, so that his caring side can also find expression. Correspondingly, we need to bear in mind, when we look at the behaviour people show towards a leader (that of a staff group towards its headmaster, for instance) that dependency and opposition are really duals of one another: for behind every rebellion there lurks the need to find someone dependable and someone who cares for one as a person; and behind submissive, dependent behaviour there lies a core of hostility and a wish to oppose.

To describe a headmaster as either 'autocratic' or 'democratic' is to beg all these questions. The problem is to use dependency, fight/flight and pairing appropriately on different occasions, and thus to free staff members to trust but not to trust blindly, to fight but not to fight unthinkingly, to pair but not to pair irresponsibly. I have at times used the word 'paternalism' in describing Denys John in those situations in which he seemed concerned primarily to offer guidance and support and to demonstrate his own dependability. I have described him in a number of other situations in which he accepted a good deal of open opposition from staff. I have also described him as someone who was reluctant to break old pairing or triangular relationships and who was more inclined to protect people from disturbing feelings than expose them to conflict and risk.

I myself had reason, throughout the years of my collaborative project with his school, to be thankful that I was working with a headmaster who could use pairing in a task-centred way. And members of his staff who had come from schools where opposition had been either stifled or explosive must have had similar cause to appreciate that he could be challenged in public as well as in private without working relationships thereby being severed. If, as I believe, his preferred mode of operation as a leader was in a dependency-pairing culture, then he was bound to have to encounter powerfully ambivalent feelings; and because he wanted people to work *with* him rather than merely *for* him, he was bound to be made to wonder whether he was giving them enough direction. Yet by refusing simply to lead his staff by the nose, he enabled those to whom he delegated authority to use it effectively in his absence. I have already implied that the role of deputy head was a difficult one to sustain in a school where other leadership roles seemed often to be overshadowing it, and I will have more to say about this later in this chapter. But it is important to make the point here that Denys John's deputy, both because he himself had the necessary inner authority and strength and because of the head's trust in him, could and did take over his role, if necessary for quite long periods.

Stability and fluidity in an expanding school

It is inevitable that the more a headmaster trusts his senior colleagues to use the authority he delegates to them, the more will he feel his own area of responsibility to be shrinking. Denys John expressed this feeling vividly on one occasion, in the presence of Robin Thomas, Joan Bradbury and myself, when he remarked that although he still signed a good many letters and still answered a good many questions brought into his room by the bursar or her assistants, there seemed to be more and more questions that other people in the school could answer better than he could and fewer and fewer questions for him to answer. Joan Bradbury responded to this by asking him whether he was saying that there were fewer questions to which he was still able to give answers, or that there were fewer questions to which *only he* could give an answer.

As I understood her at the time, she seemed to be saying something about the two-way flow of communication between a headmaster and his senior staff. If real authority is delegated by a head to others, then it follows, appropriately, that he will quite often be in ignorance about matters arising in the day-to-day life of the school. Questions relating directly to a particular section, house or subject department should therefore be taken directly to the appropriate section, house or department head, and not routed through the headmaster. Yet it need not follow that the head be kept in ignorance of important matters arising in any particular part of the school. Nor does it follow that all questions can be referred directly to a member of staff other than the head, since the number of questions about which only he has all the relevant information must be significantly related to the complexity of the institution. Joan Bradbury seemed also to be saying that the person on the outer boundary can tolerate the sense of being less needed most of the time provided he can feel really needed some of the time; the problem for the leader, at the feeling level, is that his own sense of being needed diminishes in proportion as the skills of his followers, as leaders in their own parts of the institution, increase.

As long as a school is as small and intimate as Nailsea School was during the first four years of its existence, when it had a staff group of fewer than 25 and a pupil group of fewer than 500, the head can still feel in touch with those parts of himself that different colleagues unconsciously take over in discharging their responsibilities in the school; similarly, his colleagues can still feel close enough to him to recognize his awareness of them, both in their professional roles and as persons who share with him a sentient system that is graspable within the context of the life and work of the school. But as staff and pupils become more numerous, sub-groups develop, each seeking to create its own sentient system, and the head seems to be faced with two equally uncomfortable alternatives: to become dispersed and fractionated in the attempt to be all things to all people, or to withdraw into remote un-approachability. The nature of this growing complexity is illustrated in Figure 42.

In a time of rapid change, when fundamental questions about school organization and the content of the curriculum are being asked, there is an increase of defensive attitudes as the once familiar pattern of roles and relationships is shaken into new configurations and people become uncertain where they belong within the system. Challenges from pupils inside the school and from parents outside the school produce exaggerated alignments of attitudes and a sharp polarization of opinions about what is needed. Although the head is looked to for answers, even sometimes for direct instructions, in the hope that a way out of the dilemma can be found, the polarization of attitudes itself can have the effect of immobilizing leadership. This, indeed, may be the unconscious intention behind it. Thus, staff protect themselves and one another by making it more and more difficult for the head to reconcile their own conflicting views on questions of fundamental importance, except by making dictatorial decisions. If he listens patiently to everybody and delays his decision, he may be perceived as vacillating; if he makes a decision after minimal delay he may be perceived as riding rough-shod over all his colleagues or as favouring some at the expense of others.

There were eight members of the Nailsea staff (including four of the standing committee, a house head and the heads of classics, modern languages and technical education) who had worked with Denys John since those early years, when the staff group had still been smaller than the average secondary-school class. They had thus lived through with him the expansion of the school, the change from grammar to comprehensive, and the growth of their own sections and departments. As they themselves, in the later years, assumed leadership roles in the expanding staff group, they must have experienced a bewildering series of changes in their own role relationships, both with the head and with one another. By the autumn of 1968, two of these eight were in what I have called the 'triumvirate'; three others were members of the 'section heads' meeting'; and the remaining three were members of the 'department heads' meeting'. In the months before the reorganization of the management structure, as we have seen, those who were in the first two categories had a kind of unofficial right to attend the meetings of those in the third category. Some of these eight staff members, if not all of them,

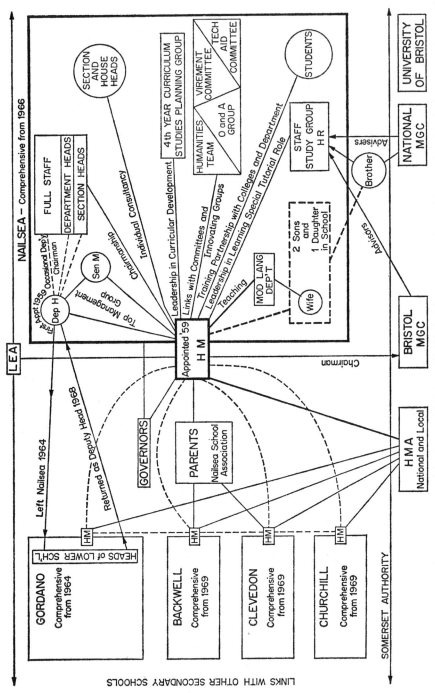

FIG. 42. The changing role of a headmaster: 1968–9.

must have had feelings about their relative status, within the general category of 'staff with special responsibility', as symbolized in their own closeness to or distance from Denys John in the overall pattern of staff consultation. To be part of a meeting attended by only nine people other than the headmaster was without doubt a very different experience from being part of the much larger meeting of twenty-eight; and even among the nine members of the smaller section heads' meeting, there must have been some envy towards the two who had weekly meetings with the headmaster alone.

Nevertheless, the fact that the eight people from the earlier years were still in the staff group of 1970-1 can in itself be taken as a piece of evidence about the capacity of the school to adapt itself creatively to changing circumstances. Despite the occasional storms, despite all the fluctuations of mood, despite the anxieties about changing boundaries, they were still there. Five of them had been away from Nailsea for varying lengths of time: Robin Thomas in a senior post in another school, the other four on secondment—Peter Atkinson for the session of 1963-4, Pip Ridgwell for the session of 1964-5, Joan Bradbury for the autumn of 1964 and Cyril Routley for the session of 1969-70. A headmaster who releases a member of his staff for secondment does so knowing that absence may loosen the roots of that person's attachment to the school, and that secondment is likely to be only a precursor to a permanent move to some other place of work, conceivably to a more senior post. Yet in the year in which this report was being written there were, in addition to the four mentioned above, five other staff members who had been away on secondment between 1967 and 1970: the head of home economics for the 1967-8 session, a member of the history and R.E. departments from December 1968 until February 1970 on a year's exchange with a teacher from Australia, two members of the English department, one for the spring term of 1969, the other for the 1969-70 session, and two members of the department of modern languages, both in the year 1969, one on an exchange with a teacher from Corsica during the spring term, the other to take up a studentship at Oxford University for the summer and autumn terms. All these returned to Nailsea and all but one were still on the staff in the autumn of 1971.

Additional evidence suggesting that Nailsea was regarded as a good school to work in and Denys John as a good headmaster to work with is to be found, perhaps, in the fact that four staff members (teaching French, technical subjects, home economics and general arts subjects) who started in temporary posts, replacing staff members away on secondment, subsequently moved into permanent posts in the school. Four others, after teaching part-time for one, two, three and four years, moved into full-time posts in the departments of history, art, music and modern languages respectively. We can add to this list one full-time teacher in the P.E. department, who, after four years in this post, married and left, but returned as a part-time teacher on the staff for the summer term of the third year to replace someone who was away on secondment.

The headmaster himself, in his report to the governors and parents entitled 'The First Ten Years', distributed in the autumn of 1969, described the 'organization scheme' at the beginning of the eleventh year of the school's existence as having 'evolved from that of a family, through a structure which might be described as tribal, to a complex pattern of interdependency'. The original nuclear 'family', metaphorically speaking, was clearly visible in the standing committee as it existed in the two years following its inception in September 1969, the parental figures being symbolized by Denys John and Robin Thomas, the two survivors in the school of the 1959 staff group of four, the surviving 'children' of this parentage being symbolized by John Harbinson, Joan Bradbury and Mike Burnham, who had taken their places on the staff in that order, and the 'adopted child' from another 'family' being symbolized by Clive Vanloo, who had come to Nailsea five years after Mike Burnham's arrival, bringing with him the experience of working in a well-known London comprehensive school.

Family and tribal imagery was powerfully present in the Nailsea culture in another, more literal, sense also, for the school was very much a neighbourhood school, and as such contained both the satisfactions and problems of multiple role taking for staff, parents and children. Several of the governors and several members of the staff (including the head) had children in the school. Denys John's wife, as we already know, was on the part-time teaching staff, and his brother came from London on a number of occasions, by virtue of his experience in the National Marriage Guidance Council, to help with the work of the H.R. staff study group. The school caretaker was the son of one of the senior members of the staff. And there were known networks of friends who lived near one another in Bristol, Backwell, Clevedon and Portishead, one member living in a flat which he rented in the house of one of his colleagues. The school bursar, who had been with the school since its opening, knew many of the parents personally, and one of her assistants in the Office had previously worked as secretary in the local infant and junior schools and had known many of the children in their earliest years of schooling. One of the department heads had been a supply headmistress for Somerset primary and secondary schools before taking up her post at Nailsea in 1963, and had in that capacity known many of the children who came to Nailsea from the primary school in the neighbouring village where she had lived since the war, and also knew socially the families of some of these children.

In this situation, the pressures on Denys John to run his school like an extended family must have been very strong. It is therefore difficult to know how far the 'paternalism' to which I referred in the last chapter was a characteristic of his own 'personal style' of leadership and how far it was reflecting the family culture that had been built into the school over the years. The determination of the staff to preserve a kind of 'generation gap' between themselves and him was reflected in the almost total reluctance of his colleagues to use his Christian name, either in addressing him or in referring to him, although he always made a point of using theirs, sometimes in combination with a surname, sometimes without the accompanying surname. The only member of staff I ever heard refer to him by his first name in his presence was Joan Bradbury, and that happened first in a meeting between the three of us to discuss a section of my internal report of December 1969. Even in the standing committee he was still 'Mr John' as though even his most senior colleagues, with the possible exception of one, wished to keep him distanced, almost on a pedestal. It was perhaps because this one senior colleague occasionally broke this convention that she was also kept at a certain distance by some of her colleagues, who went half-way between formality and informality by calling her 'Mrs B'; and the same compromise was used in the naming of another married woman on the staff who was about her age. Yet Robin Thomas was almost universally known to his colleagues, both senior and junior, as 'Robin'. It was possible for staff members to find a number of ways of referring to Denys John—both formally and casually—without actually naming him at all. Thus, because of his role, he could be variously described as 'the head', 'the boss', 'the old man'; and occasionally his initials might be used.

I myself, at times, particularly in the early stages of my work with the staff, avoided the difficulty by referring to him as 'the headmaster' (as indeed I have done in certain contexts in this book) and was aware, when doing this, that I was in an uncomfortable way depersonalizing him. More often, however, I used his Christian name and surname together in the larger meetings and his Christian name alone in the smaller meetings. As time went on, I was made to feel more and more exposed as the only person in the school who thus publicly claimed to be on equal terms with him, at least in the matter of how we addressed each other. Consequently I was always left in doubt whether his colleagues regarded this as a privilege that I had been given or as a right that I had claimed. The dilemma for me was that in using this privilege publicly I might seem to be flaunting it; yet failure to use it publicly would have suggested that the privilege was not available to the staff, although any of them could have chosen to exercise it. The apparent subservience of his colleagues in this matter always made me impatient, since it seemed like a refusal to accept their own adult relationship with him; yet my impatience was directed at him too, since I felt he had allowed himself to become trapped in a false situation by too readily assuming that he had the right to use their Christian names without really establishing that they had a corresponding right—perhaps even an obligation—to use his. And so the wish to move into these staff-room relationships socially rather than professionally, or in other words to pre-empt some kind of comfortable sentient group before embarking on the task for which the sentient group was to come into existence, produced an uneasy kind of hybrid situation, which was welcomed by some and resented by others.

If this is a common phenomenon in school staff rooms—and my impression is that it *is* common practice—it seems to indicate a deep need on the part of teachers to put the head of the school, whether man or woman, on the same kind of lonely, isolated platform that they themselves have to occupy in their classrooms, workshops and laboratories and even on the games fields. The headmaster's wife may—as at Nailsea—be accepted on Christian-name terms, but not the head himself. He may even have to suffer being addressed as 'Sir' by a colleague, or, as happened in one staff meeting at Nailsea, by the title 'Headmaster', used as though it were a name. Thus the staff recreate in their own staff group a kind of adult equivalent of the classroom situation, in which the teacher calls his pupils by their first names (or, as in some boys' schools, by their surnames), while remaining 'Mr Smith' or 'Mrs Jones' or 'Miss Brown' (or even 'Sir' or 'Madam' or 'Miss' to them) the only relaxation from this one-way formality being the abbreviated 'Mr S.' or 'Mrs J.' or 'Miss B.', or the nostalgic, perhaps affectionate, nickname.

The convention—while forcing the head into this distanced, isolated position in the sentient system of the staff group—also symbolizes an important truth about the task system; the fact that part of the head's role is to provide an educational experience for his staff. In other words, staff discussions, at whatever level they occur, are vehicles for the growth of ideas and for the development of new skills and knowledge; and in this process the headmaster is indeed a teacher, engaged in training his staff to take more demanding leadership roles, including headships in other schools. This is the hidden part of his boundary function—the part that leaves him exposed to the pain of loss, since in the very act of strengthening the leadership skills of his own colleagues, he is helping them to leave his school in search of promotion outside it.

The changing role of a headmaster

I shall be taking up this general notion of the staff group as a unit for in-service education in my last two chapters. Here we may consider how far the staff at Nailsea, during the particular two-year phase we are studying, were able to see reflected in Denys John's behaviour at different times some of their own fluctuations as teachers. For the choices that he was continually having to make as leader in the staff-room discussions about educational policies and about the specific problems of running this particular school were not, in essence, different from those that his staff were having to make as leaders in classroom, laboratory, studio, workshop and gymnasium. And just as their pupils must have seen them in many shifting perspectives, so they saw him exercising his leadership role in a variety of ways.

At times—particularly when he had been under pressure from parents or governors about standards of work, of behaviour, of dress—he would almost lecture the staff on the ways in which he felt they were falling down, though he would be careful to use the pronoun 'we' rather than 'you', thus acknow-ledging his own share of responsibility for the school's image in the neigh-bourhood. Sometimes he would offer intellectual leads, in the manner of a seminar leader, through duplicated papers on fundamental topics such as staff participation in policy making, the nature of authority, the theoretical bases of curricular development. Sometimes he would set out proposals, almost in the style of a government report or memorandum, on such problems as the reorganization of courses, the setting and supervision of homework and the standardization of assessment procedures. On some occasions he would protect people from their own feelings by avoiding staff discussion of an important event; on others, he would devote a whole meeting to the exploration of attitudes and feelings about such an event. He might introduce a discussion with a careful, detailed explanation of the theme to be con-sidered, or he might wait for others to take the initiative after only the barest of introductions, if necessary holding an uncomfortable silence. In all these situations it seemed that the staff experienced discomfort, either because they felt lumbered with his prepared thoughts and therefore inadequate by comparison, or because they felt helpless, leaderless and so at the mercy of their own uncertainty about what kind of thoughts it would be appropriate to bring forward.

During the two years, Denys John moved more and more into the role of listener and interpreter, and increasingly felt able to dispense with the pro-tective array of agenda items so that the staff could concentrate their thoughts on whatever theme was the major preoccupation at the time of a scheduled meeting. Thus the staff found, gradually, that their initial anxieties about the apparent loss of leadership would give way to a growing sense of freedom to explore with increasing honesty their real feelings about current issues. And as new ideas were examined in the context of old habits and values, it gradu-ally became possible to discuss openly how existing structures might have to be modified at some future time in the interest of important emerging tasks.

The kind of leadership taken in full staff meetings and in the senior staff meetings by the members of the standing committee underwent a correspond-ing change. It seemed that the weekly consultations with Denys John and the increased sense of corporate responsibility for the success of staff meetings and, by implication, for the work of the school, freed them from the stereo-typed notion of leadership as measurable only by the amount of verbal contribution to a discussion. Because they themselves became able to hold back, colleagues who had not formerly been in the habit of taking much part in discussions began to do so. And as more people overcame their resistance to taking part, so the members of the top-management group found themselves with real material about which, with the experience of the standing-committee consultations behind them, they could offer interpretative comments. The parallel to this progress that was going on in the meetings themselves was the development of a new kind of documentation from the head: the compilation of notes based on contributions of staff at all levels, and the setting out of proposals or of decisions that could be clearly seen as related to those discussions. I will have more to say in Chapter XI about this evolving style of written communication from the headmaster to the staff group.

It must by now be clear that the roles of the lower-school, middle-school and upper-school heads had been steadily expanding during the years; indeed, the role of 'head of middle school' was a completely new role, which had been in existence for only one term before the formation of the standing committee. But when certain roles are expanding rapidly within a structure that is changing more slowly, other roles are liable to find themselves diminishing. The members of the standing committee, in their first meeting, expressed concern that their colleagues in the middle-management roles might feel diminished by the new status accorded to themselves; and later in the same day members of the new 'senior staff meeting' expressed a similar concern that their colleagues not so named and therefore excluded from these councils, might feel diminished in the staff group as a whole. But the persons whose roles were really shrinking were the two whose status may have appeared to be the most secure: namely, the deputy head and the senior mistress.

The sex-linked roles of deputy head and senior master/mistress

The experiences of Robin Thomas and Joan Bradbury during the years of expansion cannot be studied in isolation. Their roles can be understood only if they are examined in relation to each other. In terms of the curricular/pastoral split, these two people felt themselves to be equally trapped in strait jackets—the one as 'the administrator', the other as 'the carer'. This division of strengths, with its implied distribution of weaknesses, was also a reflection of ancient assumptions about masculinity and feminity; for unlike the headships of the lower, middle and upper schools, these two posts were sex-linked. The reason for this has to be laid at the door, not of the headmaster, but of the Burnham Committee, which in successive reports has stipulated that if, in a mixed school, the deputy head is a man, one woman on the staff may carry the title and responsibility of 'senior mistress' and, conversely, that if the deputy head is a woman, then one man on the staff may carry the title of and responsibility of 'senior master'. The unconscious assumption underlying this stipulation appears to be that a head, whether man or woman, must ensure that the masculine and feminine aspects of his or her leadership are symbolized by the two most senior members of the staff. It seems to follow from this that a headmaster is not to be allowed his own feminine side or a headmistress her own masculine side, although all human beings are to some extent bi-sexual. Thus what looks like a saving clause to protect a mixed school (and a mixed staff group) from investing all its top leadership either in two men or in two women, becomes a trap both for the head's Number

Two and for the head's Number Three, binding them in stereotyped roles from which they find it increasingly more difficult to escape (see Figure 43).

At Nailsea the situation was complicated by the fact that Joan Bradbury, having joined the staff group in the school's third year as head of German, with the additional role of mistress in charge of girls' welfare, had always been promised that her position as Number Three would be guaranteed if she did not get the deputy headship. In other words, if she herself were not appointed, the post would not go to another woman. In fact, when the school reached the size at which it could carry a deputy head, in 1964, she had chosen not to apply for the post; and when the first incumbent of the post resigned to take up another appointment, she again chose not to apply. Thus Robin Thomas

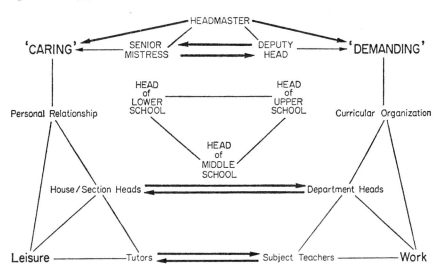

FIG. 43. Tension between caring and demanding functions and its effect on management roles.

could never have been certain whether Denys John would have preferred a woman as his deputy and whether, if Joan Bradbury had applied, he himself would still have been selected. Similarly, of course, Joan Bradbury never knew whether she would have been successful if she had applied and which of the men already on the staff would have been in her role, though as 'senior master', had she succeeded.

From the point of view of the staff group as a whole, it was only on this outer boundary of the institution that 'headship' was not seen as requiring a built-in heterosexual partnership between the head and his deputy. It is, perhaps, open to question whether Joan Bradbury ought to have been protected from the consequences of not applying for the deputy headship, since it laid the headmaster open to the suspicion that he might have *wanted* a male deputy rather than a female one, while still insisting that elsewhere in the system the principle of heterosexual partnership at the boundaries of the houses and sections must apply. The implications of this principle became apparent in the summer of 1969, when the deputy to the head of the upper school (Kitty King) left to take up a senior appointment elsewhere, and the deputy to the lower-school head (Sue Redfern) was transferred to the upper school. John Harbinson, faced with the problem of choosing a new deputy, found himself bound by the rules to select a young and recently appointed member of the staff because she was virtually the only available person; and in doing so he had to pass over a man whose experience in the area of lower-school work would have fitted him for the role, and also one of the senior women on the staff with a great deal of experience including experience in junior schools, who was ineligible because she already held office on the curricular side as head of a department.

The dilemma is evident. But it is easier to point to the dilemma than to suggest how a headmaster, given the Burnham regulations or 'recommendations', gets over the difficulty. Whichever way it turns out, he can be suspected of seeking one kind of partner and avoiding the other. The temptation to give the 'Number Two' post to the man and the 'Number Three' post to the woman, or to accept with relief the woman's decision not to seek the Number Two post, must be very strong, since men are almost expected by society to find it difficult to accept women in leadership roles.

The role of a head's Number Two and the problem of being a deputy

In the triangular relationship between the head, the deputy head and the senior mistress, the deputy head occupies the central position. Consequently, he has to be continually balancing his need to be in close touch with the head, so that he can take over his role without hesitation in an emergency, against his need to be in close touch with the senior mistress, so that he does not feel alone on the boundary of the institution without any recognizable task. He is thus vulnerable, in both these relationships, to all the processes of splitting and projection that occur in an institution that has to cope with multiple sub-tasks and often has difficulty in defining its primary task. In an expanding school the increasingly heavy administrative task is liable to be identified more and more with the deputy head, however strenuously he may resist this, however often he asserts that he shares this responsibility with the senior mistress, and however frequently she herself demonstrates her involvement in it. And just as the senior mistress may have to cope with the staff group's unwillingness to acknowledge that she has any administrative skills, so the deputy head may find himself having to cope with their unwillingness to acknowledge that he has any skills that are not purely administrative.

Robin Thomas returned to Nailsea in January 1968 in the role of deputy head, having been a history teacher and subsequently head of history and religious education in the same school between 1959 and 1964, and a head of lower school in close touch with pupils and tutors in a developing comprehensive school for the four intervening years. As the months went on, he found himself, in his new role, increasingly alienated from children and increasingly used by his colleagues as a source of hard information about organizational details or as a receptacle for information about time-tabling needs. He still taught history; yet, by one person at least, he was no longer regarded as a real history teacher, but only as a 'guest artist' in the history department—by implication already out of touch with the realities of the classroom. As a lower-school head, he had cared for children; but now he was liable to be brought into direct contact with them only as an arbiter between a baffled or angry house or section head and a difficult pupil or group of pupils. And so, while Joan Bradbury sought to escape from the stereotype of the 'mother substitute' and to be acknowledged as a woman who had administrative as well as pastoral skills, Robin Thomas was seeking to escape from the stereotype of the 'admin. man', and to be acknowledged as a person who had pastoral as well as administrative skills.

In fact his colleagues did not really deny these other skills. But they tried to preserve them for themselves as persons—friends of the old colleague of earlier times—rather than use them in task centred ways. And so he would find himself being approached as a sort of universal friend and confidant for staff, but allowed only to take disciplinary or punishing roles with pupils, as though his 'good' receptive self could thus be kept in the staff group and his 'bad' reporting self be conveniently got rid of. From time to time—as the person retrieved from a past in which he had been, to some members of the staff, simply a colleague without special status or responsibility and without special access to the headmaster—he would become aware of seductive attempts to get him back into his former role and to deny the reality of his present one. He would be told things, in the context of friendly chat, about which, in the context of the task of the school and in his real role as deputy head, he would be obliged to take some action once he knew about them. And so he would find himself having to remind colleagues who were using him in this way that he could not receive information from one of them one day as 'the nice chap' who used to be just another colleague, and then conveniently forget it the next day when, as deputy head, he might have to use the information responsibly. His difficulty, as he moved in and out of different situations in the staff group, and particularly as he moved from 'informal' conversations to 'formal' discussions, was therefore not unlike the difficulty I frequently experienced, for I too had to determine what sanction I had, to use in one situation what I had learned in another, and to try to discern the extent to which people were consciously or unconsciously placing me in this kind of predicament.

It was not only in the context of personal relationships and in this kind of interplay between the sentient groups of the past and the task groups of the present that he felt the tug of conflicting commitments, for he also stood between the school's past and future as an educational institution. Because of the four years' break in his membership of the Nailsea staff group, he symbolized for his colleagues the tension between the traditional values of the grammar school it had been and the untested values of the comprehensive school that it was becoming. Moreover, the grammar-school past was also linked nostalgically with the relative 'smallness' of a secondary school of under five hundred pupils, rising to six hundred by the time he left in 1964, whereas the comprehensive-school future was associated with expansion to well over twice that size. This past/future split in Robin Thomas was symbolized particularly in his relationships with the two house mistresses: one of these two (Catherine Walker) had been on the staff since the second year of the school's life, and had been a house mistress in the old grammar-school house system; the other (Pat Chapman) had been a tutor for two years in his section of the comprehensive school to which he had moved in 1964, a school that had begun its life, not as a grammar school but as a secondary modern school. His teaching role in the humanities course that was taught for the first time in the autumn term following his return to Nailsea laid him open to the suspicion that he might now champion the new against the old and turn his back on the colleagues with whom he had once worked; yet the younger members of the staff could have perceived him as the old grammar-school teacher who would want to preserve those traditions (see Figure 44).

If his colleagues were uncertain how he could reconcile these dual commitments, he himself lived with a good deal of uncertainty about how far the school, and particularly the headmaster and the governors, were committed to him. He had been told at his interview that he would not be expected to stay for more than four years or so. Now an observation like this can be interpreted in two ways. Did the governors (and the headmaster himself) mean to imply that they would hope to get rid of him after about four years? Or did they mean that they would not wish to stand in his way if, after about that time, he had the chance of being appointed to a headship?

In fact, the role of deputy head as a training role for a headship had been discussed at the interview. Yet two years later what was uppermost in Robin Thomas's mind was the feeling that a head might not want to keep the same deputy for more than a few years and that if he stayed too long at Nailsea he might outstay his welcome, or—more importantly—his usefulness. What he had been unable to hear at the interview was Denys John's uneasiness about the whole problem of subjecting an experienced and skilled teacher and a potential headmaster to what might well turn out to be a role tied to dull administrative chores, relieved only by occasional opportunities to deputize for himself and so to have periodic experiences of being, in effect, the headmaster. Thus, the acknowledgement, at the time of the interview, that Robin Thomas might very probably be taking on greater responsibilities in his own right in a few years' time, began, later to feel like a hint that he

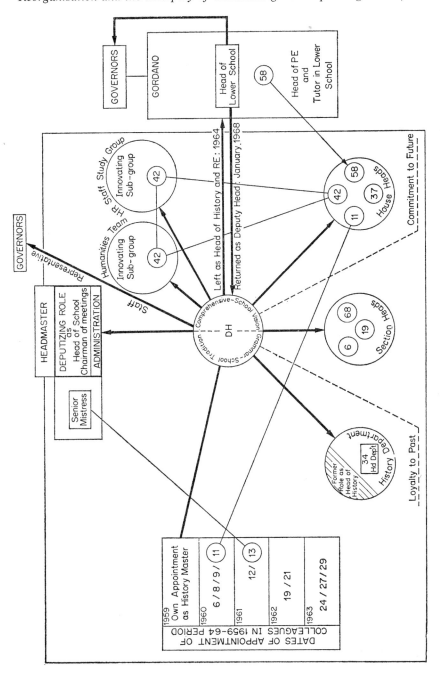

FIG. 44. The changing role of a deputy headmaster: 1968–9.

ought soon to be moving on. And once he began to feel there might be a boot—however gentle a boot—behind him, the fear that the hoped-for headship might not be available for him to go to was likely to creep up behind it. And so, ironically, the assurance to Joan Bradbury that her permanence, along with the seniority she already had, was guaranteed had unconsciously been accompanied by hints that Robin Thomas was expected to be relatively temporary.

It was perhaps this uncertainty about tenure that made him wonder from time to time whether his colleagues could really perceive the evidence that Denys John trusted him, as deputy head, with responsibilities in the leadership of the school. For him this anxiety about how others perceived his relationship with the head was linked with a comment made to him by Graham Morris in a staff meeting: 'You never disagree with the head.' Was he seen, then, as a yes-man, who at best could only step into the head's shoes and do what he had been told to do? Were colleagues able to believe that his relationship with Denys John outside staff meetings did allow him the freedom to make judgements of his own that might even bring him into dispute with the head and that on those occasions when he did have to deputize, he did so with the knowledge that he had been given real authority and could make important decisions in the head's absence?

Although he himself could have listed many occasions when Denys John had asked him to deal with an important matter on the boundary of the school, without giving him any specific instructions about how to handle it, he had the impression that his colleagues were unwilling to acknowledge that such authority really was delegated to him. This suspicion was confirmed in the concluding moments of a standing committee meeting in June 1970, in which he had deputized for the headmaster. The theme of discussion was the whole conflict-ridden subject of assessment; and it was the committee's last chance to prepare themselves for the full staff meeting in the following week, when the staff as a whole were to discuss their views about the head's controversial proposals for a standardized marking system before he made his final decision about it. Towards the end of the committee meeting, there was a sudden outburst from Clive Vanloo, who said that he did not want to discuss assessment at all, since his real concern was that they should really devote themselves to the problem of redefining the educational task of the school. He implied, in other words, that he was rejecting the head's brief. And so, in the last few minutes of the meeting, the committee, through one of its members, had really lumbered Robin Thomas, as their acting chairman, with the problem of taking back to the head some account of the meeting that would not conceal or gloss over the conflict about the relevance of his own brief, and this on the eve of a full staff meeting that was likely to be a difficult one to handle. Following Clive Vanloo's declaration, as time ran out, the committee showed an unusual reluctance to disperse. Not only did they stand around in the room continuing to talk in a somewhat desultory way with Robin Thomas, but they also made conciliatory and apologetic noises to him outside the door, leaving him with the impression that they regarded him as rather too fragile to contain the conflict that had just been put into him. This behaviour confirmed his own feelings that his colleagues perhaps doubted his capacity to stand up in opposition to Denys John either personally or on behalf of others.

In discussion with Robin Thomas after this meeting I discovered that his doubts about other people's recognition of the reality of the 'deputy' bit and therefore of the 'leadership' bit of his role had also extended to myself, since he had been uncertain whether I would even come to a standing committee meeting, knowing that the head himself would not be taking it; moreover, he had been uncertain after it whether I would have the same kind of consultation with him as I would have had with Denys John, since on two previous occasions when he had deputized I had gone straight home, thereby unwittingly conveying some kind of message to him about the ambiguity of a deputy's role. His own ambivalence about this, when he realized that I *was* on this occasion expecting to talk with him, was shown in his quick suggestion to Joan Bradbury, as she was making for the door, that she could stay for this post-meeting discussion if she wanted to. If this was an unconscious testing out of her acceptance of him as acting headmaster, he received full confirmation of that acceptance, since she made it clear that she was assuming that I would expect to talk with him alone and asked me to confirm that this was so. Thus, at the point of actually deputizing for the headmaster, he had to face also the reality that he must relinquish the pairing relationship with the senior mistress.

As deputy head in this large school, lacking any continuing leadership role that could have enabled colleagues to test his competence, it was, it appeared, very difficult for Robin Thomas to imagine that he could ever appear to them as anything more than the occasional stop-gap headmaster. In his own mind, the real task leader, the 'ideas man', the inspirational head was Denys John. It was hard for him to convince himself that he was any more than the organizational assistant who might help to get the ideas implemented, the 'man on the ground', the person to whom colleagues might bring their confusions and anxieties, or that he, too, might be someone from whom creative ideas or executive leadership could be expected. Yet, on the rare occasions when he did have to deputize in important meetings, there was plenty of evidence that he had the leadership skills required by the situations, even though his style of leadership was different from the head's.

It was not until a special meeting in July 1970, when the lower and middle-school tutors with their respective section heads and with the house heads met to discuss the whole question of lower-school organization, that he found himself doing something in his own right rather than as the 'admin. man' who occasionally had the chance to deputize for the head. For on this occasion the meeting took place under his chairmanship, at the specific invitation of John Harbinson and Clive Vanloo, who wanted an impartial chairman who was not the headmaster yet had the necessary authority to preside over a discussion that was likely to open up some difficult and even painful areas for scrutiny. This time there was no question of a deputizing role; for Denys John was in school throughout the day, knew that the meeting was taking place and that I was attending it by agreement of the three members of the standing committee concerned, and knew on the following day that these three held a long consultation with me to clarify what had happened at the meeting. Moreover he had been in the upper-school dining room when they and I had gone in, collected our meal and withdrawn to John Harbinson's room for that discussion. In fact the main purpose of that discussion was to work out how best the head could be given information about what had happened at the meeting; but at the time Denys John could not have known this, since he had not as yet even been asked for a meeting with the three people concerned. And so he had to contain his own uncertainty about what was going on and wait for events to happen. If the staff needed a demonstration of real delegation of authority to Robin Thomas—not just as acting head in his absence but to take on a special leadership role while he was in the school—they were given it in those two days.

Curiously enough, I myself was almost instrumental in keeping Joan Bradbury and Mike Burnham out of the follow-up meeting between the head and the three members of the committee who had been involved in the tutors' meeting. It was arranged that this 'mini standing committee' should meet after school on the same day as the consultative lunch-time discussion with me. It was Denys John who said, as the other three came into his room, that he was feeling uneasy about not having the whole standing committee present, even though the meeting of tutors and house heads the day before had apparently concerned only the lower and middle schools. And he went to the staff room personally to invite the other two to come and hear what the three had to report. They came immediately, bringing with them the news that the tutors' meeting had caused some curiosity in the staff room and that they themselves, as members of the standing committee, had been 'lobbied' to give information about what was going on.

Since a good deal of the meeting, at which well over half the full-time staff had been present, had been concerned with questions about the validity of the house system, which could have far-reaching effects upon future school organization and therefore on senior roles in the school, the curiosity should have surprised no-one. Why then had I accepted—even, as I remember, advocated—that the boundary of this special committee meeting should exclude Joan Bradbury and Mike Burnham, despite the fact that on other occasions I should probably have drawn attention to the exclusion of any committee member?

On this occasion, it seemed that I was no longer perceiving Joan Bradbury as paired with Robin Thomas as I usually did, but rather as identified with Mike Burnham by virtue of her tutorial role in the upper school. The confusion in my mind on that occasion, when Robin Thomas had suddenly found himself linked closely with the other two section heads in an important and indeed unique meeting that separated him from his usual partner is an example of the ambiguity of the role of senior mistress in a school which, as a result of expansion and change, can no longer offer to the incumbent of the role any certainty of what it really is.

The role of a senior mistress and the professional status of women

I have already, in earlier chapters, touched on some of the difficulties that faced Joan Bradbury during these years in exercising the authority she was capable of exercising, particularly in the new area described as 'human relationships' tutoring. Again, it would be easy for the onlooker to attribute this to a supposed lack of leadership skills in the person and to ignore the institutional side of the problem. In order to exercise authority effectively it is necessary to have a clearly definable role and to know where the boundary on which the leadership must operate is drawn. The problem for Joan Bradbury was that she had a role that had all the sanction of tradition but little definable reality in the changing situation of the 1960s. What is there left for the senior mistress to be when she is not the deputy head, is not responsible to the headmaster for the running of any bounded section of the school, and has relinquished most of the tasks that were formerly considered the responsibility of the senior woman on the staff?

In discussions about curriculum development and organizational problems Joan Bradbury had a personal authority that enabled her to contribute a great deal to the thinking that was going on. But the role of 'senior mistress', in this school as in any other school comparable in size, complexity and stage of growth, was fast becoming a non-role. Although a member of the original top management or 'triumvirate', her actual roles on both the curricular and pastoral sides of the organization had for many years placed her in a subordinate position to colleagues who were officially junior to her in the school. As a member of the modern languages department, even though still technically in charge of German, she had to accept the leadership of Peter Atkinson; as a tutor in the upper school she had to accept the leadership of Mike Burnham, eventually her colleague in the standing committee; and as senior mistress she had to accept the seniority of Robin Thomas, who had been junior to her during the years before he left in 1964.

The 'pastoral' work implied in her earlier title had long since been absorbed into new roles in various parts of the system; the two house mistresses, the deputies to the two house masters and the deputies to the heads of the lower and upper schools could all be seen as having taken over problems of girls' welfare in their different areas, as indeed the stipulation that either the head or the deputy in each section should be a woman implied. The 'welfare' part of her early role was further whittled away in the two years of this study first by the appointment in September 1968 of a new member of the office staff who was to devote a fairly large proportion of her time to welfare, thus providing a kind of first aid post within the administrative sub-system, and secondly by the appointment in September 1969 of a school counsellor, also a woman, who was to have a light teaching load so that she could give individual support to children in emotional and social difficulties in the school. The other side of the welfare task was to give advice and information on careers. Here too, the role of senior mistress had for some years included careers work for girls—the equivalent advisory service for boys being provided, until the autumn of 1966, by Pip Ridgwell. During the following year he had, as he put it, more or less 'unloaded' the careers work for boys on to Joan Bradbury; but in 1967, the arrival of Clive Vanloo changed this; for, as director of intermediate studies, he took over the careers work, first for the boys only and then for the girls also. And so, in these two areas of 'welfare' —care for those in physical or mental stress and advice for those about to enter employment—the original assumption that provision for girls' welfare must be the responsibility of a woman was gradually modified. Thus, Joan Bradbury, while freed from the over-feminized role that had somehow precluded her from offering other kinds of leadership in tasks that were assumed to be the natural preserves of men, was left with a corresponding uncertainty about what she was really in the school to do (see Figure 45).

She herself described the problem in a discussion with me as a feeling that the staff wanted to keep her in the role of a kind of 'school mum'. In fact, as I have already indicated in an earlier chapter, she had an important share in the administrative work of planning the time-table, a fact that could hardly have escaped the notice of her colleagues, since she and Robin Thomas were in continuous consultation with heads of departments every year for many weeks during the spring and summer terms. Moreover, Robin Thomas frequently pointed out in staff meetings that many of the documents that went out over his signature had in fact been the joint work of Joan Bradbury and himself. Yet on several occasions I was made aware of the reluctance of staff to recognize this side of her work. The fact that the head and deputy head were both members of the F.Y.C. planning group was twice mentioned in my presence; on neither occasion was she included in the reference, although it was made in the context of a general allusion to the top-management group and its power.

On one occasion, in a standing committee meeting, her own feelings about being passed over and not acknowledged came out in a rather dramatic way. The committee was holding a post-mortem on the senior staff meeting of the preceding day, when there had been a discussion of the whole problem of assessment, focused on a fairly provocative paper from Denys John, setting out proposals for recording assessments in a standardized form for all subjects and across all bands and sets, so that parents might receive more precise information about their children's progress in relation to the total age group than had hitherto been available to them. The scientists and mathematicians had seemed undisturbed by these proposals; but a number of people on the arts side had strongly opposed them, maintaining that their subjects could not be handled in this way. The few women in the middle management group had either remained silent or had been openly antagonistic to the idea that assessment was a shared problem that could profitably be

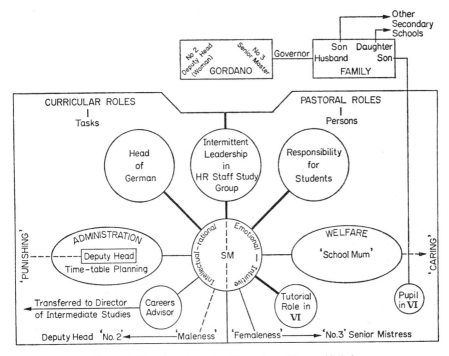

FIG. 45. The changing role of a senior mistress: 1968–9.

discussed by all the staff. Towards the end of the meeting, Joan Bradbury had made a strong, considered and quite emotive statement about the difficulties teachers always experienced in acknowledging that assessment was an integral part of their task, admitting that she herself disliked having to assess her pupils. Conferring about the meeting on the following day, members of the standing committee expressed surprise about the amount of feeling that had been displayed by some of their colleagues in the middle management group. But it turned out that emotions were running fairly high within the top-management group itself and that the irrationality could not all be left outside in the senior staff meeting. For the senior staff meeting had also contained the members of the standing committee, who were now face to face with one another in the headmaster's room.

The feelings became centred on two people in particular—on Mike Burnham and Joan Bradbury, who both expressed a sense of being outsiders in the committee, though in quite different ways and with little sense of kinship with each other. He, it seemed, was picking up and bringing into the committee the opposition to the head's paper that had been expressed in the senior staff meeting most strongly by his own colleagues in the English field; and he found himself saying, with evident difficulty, that this committee often forced him out on a limb, so that he needed to be convinced of ideas that were being supported by the other five, at the same time recognizing that if they could not convince him of the rightness of their ideas, then he might have to convince them of the rightness of his. Joan Bradbury, on the other hand, was bringing back into the committee a quite different kind of experience—not the experience of men who, in the senior staff meeting, had felt bound to stand out and resist, but that of women who had felt left out, ignored or forgotten. His declaration came early in the committee meeting; hers came near the end of it, after comments had been made, without any acknowledgement to her, that seemed to be echoing rather strongly the statement she herself had made the day before in the very meeting that they were discussing. Suddenly she remarked that she was beginning to feel that she must have been at quite a different meeting, reminding them of her own apparently forgotten or unheard contribution, and adding: 'It seems nobody takes any notice until it comes out from a different face.' Now the fact was —as she was quickly reminded—that both Mike Burnham and Peter Atkinson had in that senior staff meeting referred back to what she had said—the former in terms of disagreement and the latter in terms of support. Yet her *feeling* of having been unheard or ignored or forgotten was very strong; and it appeared to me that it was carrying something more than her own sense of frustration in the committee—something about the shared experience of women in general in a staff group like this, something about a sense of left-outness, of being considered of little account, of having to leave the major decisions to men, of denying their own capacity to take executive leadership even in a school in which girls had consistently outnumbered boys throughout the eleven years of its existence.

It seems, then, that one of the roles that may be unconsciously accepted by the senior woman on the staff is to take up into herself the difficulty that women in general have in using their leadership skills without simultaneously losing their femininity in a society that is still essentially dominated by men. We must, however, be prepared also to examine the other side of this problem and to try to understand its collusive nature. For women are themselves partly responsible for the situation in which they find themselves. Joan Bradbury's decision not to apply for the deputy headship was matched, during the years when senior posts were being advertised, by the scarcity of women applicants. As Denys John saw it in those years, women seemed willing to apply in large numbers for the less demanding posts, but preferred to leave the major responsibilities and the tasks of leadership within the staff group itself to men.

It appears that women, however emancipated today in comparison with their forbears, do not yet easily reconcile the demands of home and job, of domestic and professional responsibilities, of being committed to an institutional task on the one hand and of being home makers on the other. Or do married women in particular prefer to exercise their organizational skills in running their homes and look for other kinds of satisfactions in their teaching roles? For a man these conflicts do not normally arise. Man, the breadwinner, is traditionally expected to do his work outside the home. Is it enough to say, then, that women tend to avoid leadership roles because they fear that to accept them will imply an unnatural masculinity and a loss of their real potential as wives and mothers? And if, as teachers, they do make full use of their own 'pastoral' skills, do they inevitably collude with the assumption, often made by their male colleagues, that they have little organizational ability?

The central problem for the leadership in an educational institution is how to maintain a culture that must, because of the nature of the task, be basically dependent, without blocking off the sophisticated use of aggressive feelings. Women would appear to have a key role in this because their biological role, as potential if not actual mothers, fits them naturally to care for children in a containing and supporting institution. But in their struggle to succeed professionally in competition with men, if they *are* ambitious and if they *do* seek leadership roles, they run the danger of being cast as militant, destructive women, and so find themselves unable to use those skills that society labels 'feminine'. Thus the men in a staff group who oppose the headmaster may be able to do so in such a way that they can still be perceived as working with him towards shared objectives; but women have much greater difficulty in bringing their hostility into the open without being perceived as acting out the paranoia or the hysteria of the group and so becoming labelled as 'difficult' or even 'neurotic' members of staff whose opposition can be dismissed as 'personal', 'irrational' and 'self-centred' rather than accepted as 'objective', 'rational' and 'task-centred'.

In education, more than in any other profession, women have for a long time played a prominent part. When a greater proportion of the secondary schools were single-sex, as many women as men were needed in the leadership roles. Why then do so many of them appear to underestimate their own skills by refusing to compete with men for the senior posts in mixed schools? It seems that there is a powerful urge within the woman herself to *be* less skilful, less efficient, less masterful than her male colleague, and that any woman who does risk herself by taking leadership may find that the discomfort of accepting her in such a role is as strongly, if not more strongly, felt by the other women as by the men who have to work under her leadership and accept her authority. What, then, is the plight of the able professional woman who never even takes this risk? Having avoided seeking such a role and therefore pitting her strengths against those of men, she loses the opportunity to test any lurking suspicion that she would be discriminated against in favour of a man; and from that kind of disappointment in herself, it may not be a long step to the unconscious acceptance of the role of the 'difficult' woman who blames the institution for allowing her to be passed over. Meanwhile the woman who does seek and gain fairly high status and the responsibility that goes with it has to cope with the other kind of strain—that of being in a minority group.

Ironically, the situation of being in a minority group of women, although considered quite an enviable one in a purely social setting, and usually experienced as such, can be an extraordinarily painful one in a work setting. Nailsea was probably like many other schools in having a senior staff group in which men outnumbered women by about three to one. In the task area, it is likely to be hard for a woman to be alone, or nearly alone, among men. And it can be even harder for her to be one of a pair of women in a predominantly male group, since the presence of one other woman brings both of them face to face with the conflict between their need to identify with one another and their need to compete. Moreover, together they are exposed to the unconscious need of their colleagues to *make* them compete—even to project 'goodness' (or competence) into one of them and 'badness' (or incompetence) into the other.

Pairing and triangular relationships and the responsibilities of top management

The facts about the distribution of graded posts at Nailsea between men and women in the different age groups during the ten year period of 1959–69 and the equivalent data about the distribution of graded posts in the 1968–9 session are shown in Figures 46 and 47. It is clear from these graphs that the acceptance of special responsibility could, for women, be regarded and felt as a lonely business. Joan Bradbury, as the only woman in the standing committee, exemplified this problem of isolation more clearly than anyone else. But there was an additional factor in her particular situation which we must not ignore —a factor that may not be uncommon in neighbourhood schools like Nailsea; namely, the presence of the headmaster's wife on the staff. Ada John, as a member of the part-time staff, teaching in the department of modern languages as were Denys John and Joan Bradbury, was thus interlocked with them in a triangular situation, not only in the staff group as a whole but also in the task system of the modern languages department. Thus there was for Joan Bradbury in her permanent situation as senior mistress and head of German, as for me in my temporary situation as consultant to the staff group, a continual reminder that the headmaster and one of his part-time staff were always handling simultaneously their own private marriage relationship and their public professional relationship. And this dual situation, which had to be contained both by Denys and Ada John in their separate roles in the management structure and by all their colleagues, was an integral part of the pattern of roles and relationships in the school as a whole.

Particularly for any woman who worked closely with the headmaster, there was bound to be a treble fear: that colleagues might suspect her of trying to take the place of the headmaster's wife; that the headmaster's wife herself might feel a sense of intrusion which she would not be so likely to feel if the consultations were being held with a man; and that the closeness of the

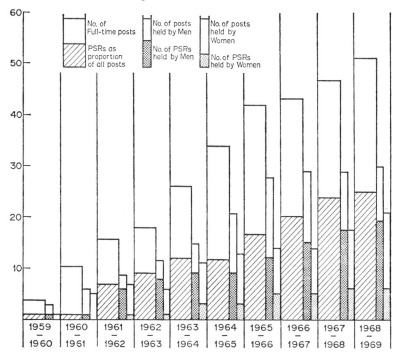

FIG. 46. Posts of special responsibility (Grade A upwards) as proportion of total number of posts and as distributed between men and women: 1959-69.

school based work partnership might actually be undermining in some way the home-based marriage partnership.

I have, throughout this book, as in the actual work I undertook with the staff, tried to use my own role as a kind of mirror in which some of these problems can be more clearly delineated. When—in the summer of 1968, before anyone was committed to this project—I learned from Denys John that his wife was a part-time teacher in the school, I experienced a kind of panic reaction which would not, I believe, have been experienced by a man in the same circumstances; and for a brief space of time I considered whether to withdraw from the whole venture rather than enter a situation with this additional complication. In fact the panic was short-lived; and I had no evidence, then or later, that the work I did in the school was adversely affected in any way by the presence of the headmaster's wife on the staff. Indeed, I felt it to be supportive. Yet, after two and a half years, I could find myself very disturbed by a suggestion from Joan Bradbury that the person who might have been diminished by my presence in the school was Ada John. Whether this was so or not, the fact that Joan Bradbury was asking herself and me this question must have been an indication that the anxiety was also present in herself; and it suggested also that the decision on two successive

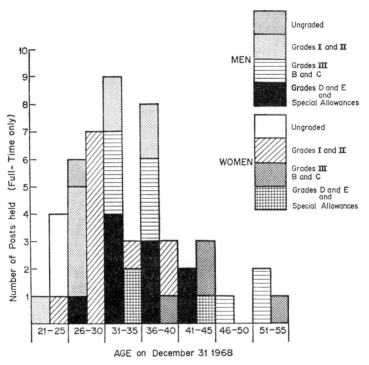

FIG. 47. Distribution of graded posts between age and sex groups: 1968–9.

occasions not to apply for the deputy headship, although linked in her own mind with the fear of putting the stability of her own marriage at risk by taking on greater responsibilities in the school, may also have been linked unconsciously with reluctance to enter into too close a relationship with the headmaster and so into a too closely competitive situation with his wife.

The fact that Ada John showed great skill and sensitivity in keeping her roles clear and that she never, to my knowledge, misused her personal relationship with Denys John in her various roles as a staff member, was itself a source of very important learning for all her colleagues. Yet the anxieties must always have been present, for the other equally uncontrovertible fact about the situation was that no-one in the staff could possibly know how much of the everyday life of the staff room was carried back into Denys John's home, since his marriage, like anyone else's, was the private concern of himself and his family. Again, however, the positive side of this complicating situation in the school, seen in the context of opportunity for learning, is that the interrelationship between the head's family and work settings, if studied rather than denied, could be used as a mirror in which many comparable problems, being experienced by all staff members could be reflected and perhaps better understood.

My role in the school must have affected Joan Bradbury more acutely than it affected anyone else in the staff group. Despite her loyalty to the task in which we were both engaged, it must have been difficult for her not to envy me my relationship with Denys John, or to wonder whether the frequency and length of my consultations with him might not have been instrumental in reducing the amount of individual contact that she—and indeed other women on the staff—might otherwise have been having with him. And so I came increasingly to believe that my good relationship with her was preserved perhaps at the expense of my relationships with other women on the staff. But if this was so, it cannot be understood simply in terms of what women might be doing to one another but must be seen as part of the more complex problem of how men and women manage their task relationships within the sentient system of the staff group. There was, I believe, a powerful force at work that made the staff group unconsciously use this male/female division in such a way that it was, on the whole, men rather than women who were able to accept leadership from me in the task of examining roles and relationships, and certain women who were left to carry, and sometimes to express, the distrust and fear of the work that I was doing and so to resist entering into any real working relationship with me. And I believe that Joan Bradbury, as the senior woman on the staff, and seen as strongly identified with me in this task, became the receptacle for the corresponding projections from both sides, with the result that she felt herself to be under-employed by men as a professional colleague and over-employed by women as someone who could absorb their complaints and their anxieties and if need be fight their battles for them.

In looking at a school staff group we are looking at a very complex institutional situation, in which sexual rivalries and feelings of acceptance and rejection must inevitably play an important part, as in any other kind of working group. If the relationship between the senior mistress and the deputy head is a good one, it will be the subject of envy. At Nailsea, Joan Bradbury —despite the frustrations of her role and despite her recurrent experience of feeling left out—did enjoy a close pairing relationship through a shared task with Robin Thomas, which was not matched, for any of the other women in her age group, by any comparable task-pairings in the staff group. The pairing relationships between section or house heads and their deputies were not really comparable, because none of the deputies, apart from David

Williams, latterly, in his other role as drama specialist, was a member of the senior staff meeting. Therefore the deputy role, in the area of middle management, was in effect a training role rather than a role linked with experience and achieved status.

One possible exception to this was the role of Mike Burnham's deputy in the upper school. The first woman to occupy this position, Kitty King, held, as we have seen, two other leadership roles, one in the task system of the history department, in which she had charge of the optional course in British Constitution, the other in the sentient system of the staff group as elected chairman of the staff common room; moreover, when she left Nailsea in the summer of 1969 it was to take up an appointment as senior mistress in a new comprehensive school. It was significant that her successor as Mike Burnham's deputy, Sue Redfern, was already experienced in the role, having been John Harbinson's deputy in the lower school since her appointment to the staff in January 1967. Mike Burnham always maintained that his deputy really *was* a deputy, not merely an assistant in a training role; and he visibly demonstrated that this was a pairing relationship on the boundary of the section by sharing his room with her, in spite of the fact that it was a very small room.

Now Joan Bradbury, for some years, had been a tutor in the upper school. Her seniority and status as senior mistress thus involved her—where upper-school matters were concerned—in a reversal of roles not only between herself and Mike Burnham, but also between herself and Kitty King up till the summer of 1969 and between herself and Sue Redfern in the following years. In the event of any prolonged absence of the head of the upper school, it would have been his deputy and not the senior mistress who would have taken over the organization of the upper school and therefore the leadership of the upper-school tutors. In the standing committee there were times when Joan Bradbury and Mike Burnham opposed each other quite sharply or subjected one another to teasing, semi-derogatory comments. And more than once in the course of that second year I had the feeling that Joan Bradbury might have been preserving her good relationship with Robin Thomas at the expense of her relationship with Mike Burnham, and that he, on his side, might be preserving *his* good relationships with his two successive deputies, who were both considerably younger than himself, at the expense of his relationship with Joan Bradbury who was a few years older than himself.

There was a further complexity in the relationship between these two members of the new top-management committee. For there had been a time when they had actually worked together for a whole term as acting deputy head and acting senior master, between the departure of the first deputy head in the summer of 1967 and the arrival of Robin Thomas as the second deputy head in January 1968; moreover, for two weeks of that term they had operated in an even closer partnership as acting head and deputy head in the absence of Denys John.

The complexity of the relationships in the standing committee when it came into existence, only two years later than that autumn term when the permanent deputy headship had been in limbo, now becomes more apparent. In the first meeting of the new committee in September 1969, there was some preliminary exploration of the kind of difficulties its members might have to face in crossing the boundary between the committee and the rest of the staff group, but little conscious reference to the difficulties of crossing the boundary in the other direction—from the staff group into the committee. In particular there was concern about how the three section heads would be able to live with the new 'top-management' parts of themselves and continue to work with colleagues, particularly those in middle-management roles. Behind this concern there seemed to be lurking the unspoken question, echoing, perhaps, the unspoken question about the relationship between Robin Thomas and Denys John to which I referred earlier in this chapter: would it be possible for anyone on this committee to disagree with the head, even perhaps to oppose him on an important matter of policy? Would the price of top management status be conformity?

It was Mike Burnham who seemed to take on most of the burden of testing these questions. I have already indicated that his mode of operation as head of the upper school was to work very closely with his deputy; and this natural leaning towards exercising leadership in a pairing culture showed itself in a similarly close association with Graham Morris, who, during the year when he was gradually moving towards a leadership role in the area of sixth-form general studies, had a desk in the room officially allocated to the head of the upper school which Mike Burnham already shared with his deputy. This triangular relationship between Graham Morris, Sue Redfern and Mike Burnham during the 1969–70 session looks strangely similar to that earlier, short-lived triangular working relationship between Mike Burnham himself, Joan Bradbury and Denys John in the autumn of 1967. Yet this experience was never referred to by any of the three in any meeting of the standing committee that I attended.

The fact that Mike Burnham had had that brief experience of being the head's Number Three two years earlier and had lost it again with the arrival of Robin Thomas and with Joan Bradbury's resumption of the 'Number Three' role, may have been playing its part in the role that he repeatedly assumed in the committee of being the one to challenge the leadership both of Denys John himself and of the committee as the top-management group. It was he who really put into words, in the meeting a few days after the first disturbing consultative session with colleagues outside the committee boundary, a fear that was probably shared by others, namely his fear that he might at times find himself in opposition to things the committee did or conclusions it might come to, and that he might consequently have to look for a way of reconciling his own personal convictions with his obligations as a member of the top-management group. It was significant that on that occasion, when he had risked his own personal relationship with Denys John by bringing this anxiety out into the open, he felt the need to stay behind in the room for a few minutes, ostensibly to remind him about some arrangement concerning the sixth form, but really, perhaps, to convince himself that the personal relationship had not, after all, been impaired. It was significant also that Denys John, in conversation with me afterwards, revealed that—whether or not the personal relationship had been impaired—he was now in some anxiety lest Mike Burnham had been trying to warn him that he might be capable of sabotaging the work of the committee outside, by denying his own responsibility for decisions made as a result of committee discussions. Yet Mike Burnham had quite explicitly stated that he would consider it very inappropriate to go round in the staff group implying that he, alone in the top-management group, did not go along with its views or approve of its behaviour. What he had done was to highlight the dilemma that he or any other member of the group might find himself in: the fear that one might avoid disloyalty to the committee only by being untrue to oneself or, conversely, that one might maintain personal integrity only at the cost of disloyalty to the committee. Only some weeks later did it become possible for people to recognize that it was loyalty to the task rather than loyalty to persons that was important in the long term.

Although no leader can easily cope with the task of leadership without being able to feel that he has the personal loyalty of those who work with him, yet the loss of a once close personal relationship, or the fear of such loss, may be part of the cost of relentlessly pursuing the real task for which a staff group as a whole and one particular part of it exists. When, half jokingly, Denys John looked across the table at the end of one of these meetings and asked with a smile: 'You still on this committee?' and Mike Burnham replied with some surprise: 'Oh yes!', something very important was really being acknowledged between them. For the reality was that if any member of the committee ceased to feel that, notwithstanding disagreement over specific matters, he *could* still accept responsibility for what the committee did, then he would have only two courses open to him: he would either have to resign, which would imply resignation from his post in the school also, or he would have to carry the committee with him and challenge the leadership in a fundamental way, if necessary to the point of pressing for the head's resignation. It was in fact in this new climate of understanding that it became possible for Mike Burnham to recognize that his own wish to oppose the head on specific issues co-existed with his wish for a good pairing relationship with him and a real fear of losing this. The anxiety about the dilemma of how to cope with conflict in the committee thus sprang from a fear that one might damage the 'good' headmaster whom one wanted to preserve in the very act of attacking the 'bad' headmaster whom one might at times want to destroy.

What he in particular was struggling with in that committee was a reflection of much that had been happening in full and sectional meetings between the headmaster and certain members of the staff. I have noted in an earlier chapter that some of those who challenged him most strongly were either connected with me as former students or with the teaching of English or both. And it seemed that Mike Burnham, both as former head of English in the school and as a former student of mine many years earlier, was representing in the committee that group of staff who acted out the ambivalent feelings towards the head, by supporting his ideas about future educational developments and at the same time questioning his methods of implementing those ideas; and this, after all, was a duality that was present in my relationship with the head also, since I shared many of his convictions about education, yet challenged his thinking about how he should operate as headmaster.

Sixth-form power, post-primary-school dependency and the contrasting roles of an upper-school and a lower-school head

It was not only the 'head-of-English' part of Mike Burnham that made him a ready mouthpiece in the committee for the questioning attitudes of his colleagues outside it. As head of the upper school he was in the peculiar situation of being responsible for the section most likely to be lost to the school if the county reorganization scheme demanded at some later date the setting up of separate sixth-form colleges. Moreover, it was in the upper school that the most striking changes in the relationship between staff and pupils were taking place, the recent abolition of school uniform in the upper school and the new sanction for boys and girls alike to wear jeans in school if they wanted to, giving visible prominence to this change. The lessening of adult control was also demonstrated during that year in the publication of a sixth-form magazine in which certain material had appeared that had given offence to some of the parents and staff and had created a rift for a while between Denys John and Mike Burnham over the subject of where liberality ended and censorship began.

The fundamental problem here was about how far the school was prepared to allow pupils to threaten the relations between teachers and parents by indulging in behaviour that, in some parents' eyes, ought not to be sanctioned by teachers, but that might, in the eyes of some of the teachers, have to be contained as part of the process of growing up and testing the limits of adult authority. In this conflict between the headmaster and his head of upper school over the rights of the older pupils, there seemed to be an echo of earlier conflicts between the headmaster and the staff over the rights of teachers, in which Lewis Smith and Tony Frost had been prominent. And now it was Lewis Smith's colleague, both in the English department and in the upper school, who had to defend the right to be bad, and, by doing so, demonstrate that it was safe not only for pupils to be 'bad' in the upper school, but also for staff, even if they were in the top-management group, to be 'bad' in the standing committee.

History was perhaps playing a part in this situation in another way also. For—apart from Clive Vanloo, who was a recent appointment to the staff—Mike Burnham was the last of the committee members to acquire the status that assured him his place on it; yet he had been in the school seven years by the time it was set up. He had once said to me that when people asked him what it was like to be head of the upper school he had sometimes said: 'Well, you're a sort of baby headmaster.' The image, even though he no longer used it, was perhaps an indication of the nature of his struggle to define and understand the new relationship with Denys John, now that he had to share with him some of the responsibilities of top management. It would have been easier, no doubt, to be head of the upper school, even at a time when sixth-form militancy made headlines (as did the action of headmasters who disregarded the liberties of their adolescent pupils), if the problems arising there could be handled as though they were unrelated to the tasks of the other two section heads. Thus his own wish to let the head be the bad object to the pupils when things were difficult, in order to protect his own good relationships with them, reflected on the one hand his own uncertainty about how to liberate young people without abdicating and on the other hand a fundamental problem about the delegation of authority within the staff group. If he was to be something more than a 'baby head-master', he had to work out with the real headmaster and with his senior colleagues how much authority was really being given to him and also how much he himself was really prepared to take.

The tension between himself and Denys John that became evident during the 1969–70 session from time to time over questions about pupil behaviour in the upper part of the school was not, it seemed, matched in the relationship between Denys John and John Harbinson. This difference is more understandable if we can see it in the context of a headmaster's experience of being on the outer boundary of a large school rather than simply as a question of compatibility or incompatibility between persons. The head's position makes him vulnerable to the critical comments of governors, parents, local residents and local employers, particularly over the 'sixth-form image' that is created in the neighbourhood (and for visitors from further afield) by the oldest pupils. For it is as products of the whole school rather than only of the upper part of it that sixth-formers will be judged by the outside world. Thus, in the context of a three-tiered system of secondary schooling, a headmaster is likely to be on easier terms with his lower-school head than with his upper-school head. In other words, he will probably find it easier to give full authority to a lower-school head, whose pupils seem comfortably distant and securely contained within the school boundary, than to an upper-school head, whose pupils must often seem uncomfortably close and dangerously near the point of breaking loose from that containment. Moreover, the inhabitants of the first forms tend to be perceived, both inside and outside the boundary of the school, as products of the primary schools and of the homes and neighbourhoods from which they have come rather than as products of the school they have only recently entered. If we can accept a little industrial imagery, we can say that a headmaster does not have to take responsibility for the quality of the raw material his school takes in; but he does have to accept responsibility for the products his school sends out, year after year, in the form of leavers from the senior forms (see Figure 48).

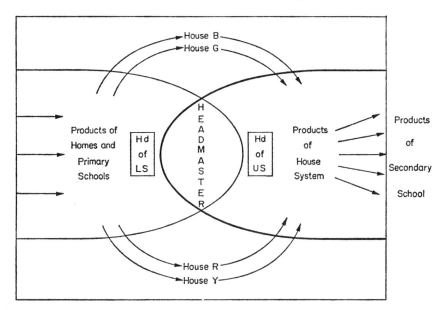

FIG. 48. Lower and upper schools in relation to input and output of pupils.

In terms of the import-conversion-export model, a head of lower school controls the import system and a head of upper school controls the export system. The fact that there are problems of import and export in each of the three sub-systems, and indeed in each year group, is something that will be taken up in succeeding chapters. Meanwhile it is enough to note that Mike Burnham, besides controlling the export system of the school as a whole, had to take in pupils both from the middle-school system inside the school and from other schools beyond the neighbourhood. Similarly, John Harbinson, besides controlling the import system of the school, had to manage the export of second-year pupils to the middle-school house system, and was not therefore free from the anxieties of having the products of his own sub-system judged by those who received them into the middle sub-system.

For Denys John, the lower school, although physically located in the main building and therefore quite close to his own room and to the school office,

T.S.T.M.—9

was in another sense more remote than the upper school. Perhaps because of this, John Harbinson seemed to personify the 'splendid isolation' image of headship rather than either its vulnerability to critical attack or its search for dependable pairing relationships through which the strains of leadership could be shared. In contrast to Mike Burnham, he did not share his room with his deputy; nor did he, up until the formation of the standing committee, hold consultative meetings with the tutors in his section. But he had been in the habit of holding a weekly meeting with them—a short, sharp one, teasingly described by Mike Burnham on one occasion as a 'parade'. By the summer of 1970, however, these meetings were becoming longer, mainly because requests from tutors themselves for longer meetings awakened him to the reality of the need to explore more deeply some of the problems of managing a lower-school section.

It is probable that John Harbinson's natural preference was to exercise leadership in a dependent mode, offering both staff and pupils the security of a system in which he gave clear instructions and did not make demands upon colleagues to expose problems in consultative meetings. But we must recognize that in a section where pupils are relatively young, many of them being still in the pre-adolescent phase of development, there is a real need in educational terms to provide security, stability and reassurance. In providing such an environment, the section head has to guard against two dangers: firstly, the danger of over-protecting the pupils; and secondly, the danger of wasting the resources of the teachers by giving them too little scope for examining as a corporate group the problems they are encountering within the section. In the upper school, the basic problem for the leadership is to contain pupils who have been in the school for a long time and are experiencing rebellious, anti-adult feelings, and to contain them in such a way that they can recognize also their continuing need to look for dependable adults who can tolerate their opposition without retreating into abdication. Conversely, in the lower school, the basic problem for the leadership is to contain pupils who have recently experienced what for some of them may have been a fairly traumatic up-rooting and who are entering an unknown and perhaps alarmingly large community, where they will need firm boundaries within which to develop their potential. For tutors in the upper school there may appear to be a choice between two equally disastrous modes of behaviour— repression of the young and over-identification with the young. For tutors in the lower school there is less likelihood of such polarization, because the child/adult boundary is not yet becoming blurred; the need for tutors' meetings may thus be far less apparent than in the upper school. Moreover, there may be corresponding pressure exerted unconsciously upon the head of the lower school to maintain the system as a sort of benevolent dictatorship. So it is not surprising, perhaps, that after my first year as consultant to the Nailsea staff group, I wrote about the heads of the lower and upper schools in the following terms:

The Head of Lower School emerges, then, as a sort of benign autocrat, making relatively few demands on his tutorial staff to discuss policy-making with him, and, it seems, encountering little opposition. The Head of the Upper School emerges as a kind of charismatic leader, working through younger colleagues and encouraging pairing relationships between himself and them rather than choosing to remain isolated, yet, at the same time, facing a good deal of opposition from other members of his tutorial staff, who hold different views.

That was written during the autumn of 1969. But by that time the standing committee was in existence, and these two people were, for the first time, working alongside one another in a top-management group that was identifiable to their colleagues as a working group. Because of this, the stereotypes into which these two had perhaps allowed themselves to be confined could be tested and the more complex experiences they represented could be allowed to emerge, as could the sides of their own personalities that had previously been suppressed.

I have suggested in an earlier chapter that John Harbinson appeared to be relatively free from the curricular/pastoral split in his area of school management, and that his role was probably perceived from the beginning as being concerned with both sides of the educational task. The increasing integration of tutorial and teaching functions through extension of the work done in tutor groups made his task of leadership in relation to the tutors in his section both less ambiguous and more complex. For, paradoxically, the staff who did both their tutoring and the bulk of their teaching in the lower school saw this identification with the task of educating the youngest children as a possible threat to their status within the school as a whole. At the same time, the presence—as tutors in this section—of the heads of the departments of art, biology, modern languages, music and technical education points to the other side of this feeling: the pleasure of being associated with the youngest children in the school and therefore with the responsibility of helping them to cope with the transition from primary to secondary education.

The importance of this aspect of the lower-school task affords an additional clue to the remoteness, if we can call it that, of John Harbinson's mode of operation as a section head. As head of the lower school he spent a great deal of his time in consultation with parents. But his contact with the environment outside the school extended not only into the families it served but also into the primary schools from which its pupils came. In the subject areas of modern languages and mathematics in particular, where important new developments, cutting across the primary/secondary boundary, were taking place, consultations were going on throughout this period involving the heads of the mathematics and modern language departments at Nailsea, the specialists in the primary schools and some of the local education officers. Thus John Harbinson's work on the boundary of the import system of the school was bringing him into a relationship with parents and with colleagues in the primary schools that could lay him open to charges of interference and that raised many questions about boundary control both for himself and for those with whom he was conferring. Hence perhaps his need to keep the situation inside the school boundary conflict-free by holding it under a fairly tight rein, so that he could cope with the potential conflicts outside. Yet, to those inside the school, the relationships between a lower-school head and parents had a far more paternalistic flavour than did the sometimes difficult encounters between the middle and upper-school heads and parents, which were often linked with emerging problems about behaviour or about standards of work and career expectations.

My own relative ignorance about the nature of John Harbinson's work and my feelings of being denied any real consultative role in his section of the school came about through a combination of circumstances. It was perhaps in keeping with his own preference for a basically dependent mode of leadership that he continued for some time to assume that it was my place rather than his to suggest a way in which such a consultative relationship might be opened, even though I had made it clear that I would attend meetings only at the express invitation of the staff member responsible for them. Thus he would perhaps—in the early stages of my work with the school—have preferred a more dependent relationship with me than I was prepared to offer. But chance entered into the situation too: for there were two occasions in the spring of 1970 when he did want me to attend meetings he was by then having with his tutors, once when I was already committed to a different one and once when I was ill and unable to take up his invitation.

In examining his role as head of lower school and his personal way of exercising leadership in that role, I have contrasted his situation and his response to that situation with Mike Burnham's way of exercising leadership in the upper school. In other contexts I have repeatedly emphasized the need to take account of historical factors as well as of personal and institutional factors in studying these problems about the exercise of authority. Both these two, as we have seen, had formerly been heads of subject departments within the school. Mike Burnham's successor, Lewis Smith, originally a member of his department, was one of the upper-school tutors and the room he occupied as head of English was next door to the one that Mike Burnham, along with his deputy, occupied as head of the section. But John Harbinson's successor as head of P.E. had come to the post from another school; and he was a tutor, not in the lower school but in one of the houses in the middle school. Perhaps because of these important differences between the two situations, there was a marked contrast between the way in which the one section head used his 'English teacher bit' and the way in which the other used his 'P.E. teacher bit' in the standing committee. It seemed very difficult for Mike Burnham to refrain from springing to the defence of the English department, from speaking on behalf of Lewis Smith (even while asserting that he could not do this) and from taking up attitudes that forced him out on a limb in some of the discussions, particularly those focused on teaching objectives, time allocations and assessment procedures. John Harbinson, on the other hand, seemed much more free to use his experience in the field of physical education without becoming the protector of the P.E. department, even raising questions on one occasion about whether the annual sports day ought necessarily to be regarded as an event that all pupils attended compulsorily. Indeed the fact that Bob Miller chose to bring all the members of the P.E. department with him, when he visited the standing committee to discuss some of the implications of the changing pattern of the department's work, suggests that he and his colleagues may unconsciously have seen the former head of P.E. as needing to understate his links with them in order to maintain his role as head of lower school.

The relative ease and difficulty with which the lower and upper-school heads relinquished their leadership of the P.E. and English departments respectively seems to have been reflected in the ease and difficulty with which Denys John had delegated to these two men his authority as head of the whole school. The change of Mike Burnham's title from 'master in charge of sixth-form studies' to 'head of upper school' was far more than a mere name change. It implied a considerable strengthening of his powers and must inevitably have left Denys John with a sense of having relinquished some of his own power, in the very area that seemed closest to the boundary of his school. It was as though—five years after handing over the task of organizing the sixth-form *studies*—he now had to hand over the 'pastoral bit' that he may have unconsciously hoped to keep in himself in so far as the senior pupils were concerned, even after Mike Burnham's role ceased to be linked only to curricular matters. Looking back through the other end of the telescope, we can see that much of Denys John's uncertainty about how to exercise pastoral leadership with near-adult pupils was in fact shared by his upper-school head, even though this was the main area of conflict between the two. Both were uncertain where precisely lay the boundary between tolerance and indifference, between liberalism and irresponsibility. Thus each projected into the other, at times, what he could not easily accommodate in himself. Denys John, who once said rather sadly, 'We can't all be A. S. Neills', may at times have unconsciously attributed to Mike Burnham his own latent wish to be more revolutionary, thus suppressing it in himself in order to preserve his relationships with governors and parents. Similarly, Mike Burnham, who must often have looked back with nostalgia at the conventional grammar-school sixth forms of his own youth, may at times have attributed this kind of nostalgia to Denys John, thus suppressing it in himself in order to preserve his relationships with his pupils.

Problems of boundary control and the role of a middle-school head in a house-tutorial system

Clive Vanloo, as head of the middle school, also had difficulty in defining his role at the boundary of his section, because the pastoral leadership in that section had been split off two years before and put into the four house heads. During those years the authority over curricular matters had been distributed even more widely between the heads of subject departments. The house heads themselves, paying the price of the independence they enjoyed in their own areas, had been left virtually leaderless; hence the building in of the weekly consultations alternately with the head and the deputy head of the school. The problem about leadership within their section had always been present, for the possibility that one of the four might in due course be appointed as 'senior house head' had been openly mentioned when the house system was first set up. There had certainly been some conjecture about which of the four would be seen as the appropriate person to take this role. Graeme Osborn, who was some years older than the other three and was perceived by some people as an ambitious man, must have at least wondered, as must his three fellow house heads, whether the mantle would eventually fall on him.

Not unnaturally, these speculations and half-formed hopes and fears within the group of house heads had their effects upon Clive Vanloo himself as he moved into his new role and as he took his place, a few months later, in the new standing committee. Although he fairly quickly established his own weekly meetings with the house heads—meetings in which, as we shall see in the next chapter, it became possible to examine some of these problems— it was not until near the end of the 1969–70 academic year that he succeeded in having a meeting of all the middle-school tutors. If the headmaster was already beginning to fear, by the autumn of 1970, that he might soon be feeling like the Pope who was occasionally brought down and shown to the people, and be losing touch with the rank and file of the staff group, the head of the middle school, during the preceding few months, must sometimes have felt like a Pope who had scarcely been seen by his people at all and whose election, despite the puff of white smoke, was still in question.

Yet it is hard to say whether the long delay in holding a tutors' meeting was due primarily to Clive Vanloo's reluctance to test his own leadership skills in the presence of the house heads or whether it was due primarily to the reluctance of the house heads to let him demonstrate his authority over them in the presence of their own colleagues in the houses. Indeed, there appears to have been some collusion between the house heads and himself to perpetuate the delay. To what extent this was a conscious collusion it is difficult to say. Clive Vanloo was aware of the need to give the house heads time to adjust themselves to the new situation. Yet he would not have pretended that it was only to protect their self-respect that he hesitated to subject himself and them to this public test of their tolerance of one another; for he recognized his own fear lest his role performance should prove inadequate to meet the demands upon it once he was face to face with four house-tutorial groups, each equally anxious, no doubt, to make a creditable showing in the eyes of the other three.

In the standing committee it was he rather than either of the two more established section heads who seemed to be most closely identified with Denys John, perhaps because he was experiencing more than they were something akin to the role of a headmaster. The complexity of his own relationship with the four house heads mirrored to some extent the complexity of the head's relationship with the five members of his standing committee. On one occasion, through a slip of the tongue that only I appeared to notice, Clive Vanloo actually referred to the four house heads as 'the standing committee', when he was reporting on a discussion that he had recently had with them and to their wish that the matter that he was now raising should be discussed in the top-management group. On another occasion, two days after I had had an unusually long discussion with him after one of his house heads' meetings, Denys John remarked to me with a smile, as I was sitting down for the weekly standing-committee meeting: 'I hear you had a late session with Clive the other day.' As he said this I had a slight feeling of guilt, and a sense that, even while Denys John welcomed the news that the head of the middle school was working closely with me, he might be half fearing that this member of his standing committee could symbolically usurp his place as head of the school by engaging me in discussion about school-wide problems rather than limiting his consultations with me to matters concerning the middle school.

It was not, I think, a mere coincidence that this half-pleased, half-anxious reference to my 'late' session with Clive Vanloo was made exactly a week after a rather stormy staff meeting, in which my comments—on the subject of difficulties in establishing section identities—had met with a good deal of hostility; for after that meeting ended, a group of the new staff members had succeeded in holding Denys John in the staff room for so long, discussing with him, as I learned later, the possibility of holding a special meeting with him on their own, that I left the school without having my usual post-meeting discussion with him, and feeling very uncertain whether he wanted it or not.

I have mentioned earlier that Mike Burnham, in the standing committee following the head's subsequent meeting with the new members of staff, told Denys John that he was 'a good headmaster but a bad public relations man' and—as it seemed to me at the time—tried to lure him into the role of the charismatic leader by suggesting that he should make a public statement about his policy to the whole staff and run a 'headmaster's seminar' for new staff. Clive Vanloo's description of the head in that same committee meeting was quite different. He saw him, he said, as someone who was 'walking on a tight rope'. The image conveyed something about exposure to watching eyes, a precarious position from which one might fall as a result of one false step, a sense of being watched by people who both needed the tight-rope walker to succeed yet wanted to see what would happen if he failed. Was this something, perhaps, about Clive Vanloo's own exposed position as the occupant of a new role, watched particularly by the four whose own roles were most affected by his appointment?

He was very much alone on his tight rope. For, unlike the other two section heads, unlike the four house heads, and unlike the headmaster himself, he had no deputy. Yet his section—with 545 children on the roll in September 1969 and 619 in September 1970—was far larger than any other. The corresponding figures for the lower and upper schools respectively were 366 and 207 in 1969 and 414 and 224 in 1970. The house heads probably felt that there was no need for a deputy head in their joint section of the school, assuming that the situation, in the event of Clive Vanloo's prolonged absence or sudden departure or death, would simply revert to what it had been before the spring of 1969: the middle school would, at least for an interim period, fall back into its four 'sections', each now containing between 145 and 165 children.

With no one of the house heads officially designated to take over Clive Vanloo's role in an emergency, the leadership role in that section remained fragmented, the pastoral leadership in each of the sub-sections being assured, but the curricular leadership in each of the three year groups remaining in doubt. He himself, although undoubtedly exercising leadership in both the curricular and the pastoral areas, was nevertheless caught in a system that either put him in the role of a kind of curricular adviser to four house heads or put them in the role of pastoral advisers to him as a section head. We shall see in the next chapter that this dilemma had its counterpart for a while in three other middle management roles in the system: namely, those of the head of remedial education, the head of sixth-form general studies and the school counsellor.

Now in fact I had been strongly aware during that 'late' session with Clive Vanloo of difficulty in maintaining the boundary round it and had found myself more than once pulling the discussion back to the specific problems that concerned his own role and task. It was evident that he himself was having difficulty in defining just where the boundary round the 'middle school' was and therefore in locating precisely which boundary he was operating on as head of the middle school. But this difficulty had its basis in some of the facts about the overlap between his section of the school and the two other sections between which it was so uneasily poised.

In the first place the difficulty was related to the uncertainty of the house heads about the extent of their own areas of control, and also about when— for a child—the link with a house head really began or ended. For although in theory the house system was supposed to be providing for every pupil a set of stable and lasting relationships throughout his or her journey through the school from entering it to leaving it, however long or short the journey might be, opinions differed about the reality of the house links for pupils who were still in the lower school or for those who had moved on into the sixth form. Were these 'permanent' relationships based on curricular concerns, pastoral concerns or social concerns?

The extent to which Clive Vanloo's functions—even after his appointment as head of middle school—were still perceived as primarily curricular, and perhaps also as located mainly in the area of the new non-grammar-school part of the comprehensive intake, was reflected in his own recollections of his first year on the Nailsea staff, when he had been a tutor in the lower school, though carrying his main responsibility (and his official leadership role) as director of intermediate studies in the third, fourth and fifth years. He recalled that he had felt himself, at that time, to be very divided, as though he could offer 'care' only in his role as tutor and therefore only with younger pupils, and as though he must always be narrowly focusing his attention on 'studies' where older pupils were concerned.

The geographical location of his room also emphasized his links with the curricular system and weakened his links with the pastoral system of the middle school, on the boundary of which his eventual leadership role placed him. This room was next to John Harbinson's on the ground floor, not far from the entrance to the main building. Thus they both shared the problem of being separated from their sections. But the effects on the two leadership roles seemed rather different. For the lower school, the slight distancing of John Harbinson from the tutorial rooms on the floor above had the effect of leaving the leadership very firmly in his own hands: he was accessible, but not too close. For the middle school, the much greater distancing of Clive Vanloo had quite a different effect. The siting of his room near classrooms used by middle-school pupils, but at a distance of several minutes' walk from any of the buildings in which the house-tutorial rooms and dining-rooms were situated, emphasized the distinction between the 'curricular' role to which *he* had initially been appointed and the 'pastoral' role to which the house heads had been appointed. It was therefore easier for colleagues teaching in his particular subject area to see him as non-threatening (and indeed as helpful) than it was for house heads to see him as non-threatening in their family-like house blocks, where his presence raised questions about the 'autonomy' they had formerly enjoyed. For it was far from easy for the house heads, at first, to recognize that the move from their earlier leaderless state had within it the promise of greater richness and stronger mutual support, or even that the old autonomy, in so far as it had ever really existed, had involved for each of them a certain degree of rather painful isolation. In the next chapter we shall be examining the process by which this modification of their own attitudes to the new situation became possible.

It was not the house system only that blurred the boundaries between the middle school and its neighbouring sections on either side. The curricular pattern also did this in several ways. The Option B courses which had formerly started in Year II, were pushed back to Year III in 1970, following the discussions about the curriculum as a whole, thus necessitating a handing-over process from John Harbinson to Clive Vanloo at the transition from the lower school (Year II) to the middle school (Year III). At the other end of the middle-school phase, there was the continuation into the sixth-form curriculum of CSE and GCE O-level courses, necessitating a similar handing-over process from Clive Vanloo to Mike Burnham. Furthermore, the changing ethos of the upper school from the old grammar-school sixth form to the comprehensive sixth, seventh and eighth years, produced an increasing amount of overlap in the whole context of careers work; for although the provision of information about university entrance and entrance to colleges of education was handled by Mike Burnham and his deputy respectively, the provision of information about courses in colleges of further education, needed both in the middle school for pupils leaving from the fifth year and in the upper school for later leavers, was still being handled by Clive Vanloo.

As a subject teacher he, perhaps more than anyone else on the staff, was liable to find himself holding the tension between the arts and the sciences. He was the only member of the standing committee who had not previously held office in this or any other school as head of a subject department. His own teaching area was wide, taking him into various territories, including English, history, geography and economics, through his interest in organizing and teaching integrated courses in humanities, social studies and economic studies. Although he did not actually teach science he had been trained in the physical sciences. Curiously enough, it was not until the early part of 1971 that he acknowledged this fact even in the standing committee. On the other hand, he referred more often than any other member of staff to the need for scientific rigour in planning, evaluating and reporting educational research and for clarity and precision in determining teaching objectives and in devising methods of assessment.

It often seemed to me—particularly when I myself was the target of his challenging questions or critical comments—that he was having to hold the balance between the sciences and the arts on behalf of his colleagues, as perhaps he was having to hold the balance between the lower and upper schools on behalf of the headmaster. As far back as the staff meeting of July 1968, when I first met the staff group to discuss with them the proposed collaborative study of change and innovation in the school, he had put to me a very direct and testing question about the theoretical background to the work I hoped to do with the staff group and about the extent to which this could be regarded as a theory that had already been tested in comparable fields. It was also he who, on various occasions, pressed me to justify the scientific validity of my methods by defining the sense in which I used the word 'evidence'. Yet he did not, as the months went on, deny the importance of examining the evolution of new management structures and new teaching approaches in the school. He probably expressed more than any of his colleagues the problem of reconciling the pull of apparently opposite demands —the demand for scientific rigour and the demand for artistic sensitivity.

And so, on more than one occasion, he and I found ourselves taking up polarized attitudes, as on one occasion, in a discussion about assessment, when he declared sharply that we needed more 'science' in the process and I retorted equally sharply that we also needed to leave room for the 'poetry'. Yet there was abundant evidence that he was no more blind to the usefulness of imagery than I was blind to the importance of facts. At times he would swing from strong support of the work that I was doing to powerful attacks upon it. Both of these attitudes, it seemed to me, were equally genuine, however puzzling and even disturbing the switch from one to the other might be. He was not simply 'being himself' on one day and 'acting a part' on another. The ambivalence he expressed towards me in my role as consultant was not unlike the ambivalence that Mike Burnham expressed towards Denys John in his role as headmaster. In both cases, a staff member who was at the receiving end of strong ambivalent feelings about his own leadership role in a section—the one from his near-adult pupils in the upper school, the other from his closest colleagues in the middle school—was able to give expression to similarly conflicting feelings, the first in relation to Denys John as headmaster, the second in relation to myself as consultant.

Figure 49 shows, in diagrammatic form, some of the complexities of this shift from the role of a director of intermediate studies to the role of a head of middle school as it was experienced during the years about which I have been writing.

Conclusion

In these two chapters I have been describing the evolution of a top management group and trying to show how the roles of a headmaster and his five most senior colleagues reflected different facets of the primary task of a school that was catering for an increasingly diverse population of children and adolescents between the ages of eleven and nineteen. We have seen how the members of this group, as they examined more and more closely the interdependence of their tasks, found themselves able to question some of the assumptions with which they had operated in the past and thus brought to their roles a deeper understanding of their own particular modes of leadership. We have been exploring also the ways in which a headmaster may experience the loss of parts of himself into his senior colleagues as he delegates to them important parts of what used to be regarded as the sole responsibility of the head.

In examining these dynamic processes within a complex institution it is never easy to be sure when we are describing persons and when we are describing roles, or to know with any certainty where a conscious deliberate intention can be differentiated from an unconscious mechanism being used by the members of a group. When we study the development of a working committee over a period of time we are looking both at a process of redefining and differentiating between the sub-tasks undertaken by the members of the group and at the growth of a sentient system within the group itself.

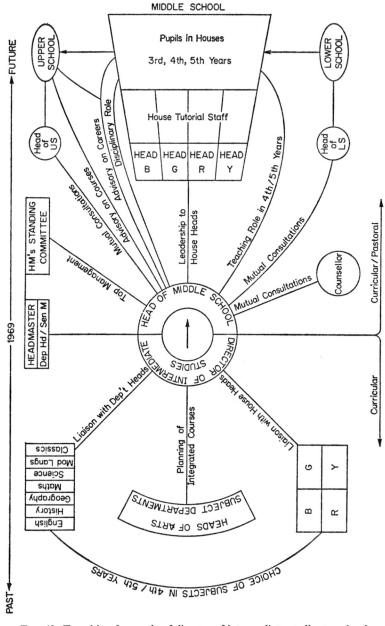

FIG. 49. Transition from role of director of intermediate studies to role of head of middle school.

In so far as such a group will seek to preserve the sentient system by avoiding conflicts arising from the management of the task, so far will the task itself be in jeopardy; yet the examination of the conflicts in relation to the task may in itself strengthen rather than weaken the sentient system that supports that task. For at least three members of the particular top-management-group that we have been studying, there was a corresponding necessity to ensure that the separate task systems for which they were responsible in the school as a whole were strengthened rather than weakened by the sentient systems with which, in varying degrees, they coincided.

Change in one part of a system is always accompanied by changes in other parts and indeed in its whole configuration. The growth and development of a school in which staff recognize the need to modify earlier views of the nature of their primary task will inevitably be accompanied by changes in role definition at all levels and in staff deployment in different parts of the system. In the next chapter we shall be examining—again in the perspective of the whole period under review—the experiences of those in the middle-management roles and the tasks they found themselves called upon to tackle.

CHAPTER IX

Deployment of Skills and Experience in the Area of Middle Management

Replacement and redeployment in relation to status and salary

When a school superimposes upon an existing departmental system an additional house-tutorial system, and then builds in further divisions between sections, terminology may become ambiguous and role distinctions blurred. The management structure grows by accretion, and as new roles become necessary for the efficient functioning of the institution, some of the old ones become expendable. All this has to be seen realistically in the context of a salary structure that is not necessarily supportive to the emerging ideas about how a school should be organized. Redeployment of senior, experienced members of a staff group in accordance with new policies is therefore related to two concurrent processes: on the one hand it depends on the availability of money for new posts as a result *either* of expansion *or* of discontinuation of existing posts when their holders move to other schools; on the other hand it depends on the growing willingness of senior staff remaining in the school to use their leadership skills in new ways so that they can undertake different roles without losing seniority in consequence of such change.

A headmaster who recognizes that the system as it has existed hitherto may require modification or even radical reorganization must therefore be prepared to work with the feelings of his established staff about the implications of the new appointments being made in his school. For as colleagues move away to new posts, their replacements may join the staff group with lower status, with the same status or with higher status. Consider the following examples. A head of science leaves the school and is replaced by a new head of science, but on a slightly lower salary scale; at the same time a head of physics leaves, but he is replaced by a young assistant teacher without the title or salary of a department head. A drama specialist who leaves the school has had a scale allowance, not by virtue of his drama specialism, but because of his 'pastoral' role as deputy to one of the house heads, being ranked, in the curricular system, as an assistant teacher in the English department; but because of the change in the status of drama brought about during his term of office in the school his replacement comes in as 'head of drama' though without a salary grade as a head of department. A head of history leaves, and

254

her role is taken over by one of her more experienced colleagues, but at the level of a 'subject organizer' and not of a 'head of department', since historical and geographical studies are to be subsumed under the heading 'Environment' in a broader-based department headed by the former head of geography. A house head continues to be graded by virtue of his pastoral responsibility, but—because of the departure of the former head of physics—begins to resume responsibility in that area of the curriculum, drawing on his earlier experience in the same school when he himself was head of physics. A fellow house head, similarly, continues to draw his salary on the grounds of pastoral responsibility, although his leadership task in an expanding two-year humanities course is probably engaging him more fully as a person working in a new curricular field. A number of staff in middle-management roles move to other schools or institutions: a head of physical education to become a housemaster, a drama specialist to become head of a lower school, two historians (the head of department and a colleague who has been deputy to a section head) to become senior mistresses, two house heads, a man and a woman, the former to become a deputy headmaster, the latter to become a senior mistress, a head of physics to become a head of science, a head of chemistry to become a lecturer in a university school of education, and a head of science to become a county adviser. The race for promotion is always going on; but what looks like promotion to one person may look like side-stepping, or even leaving the race altogether, to another.

It must already be apparent that my examples in the last paragraph are not fictitious. All these things happened at Nailsea; some of them indeed have been referred to in earlier chapters. The processes of examining and modifying existing structures and of facing the possibility that more radical changes may follow at some future date must always be affecting the decisions a headmaster and his governing body make about the replacement of lost staff and about the creation of new posts. A head of biology who sees the once established post of 'head of chemistry' disappear at the end of one academic year and the once established post of 'head of physics' disappear at the end of the following academic year, may be able to accept, at the thinking level, that the whole area of science can be freed to work in a more flexible way once the relationships between its constituent parts rather than their separateness can be reflected in its internal organization; yet, at the feeling level, the questions 'What is going to happen to my bit?' and 'How much longer will "head of biology" be a viable role?' are nagging reminders to the biologist that the 'department of biology' as such may soon lose *its* identity too.

During the early phases of a school's transition from grammar school or secondary modern school to comprehensive school, when teachers are finding themselves preoccupied with problems of child care in large institutions, new patterns of pastoral organization creep up over the established curricular or departmental structure. But in the later phases, when it is the quality of the learning experience itself that comes under fire, new patterns of *curricular* organization begin to creep up over the supposedly established pastoral structure. The staff of such a school thus find themselves having to search for new ways of interpreting their roles. Where formerly the system seemed to expect them to protect either their subjects or their pupils, according to whether they were heads of departments or heads of sections, they now have to strive for a new kind of partnership, which does not force them to put the development of scholarship and the care of scholars into opposed categories, for only thus can they work together at the fundamental problem of how to fit curricular development to the changing needs of children and adolescents as they move through the school system.

Ambiguities about authority and responsibility

The progress towards this reintegration of the curricular and pastoral functions and responsibilities in the Nailsea staff group brought into sharper focus another kind of problem that was in a sense the obverse of splitting: namely, the problem of false blurring and homogenization. For as those members of staff who held key leadership roles in the school began to acknowledge the realities of their shared responsibility, so they had to face the implications of their own seniority, and hence of the differentiation, in terms of their various boundary functions, between themselves and their junior colleagues. And this necessitated a firmer control of the relations between the task and sentient systems, both in the staff group as a whole and in the various overlapping sub-sections.

I have referred in an earlier chapter to the Nailsea journal—a small handbook, compiled annually and distributed to all parents, pupils and staff at the beginning of every school year, containing information about the members of the institution and the offices held, at both staff and pupil levels. The journal contained the names of the school governors, the full-time, part-time and visiting members of the teaching staff, the secretarial and technical staff, the school-council officers and representatives and the house officers, and the members of every tutor group in the school. In the journal for the 1968–9, 1969–70 and 1970–1 sessions, the names of the head, deputy head and senior mistress were printed at the top of the complete staff list and the rest of the full-time teaching staff followed in alphabetical order, each recognized area of responsibility being identified by the addition, in brackets, of the name of that area after the name of the staff member who was responsible for it. These staff lists appeared at first glance to provide all the information needed to identify any staff member's responsibility. Closer scrutiny, however, revealed some quite surprising discrepancies.

In all three of these journals the identities of section and house heads, their deputies and the tutors responsible to them were given on a separate page. But in the 1968–9 journal none of these 'pastoral' leadership roles was given in the complete staff list itself, although the areas of responsibility of the subject department heads, including Clive Vanloo's responsibility for intermediate studies (in other words, the 'curricular' roles) *were* indicated. In the 1969–70 journal this was changed. The names of Mike Burnham, John Harbinson and Clive Vanloo in the alphabetical list were followed respectively by 'Upper School', 'Lower School' and 'Middle School' in brackets; the names of the house heads were followed, not by the name of a house or area of responsibility, but by the title of 'Housemaster' or 'Housemistress'—terms which were not normally used in the school. This difference in terminology in identifying the areas of responsibility of the section and house heads seemed to be reflecting some unconscious wish to distinguish between an 'administrative' area as symbolized in the role of a section head and a 'pastoral' area as symbolized in the person who looked after a house, thus suggesting that the difference between the two roles was a difference in kind rather than in scope of responsibility.

Changes appeared also during these three years in the descriptions of some of the subject department heads. Already, by 1968, Allen White's name had 'Geography and Geology' after it, and not only 'Geography'; but it was not until the following year that the names of Joy Sollars and Gwen London were followed respectively by 'History and Citizenship' and 'Biology and Rural Science', rather than by 'History' alone and 'Biology' alone, as in the previous year.

Of all the changes in ways of designating an area of responsibility in the journal, those connected with Reg Clarke were perhaps the most noticeable. In the 1968–9 journal and the 1969–70 journal his responsibility was located in 'General Subjects' and 'General Arts Subjects' respectively, the change in the second year corresponding with the temporary responsibility given to him for the second phase of the lower-school humanities course. In the following year, when his responsibility for remedial work throughout the school was being more clearly identified in the staff group itself, his name appeared in the journal without any indication that he had a special role of any kind, 'General Arts Subjects' being replaced not by 'Remedial Education' but by a blank. The difficulty about naming such an area in a public document seems to have been related to Reg Clarke's own reticence about exposing children as needing such help. This had been expressed by him some time before my work with the school began, when he had requested that the title 'Head of Remedial Education', originally on the door of his room, should be replaced by his name, and that his title be known as 'head of general subjects', on the grounds that the less able children for whom he was responsible worked within a pattern that included all subjects, rather than in separate subjects taught by different teachers.

These modifications, additions and omissions can hardly have been accidental or without their effects on the feelings of the persons concerned. They seem, indeed, to have been reflecting the kind of uncertainty that teachers in any school are likely to have about their relative status in the eyes of colleagues inside the school and of parents, governors and local authority officers outside it. In noting them, I have to recognize that I—like others who studied and used these journals—had no knowledge of the processes through which decisions about what should be printed had been arrived at in those particular years. The compilation of the journal, as I later learned on enquiry, had always been necessarily very hurried because of the narrowness of the time gap between the allocation of roles for a coming year and the dispatch of copy to the printers. Consultation with colleagues may therefore have been inadequate, perhaps even avoided on both sides.

Was the compilation of the journal just a 'straight administrative job', a chore even? Or was it something more? The member of staff who undertook the task of editing it during those years was Graeme Osborn; and the fact that he was, in the 1968–9 session, the one house head who still held office as a department head must, if only at an unconscious level, have had something to do with the editorial change of convention in the following year, when he himself no longer had this dual role but had handed over his departmental responsibility to a new member of staff. Even if the proposal to include reference to the pastoral as well as to the curricular responsibilities in the combined staff list came from someone other than himself as its compiler, the change carried an important implication. For in the context of the school's task there was, not unnaturally and in work terms quite appropriately, a need for all those who held senior posts to have their roles identified in any document that would be read and would be used continuously as a reference source by pupils, parents and governors of the school.

But the feelings about seniority were evidently far from simple. Within the sentient system of the staff group, there was an equally strong need to suppress or blur these status differences, springing from a fear lest friendship patterns might thereby be disturbed. This reluctance to acknowledge one's own seniority in the personal, face-to-face situation of the staff room was expressed vividly by one of the department heads in the very first meeting of the combined senior staff group in September 1969, when he said—interpreting the general uneasiness about the new name 'senior staff'—that he liked to feel that he was 'just Tony Frost' in the staff room, even though he had to be and act as head of music in the teaching block or in a staff meeting like the one he was attending then. In saying this he was highlighting for all his colleagues the perpetual dilemma of having to acknowledge both what one is as a person and what one must do in taking a particular role, and the uncertainty about how much of oneself can be made available in the performance of that role, despite the constraints imposed by it. Tony Frost, in asserting that he could split himself off as a person from his own behaviour in the role of a department head, was trying to deny that his colleagues, whether they were working with him in a staff meeting or talking with him in the social setting of the staff room, were responding both to the 'Tony Frost' part and to the 'head of music' part of himself. Reg Clarke's reluctance, some years earlier, to have 'Head of Remedial Education' (or even, presumably, 'Head of General Subjects') on the door of his room and his request that this should be replaced with his name, was perhaps another example of the fear that the person might become submerged by the role. The counterpart of this wish to shed the role in order to be perceived more simply as the person could be seen in the pressure to keep the headmaster so tightly constrained in his role that his colleagues could never allow him to be 'Denys' but always insisted that he be 'Mr John'. If he could symbolize the constraints of the role, it seemed, the rest of the staff could feel themselves able to preserve *their* freedom to be persons.

The anxieties of the senior staff about their newly named status in the autumn of 1969 had a somewhat ironical reversal for some of them just over a year later, when—as it was reported to me—the heads of departments were considerably shaken to discover, in the course of a senior staff meeting, that the amount of free time allocated to them by virtue of their responsibilities in the curricular area (and, by implication, of their seniority in the staff group) was no greater, and in most cases was actually less than the amount of time given to the deputies to house and section heads, who were not among those entitled to attend the senior staff meeting. This revelation brought home sharply to the senior staff, including the top management group, that higher salary did not, in itself, carry the assurance that one's contribution was valued. Time, it seemed could be as precious and as real a reward as money. Did the section and house heads, then, regard their deputies, however junior their status in the staff group, as more important colleagues than the department heads with whom they shared the label 'senior'?

Denys John acknowledged in the first combined senior staff meeting of 1969 that it would have to be his responsibility to make it clear to all staff where the boundary round the senior staff group was drawn—in other words, which members of staff were in that group and which were not. In terms of defined responsibility within an area, rather than of the former split terms 'department head' and 'section head', there was now both greater flexibility and greater precision in defining the position of this new boundary. Thus people in service roles, like the head of remedial education, the school counsellor, the librarian, the bursar and the head technician could be members by right of these special roles and responsibilities where formerly they could have been perceived as attending meetings of section or department heads only by courtesy.

This, in its turn, required of the headmaster and his standing committee a new kind of precision in deciding which of those staff in service roles were to be regarded as operating within the first-order system of management and which fell within the second-order system, or, in other words, which were responsible directly to top management and which were operating only in one sub-section and therefore responsible to the leadership in that section. The location of Ethel Hawker and Bill Smith in the first-order system had already been clearly recognized as entitling them both to membership of the senior staff meeting. But when in the autumn of 1971 the new structure, based on the year-group organization and the modified departmental system, was introduced, certain painful decisions had to be made about persons in the staff group, because of increased differentiation in the levels of responsibility of staff members.

Cyril Routley again became a key person in this reorganization, not this time as someone given a temporary role that would inevitably have left him later in a no-man's-land, as his earlier role of head of the fifth year had done, but as someone taking a permanent new role as controller of and adviser on resources. In a school system that was attempting to plan its use of new materials (both 'soft-ware' and 'hard-ware') in teaching situations that were becoming more and more complex as a result of moves in the direction of integrated courses and mixed-ability teaching groups, this was likely to become an important service. But if Cyril Routley's new role was to give him real authority in this complex area, a question was bound to arise about the role of the librarian. Was she to be regarded as responsible for part of the general area of resources? Or was she to be regarded as being in charge of an area that existed still in its own right, as it had done (under a different librarian) during the two years before this second change in the management structure took place? It was upon the answer to this question that depended the decision about whether or not she should be included in the senior staff meeting, along with Cyril Routley.

In fact the decision was that her role fell outside the boundary of the senior staff meeting, though inside the boundary enclosing named responsibilities in the general area of middle management. And so, in the 1971–2 journal, her name appeared at the end of a list headed 'Subject Organizers', thus recalling the earlier situation, when Graham Morris, as 'head of library' in the absence of a full-time librarian, had somewhat illogically been included in the category of 'heads of departments' and had attended their meetings, during the 1968–9 session, by virtue of a role that had nothing to do with responsibility for a subject.

Temporary leadership roles in times of change and transition

At times of transition from one pattern of management to another, new roles that have a certain air of temporariness about them may be introduced into the structure, reflecting uncertainties about where the new boundaries should be drawn. Before the formation of the standing committee and the amalgamation of the section heads' and department heads' meetings, Reg Clarke and Graham Morris, it will be recalled, occupied for a short time two new roles as 'curricular advisers' to the lower-school and upper-school heads. The changing roles of these two men illustrated rather dramatically the nature of the struggle that was going on at all levels in the staff group to bring the curricular and pastoral sides of the educational task into a closer and more fruitful relationship. The functions of a curricular adviser threw into sharper relief the assumptions that were being made about the nature of the other 'Number Two' role in the management system of the lower and upper schools, namely the role of the deputy to the section head. For if John Harbinson and Mike Burnham were perceived as needing curricular advisers, the roles of their deputies must have been perceived as mainly pastoral. The introduction of these two new roles seemed also to be an attempt to differentiate between the supportive or assisting functions of the 'deputy', implying some kind of training to be given to her *by* the section head, and the organizational or consultant functions of the 'adviser', implying relevant experience and expertise that were to be made available *to* the section head. For Reg Clarke the new role was the stepping stone to a clearer recognition of the nature of his responsibility as head of remedial education; for Graham Morris the new role was related to the need for clarification about the nature of his new leadership role as head of general studies.

Reg Clarke's appointment as head of remedial education in 1966 had coincided with the first comprehensive intake of children into the lower school. Yet by the autumn of 1968, when these children were moving into the middle school, he was, despite his official title 'head of general subjects', still associated in the minds of his colleagues, and probably also in the minds of parents, with the youngest children only and with only a small number of them, since he was working with the special group that included, along with those needing remedial help, others who were sometimes described as 'fringe remedial'. The term 'general subjects', although not intended to apply only to less able children, had thus come to be associated with the teaching of children who, in the pre-comprehensive era, would have attended secondary modern schools. But by the winter of 1968 the way was open for the term 'general subjects', in the context of the lower-school curriculum, to acquire a much wider meaning and to lose its 'remedial' and 'ex-secondary-modern-school' connotations.

It was, I believe, with the intention of giving Reg Clarke authority to extend his own leadership role in this direction that Denys John offered him in the spring of 1969 the additional title of 'curricular adviser to the lower school'. It was only during the following year that it became clear that this title, by somehow tying him to the lower school, was denying his real role as head of remedial education throughout the school and was substituting for it an unreal leadership role that reduced him to being John Harbinson's 'curricular arm'—a term that was actually being used towards the end of the 1968–9 session. Only later was it recognized that the head of a remedial department, like a school counsellor, has to be perceived as a person qualified by training or experience or both to offer a service to all children in the school who may require it. This implies also that he offers a service to his colleagues and that he, like anyone else in a service role, may also occupy a leadership role in relation to other members of the staff who assist him in providing this service.

For Graham Morris, the new title of 'curricular adviser to the head of the upper school' (sometimes described as Mike Burnham's curricular arm) accompanied a genuine change of role when he was officially appointed to a new post of responsibility in the school (having been interviewed along with other applicants) as head of general studies in the sixth form. The term 'general studies' unlike 'general subjects' already had academic respectability in the educational world, since it named an area that could be associated with pre-university sixth-form work. In the lower school, 'general subjects' had to lift itself out of the realm of remedial education and take its place alongside science and modern languages and other subjects as work in which academically able children took part. In the upper school 'general studies' had the converse problem, since it had been perceived as an area in which pupils who did not take readily to academic work might show talent and commitment. Thus, whereas Reg Clarke's changing role demanded of him the capacity to work with abler children than he would have encountered in a secondary modern school, Graham Morris's changing role demanded of him the capacity to work with children who would not until recently have reached the sixth form at all.

In Figure 50 the changes in Reg Clarke's role between September 1968 and September 1970 are shown in relation to a time scale indicating how his functional isolation as the remedial teacher with his remedial group in the earlier years contrasted with the liaison work he had to undertake later with his colleagues. But this new kind of role was not reached without loss. Because backward children are often also emotionally unstable and may be suffering from various kinds of deprivation in their homes, the remedial work demands of the teacher that he provide a good deal of comfort, security and assurance. He may thus be associated in the minds of his colleagues more with pastoral care than with subject teaching. This in itself creates a dilemma, for it is never easy to know just how far the special environment provided by the remedial teacher is becoming over-protective and therefore perhaps weakening the less able child rather than strengthening and developing whatever capacities he has.

Part of the problem is that this very dependency is emotionally rewarding for the teacher as well as for the children, and may therefore be relinquished only with pain. As we saw earlier, the autumn of 1969 brought a radical change into the pattern of remedial work in the school—a move away from the method of providing remedial help by creating a protected 'remedial group' as in former years, towards the new method of withdrawing children as necessary from the mixed-ability teaching groups through which they were henceforth to be dispersed. Because of this Reg Clarke's work took on a new significance in relation to other department heads: for whereas formerly he had been in an isolated position in the curricular field, though perceived as

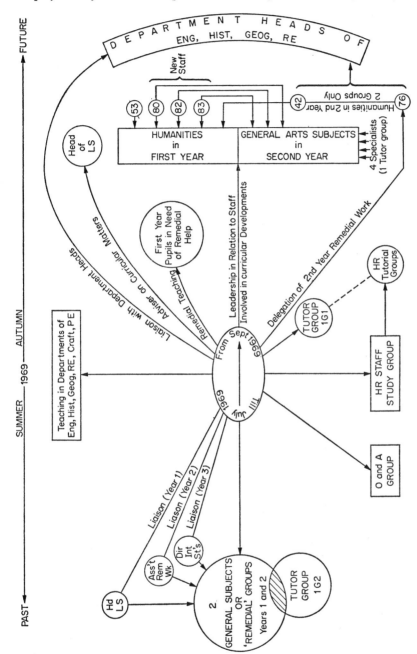

FIG. 50. The changing role of a head of remedial education.

related very closely with the particular group of children for whose work he had been responsible, he now found himself having to work more and more closely with heads of departments and also with tutors in order to organize an effective system of groupings for children who were no longer in his charge throughout the school day. Thus within the culture of the lower school he had to relinquish some of his old concern for pastoral care of children in need and to strengthen his concern for curricular developments across the board.

For Graham Morris the development was perhaps rather more from a concern about how to teach a particular subject, namely English, to a concern about how to enable young people with a wide range of abilities and varied interests (not all scholarly) to learn more effectively, not just in the field of 'English' but in overlapping areas of study. Thus he too had to move into a situation in which new working relationships with colleagues were to be of paramount importance to his work with pupils. Figure 51 shows the changes in his role against the same time scale as was used in Figure 50. In contrast to Reg Clarke, who seemed to move through a middle phase when he was more isolated than before, Graham Morris moved through a middle phase which brought him into a close-knit group with Mike Burnham and Sue Redfern, with whom, as I indicated earlier, he shared the room officially allocated to the head of the upper school. In the autumn of 1970 he was able to establish himself in a separate room, now available for him as head of general studies, and thus he accepted the measure of isolation that leadership in this area as in any other demanded.

Although for a while his new role looked like the counterpart in the upper school to Reg Clarke's role in the lower school, in fact it resembled much more closely the role that Graeme Osborn subsequently accepted when he took over the direction of the lower-school humanities course. Graham Morris's teaching team, though numerically smaller than Graeme Osborn's, was comparable in complexity, since it contained the deputy headmaster, the senior mistress, the upper-school head and two department heads—a situation that must have presented to all concerned quite formidable problems of role reversal. There was also a further risk in the work that he was undertaking. In connection with the general studies course, appropriate activities outside the physical boundaries of the school had to be organized. If the pupils were to grow through this experience they had to be left unsupervised to a considerable extent. This carried its own kind of strain for him as the staff member responsible not only to Mike Burnham but also to Denys John —a kind of strain which Graeme Osborn in the lower-school framework was not called upon to accept, since any activities outside the boundary of the school that were connected with the lower-school humanities course were bound to be more closely supervised.

In their different ways these three, like the new school counsellor, were all struggling with the problem of defining their leadership roles in the school,

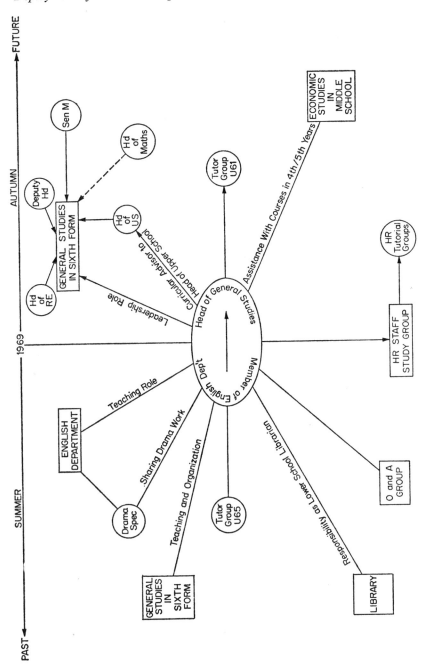

FIG. 51. The emerging role of a head of sixth-form general studies.

not only in relation to pupils within a particular context of learning but also in relation to colleagues. Because of this, I saw them in the autumn of 1969 as shadowing in some way the changing roles of the three section heads, whose leadership was coming to be recognized as being neither pastoral nor curricular but rather as embodying the authority delegated to them by the headmaster. In the middle management group, as in the new top management group, the question that needed to be faced, as the 1969–70 session approached, was how those in the leadership roles could move away from the traditional struggle to protect their own empires and turn their attention to the fundamental problem of determining what kind of school they really wanted for their pupils, not just in the years immediately ahead but during the coming decade which would see the retirement or the departure to more senior posts elsewhere of many members of the present staff group.

House leadership in relation to section leadership in the middle school

Nowhere was the problem of adjusting to the new pattern of management more acute during those months than in the newly identified middle school. I have suggested in an earlier chapter that Clive Vanloo, in taking up the role of its head, found himself in a situation of great complexity, without a deputy to share the administrative tasks of leadership but with four senior colleagues who might have been described, in parallel with the 'curricular advisers' to the heads of the lower and upper schools, as 'pastoral advisers' located in the separate houses in the middle school.

My impression during the summer of 1969 was that he himself felt that his new robes were sitting uneasily upon him, not through any sense that his leadership in the curricular field was being questioned, but rather in the sense that it might be difficult for him not to collude with his colleagues' unconscious wish to keep him confined within the curricular boundary and thus to deny the reality of his overall leadership of a large section of the school. It was not until the autumn term, however, that he was able to explore this problem directly with the four house heads. Between the middle of September and the middle of November I attended five of his meetings with the house heads. One of these was confined to fairly routine administrative matters, but the other four were concerned with fundamental questions about the way in which the roles of the house heads were being affected by the recent change in the management structure.

The elevation of Clive Vanloo to his new role, with his consequent inclusion in the standing committee, was not the only change that threatened the autonomy of the house heads, for the autumn term brought yet another new element into the situation: namely the appointment and arrival of Margaret Fisher as school counsellor. Because the role was new both to her and to the school, her coming had inevitably brought a great deal of discussion and puzzled enquiry about how the staff could best use her help with children who presented behavioural problems.

It was somewhat ironical that at the very time when the management structure in the staff group was being radically changed with a view to re-integrating the curricular and pastoral functions, the problem of pastoral care for children in difficulties should appear to have been hived off into a new member of the staff who had not experienced the events leading up to that change. It had already been evident in the first staff meeting of that term, part of which was devoted to discussion about the role of the counsellor, that problems were likely to arise both for tutors and for Margaret Fisher herself over the question of confidentiality. In the middle school this problem had an additional dimension since she would be accountable not only to the tutors and the section head as in the lower and upper schools but also to the house heads.

The exploration of this problem between the house heads and Clive Vanloo in two consecutive meetings, the second of which was attended by Margaret Fisher, exposed the danger of another kind of splitting between 'teaching' and 'caring for' children. Peter Chapman expressed a fear that the head of the middle school might have to adopt a punishing attitude to a difficult child in his house and thus unwittingly obstruct the work that he and the tutor and the counsellor might be trying to do together on the counselling side. Later, Graeme Osborn made a similar reference to 'disciplinary action' that might have to be taken at the top. Curiously enough, Clive Vanloo himself did not apparently feel any danger in these suggestions perhaps because they were felt to implicate 'subject teachers' who might put pressure on him to punish rather than himself as a punishing kind of person. Yet the house heads, who had probably experienced similar pressure from their tutors to be the punishing figures in the houses, seemed prepared to recognize that there might be some danger in this kind of polarization, and that they and their tutors, like the children in their houses, might be tempted to put the caring part of leadership into Margaret Fisher and the punishing part into Clive Vanloo—a kind of splitting that Robin Thomas had sometimes felt was being done by colleagues to Joan Bradbury as senior mistress and himself as deputy head.

Because Margaret Fisher carried a service role in relation to the house heads, and was not someone in authority over them as Clive Vanloo was, the temptation to see her rather than him as the one with whom they could collaborate in the care of disturbed children was very strong. In doing this, they were unconsciously pushing him further out as someone who supposedly exercised a kind of authority that might exclude care. In the second meeting, when Margaret Fisher was actually present, she was at one point unwittingly increasing the distance between Clive Vanloo and the house heads when for some minutes she referred to them by their christian names and to him as 'Mr Vanloo'. Thus it seemed that she found herself caught up in something that the house heads had tried to do to him in an earlier meeting, when they had raised all kinds of objections to the idea that he could hold meetings of the middle-school tutors. Even when he had pointed out his need to be in touch with the tutors in his section if he was to represent them adequately in the standing committee, the house heads seemed unwilling to entertain the idea that he should hold tutors' meetings except in relation to specific curricular matters.

It seemed, then, that both in relation to Clive Vanloo as the new section head and in relation to Margaret Fisher as the new school counsellor, the house heads felt that their own internal relationships with their tutorial staff groups, built up carefully over the years, might now be in jeopardy. It seemed also that they were unconsciously united in a wish to keep him at a safe distance at least from their tutors, but to seek a partnership with her within their houses and along with their tutors. In fact, by the middle of October, Graeme Osborn had already established a working relationship with her by inviting her into his house to talk with him and his tutors about the work she hoped to do and about the children in their house, a gesture to which she made public reference both in a full staff meeting and in the meeting of the house heads to which I have just been referring. He subsequently followed up this move by having fortnightly meetings with her in her room to discuss her work with children in his house.

The anxieties about how much of a child's situation could be shared between the counsellor and the tutor or house head (or both) and how much would have to be regarded as 'confidential' were evidently masking a similar anxiety that would have existed whether or not the school had acquired a counsellor: namely, the fear that matters hitherto contained within a house might have to be shared and discussed not only with the head of the middle school but also with fellow house heads. This perhaps was why the house heads tried, in various ways, to perpetuate the fantasy that Clive Vanloo would not even want to be involved with anything that could be described as the 'counselling' of children in difficulties. Yet a very clear piece of evidence that his role *would* (and already did) include this kind of concern was there for them all to see at the beginning of the meeting that was attended by Margaret Fisher; for when they arrived for that meeting, he was on the telephone receiving information about a difficult situation that had arisen that very afternoon in connection with a girl in the middle school. After he had replaced the receiver and exchanged a brief word with the house head concerned, merely indicating that they would need to discuss the matter later (by implication, in private), the meeting proceeded as if no-one there had overheard a word of this conversation.

The main theme for the meeting was the problem of liaison between the counsellor, the house heads and the tutorial staff; yet the knowledge that Clive Vanloo at that very time was in possession of information that none of the others yet had was totally ignored, until, quite late in the meeting, I drew attention to the way in which their abstract discussion about situations that had not yet arisen was covering up the concrete reality of the situation there in their midst. This forced the house heads to recognize that they, like members of the standing committee and like Margaret Fisher herself, would frequently be faced with the necessity to make choices about whether they would consult colleagues or keep them in the dark about problem cases, and equally that colleagues would be making choices about whether to consult them or keep them in the dark.

The subsequent sharing of information, in that same meeting, about the particular incident that Clive Vanloo had been discussing on the telephone when the meeting was due to start enabled the house heads to look more closely at their own ambivalence about the new situation in the middle school. Graeme Osborn acknowledged that the 'autonomy' that they had so prized in the past had also involved a kind of isolation; and he predicted that the necessity to exchange more information with one another about what went on in the houses and to expose more to one another about the problems they encountered might have a value for them that would compensate at least in part for the loss of that earlier autonomy, about which Peter Chapman had spoken nostalgically, as I recalled, in an earlier meeting.

Along with this acknowledgement, however, there was a strong urge to question the wisdom of such self-scrutiny and an equally strong need to take me severely to task for having exposed conflicts instead of colluding with their wish to deny conflicts—a need that was at first expressed privately to Clive Vanloo and then, on his advice, taken up directly with me in his presence. The confrontation between the house heads and myself in a later meeting—following the painful exposure of these complex feelings about the nature of leadership and consultation—opened the door for further exploration both of Clive Vanloo's difficulties in taking over his new leadership role and of their difficulties in accepting that leadership. To the surprise of the other four, Clive Vanloo then found himself able to say that he perceived the situation between himself and them to have been improved rather than worsened by the exposure of the conflicts, and that he now found it easier to work with them because what had been private and inaccessible had become public. Ten weeks later, in the full staff meeting that followed the distribution of my internal report of December 1969, the difficulties that the house heads had experienced were made even more public, when Peter Chapman, acknowledging his discomfort and anger at the time of those meetings, also acknowledged the learning that had accompanied or followed the discomfort.

Uncertainties of senior staff about the validity of their roles in a changing school culture

During the months that followed the change of structure in September 1969, the department heads too were experiencing a sense of loss. Like the house heads, they were losing, to Clive Vanloo in particular, part of what they had hitherto regarded as their autonomy; they were having to hand over to incoming young and inexperienced teachers some of the teaching tasks that they had enjoyed carrying out in the past; and they were seeing their specialized curricular roles being submerged in the integrated courses that were gradually finding their way into all three sections of the school, bringing with them new problems about leadership and boundary definition.

As I showed in Chapter V, the structure of management before the autumn of 1969 had made it difficult for senior staff in different parts of the system to test their relationships with one another, because the separation of 'pastoral' from 'departmental' concerns had been enabling those on the two sides of the dividing line to perceive one another's tasks as more distinct and separable than they really were. The dissolution of these separate meetings and their replacement by the combined senior staff meeting gradually freed both the department heads and the house heads to find new ways of working constructively together to bring about appropriate kinds of change rather than continue the struggle to defend personal empires. The fact that such a radical change as the abolition of the house system in favour of a year-group system in September 1971 could be brought about was evidence that this had indeed been happening during the intervening two years.

But again, as with the top management group, itself a part of the senior management group, the process was slow and difficult. And all the time the staff, from the headmaster to the most junior teachers, from the most 'traditional' to the most 'radical', were having to handle pupils who were testing out their authority in all kinds of ways and parents who often threw doubts on the ways in which these tests were being met. For if the testing out of the headmaster, particularly by those in the middle management roles, had been severe during the winter and spring of the 1969–70 session, the testing out of the authority of the staff, particularly in the upper school, was equally severe during the winter and spring of the 1970–1 session. Much of this was perceived by the staff to have stemmed mainly from the abolition of school uniform for the upper school in February 1970.

It was ironical that this decision had been made hurriedly, with very little consultation, during the very term when the standing committee was spending hours of time, almost every day of the week, consulting with colleagues about decisions concerning the curriculum. It was even more ironical that over the matter of school uniform, the effects of which were going to be more visibly obvious to parents and indeed to the entire neighbourhood than any decisions about the curriculum could be, Denys John and Mike Burnham had been equally reluctant to take the responsibility of working the whole question through with the pupils themselves and with the staff. Almost overnight, it seemed, the inhabitants of the old sixth-form territory, with its grammar-school associations, had begun to look like students in a college of further education.

Some months later it was not only a change in clothes that was making itself apparent, but also changes in behaviour. Students complained that pupils were casual, new members of staff that they were unmannerly. The senior staff found themselves hesitating to interfere lest they antagonize the young. Some of them looked for someone to blame and one or two implied, or stated openly, that they had not been consulted about the decisions and were at a loss to know what to say to parents who made disapproving comments on the change in the general appearance of the older pupils in the school. Was it Mike Burnham's 'fault' or the head's 'fault'? Joy Sollars—perhaps making a gesture on behalf of others besides herself—formally asked to withdraw from tutoring in the upper school, because she found herself, as she put it to me some months later, 'out of step' with the general ethos of the upper school as it was then developing.

Yet the depression being experienced by many members of the senior staff about this fear that they might be abdicating was very difficult to reconcile with the increase of their skills in discussing in public the real issues with which they had to deal. The difference between the atmosphere of the former section heads' and department heads' meetings and one particular senior staff meeting that I attended in February 1971, was to me very striking, even though I was aware that there were great difficulties being faced.

The difference seemed to be that it was no longer considered unwise or unprofessional to acknowledge such feelings as uncertainty, depression or fear of inadequacy. The problems of being in the middle-management group rather than the top-management group, and of being in the senior-staff group rather than the rank and file, were being explored at greater depth. Where people would, perhaps, have been saying formerly that they were not being consulted or that the head was failing to offer decisive leadership, they were now asking themselves why they should be *feeling* unnecessary, or why they were so puzzled about how best to use their leadership powers in the difficult circumstances in which they so often found themselves, both with colleagues and with parents, and indeed also with pupils. There were references to the problems of being representatives acting or speaking on behalf of departments or areas of the staff group and of reconciling oneself to being 'senior' to colleagues who, in other respects, were just as essential to the work of those departments. Nearly two years earlier (in May 1969) when Denys John had put on the agenda for a department heads' meeting an item that he had called 'the role of a head of department', Lewis Smith, himself absent from the meeting but using Mike Burnham as his proxy, had sent in a counter question about what, in relation to the full staff meeting, the role of the department heads' *meeting* really was. In fact at first that question had been misheard, apparently by everyone there apart from myself, with the result that, although it did in the end precipitate a useful exploration of the problems of how department heads and section heads handled their relationships, the discussion had for quite a long time been deflected into the much safer theme of the current difficulty in finding time to hold departmental meetings within subject groups, with consequent avoidance of the task of examining the relations between the headmaster and the department heads *as a group.*

On the later occasion, in 1971, it was Denys John himself who requested that the whole meeting be devoted to discussion about what the senior staff meeting was really for. Thus the way was open for a far more honest exploration than had been possible on the earlier occasion, or even in the first meeting of the combined senior staff group in the autumn of 1969— an exploration of the relationships between the middle-management and top-management groups. This involved some consideration of how the members of middle management and the standing committee handled their relationships, not just within this combined group in the monthly senior staff meetings, but publicly in the staff group as a whole, and in the still wider context that included staff, governors, parents and students.

At the first senior staff meeting eighteen months earlier, Lewis Smith had asked the head a direct question which could easily have trapped him into giving a false assurance that the standing committee would be only an agenda-forming body rather than one which would have power to work closely with the headmaster over his final decisions and thus be a council in which he might actually make decisions. That attempt was now recalled by members of the standing committee, denied at first by the middle-management representatives who had been on the staff at that time, and then quite seriously examined. Denys John acknowledged that, as it turned out, the standing committee had unwittingly become the body that, among other things, decided what the agenda for both full and senior staff meetings should be—in other words, that the committee had accepted as part of its role the function to which others had wanted it to be restricted. Mike Burnham then pointed out that it had always been open to any member of staff to suggest agenda for meetings. Why, he wondered, had none of his colleagues taken this kind of initiative? A few minutes later Lewis Smith parried this thrust by announcing that while Mike Burnham had been talking he had thought of five topics that he would like to propose be put on the agenda for future senior staff meetings. Soon after he had read out his list, another department head, as though implying that it was probably falling on deaf ears, said something to the effect that there was no machinery for proposing agenda. Two members of the committee countered this—Mike Burnham by pointing out gently but emphatically that Lewis Smith had just shown that the machinery did exist, since he had used it, Joan Bradbury asking her colleagues with some indignation whether they were imagining that these suggestions would now be lost without trace, in other words that the standing committee would ignore them. In fact the committee subsequently spent a good deal of time working out a series of related themes for staff meetings that incorporated all those suggestions.

One topic that did not appear in Lewis Smith's list was the whole burning question of the validity of the house system and the growing need for some form of year-group leadership. This question had been discussed in two special meetings seven months earlier—one centred on lower-school tutors along with the house heads, chaired by John Harbinson and attended by Clive Vanloo; the other a combined meeting of the lower- and middle-school staff groups chaired by Robin Thomas. There was at least some slight evidence that this question was in the air during this senior staff meeting of February 1971 however. The meeting was being held in a larger room than usual, a room in the Further Education block, in which up to forty people could sit round in a circle in comfortable chairs. Yet two of the house heads (the two women) coming in at the last minute sat together on hard chairs outside the circle near the door making no contribution to the discussion, although there were comfortable chairs in the circle still empty, chairs that were in fact occupied eventually by still later arrivals. I had a strong impression, throughout the meeting, that the other two house heads, both of whom were by then taking responsible leadership roles in the curricular system as well as the house system—Graeme Osborn in the humanities course, and Peter Chapman in the physics department—felt more integrated within the senior staff group than did their two female colleagues. Moreover, both the men had on certain occasions expressed some doubts about the continuing validity of the house system.

Three weeks later the house heads were invited to attend a joint meeting over lunch with the standing committee, to examine the whole problem of structure, and to exchange as freely as possible their views and feelings about the existing house system as compared with the possible alternative year-group system. On this occasion there was a visible division of interests—not this time between the two men and the two women but between Graeme Osborn and the other three. Sitting between Clive Vanloo and John Harbinson on one side of the table, he remained silent for much of the meeting, apparently holding much of the ambivalence towards the house system. The other three, sitting opposite him, spoke strongly in favour of retaining it. The two women spoke first, basing their argument mainly on the need to preserve, within the institution, units that could resemble the family structure, in the sense that each house had a mixed age group within it. Peter Chapman began by recalling something he had said when he was interviewed for the post of housemaster, about his 'love' of children, and emphasized the need of each child for love and care, suggesting that the house system made it possible to provide this; but the more telling argument he put forward was not about his love of children but about his fear of them—his fear that a year-group system might strengthen the 'bad elements' by isolating thirteen, fourteen- or fifteen-year-olds as year groups and thus massing them together, as potentially violent individuals, in large numbers. This argument received support from the two women, Pat Chapman pointing out that some of the

T.S.T.M.—10

recent outbreaks of bullying in the middle school had occurred after the fourth-year pupils from all the houses had had a joint afternoon on the games field.

For this special meeting between the standing committee and the house heads, Denys John had—skilfully it seemed, though in fact, as he later told me, quite unconsciously—avoided reconstructing the old visual pattern of the pre-standing-committee years. The ten people who took part in this joint meeting were the same ten people who, as 'section heads', had met every other month in his room, not over lunch but in the late afternoon, before the reorganization of the management structure in September 1969. He had recently rearranged the furniture in his room so that the tables formed a large square in place of the former long oblong, with its twin suggestions of the board meeting or the refectory meal. For this occasion he restored the long table; but he arranged it in a different part of the room, head on to the long side of his desk and reaching almost to the door. It was, I think, an indication of how far the examination of the real role relationships in the staff group had gone during the intervening months since the last of the old-style section heads' meetings in the summer of 1969, that I did not once feel this meeting to be turning the clock back. Nor did it once occur to me consciously before or during the meeting that these *were* the same ten people whose regular meetings I had attended during the 1968–9 session. All I was aware of as I entered the room was a certain nervousness which I was at a loss to account for and which found expression in my remark 'It looks like a board meeting' as I sat down. The next two people to arrive—both members of the standing committee—expressed a similar nervous apprehension by commenting on the table formation as they sat down, the first referring to an interview, the second merely remarking 'Bit of a change!' The nervousness was not, it seemed, confined to me. Indeed Denys John himself seemed anxiously preoccupied, as people were arriving, with the task of ensuring that everything was arranged so that the work of the meeting could be tackled in spite of the distractions of eating lunch together in what could easily have become a nostalgic recreation of past relationships.

In fact the discussion, firmly based on the present realities of the existing management structure, was sophisticated and forward-looking, and the meeting felt like the meeting it was intended to be—a joint meeting of two important sub-groups of the staff, in which motives for wishing to preserve one system or to introduce another could be questioned and studied. It even became possible for the two single women in the group of house heads to consider whether their wish to preserve a 'family-like' house structure might have more to do with their own need to find in their work, through a leadership role in relation to a family-sized staff group, a kind of substitute for the family they did not have in real life, than with the actual needs of any unit of 150 or so children. There was also some examination of the wish to perceive the leadership of a year group as 'administrative' rather than 'caring', and the leadership of a house group as 'caring' rather than 'administrative', and thus to avoid the reality that any form of leadership or administration must involve both caring and organizational functions, whether it occurred at the boundary of a house or at the boundary of a year group.

Fairly near the end of the meeting, Clive Vanloo, referring to some of the opinions that had been put forward, spoke of the splitting apart of the curricular and pastoral functions that the house system encouraged. This released Graeme Osborn to express some of his own ambivalence towards both sides of his work, by saying with some feeling that if one was a department head one was left alone to get on with it, whereas being a house head forced one into a tightly structured system. On the face of it this could have implied that he felt it was preferable to be left to get on with it; and that he experienced the 'tightly structured system' as something that robbed him of independence. Later, however, it emerged that what he had really been trying to identify was the problem of moving away from the structured *support* system—as he had experienced it through the section heads' meetings and through the house heads' meetings with Denys John, Robin Thomas and Joan Bradbury—into the potentially isolated position he was now beginning to experience in taking charge of the expanding humanities programme. And he, more acutely than any of the other house heads, had been and still was in a position to experience the ambiguity of these two contrasted positions —the comforting support and the possible constriction in the one case, the enviable freedom and the accompanying fear of isolation in the other.

Conflicts between parents, teachers and pupils over the setting of homework

So far in this chapter I have been concerned only with relationships between those in middle-management and top-management roles. But to understand the nature of the tensions between these two levels of management and between heads of departments and those in pastoral roles, whether as tutors or as house or section heads, we need to bring in a third group of adults— namely the parents. The problem—for all the staff—of containing the anxieties about the triangular relationships between parents, teachers and children was particularly noticeable whenever discussions arose about the apparently trivial theme of 'homework', since this always uncovered uneasiness about the obligations of parents and teachers both to the child and to one another about how any two exchanged information about the activities of the third.

It is very difficult to describe the nature of the tensions between tutors and subject teachers, particularly at the level of section and department leadership, because the same staff could, at different times, perceive the same problem from different standpoints—hence, perhaps, the urge to deny that the difficulties ever existed. Such areas were often found to be somewhere on the boundary between school and home. Parental anxieties about standards of work could induce a state of friction—even of mistrust—between a house head and a subject department head. It was not surprising, therefore, that problems arose on two occasions in the earlier department heads' meetings and again some months later in the combined senior staff meeting over this vexed question of homework. Again, I must take my readers back along the time scale in order to illustrate, through this particular recurring theme, the increasing openness and sophistication of the consultative process in the staff group.

At least one BBC television programme has given enough attention to this issue to justify the conclusion that it must be giving rise to conflicts between parents and teachers and between teachers themselves in many schools, and that it may be particularly acute in schools that are 'going comprehensive'. Parents, it seems, are very ambivalent towards this matter. They grow anxious and protective if they see their children being overworked and may protest to the schools that too much homework is being set, or that the work set is inappropriate. Equally, however, they grow anxious if they feel that their children are being underworked and they may then protest that too little is being set. The second kind of complaint is by far the more damaging to the morale of teachers and to their relations within the staff group, since to set too much homework implies conscientiousness and a wish to harness the pupil's effort, whereas to set too little (or to be accused of setting none at all) implies laziness and lack of concern about whether the pupil learns or not. A child who assures his mother that Mr X did not set him any homework may be communicating only half of the truth; or he may be lying to protect himself. Moreover, in a school that is having to change its image from that of the grammar school it used to be to that of the comprehensive school it is striving to become, such complaints from parents are difficult to interpret because they may have less to do with the value of 'homework' than with feelings about lost grammar-school status.

Complaints about the non-setting of homework may come direct to the headmaster; or they may come to the head of a section, or even perhaps to a child's tutor. And immediately a dilemma arises. If the complaint has come to the headmaster, what does he do? Does he take the matter up with the tutor or with the section head, leaving one of them to follow it up with the subject teacher concerned? Or should the matter be raised first with the head of the subject department to discuss with him or her how homework tasks are viewed functionally within that department and to find out how the parent's complaint is likely to be interpreted by the teacher concerned? Alternatively, does the head avoid going to individuals and raise the question in a general way during a staff meeting?

Whatever he does it will be hard for the staff not to feel that they are being reprimanded. And at the level of a reprimand, or even of a benevolent kind of injunction, the question of homework can take on a certain triviality and arouse feelings of irritation on both sides. Yet the whole issue of homework is really very central to the problem of how teachers and parents cooperate in the education of children; for it symbolizes an almost nightly meeting point where parents, pupils, tutors, subject teachers, senior staff members and heads can use one another in all kinds of divisive ways. In any of the triangular situations that develop—between head, section head and subject teacher, or between parent, headmaster and section head, or between parent, child and tutor—it is fatally easy for two of the three to find themselves almost ganging up against the third. Thus, two of the three parties to the argument may combine to protect each other against the third; or two of them may combine to put pressure on the third or to blame the third for what has happened.

Faced with this kind of problem, it may seem to a headmaster that the best way to handle a growing number of complaints or queries from parents is to depersonalize the problem by delivering a kind of sermon in a staff meeting and appealing to his colleagues to tighten up their procedures for the setting and marking of homework. Yet it may be that what is really needed is a full discussion about the whole matter, in terms of how tutors and their section heads on the one hand and subject teachers and their department heads on the other handle their communication system so as to avoid colluding with the splitting devices unconsciously being used by children and by their parents and indeed by themselves.

If teachers avoid examining these problems—particularly at the middle management level, where they are probably most acute—it becomes increasingly difficult for anyone to know at what point a search for information or evidence becomes an act of spying, or at what point the act of providing information becomes a kind of betrayal. Once it becomes possible to open up these fears and suspicions in the staff group itself, the real underlying problems can be uncovered. And these are questions about what it means to have responsibility for the teaching of a particular section of the school, and about what it means to be responsible on the one hand to a department head and on the other to a section head for the kind of contribution one is making to the growth and learning of one's own pupils.

Every member of the middle-management group at Nailsea experienced both these situations: for everyone was simultaneously in a leadership role in one part of the system and a member of a team (or of two or three teams) in another part of the system. In the year before the combined senior staff meeting came into existence, the issue of homework came up twice in department heads' meetings, first in January 1969 and then in July of the same year. On the first occasion, Denys John tried to deal with the problem by the 'sermon' or 'injunction' method, appealing to his colleagues to recognize that they had a kind of contract with parents and must fulfil the expectations aroused by that contract by setting homework according to the agreed schedule, a schedule that was based on their own requirements in the various subjects for which they were responsible. The staff had been discussing the matter in a somewhat desultory way, some people pointing out that in some subjects the actual setting of a piece of homework did not necessarily contribute to real learning, whereas in other subjects homework might be a necessary sequel to classwork. They listened in silence to what the head said, and no further discussion took place.

As the meeting moved on to the next item on the agenda I found myself uneasily wondering whether the parents who had been registering the complaints had somehow split the staff from their headmaster, thereby worsening rather than improving the situation. The real problems, it seemed, lay buried under the mask of polite acquiescence. Ironically enough the next item on the agenda for that meeting also concerned communication with parents: namely, the urgent need to communicate to them by letter, later that week, the recommendations of the staff about which fifth-year pupils should be entered for GCE and which for CSE examinations. This item also touched on another raw spot in the middle-management group—the effect on department heads of the key role of Clive Vanloo (still at that time 'director of intermediate studies') when decisions of this kind had to be made. The opinions of the heads of departments about the capabilities of the present fifth-year pupils as candidates for GCE or CSE were, it became clear, being based partly on the mock GCE and CSE examinations still going on during that week, examinations that were regarded by some staff, if not by most, as diagnostic in their purpose rather than as the rehearsal for the real thing that the pupils took them to be. The argument that ensued over the difficulties of supplying Clive Vanloo with the information he needed, in order to make the final decisions having collated the evidence from the department heads, was in marked contrast to the lack of protest following Denys John's injunction about the provision of homework.

At the time I did not connect the suppressed hostility over the homework issue with the open turmoil over the examinations issue, but saw the latter only in the context of the difficulty over Clive Vanloo's leadership role. But there was some evidence that the problem of communication with parents was causing a division between those with curricular responsibilities and those with pastoral responsibilities, since it was one of the house heads who suggested that the school did a poor public relations job with parents and said that she feared they were in danger of appearing to 'consult' parents about what examinations their children should be entered for when they had really already made up their minds and wished only to present the parents with a *fait accompli*.

When the problem came up again seven months later it was in a different context, though still in relation to children's allegations, via their parents, that certain members of staff did not set homework in accordance with the agreed schedule. From Tony Frost, who himself had children in the school, came the other side of the problem: the fear that the demands on pupils were becoming too heavy as they progressed through the school. He expressed concern, as others did in response to him, that the homework schedule for the coming year, prepared by Joan Bradbury and circulated to the staff before the meeting, showed an alarming increase from fifteen hours per fortnight in Year III to twenty-four hours in Year IV.

But the important thing that emerged from the discussion on this second occasion was the uncomfortable discovery that tutors were somehow being manoeuvred into a position in which, in the process of checking up on children to ensure that they were doing the homework that had been set, they imperceptibly found themselves checking up on their colleagues to find out which of them were neglecting to set homework. One department head reported that a tutor in one of the houses in the middle school had claimed to have accumulated in the course of one term about 2000 pieces of paper, all noting cases of children who said they had been given no homework or whose parents had complained that particular teachers were not setting it. Thus a department head might find himself having to act on a tutor's report of such a complaint by setting up with a particular member of his department an enquiry about whether or not the allegations of child and parent were true, and if true whether the non-setting of work to be done at home was justifiable in terms of the kind of work being done at school. The same department head, of course, in his role as tutor—particularly, it seemed, if he tutored in the middle school—might have to make similar reports to other department heads; and he himself, as a teacher of his subject, might at times be named by a parent or a child as one of the backsliders.

The revelation of these difficulties in carrying out supervision—whether as a tutor in relation to children or as a department head in relation to staff —produced from Graham Morris (who, it will be recalled, was not at that time technically a head of either a subject department or a section, but attended department heads' meetings as head of library) a sudden sharp question: 'Is this a check on children or a check on teachers?' echoing exactly my own thoughts and feelings about the developing situation. Denys John attempted to reduce the tension by declaring that although the situation might look like that, it was not really a check-up on teachers that was going on. But the anxiety could not be allayed as easily as this; and it was perhaps important that it should not be allayed, since the reality of the supervisory part of a department head's role and of a section or house head's role was something that did, in the end, have to be examined.

At that stage, the important distinction that was beginning to emerge was that it might be possible for tutors (and house or section heads) and subject teachers (and department heads) to move away from the situation in which people had to check up on one another and by implication defend themselves against one another, towards a situation in which they could share information with one another. Thus the parent's anxiety about the amount and quality of work being done at home could be perceived as the natural counterpart of the teacher's anxiety about the amount and quality of the work being done at school, since the real objective in all exchanges of information and evidence, about homework as about other matters, was to find out how far each child was using his opportunities and developing his potential.

When the homework issue reappeared for the third time, in the senior staff meeting of February 1971, Denys John prepared a detailed statement, covering two sides of a page, setting out the problem in terms not unlike those he had used verbally in the earlier meetings, but in the context of a problem to be tackled rather than of a simple wrong to be put right. He proposed as an approach to the problem that a specific procedure be adopted so that everyone would know what the agreed sequence of action should be when a tutor, a house head or a section head became aware of a conflict between home and school over this matter. To me, seeing the document in cold blood as it were, and without the experience of the senior staff meeting in which it was discussed, it looked alarmingly dictatorial and seemed to be setting up staff members, in their tutorial roles, as informers to the heads of departments, and to be subjecting the same staff members, in their subject-teacher roles, to the surveillance of the three section heads who were, if necessary, to alert the department heads to the need to investigate or offer help.

My impressions about staff reactions to this document, gleaned from what I was told by Denys John and Robin Thomas, was that they were strongly ambivalent. The positive side of the ambivalence was expressed by certain department heads who individually, outside the meeting, admitted to considerable relief that a procedure was being offered. The negative side was expressed in the senior staff meeting in a certain amount of anger over the threat to friendly relationships implicit in the proposals. But again, the very fact that the handling of the situation made the expression of these mixed feelings possible, brought with it an exploration of important realities. For the senior staff were forced to ask themselves what their responsibilities were towards younger and less experienced staff and what authority they had to exercise leadership in an active way, even by using supervisory powers and by finding ways of offering supportive, if critical, advice to colleagues who were in difficulties. What Denys John had in fact tried to emphasize in his document was that young teachers, or even older ones who were encountering problems in their work, could ask for help without losing face, since part of the responsibility of senior staff was to provide such help.

Ironically, however, the work that was done on this problem during the senior staff meeting was done in his absence. For it was scheduled during a two-week period when he was not only absent from the school but out of the country, working in France on behalf of the D.E.S., interviewing French assistants for the 1971–2 session. Thus it was Robin Thomas, deputizing for him during that fortnight, who experienced the bad feelings of the senior staff group about the head's 'Homework' manifesto, while Denys John himself was far away in France assuming that it had come to them as a needed directive in a confused situation. Moreover, it was at the very end of that meeting that reference was made to the amount of time given to department heads to carry out the kind of supervisory task outlined by the head, as compared with the amount of time given to the deputies of the section and house heads. It must have been clear to many people at that time that the ambivalence towards the document and towards the headmaster himself in this connection was far stronger, even by the spring of 1971, and far more difficult to express directly to him than anyone was yet prepared to admit.

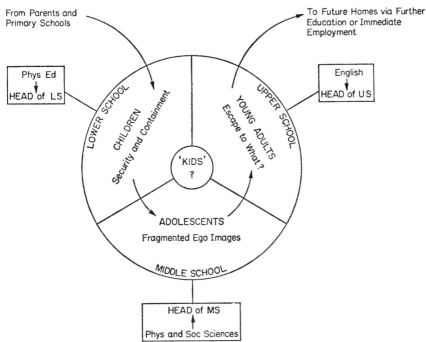

FIG. 52. Section leadership and changing pupil needs.

It is becoming evident that we cannot examine these problems of role relationships either at the level of top management or at the level of middle management, without being involved in frequent shifts of perspective. For the kind of analysis in which we are engaged reveals a continuous state of tension between those divisions or 'departments' that are based on areas of knowledge and those divisions or 'sections' that are based on phases of growth (see Figure 52). The content of this chapter has overlapped with the content of the next one in at least two ways: for it has already touched on the differentiation between those management roles that included member- ship of the senior staff group and those that did not, and it has drawn attention to the problem experienced by many staff members in reconciling a commitment to the task of one of the three main age-based divisions of the school with the need to feel identified with the institution as a whole. Both these questions are intimately related to the overall theme of the five chapters in this section of the book—the way in which a headmaster and his staff manage their consultative and decision-making procedures.

In the next chapter I shall consider how successive distributions of tutorial staff between the three main sections of the school may have been affecting people's perceptions of one another and bringing into existence certain assumptions about value systems in one section as compared with those in another. I shall then take up some of the implications of the second major change of structure, when the house system was abandoned in favour of a year-group system and the departmental pattern was modified to allow for some differentiation between 'subjects' and 'curricular areas', with further differentiation between middle-management roles and further building in of training roles in all the major areas of responsibility.

CHAPTER X

Section Identity in Relation to School Identity in a Three-tiered System

Consultation as an aspect of management

The four preceding chapters have been concerned mainly with the problems of defining and differentiating between top-management and middle-management tasks. In other words, it can be said that we have been looking at the management group within the staff group. But the staff group as a whole, viewed within the institution, is itself a management group in relation to the pupils. And so when we study the problems of consultation we are concerned with something more than the steps taken by heads and their senior colleagues to keep their junior colleagues happy. Essentially the point of consultation is to find more effective ways of using management skills at all levels in the staff group.

It is perhaps a truism to say that the amount of consultation that goes on in the sub-sections of any staff group will vary in proportion to the amount that goes on between the head and his senior colleagues. But it is not the head alone who controls this, for we have to bear in mind that the word itself implies effort on both sides. The headmaster or the head of a section or department, it is true, may have to be the initiator in setting up a structure or programme within which consultative meetings can take place. But the members of staff themselves must be prepared to initiate processes by offering themes for discussion in regular meetings, asking for special meetings when the need for these arises, even perhaps proposing alternative kinds of structure. Thus the responsibility to take initiative is continually balanced by the responsibility to respond to initiative; and those in leadership roles, if the system is flexible enough, will find themselves moving back and forth between these positions, as will those to whom they give leadership.

How then does the school mobilize its junior management to take part in creative reconstruction and the rethinking of educational objectives? Does this happen predominantly within subject departments in relation to innovatory practices in classroom, laboratory or workshop and in relation to the redesigning of syllabuses? Or does it happen predominantly in tutorial staff groups within the section boundaries that enclose particular age groups of the pupil population? If it is happening in both areas, how can the contribution of younger members of staff (and of older ones who for one reason or another are not in senior roles) be made part of the overall planning and policy-making in the staff group as a whole?

Already in earlier chapters we have had examples of staff members taking various kinds of initiative by promoting discussions on themes which, but for their initiative, might never have been formally discussed at all. Seven of those who asked for meetings with the standing committee during the spring of 1970, when the whole curriculum pattern was under review, were colleagues who did not hold senior positions as heads of sections, houses or departments. One, a temporary staff member, who left at the end of the year, raised some of the problems of liaison in the humanities work. The other six were: David Williams, who took up again in the changing situation of that term the problems about drama which, as a result of his own earlier initiative, had been discussed in the special meetings described in Chapter IV; John Phillips, who outlined proposals for a possible course in creative technology to be taught within a scientific framework; Pat Richardson, who raised questions about a new kind of linguistic study for especially able children who were not being sufficiently stretched by their present courses; Valerie Weyman, who presented views about how the teaching of geography could be enriched through links with the empirical disciplines of the physical and social sciences; Janet Roberts, who proposed an integrated course for less able middle-school pupils, in particular for early leavers, that would cut across science, technology, home economics, citizenship and (possibly) humanities; and Sue Moth, who put forward ideas about collaboration between the English, art and music departments. All but one of these initiatives, while appearing to be springing from particular scientific, linguistic, environmental, literary and artistic interests, seemed also to be linked with a concern about children who were in a particular phase of their journey through secondary school, and perhaps because of this, to be concerned with exploring the possibilities of collaboration between adjoining areas rather than with the rigid maintenance of existing subject boundaries.

The first three people in the above list spoke of courses that were or might be located in the lower school. The next three were concerned particularly with the middle school and with the problems surrounding the transition either of the high achievers to sixth-form courses and university education or of the low achievers to early employment and home making. The remaining one, who was not at that time a tutor in any section of the school, seemed to be concerned more with the overall possibilities of collaboration between the English department (of which she was a member) and the specialists in art, music and drama, than with any particular age group of pupils. None of the seven people listed here was a tutor in the lower school. Of the five who did have tutor groups, four were located in the middle-school system, the two men being deputies to two of the house heads, and only one, Pat Richardson, was a tutor in the upper school. What evidence can we find from the expressed concerns of these people about how tutorial interests, which in any one year had to be based in a section, were being influenced by subject interests that were, or could be, school wide?

Choice versus chance in the distribution of tutors between sections

It may be useful first to recall the evidence, discussed in Chapter V and mentioned again in Chapter IX, about the distribution of senior staff between the lower, middle and upper-school tutorial teams during the 1968–9 session. At that time all but two of the heads of the academic subjects were located in the upper school, the heads of modern languages, biology, art, music, technical education and remedial education in the lower school, and the head of physical education, as the sole representative of the department heads, in the middle school. Looking at this distribution through the other end of the telescope as it were, we find that three out of the twelve upper-school tutors, seven out of the thirteen lower-school tutors and twelve out of the fourteen middle-school tutors were of junior status, in the sense that they were not entitled to attend meetings of either the section heads or the department heads. Because of the particular circumstances that had surrounded the building up of the house-tutorial teams since 1966, it was difficult to know how far chance opportunity rather than deliberate choice had operated for any particular member of staff when a move from a tutorial role in one section to a tutorial role in another section took place, particularly since section heads themselves exercised some choice in selecting their tutors or at least in bargaining to get some of the tutors they wanted. Nevertheless, given the evidence that people were consulted about any reallocation of roles that would affect them personally, it is reasonable to suppose that tutors could exercise at least some choice in moving into or out of any particular section of the school. Gwen London and Tony Frost, both heads of departments, had, as I was told, moved at their own request from the sixth form to the lower school at the beginning of the 1967–8 session. It is of interest therefore to return now to those non-senior permanent staff members who sought interviews with the standing committee in the spring of 1970, and to follow up their subsequent movements.

John Phillips and David Williams, the two deputies to house heads within the 1968 to 1970 period, left the school in the following year, the former to become a head of science, following up his special subject interest, the latter to become head of a lower school, following up his interest in section-based tutorial work. Janet Roberts, who had shown a deep concern over the needs of early leavers, remained in the middle school in the two years following the summer of 1970 as a fifth-year tutor. Pat Richardson and Valerie Weyman, who had shown an equally deep concern over the conceptual problems of teaching linguistics and geography, and therefore, by implication, with the needs of pupils who would pursue special studies in those areas, were both upper-school tutors during the two years starting in September 1970, the latter being transferred into the upper school from the middle school in that year. Sue Moth's destination, after her year without a tutor group, was also, as it turned out, the upper school.

It would be easy to suggest that staff members in general felt themselves to be drawn to one section of the school in particular and that the strongest allegiances were to groupings based on the developmental stages of pupils rathe. than to groupings based on subject interests. But the feelings about section identity and about subject identity were much more complex than this. We have seen that the upper-school tutorial staff during the 1968–9 session was heavily weighted with heads of academic departments from both the science side and the arts side. By 1970 this kind of imbalance had disappeared, but a new one had appeared to take its place, in the shape of a sub-group with a strong 'special English' bias, since Mike Burnham, Lewis Smith and Graham Morris had been joined in that section by Sue Moth and the new drama specialist.

Scrutiny of the tutorial staff groups in the lower, middle and upper schools in the 1971–2 session brings to light another kind of weighting: namely, the predominance in that year of new staff members in the list of middle-school tutors. Now in fact there was a greater influx of new staff in that particular year than ever before—sixteen as compared with thirteen in September 1969 and twelve in September 1970. For me, as perhaps for parents of children who were moving into their third, fourth or fifth year in the school, what was striking about the 1971–2 list of middle-school tutors was the large number of new names, twelve out of the total of twenty being new members of staff in September 1971, and two others being relatively new, having joined the staff only the year before. In contrast to this middle-school picture, only three of the thirteen lower-school tutors were newcomers in that year, two others having joined the year before; and the pattern in the upper school was the same, except that one of the newcomers was a head of department, namely Lewis Smith's successor. If, as may be surmised, the staff who were already established in the school had preference of location for their tutorial work with pupils, the lower and upper schools must have been regarded as more attractive sections than the middle school in which to do tutorial work. We are left with a fairly urgent question about what message this preference pattern may have been conveying to the adolescent pupils of the third, fourth and fifth years.

To the child who enters the school at the age of eleven or who is transferred into it from another secondary school at a later stage, the hierarchical relationships between staff members as I have been describing them may mean very little. The most important person for him in the department of mathematics or modern languages will not necessarily be the head of either of those departments but the particular man or woman who teaches *him* maths or French. Similarly the head of his house or section, except at times of crisis or in a ritual assembly, may be a very shadowy figure compared with his own tutor. The members of a tutor group, as it acquires an identity and a cohesion vis-à-vis other tutor groups, will nevertheless have some awareness as the years go on of the comings and goings of staff members whom they know or about whom they have heard stories or rumours. They will therefore have their own ideas about the relative importance in the staff group of the tutors and subject teachers they encounter in the course of time; and the newness of a staff member to the school may be more significant to them than that staff member's relative seniority in the management structure of the staff group. In other words, the things that are most important in the task and sentient systems of the staff group are not necessarily the most important to the pupils.

Perception of pupil groups as vertically or horizontally organized

I have been talking of pupils as progressing 'through' the school or 'through' the years, deliberately avoiding the use of the preposition 'up'. Yet the terms 'lower', 'middle' and 'upper' schools, which I cannot avoid using, themselves imply an upward movement rather than a through process. This ambiguity in the language commonly used in schools to indicate the beginning and ending of a school career is reflected also in the terms commonly used to describe different kinds of pupil grouping. One of the most striking ambiguities in the dialogue between the Nailsea staff and myself throughout the period of our work together centred on the way in which they and I used the words 'horizontal' and 'vertical'. I noted in my first chapter that systems of house-tutorial groupings were usually perceived by teachers as 'vertical' and divisions into year groups or into lower, middle and upper schools as horizontal; but for me it was the year groups and the sections that were vertical and the house groups that were horizontal. It became evident as time went on that the staff and I were faced here with a real difference between their perspective and mine. In common, I fancy, with the great majority of secondary-school teachers, the staff appeared to have a mental picture of a school in which children moved up from the lowest forms to the highest forms, whereas I saw children as moving across the time scale from the first years to the last years.

The question at issue is a fundamental one. Are we looking at an educational ladder with a top series of rungs reached only by a chosen minority? Or are we looking at a flow of pupils through an institution with exit points through which pupils pass out of the institution after four, five, six, seven or eight years? The first model, as depicted in Figure 53, suggests a movement upwards, by implication from a low-status position to a high-status position. The second model, as in Figure 54, suggests a movement through a series of age-based systems, corresponding to phases in growth and development from childhood to adulthood. The first model puts—for teachers—a special

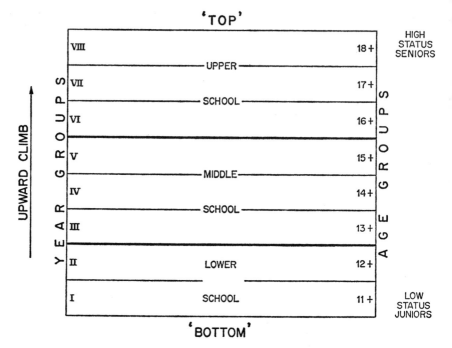

FIG. 53. Secondary schooling perceived as an educational ladder.

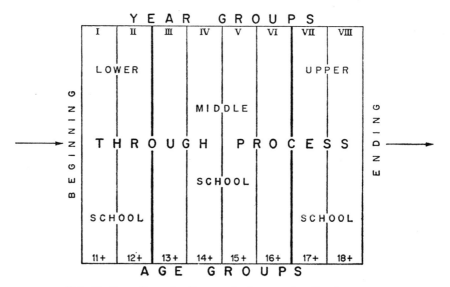

FIG. 54. Secondary schooling perceived as an educational process.

value on work with older pupils, and arouses corresponding anxieties on behalf of pupils who, similarly caught in the pursuit of status, are seen to be in need of security in the form of pastorally organized house or tutorial systems. The second model, although it does not suggest that teaching the young implies low status and teaching the old high status, does demand of teachers a realistic exploration of the kinds of skill and expertise that are needed for the different phases of a child's education and a willingness to match persons to roles in the light of what is known about the different strengths and weaknesses in the staff group.

Once we can perceive the year groups as vertical, in the sense that there is bound to be some discontinuity in the system each time a group of children moves on into another academic year and into a new pattern of courses, then we can begin to perceive the child's progress as a through-process rather than as an upward climb. In other words, it is the verticality of groupings that gives strength to the idea of movement through a time scale that is linked to natural growth and development. The concept of the educational *ladder*—in which groupings appear as horizontal and educational progress as vertical—puts a premium on climbing to the top and sees those who leave from the fourth or fifth years as 'early leavers' who have fallen off the ladder. The concept of the educational *process* recognizes that the loss of pupils at one time rather than another has to be evaluated not simply in terms of the pupil's ability or inability to stay the course but also in terms of the institution's ability or inability to provide for the growth needs of children as they pass through adolescence into adulthood. This in itself must raise for the school questions about where it should be defining the limits of what can reasonably be tackled within a single bounded institution.

The teacher, as he tries to make a choice about where to place himself in the system or come to terms with the decision made by others about his placement, is likely to experience conflicting feelings. For although attachment to the senior or 'upper' section of the school may have the lure of apparently high status and confinement to the junior or 'lower' section the implication of low status, work with younger children has nevertheless an attraction of its own that has nothing to do with status—the attraction of being in touch with children who still have the freshness and spontaneity that we associate with preadolescence, with good primary schools and lively homes. 'Going up' through the school, whether as a pupil or as a teacher moving 'up' with a group of pupils, thus has the double possibility of a sense of increasing stature and authority if pupils develop into mature scholars and a sense of disappointment and let-down if they deteriorate into resistant non-learners.

One of the problems about the three-tiered system, as it has been emerging from this study, is that the middle school is liable to be at the receiving end of projections from both the lower and the upper schools. Because of its position in the middle of the eleven-to-eighteen age-range, in the particular kind of secondary school we are examining here, it has to cope with two very different groups of pupils. It must contain both those who are just emerging from childhood (and from the more protective educational framework of the lower school) and those who are just moving towards adulthood (and, if they stay on at school, into the traditionally pre-university world of the sixth form). Viewed from within the school, the disturbance at these two points of transition or 'discontinuity' interrupts the natural continuum of the pupil's growth progress. The middle school, as a sub-system of the whole institution, may therefore find itself perceived simultaneously as the receiver of promising material at the third-year end and as the exporter of deteriorating material at the fifth-year end. The lower school and the upper school alike can thus rid themselves of 'blame' when promising pupils disappoint their teachers in later years. The fact that not all third-year pupils entering the middle school are equally eager to work and that not all fifth-year pupils leaving it are equally work-shy can easily be submerged in feelings about lost potential rather than recognized as concurrent evidence about both good and bad performance in all three sections.

Nowhere did expectations about standards, both of work and of behaviour, clash more loudly than in the meetings of the sixth-form tutors during the months that preceded and followed the reorganization of the management structure in 1969. It was, after all, in the sixth form that specialist teachers (and perhaps heads of academic departments in particular) sought the fulfilment of their hopes in the shape of good A-level results and in the accompanying signs that the pupils they had been teaching for some years would be a credit to them in their college or university careers. In view of the concentration of senior staff in the sixth-form tutorial team in the 1968–9 session, it was not surprising, perhaps, that it was through the sixth-form tutor's meetings in the early spring of 1969 that I began to receive confirmation of my own earlier sense of hostility between the upper and middle schools. It was difficult to say whether this was arising from role conflicts between section and department heads or from the problems of transferring children from the tutors in the houses to the tutors in the sixth form. Since the evidence, according to my own perceptions, appeared both in the sixth-form tutors' meetings and in the section heads' meetings of January and February, it seems probable that the confused feelings about section identity were related both to the pastoral-curricular split in the management system and to the divisional split based on pupil age differentiation.

The challenge to scholastic values in the upper and middle schools

By January 1969 Mike Burnham had begun to hold regular meetings with the tutors in his section to discuss problems that were arising with the changing character of the sixth-form entry (already augmented by pupils from neighbouring secondary modern schools) and to prepare for the even greater changes that would come when the comprehensive intake in the school itself reached the sixth year in the autumn of 1971. It soon became apparent that the major preoccupation of the tutors in that section was with the 'under-achievement' of the sixth-form pupils, and that the blame for this state of affairs was being attributed to the house system.

For the two February meetings that I attended the tutors had before them for consideration two papers. The first of these had been prepared by a sub-group consisting of Lewis Smith, Pat Richardson and Graham Morris. The second had been prepared by Graham Morris on his own. In it he reported on his enquiry into the school's records of V.R.Qs (verbal reasoning quotients) measured at the time of the eleven-plus transfer into the school of 53 out of the 77 second-year sixth formers at that time, the remaining 24 being pupils who had entered the school later, either as selected pupils from other selective schools or by transfer at the sixth-form stage from local secondary modern schools. Putting his evidence alongside published facts about the national position, he had come to the conclusion that the Nailsea sixth form was peopled by students of a wider ability range than would be found in the majority of secondary schools with sixth forms.

What Graham Morris personally emphasized in his paper was the danger that sixth-form teachers might be misled by unrealistic expectations, based on their own experiences as pupils in selected sixth forms associated with grammar-school traditions if not actually in grammar schools. Yet as a member of the sub-committee that prepared the other paper he was also involved in a different kind of statement, in which the cause of the under-achievement was being attributed to the policy in the school as a whole and in the middle school in particular. In other words the two papers seemed to be representing the struggle between a wish to accept in the upper school an intake of pupils who were not all committed to intellectual pursuits and a wish to 'blame' other sections of the school for anti-work attitudes in their section of it.

Now in fact the first of these two meetings started with a consideration of two other items: the possibility of strengthening the 'custodial' roles of sixth formers in relation to tutor groups in the lower school by giving them the opportunity to take part in tutorial work almost as assistant tutors: and the possibility of reducing the 'gulf' between the lower sixth and the upper sixth by having tutor groups including the whole sixteen-to-eighteen age-range. Later in the meeting and increasingly in the one that followed it ten days later, I had the sense of a staff sub-group that was hardening its boundaries against the middle school and was seeking to use the lower school as allies in this process. Months later John Harbinson suggested a different interpretation of this behaviour, telling me that he had seen the sixth form as wishing to adopt, at that time, the role of the kindly elder brother or protective policeman in relation to the lower school. Either way, the result could have been to isolate the middle-school house system.

It seemed to me, therefore, that the gulf between the lower sixth and the upper sixth was symbolizing the much greater gulf between the upper-school tutors and the house heads and tutors of the middle school, and that the wish to strengthen the pairing relationship with the lower-school tutors was concealing a wish to set up a protective alliance against the middle school. Through such an alliance, it seemed, those most closely associated with the incoming and outgoing pupils of the school were able to project into the middle-school house system many of their own problems—problems concerned with building effective work relationships with the very young at one end, who might be kept over-dependent, and with the near adults at the other end, who might be feared as potential rebels.

At the same time this meeting was giving me a mental image of two groups of staff separated out on either side of a diagonal line that seemed to run straight through the middle school. On the upper side of this line I saw the director of intermediate studies, linked as it were to a group of 'faculty-based' tutors and to the master in charge of sixth-form studies. On the lower side I saw the house heads, linked with the head of the lower school and his team of tutors and to sixth-form pupils acting as shadow tutors to lower-school children (see Figure 55). If the sixth-form pupils were being described as

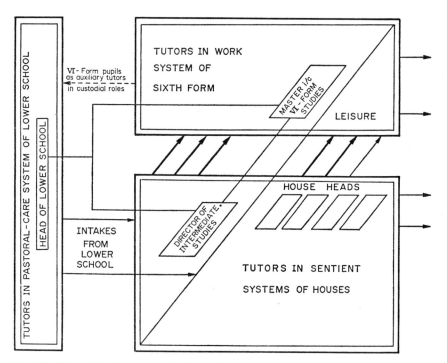

FIG. 55. The tension between curricular and pastoral roles on the boundary between the middle and upper schools.

custodians in the lower school, sent down there to take a parental or pastoral role in relation to pre-adolescent children, their tutors, it seemed, were seeing themselves as the custodians of learning, of intellectual rigour and of academic standards.

I should, however, be giving a false picture of the mood of the sixth-form tutors at that time if I were to imply that they had no awareness of a conflict between their own teaching or 'curricular' roles and their own tutorial or 'pastoral' roles. The problem of reconciling these two functions was indeed the subject of much of their discussion in the second of the two February meetings. This discussion arose out of a careful, painstaking elucidation by Pat Richardson of her own concern about the apparent absence of serious thinking other than that required to pass A-levels among these older pupils in the school. What she seemed to be expressing on behalf of her colleagues was a kind of disappointment that these boys and girls should be equating leisure with trivial and frivolous pursuits; and it seemed that the feeling was growing that the triviality and the frivolity had its roots in the house system, which was perceived by some tutors as being concerned more with social than with intellectual values. Within the sixth-form tutors' group itself the awareness of the conflict between curricular and pastoral responsibilities became, as it were, encapsulated for a while in a dialogue between Mike Burnham and Lewis Smith about the difficulties each experienced in reconciling his pastoral and academic responsibilities within the system. It was as though Mike Burnham saw the intellectual part of himself as a teacher and the pleasure in taking curricular responsibility as lost to his own successor as head of English, and as though Lewis Smith saw the caring side of himself as a teacher and the pleasures of taking pastoral responsibility as lost to the head of the upper school.

Now the sixth form, or 'upper school' as it came increasingly to be called in later months, was at that time facing a kind of crisis of survival, for it was known, certainly to Mike Burnham and probably to all tutors, that consideration was already being given in the county to the idea of separate sixth-form colleges. Indeed Mike Burnham was himself involved outside the school in a working party which was looking at this question, among others. He was therefore very conscious of his own need to justify the existence of his section of Nailsea School by providing a viable programme, not just for intending university and college students, but for young people with a wide diversity of interests and skills who would be entering the upper school for a variety of reasons, including the need to stay on simply to do some more growing up.

Thus the upper school, just as much as the lower and middle schools, faced the urgent necessity to redefine its primary task. Four later meetings of its tutors that I attended in the summer and autumn of 1969 and in the spring and summer of 1970, were very much focused on this task. In other words, as time went on, the upper-school tutorial staff took back into themselves a great deal of the conflict which I felt they had previously been projecting into the middle school. In those later meetings—or at least those that I was able to attend—the earlier somewhat self-righteous concern about sixth-form under-achievement turned into a much more open exploration of conflicting attitudes within the staff group towards pupils who presented them with problems. In one meeting the split seemed to be between the heads of science and geography, to some extent including the head of mathematics, on the one side, and those who were concerned with the teaching in the arts sector, though not the heads of departments, on the other. The first group was championing the rights of the academically more able pupils to be protected against the disruptive influences of pupils who showed little interest in academic learning; the second group was urging the claims of the less academically able pupils to be contained and indeed educated within the framework of the upper school. In that discussion it was noticeable that Lewis Smith remained silent and withdrawn, as though he could cope with this conflict of aims only by opting out of the argument. He, as head of English, must have been peculiarly torn between his wish to defend the intellectual integrity of his subject and his wish to proclaim its possibilities as a medium through which children and young people could be helped to learn about themselves as *feeling* persons.

It seemed to me that in these later discussions there was a danger that Mike Burnham, Sue Redfern (by then his deputy) and Graham Morris were being seen as identified with the pastoral, even therapeutic, objectives of the school as against certain other members of the group who were finding themselves pushed further and further out on the other side. Yet it was noticeable also that Robin Grist, who had formerly allied himself with the scientists, was now expressing a kind of puzzled ambivalence because he had seen evidence in the general-studies work, to which he had made a contribution, that at least one of the difficult boys being discussed had shown a real commitment in that area of his work. Thus he was beginning to see the problem as something much more complex than protecting the boundaries of the A-level work to which he, as a mathematician, was committed, namely the problem of understanding how the boys and girls who were still in the school after attaining the age of sixteen were coping with the process of growing up and reaching towards the adult world.

Affiliations and antagonisms to sub-groups within the system

Back in the early weeks of 1969 there had been sporadic evidence that Mike Burnham's own feelings about the attitudes of his tutors towards the tutors in the middle school were far from simple. During the stormy month of January, I became aware during a section heads' meeting of a marked split in the group, which seemed to be symbolizing the other side of the middle-school/upper-school relationship that I was to sense a few weeks later in the sixth-form tutors' meetings. In that earlier meeting of the section heads I was acutely aware of an undercurrent of bantering, almost flippant, talk that was going on intermittently between Mike Burnham and the house heads, in conflict with the open discussion between Denys John and other members of the group—a phenomenon that never occurred in any other meeting of the section heads that I attended.

On that occasion Mike Burnham was sitting at the end of the long table round which the ten members of the group along with myself were seated. The house heads were, it seemed, clustered round him at his end of the table; Clive Vanloo was seated—uneasily, as I thought—amongst the former 'triumvirate' and the well-established head of the lower school; and I was balanced equally uneasily between the two sub-groups. Later on it occurred to me that this situation—trivial enough on the surface, perhaps—might have been reflecting something important about Clive Vanloo's sense of alienation from the former joint heads of the middle school. I also found myself wondering whether Mike Burnham's social friendliness towards the house heads in that meeting—taking a form that was at variance with the task—might have been difficult for him to restrain at that particular point in time. It was evident from my subsequent discussions with him that he was not himself conscious of any connection between this situation in the section heads' meeting and the current attitudes of the upper-school tutors towards the middle-school house staff. Yet he did come to realize that he had allowed himself to be trapped by the house heads into accepting a social role that was inappropriate to the task of that meeting.

Again, a month later in the February meeting of the section heads, Mike Burnham expressed the positive side of his ambivalent feelings towards the middle-school house system when he reported on his own impressions of another kind of architectural school plan that was based on curricular activities rather than on houses. This question had arisen in the section heads' meeting because of the imminent visit of a group of architects and administrators in about a fortnight's time. Although Denys John emphasized that he did not want the staff to feel that they were bound to defend their own house system, but rather to be open to discussion with these people about the real issues, it was noticeable in this preliminary internal discussion that not only the house heads but also Mike Burnham, notwithstanding the attitudes of his tutors towards the houses, became very protective towards the existing house organization.

The confused feelings about people's affiliations to one or other section of the school did not really come out into the open in a full staff meeting until October 1969, following Denys John's action in setting up the standing committee and the senior staff group. At this meeting the staff were asked to consider the proposal that tutorial staff should have formally scheduled meetings in the lower, middle and upper schools, these to replace some of the monthly full staff meetings. In other words, what was being sought was a break-down of the large staff meeting into divisions that were not simply based on seniority. It must have been generally known that section meetings were already taking place in the upper school; and Mike Burnham, in the standing committee only a week earlier, had stipulated that, in the event of section meetings being scheduled into the calendar, he would want to continue holding what he called his 'working-party' type of tutors' meeting in addition to these, because of the special problems the upper school would have to face in the future. For him, at least, it seemed that scheduled meetings offered some kind of threat to his autonomy and aroused some fear lest the real concerns of his section might not be regarded as appropriate agenda for those meetings.

In fact the idea that section meetings should be institutionalized rather than left to chance (or choice) aroused in the full staff meeting an unexpected hostility. There were explosive remarks about the concentration of 'nearly all the department heads' in the upper-school tutorial team and of 'all the P.E. staff' in the middle-school team. Towards the end of the discussion Reg Clarke—himself a lower-school tutor who was at that time acutely aware of the problem of being over-identified with one part of the school—suddenly protested hotly: 'But we don't want section identity! We belong to a *school* staff.' The objection to regular meetings within sections seemed to be related to two problems: first, that Denys John, if he did not himself attend those meetings, would by implication be giving the section heads more power than they had hitherto been seen as having and that he himself might be seen as abandoning the rank and file of the staff; and secondly, that those who taught in two or even all three sections would feel themselves suddenly to be confined within the section in which they happened to do their tutoring and so denied access to the deliberations of other sections in which they had roles as subject teachers. It was hard to know whether the strong feelings that were expressed in that meeting were springing from rivalries between sections or whether they had more to do with unresolved problems about the recent changes in the management structure and the consequent elevation of the three section heads to top-management status.

Despite all this resistance to the idea that—by some means if not through scheduled section meetings—the sections might be needing to establish their own separate identities, I sensed in the senior staff meeting that took place less than a week later indications of a need to protect section boundaries by ensuring that the conflicts between colleagues in any one section were not made public. The theme for discussion in that meeting was staff deployment and the problems of accommodating those courses, mainly craft subjects and options, that were expensive of staff time either because they necessitated small sets, or because pupils had to be given such a wide range of choices that a large number of teachers had to be concurrently teaching relatively small groups. The discussion produced a good deal of in-fighting between subject departments. Yet I had an impression that the fighting had far less to do with feelings between departments than with feelings about the boundary that separated the life of the sixth form or upper-school section and the rest of the school.

During the meeting itself I was struck by the fact that although certain individuals opposed and challenged each other quite strongly, none of those who combined their senior-staff functions with an upper-school tutorial function opposed each other at all. This was the meeting in which Robin Grist raised with Denys John questions about the very large mathematics sets at the top of the ability range in the fourth and fifth years; yet when this problem was related back to the science department's need for small sets for their 'Science for the Young School Leavers' course, it was not Robin Grist who challenged Phillip Armitage about this, but Graeme Osborn—not, in other words, the fellow tutor in the upper school who was directly affected by the demands of the science department's setting and banding arrangements, but a middle-school house head (an arts man) who was not affected by them at all. Similarly, when Lewis Smith pointed out that English too might need small sets to accomplish its work satisfactorily, it was not his fellow tutors Phillip Armitage and Dennis Johnson but Pip Ridgwell, a lower-school tutor, whom he challenged—asking him to justify his insistence on small sets for practical work in the technical workshops, and even using the somewhat bizarre argument that English, too, might be described as a 'practical' subject.

The separateness of the upper school as the privileged sixth-form sector had been emphasized by Denys John in his opening remarks at the beginning of this meeting, when he pointed out that it was really because of the existence of the sixth form that the operational teacher-pupil ratio of 1:27—arrived at after the various allowances of free time for marking, preparation and non-teaching responsibilities had been calculated—was favourable enough to allow for the small sets for options and practical subjects, and to allow tutor groups, at least at their starting points in the first year, to be kept below rather than above thirty. The logistics had been set out in a paper, distributed for this meeting, the mathematics of which eluded me, as it evidently eluded many of the staff. Nevertheless some of the issues that required to be discussed were clearly put forward in that paper. And one of the urgent matters, to which reference had been made in the standing committee earlier the same day, was the need to find more time for general studies in the sixth form, the proposal being that this time should come out of the ten hours per fortnight hitherto allocated to A-level subjects. Robin Thomas had predicted that this proposal would arouse severe opposition, especially from the scientists, who had always maintained that they must have the full ten hours in order to ensure that enough time was available for laboratory work. But the issue was not raised at all in the meeting. I myself only recalled afterwards that the standing committee had expected it to be discussed at some length. Why, I wondered later, had Graham Morris not raised the matter? It seemed at least possible—in view of the other indications that the sixth-form tutors were wishing to preserve their solidarity—that he hesitated to do so lest he should find himself in open conflict with his fellow tutors, several of whom, in their roles as department heads, would have been likely to defend the current allocation of A-level time.

If the upper school had to be seen as benefactors to the middle and lower schools, the feelings towards those who tutored and taught in it must have been somewhat complicated, since nothing arouses hostility more than an enforced sense of obligation; and Denys John had appeared to be saying: 'We ought to be grateful to the sixth form'. Thus the disapproval expressed, in their own meetings, by the sixth-form tutors about the value system of the rest of the school (and the middle school in particular) was probably matched by the half envious, half contemptuous attitudes of staff who were based mainly in the middle school towards colleagues who enjoyed the privilege of working mainly in the perhaps rarified atmosphere of the sixth form, where tutor groups and teaching groups were relatively small and supposedly selective in comparison with those in the fifth year and below.

Ambivalent feelings are uncomfortable to live with. It is easier to split them and let certain individuals or sub-groups express the polarized attitudes than to contain and tolerate the conflict within oneself. We have seen in this and earlier chapters how attitudes were polarized between sub-groups, certain people being pushed further and further towards the kind of rigid, uncompromising scholarship and discipline that could be condemned as hostile to youth, while others were being pushed further and further towards the kind of liberality and indulgence that could be condemned as hostile to learning.

Both the upper and middle sections, it seemed, were vulnerable to the dangers of this kind of splitting and projection. For just as the science, geography and mathematics department heads, in their roles as tutors in the upper school, had found themselves at times ranged against the arts teachers in arguments that seemed to be about *intellectual* standards, so the house heads had at times found themselves ranged into opposing pairs, not always the same pairs, in arguments that seemed to be about *social* standards. I am suggesting really that the staff group as a whole may have been unconsciously projecting its concern about the intellectual progress of pupils into the upper-school tutorial group and its concern about the social and emotional development of its pupils into the middle-school house-tutorial groups.

Divided responsibility and anxieties about the third year

If the upper-school tutors were disturbed about the transition of sixteen-year-olds into the sixth form, the staff in general seemed disturbed about the transition of thirteen-year-olds into the third year. On several occasions, in different kinds of meeting, I had a sense of people experiencing a kind of mental gear change when they shifted their sights from the lower school to the middle school. Often, this shift of focus would be related to problems about the effects on later studies of integrated courses, new methods of teaching and mixed ability groups associated with the lower school. It was as though people could acknowledge the attraction and even the educational effectiveness of the escape from the rigid subject boundaries and from the graded teaching groups as long as they were thinking only of children below the third year. But the third year itself was shadowed by the necessity to make difficult decisions about individual pupils who must be sent along separate paths, the more able to the GCE camp, the less able to the CSE camp, regardless of the respective merits of the two examination courses as educational experiences in themselves. So strongly did the staff feel this need to 'change gear' as soon as a third-year syllabus came into sight that the third year itself came to be described in the staff group as 'the diagnostic year'.

For me during the 1968–9 session it was hard to determine whether this label became attached to the third year because of the necessity to start preparing for fifth-year examinations as soon as the third year was completed (or in some subjects as soon as it was begun) or because the first comprehensive intake was then in its third year, presenting staff with new anxieties about the harvest of examination results they would be reaping two years later. But in fact this anxiety recurred after that particular year group had moved out of the third year. It was not until much later that I began to associate the 'gear change' with problems about a house system that seemed in some ways to be militating against any sort of work-centred identity for the emerging middle school. And increasingly I came to feel that the preoccupation with the third year had something to do with relationships between the tutors in the lower school and the tutors in the houses, and perhaps also with relations between the lower-school head and the house heads.

The discussions about the third year often seemed to imply that it was in this year that children first experienced the effects of the fragmentation of tutor groups for much of their work through the banding and setting arrangements described in Chapter IV. In fact this differentiation, already beginning in Year I, was considerably increasing by Year II, with the additional groupings that accompanied the second-year options—a fact that was, as we saw, commented on with some heat by two of the lower-school tutors during the 1968–9 session. Yet staff would sometimes talk as if it was not until the third year that children had to face the harsh realities of ability groupings and as though the organization of the lower school did nothing to prepare them for this change. Was the anxiety about the increasing fragmentation of the working groups of pupils as they went through the school perhaps the clue to the relative unpopularity of the middle school as a base for tutorial work, despite its attractions as a system in which small, family-size staff teams could be set up as sentient groups within the institution?

The movement of tutors between the three systems during the 1966–70 period showed a marked absence of movement of established staff into the middle school. Sue Redfern, after her transfer from the lower to the upper school to replace Kitty King as deputy, was in little doubt that many of her colleagues perceived this move as a kind of promotion, even though her role had not changed, but only the location in which she operated in that role. Three others—all senior staff—had overleaped the middle school in this way, although moving in the opposite direction: Pip Ridgwell, a fifth-year tutor in the 1966–7 session when the fifth year was in limbo, became a lower-school tutor in September 1967, along with Gwen London and Tony Frost, who moved into the lower school from the sixth form. The only person, according to my records, who ever sought a transfer *into* the middle school (apart from the house heads and possibly their deputies) was a biologist, Brian Vincent, who in September 1969 moved from the lower school, where he had been a tutor for four years, into Pegasus House, where two fellow scientists (Peter Chapman and another physicist) and one of the mathematics staff were already based. He saw this move, as he described it to me later, as one in a sequence of possible moves that would give him experience of tutoring pupils of different ages, including perhaps sixth-formers two or three years later. Did he regard this transfer to one of the houses as a stepping stone to the 'promotion' of a later move into the upper school? Or was it the contact with the older pupils, as a natural sequel to his earlier work with the younger ones, that attracted him more than any sense of promotion?

The earlier concentration of biologists and of non-academic department heads in the lower school and the later convergence in the upper school of tutors associated with the teaching of English or drama, and indeed the convergence of the P.E. staff in the middle-school house system as a whole (Eva Tucker, the head of girls' P.E., remaining in Pat Chapman's house throughout this period), now begin to look less surprising. As we trace out some of these concentrations of subject specialists with the same interests in the tutorial groupings in different houses and sections, it seems that we are finding evidence of the other side of the pastoral-curricular split: namely the wish to come together in one working group with people who share both one's own interest in a special subject and one's own interest in a particular age-group of children. But the middle school offered less probability than either the upper or lower schools of being both 'teacher' and 'tutor' to at least a sizeable proportion of one's tutor group (except in art, crafts, music and P.E.); for the dispersion of the members of any one tutor group into different sets according to abilities and according to subject or course preferences was greater in the third, fourth and fifth years than in the first or the sixth, and greater in the fourth and fifth years than in the second and third.

By the third year it was not only the relations between members of any one tutor group but also the relations between the tutor groups themselves that were being affected by the processes of fragmentation. For in that year, as the B, G, R and Y groups went their separate ways to join Pegasus, Dolphin, Pelican and Lion in the house blocks, it was the year group itself that was being fragmented. Thus no house head, however strong his or her interest in an academic subject might be—and we must remember that the four included the former head of physics, the present head of religious education and a mathematician who taught O and A-level courses—ever had more than a small proportion of any one year group in the house; indeed a house might in certain sessions be without any children from a particular year. This meant that no house head could really speak with authority about the curricular needs of a complete year group of pupils. It was not very surprising in view of this fragmentation of the year groups that the house heads appeared often to be going into collusion with those who did not expect them to be concerned about curricular matters. Particularly after the 1969 reorganization and even to some extent before it they must often have felt trapped in a kind of no-man's-land between the section heads and the department heads and thus unsure of their status in the senior staff group. In the two F.Y.C. group meetings that I attended, Pat Chapman, as representative of the house heads, seemed to be present, as Dawn Castell, the new tutor in her house, was present, as a more or less silent observer rather than as an active participant. I have already mentioned the way in which the house heads, apart from Graeme Osborn, would withdraw from any department heads' meeting they attended (up to the summer of 1969) as soon as the item 'relevant' to house concerns had been discussed. And I have referred to the decision—implicit if not explicit—not to seek a discussion with the standing committee, in their roles as house heads, during the consultative meetings about curriculum development in the spring of 1970. A fourth indication that it was difficult for them to contribute directly to such discussion was their non-attendance, presumably because they were not invited, at a special meeting that was held in July 1970 to discuss the particular problems of the third-year curriculum, a meeting that was attended by nearly all the department heads concerned and by all the members of the standing committee.

In view of the recurrent preoccupations about the curricular organization in the third year it was to me surprising that the department heads who attended that special meeting, brought together so that some of the problems about options and integrated courses that had been raised with the standing committee during the spring term could be examined, did not discuss the curriculum as such at all. The focus of the entire meeting was on the use of time, and it was not until many months later that I understood why this apparent deflection into quite a different topic had occurred. In fact it had by then been generally agreed that the options that were to start in the third year should include drama; but in order to put this agreement into effect an additional five hours had to be found. Rather than take it out of the existing time given to art, music, crafts, P.E. and games, the staff were being asked to turn their attention to the possibility of reorganizing the school day. But this could not be done for the third year in isolation: it had to be done, if at all, throughout the school. In fact, as a result of this meeting, the school day was changed to provide 60 fifty-minute periods per fortnight instead of the 50 sixty-minute periods used in the past few years.

To me, at the time of the meeting itself, it was the mood of the staff that was of special interest. The merits and demerits of the sixty-minute period then in use were being compared with the discarded forty-minute period that many of the staff had known some years before. There was great reluctance to provide the necessary additional periods by restoring what had been found unsatisfactory in an earlier period of the school's history; yet there were divergences of opinion about the effects on the working day of the long sixty-minute periods. Some people wondered whether the school day was too leisurely, even admitting that they usually wasted part of the sixty-minute period and fearing that they did not put enough pressure either on themselves or on their pupils; others declared that they used time right up to the last available minute and did not feel that the sixty-minute period had any slack that they could afford to lose. In some ways this exchange of boasts and confessions was reminiscent of the earlier anxieties about parents' suspicions that their children were not being given enough homework: for what some of the staff were implying was that the pressure on children to work at school might similarly be too low rather than too high. But it was also echoing the fears, then current in the sixth-form tutors' group, that leisure, rather than work—associated with ping-pong, pop music and dating—was at the heart of house membership.

The reluctance of this meeting to consider anything except the mechanics of time-tabling was symptomatic of the problems created by a structure of management that did not yet provide any over-all leadership at the level of any one year. In the first and second years the leadership could be identified with the role of the lower-school head; but in the third year, even after the clarification of Clive Vanloo's role as head of the middle school, the splitting of the year group itself between four scattered locations, both physically and psychologically, meant that there was no one person who had an over-view of the problems of that particular age group or of any particular intake of pupils at this stage. Hence perhaps the anxious preoccupations about identifying it as a 'diagnostic' year, and the suggestion made on one occasion that it should perhaps even be regarded as a 'year in limbo', belonging neither to the lower school nor to the middle school. In a sense each year was in some degree diagnostic for most children, as each year could, for different reasons, be regarded as 'in limbo', or suspended between the phase that preceded it and the phase that followed it.

Confusion over section and house boundaries

The anxieties about the third year contained questions—gradually becoming more explicit as time went on—about what kind of boundary the second-year children were being required to cross in moving into the house blocks. Were they already, psychologically if not physically, 'in' the houses from the moment they entered the school, as the naming of their tutor groups suggested? Or had these house links been meaningless during those two years, except in so far as they provided the groupings for competitive games?

In fact there was considerable uncertainty both inside and outside the middle school about where the house boundaries really were. The main argument usually put forward in support of the house system was that it provided for every pupil a set of stable and lasting relationships throughout his or her journey through the school, from entering it to leaving it, however long or short the journey might be. The allocation to the house-linked tutor groups in the first year was to ensure the formation of these relationships; and it was assumed, at least by some people, that by the time the tutor group was disbanded at the end of the fifth year, the associations would be strong enough, for those who went on into the upper school, to persist despite the regrouping into new sixth-form tutor groups.

The implication of this argument was that the bounded region as perceived by the house heads cast a set of shadows across the middle-school bounded region as perceived by Clive Vanloo, and that these shadows extended downwards (or backwards) into the lower school and upwards (or forwards) into the upper school. Clearly there was, for some members of the staff a wish that these house identities should be regarded as paramount for the pupils. But others were not so sure. In the special meeting of lower- and middle-school tutors along with the house and section heads, held in July 1970, John Harbinson expressed some disquiet about the assumption that the house identity should be school-wide, and noted with surprise that although people were talking a great deal about such 'house identities', no-one seemed to be raising any questions about what might be called a 'lower-school identity'; and he wondered to what extent he and his colleagues in the lower school might have been inhibited, because of the tutor-group links with the houses, from doing anything that might strengthen that identity.

On another occasion it became evident that Peter Chapman and Graeme Osborn held quite different views about whether these so-called links did or should persist in the sixth form, and that sixth-form tutors themselves had mixed views about this question. Peter Chapman saw the maintenance of the links as valuable to the boy or girl after the disbanding of the old familiar tutor group at the end of the fifth year, and was assured by one of the upper-school tutors that some sixth-formers did value the association and enjoyed 'going back' into the house blocks to pick up the old threads.

It was also suggested that these links gave sixth-formers opportunities to take leadership roles in relation to the younger people coming up through the middle school in out-of-school activities including competitive games. Graeme Osborn's views on all this were quite different. He considered that fifth-year pupils had to face realistically the ending of their life in the houses and cut the connection entirely when they entered the upper school, just as they would have to face the ending of their school life when they left a year, or two or three years, later. For him, every stage in the journey through school had to be regarded as a preparation for moving on to the next stage. Any clinging to the preceding stage must be seen, therefore, as a sign of immaturity rather than of growth.

This conflict between the nostalgic longing for the dependency of childhood and the urge to seek freedom by breaking away from old bonds— expressed so vividly by these two house heads and by certain upper-school tutors in the debate about the house system—was a central problem, as much for the staff in their professional 'growing up' as for pupils in their personal growing up. Much of the uncertainty about whether or not people wanted to be identified with one particular section of the school was related to this double need for security and for freedom, even at times when the two seemed incompatible.

Discussions that exposed uncertainties about the rationality of the divisions between lower, middle and upper schools and the further divisions within the middle school were bound to be more disturbing for the section and house heads than for any other members of the staff, since the preservation of their roles depended on the belief that these divisions were justifiable in rational terms. It was not only the house heads who were vulnerable. The suggestion that the third year was perhaps not appropriately placed either in the lower school or in the middle school, when it was juxtaposed against the memory of the fifth-year group in the 1966–7 session that had been in neither middle school nor upper school, was very quickly seen to be raising a much more far-reaching question: whether a two-tiered rather than a three-tiered system might not be more appropriate to the developmental pattern of an eleven-to-eighteen age range. And it needed little imagination to perceive that such a question put Clive Vanloo's role in immediate danger, since in the event of such a change it would be his section that would disappear. Despite the implications of these questions for individual members of the staff group, they were in fact by the summer of 1970 being explored publicly in the presence of the very persons who would be most affected by any changes of this kind.

Change, loss and compromise in the reallocation of roles in a revised management structure

The reorganization of the management structure in September 1969 had concerned only the senior staff and had been brought about as a result of Denys John's own decision, arrived at during the summer holidays. The second reorganization, two years later, concerned everybody, and the whole staff group was involved in the rethinking that led to its implementation. Once the leadership of top management *vis-à-vis* middle management had been established, the way was open for clarification of the leadership functions of middle management in relation to the rest of the staff, including those who also held leadership roles but in smaller areas of responsibility.

Broadly, the new structure involved the introduction of two levels of leadership in the general area of the organization of resources for learning, and the establishment of an entirely new leadership role in every year group up to the seventh, each year-group head having overall responsibility for the curricular and pastoral concerns of all the children in his or her year, and thus, by implication, for the work of the tutors in that year. The reorganization of the old subject departments into nine major curricular areas was clearly a sequel to the series of curriculum discussions between the standing committee and its visiting colleagues in the spring of 1970, as the setting up of the year-group system was a sequel to the meetings of the house heads with the lower-school tutors, the lower and middle-school tutors and the standing committee in the summer of 1970 and the spring of 1971.

The allocation of these new or modified roles could not have been accomplished at all without careful scrutiny of existing placements of staff members on the salary scales, without the weighing and matching of skills, experience and expertise, or without imaginative consideration of potential as yet untested and untapped. For they were now having to tackle on a large scale what they had tackled together, two years earlier, when they had made a decision about which colleague ought to be asked to take on the leadership of the humanities course: the matching of persons to roles, not in order to keep people happy but in order to ensure that the right people were doing the right jobs.

Much of the work was done by the standing committee in its weekly meetings; and the allocation of persons to roles had to be undertaken by them. But the struggle to produce possible models which would allow for some real modifications without sacrificing individuals, was a task that was shared to some extent by all the staff. Inevitably in the pattern that emerged there were compromises, inconsistencies and unknowns. But that it did have a new look was incontrovertible. And the pattern seemed to have within it the possibilities of further modifications as experience with the new system and the inevitable loss of old colleagues and assimilation of new ones might suggest.

I am now moving into the area of conjecture. But before leaving this theme, I should attempt to spell out what kind of change the staff experienced as they moved into the 1971–2 academic year after that summer of scrutiny, private and public consultation and shared planning and decision-making.

T.S.T.M.—11

To what extent did the new organization meet the conflicting needs of those who would be working in it? How were people going to experience, at the same time, a sense of continuity in the institution as a whole and a sense of belonging as persons to their own identifiable sub-sections of that institution, in which sentient systems could be felt to be related to manageable tasks? What gains or losses, promotions or demotions, clarifications of formerly ambiguous roles and statuses were evident in the pattern of reallocation that took shape that September?

Of the nine new 'departments', four—namely, English, mathematics, physical education and religious education—remained undisturbed. Thus the two universal tool subjects of English and mathematics—the former concerned with literacy, the latter with numeracy—and the two subjects that catered for the physical and moral well-being of children, were left as a kind of stable framework within which other things could be changed. Science experienced minor changes within its undisturbed outer boundary: chemistry as a sub-section of the department had no separate organizer; but 'secondary science', a new course, was given the status of a 'subject' to be organized on behalf of the science department by Janet Roberts on whose initiative it had been set up; alongside her as 'subject organizers' were a young physicist, new to the school, and Gwen London who, despite her seniority in the staff group, had opted for the role of subject organizer in biology rather than the more senior role of a year-group head, thus sacrificing her former membership of the senior staff meeting in order to retain her particular responsibility for biology. The other 'giant' department, modern languages, became the more broadly based department of 'Languages', headed by Peter Atkinson, with European studies and Latin under separate organizers. History and citizenship, geography and geology, and commerce disappeared as departments, being amalgamated into the new and more complex department of 'environment', headed by Allen White, with four subject organizers responsible to him for the separate areas. Similarly, art, music, home economics, and technical subjects were subsumed under the new department of 'Creativity', headed by Tom Purvis, with four subject organizers responsible to him for the constituent subjects. 'Humanities', now promoted to 'department' status, headed by Graeme Osborn, made up the nine, doubtless arousing questions in many minds about how it was to stand in relation to English, religious education and the new department of 'environment', originally seen as the ingredients, or contributing disciplines, for the first-year humanities course. Was the department of humanities now to carry the uncertainties about whether teachers should be section-based or subject-based, as the earlier humanities course had carried the uncertainties about mixed-ability teaching and the thinning out of the subject boundaries?

The displaced department heads, with two exceptions, remained in the senior staff group as year-group heads. Pip Ridgwell and Tony Frost, formerly tutors in the lower school, took over the headship of the youngest and oldest year-groups in the school (Year I and Years VII and VIII); the two Chapmans remained in the middle school, Peter Chapman with Year IV and Pat Chapman with Year V; Graham Morris, while still organizing general studies, became head of Year VI; and Margaret Smith and Tina Bateman accepted promotion to senior-staff status as heads of Years II and III. Margaret Smith brought to the leadership of the second year the experience of being John Harbinson's deputy during the previous two years; Tina Bateman brought to the leadership of the third year her experience, first as a part-time and later as a full-time teacher, of working in the departments of modern languages, history, geography and religious education and of teaching in the extended humanities course in the first and second years.

Of the former deputies, apart from Margaret Smith, three left in the summer of 1971, Sue Redfern to start a family and (later) pursue advanced studies, the other two women to take up posts elsewhere; the two men moved into what we may now describe as 'lower-middle-management roles' as subject organizers.

The case of Eva Tucker in the P.E. department raised in what may have been a particularly difficult form the problem of the boundary between the lower-middle-management group and the senior-staff group. Although, in the earlier system (up to the summer of 1969) she had been included among those who attended the meetings of department heads, and had attended the subsequent senior staff meetings between September 1969 and July 1971, there had evidently been some ambiguity about her position, because of the distinction between Bob Miller's appointment as 'head of P.E.' and hers as 'head of girls' P.E.' This ambiguity had caused some embarrassment on the occasion of a special meeting about the curriculum for the third year, when Denys John, surprised to discover that Eva Tucker was not present, had found himself having to assure Bob Miller that he had in fact sent her the same invitation as he had sent to the people who *were* present. In the later management structure (set up in September 1971) it had to be made clear that her role put her on the boundary of a sub-section of the P.E. department and not on its outer boundary, and that she was responsible to the head of P.E. for the organization of those activities in which girls were catered for separately from boys. This later clarification of her status in the staff group may well have uncovered a more fundamental problem about the perpetuation of a pattern that placed the male successor to Bob Miller in a position of seniority in relation to her. Was there, in this appointment, some implication that only a man could take overall responsibility for physical education as one of the nine major curricular areas in the school? This, certainly, was my own perception of the situation, until I learned from Eva Tucker herself, much later, that Denys John had assured her, when the post was being advertised, that men and women would be equally eligible for it—in other words, that she herself could apply. Her own decision not to apply was dictated by a number of reasons, one of which was that the post of 'head of boys' P.E.', where the overall head of the department could be a woman, might not attract the kind of candidate who would apply for the post of 'head of P.E.'. Evidently the culture makes it difficult for a woman who teaches P.E. in a mixed school to accept the risks of professional advancement, even under a headmaster who is willing to give overall responsibility to a woman in this area. It seems that there is a quite powerful collusion at work to maintain the man as the one who shoulders the main administrative burden of managing the department, and to maintain the woman as the one who is protected from this necessity. Yet it is women, working in girls' schools and women's colleges, who have taken the lead over the country as a whole in some of the more creative developments in this field.

The three major service roles on the teaching side—namely, the management of resources, counselling and remedial work—were clearly located in the senior management in the new structure, along with the roles of the bursar and the head of the technical department, who were identified as being responsible for 'supporting services'. The dilemma over the role of the librarian has already been mentioned in another context. The question that perhaps remained—in the minds of her colleagues if not in her mind—was whether the decision to place her in the lower-middle-management group along with the subject organizers, and to regard her area as a constituent of the general area of resources, had been based on a judgement about the importance of the job or on an assessment of her own experience relative to that of her colleagues.

All these role allocations were clearly set out in the new journal of 1971–2. The hidden roles within the list of 26 assistant staff were the nineteen who were to be 'assistants' to the heads of departments and heads of year groups, these now being identified as training roles, thus symbolizing the responsibility of the senior staff to undertake the training of their own successors or future colleagues in the educational system as a whole.

We are already moving into the theme of the final section of this book. For what this new organization—despite its inevitable flaws, inconsistencies and hidden problems—highlights more than anything else is the growing recognition that the system that any school sets up to cater for the needs of its pupils must be nurturing new talents and competences in the staff group as well as exploiting existing ones. A school like Nailsea was increasingly bound to lose its experienced people to other developing schools. If the management within the staff group had done nothing during those years but maintain the *status quo*, it would have kept experienced staff members strait-jacketed within their own limited expertise. By testing out new roles, even at the cost of letting old ones disappear, the institution was giving opportunities for the self-development of persons in the system as well as for the reshaping of the management structure as a whole. During the discussions that preceded these changes, it had become possible to recognize that the emerging year-group organization might not prove to be the right

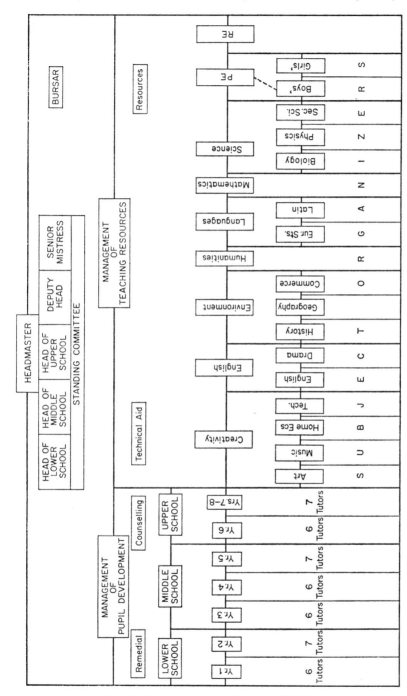

FIG. 56. The management structure: 1971–2.

one for the changing needs of the school, any more than the house system had been, and that there might be a better system that no-one had yet thought of. The only certainty that even the strongest adherents to the untried year-group system had was that it should at least be tried. The upheaval of the familiar pattern of roles and relationships could hardly have been envisaged, let alone undertaken, had not the staff group been moving gradually into a situation not unlike that of a kind of permanent college of education within the school and neighbourhood being served by its members. In the final section of this book I shall be taking up in this context of in-service education the experiences of this particular staff group and the lessons that can be drawn from those experiences.

C. The Staff Group as a Unit for In-service Education

Introduction

I have been looking at the staff group from a series of different perspectives and teasing out some of the complexity of its role relationships in the task system of the institution. This has necessitated looking at the parts, sometimes in terms of different levels of leadership, sometimes in terms of subgroups concerned with different sub-tasks. It is time now to restore the whole and to consider how the staff group counteracts the danger of fragmentation by sustaining its own growth processes.

In this final section of the book we shall be concerned with the struggle of the staff group as a whole to define its own containing boundary by regulating its relations with the outside world. The search for a new image that will be appropriate to the 1970s is reflected in the evolution of new procedures for staff discussion, in the attempts to understand the nature of the partnership between the schools and the training institutions and between practising teachers and students in training, in the testing of the capacity to assimilate newcomers and to cope with the loss of parts of itself to other schools and institutions, in the discovery of a growing need for closer relationships with parents and governors, and in the pursuit of a deepened understanding of the needs of its pupils.

CHAPTER XI

The Evolution of the Continuous
Staff Conference

Staff relationships and institutional growth

It has been my thesis throughout this book that the process of learning about the changing demands of the schools, if it is to be effective in the long run, must be strengthened by the examination of relationships within the staff group itself. We cannot learn about the effects of streaming, setting and banding without examining our own fears that we are somehow grading and assessing one another as 'A', 'B' or 'C' teachers. We cannot learn about curriculum development and the organization of knowledge without examining the double pull within ourselves from the attraction of a subject area to which we have become committed and from the claims upon us of children or students who may not share our commitment to that subject. We cannot learn to understand the problems of deviant, delinquent or emotionally disturbed children without recognizing the elements of deviance, delinquency and emotional disturbance in ourselves as staff members.

We tend to assume that the best way to offer able teachers the opportunity to study all these problems in greater depth is to take them out of the schools and away from the distractions of the day-to-day work in the classroom. Conversely, many people feel that initial training should be far more school-based than it is at present. There is much to be said for both these arguments. But the danger is that we may find ourselves recreating in a somewhat new form the old practice-theory dichotomy by saying that we give training for practical competence in the classroom at the early stage and a theory-based process of re-education at the later stage. Such a dichotomy implies that a kind of distancing or removal from the practical distractions of the school institution is a necessary condition for theoretical study of the fundamental problems of education. Yet throughout the lifetime of teachers now approaching retirement the most crucial problem of all has been one of communication between people who are teaching together in the same school about the principles upon which they base their work. And I do not believe that these problems of communication occur only between the long-established members of the profession and those who are just entering it. Much of this polarization of attitudes between the veterans and the novices results from an unconscious

312

wish to simplify relationships, and thus to falsify them, by introducing sharp dichotomies between extreme purposes and views, thus masking the much more uncomfortable truths about ambivalence and uncertainty.

A good deal of the current public discussion about school management, both at the level of talk and at the level of print, turns on the question of a headmaster's authority to make decisions about how his school should be operated. This question is frequently seen as an all-or-nothing matter. It is implied that either the head makes all the decisions or the staff make all the decisions. One headmaster, much quoted, is alleged to deny that he is the leader of the staff group, although he does not deny his obligation to represent the school (and therefore the staff) in all dealings with governors, local authorities and the outside world in general. Yet offering leadership to the staff group within the school and being its voice outside the school are really two aspects of the same task of headship. Furthermore, since over-all leadership implies the necessity to delegate authority, the same kind of dual responsibility is essentially present in all leadership roles within the staff group, on the boundaries of the various sub-task systems within the organization.

Yet the act of delegation always arouses, on both sides, strongly ambivalent feelings. A head both wants and does not want to pass on part of the burden of his task; his colleagues both want and do not want to accept full responsibility for their share of this burden. When a headmaster delegates to a member of his staff the authority to carry out a particular task and therefore to make decisions relating to that task, this delegation may be felt by the teacher concerned to be real, or it may be experienced as hollow. Similarly, the notion of 'consultation' within a staff group as a whole can imply for one group of teachers a genuine expectation that they will become personally and professionally involved in the struggle of policy-making, or for another group an empty assurance (which they cannot believe) that their opinions will count for something. The problem is not simply that different schools experience 'consultation' in these contrasted ways, but that different sub-groups in the same school can experience it differently and even that the same staff member may have to cope with disturbing oscillations between his belief in the reality of the consultative processes and his suspicion that they are hollow and false.

Consultation is in reality something far more complex than 'having a say in decision making', although of course it includes this. Essentially, it is a kind of self-education. It therefore involves a commitment to learning that is bound to entail pain, struggle and risk. For learning, if it reaches any depth, exposes one's own inconsistencies, anxieties and double feelings. We talk easily enough about the need for 'good' relationships between pupils and teachers, between students in training and the teachers who supervise their work, between probationary staff and established staff, between staff and parents, between the school and its governing body, and of course between the headmaster and all these people. But what exactly do we mean by 'good' relationships in any of these contexts? Do we mean that they should be unfailingly harmonious? Or do we mean that they are always honest? Or should we really be talking about the problem of exploring reality—a reality that will inevitably contain both harmony and disharmony, both cooperativeness and competitiveness, both the sharing of truth and the withholding of truth, and indeed ignorance of what the truth is? On the whole, schools prefer to preserve the illusion that unruffled happiness—or apparent happiness —in the staff means that everything is well in the best of all possible worlds. To ask probing questions of oneself and one's colleagues is to expose the underlying uncertainties that have been there all the time, to discover the mixture of good and bad that every school has to contain, and to face the necessity of trying to understand the bad as well as appreciate the good.

The effort to identify what is inadequate in the system and to replace it or augment it with something new inevitably brings conflict in its wake. For innovation—be it undertaken by an individual teacher working in isolation, by a group of teachers working together in one school or in a number of different schools, or by the whole staff group in a particular school—is likely to result in some sacrifice of personal security, since to turn from known policies to untried ones demands an act of faith and offers no guarantee of successful outcomes. Consultation about what shall be changed and what shall be preserved unchanged is thus inseparable from the continuous process of re-education within the staff group. And it is in this sense that I am using the concept of 'in-service education' in this final section, not as a substitute for the evolving pattern of college and university education of teachers but as an indispensable part of that pattern.

Every staff group has within it the ingredients of a kind of continuous educational workshop. For it is in the staff group itself that meeting points can be found between student and practitioner, between the young and the middle-aged, between the inexperienced and the experienced, between the enthusiasts and the cynics, the optimists and the pessimists, between the so-called 'pupil-oriented' and the so-called 'subject-oriented' teachers. Some of the paired, yet mutually contradictory, terms I have just used may appear to imply an acceptance of the very dichotomies I have been trying to reconcile in this book. Are these sub-groups in the staff room imaginary? Or do they really exist? Is the polarization to which I am drawing attention inevitable? Or can teachers, by recognizing some of the unconscious mechanisms that create them, take steps to remove them, so that individual members of a staff group can escape from the kind of trap they are put into by their colleagues? Does it lie within the professional competence of teachers to reduce the element of polarization in their own working groups?

What we really mean by 'polarization' is an unconscious mutual agreement to take up entrenched positions at opposite ends of an argument, a hardening of apparently irreconcilable attitudes, springing from a profound human reluctance to acknowledge the co-existence of conflicting views about important issues, and arising most sharply in times of crisis. During the Suez crisis friends became unsure how to talk to each other, and the persons who probably suffered most acutely were those one-time aliens who had taken British citizenship and no longer understood what they had embraced in their country of adoption. The deeply divisive effects of a student sit-in, as experienced by the members of a university, cannot really be understood by those outside it. In the educational world the repercussions of a controversial book or film are felt very differently by those who view the controversy from outside and by those who, because they belong to the institution held responsible, have to contain conflicting feelings of anger, guilt, pain and bewilderment.

Personal maturing and professional advancement

To many people outside the world of school, teaching implies restriction to the society of the immature. The teacher can thus be parodied as a man among boys and a boy among men—as someone who can exercise authority only over children. Joseph Wicksteed, in comparing the roles of teachers and parents, once described this state in a more idealistic way, using an appealing image, by saying that it was the teacher's privilege to 'dwell at the headwaters of the fountain of youth' while the parent travels 'down the watercourse'.[1] In fact many teachers also travel 'down the watercourse', and few of those who make a career in education remain throughout their working lives with the same age group or operate as leaders only in relation to their pupils. With the growing complexity of the educational system, a teacher may find himself, within the compass of forty years, working successively with pupils in pre-adolescence, early adolescence and late adolescence, with young adults in student roles in colleges or departments of education, with experienced teachers in their late twenties and early thirties, with middle-aged teachers in senior staff roles, even with head teachers in charge of large schools who are studying the tasks of management.

It is a rather remarkable fact that a secondary school may contain within its total age span of pupils and staff nearly all ages between ten and sixty. Thus for the oldest members of a staff group—those approaching their sixties —some of these colleagues already in senior roles as heads of sections or departments could, symbolically speaking, be their sons and daughters, while pupils entering the first year could, symbolically speaking, be their grand-children. This experience of watching pupils and young colleagues growing and acquiring new skills, and the experience of influencing this growth, is part of the satisfaction of teaching; and for a whole generation of childless women, during the middle part of this century when marriageable women greatly outnumbered marriageable men in the population, it must have been providing at least vicariously some of the pleasures and the pains of emotional

[1] Wicksteed, J. H. (1936), *The Challenge of Childhood*, Chapman & Hall, p. 25.

investment in a future generation. Teachers, like parents, have to learn to help the young to attain the independence they seek and thus to be prepared to lose them, and this means that they themselves have to come to terms with their ageing processes, accepting the growing burdens of responsibility in middle age and the relinquishing of those burdens in old age. We talk comparatively easily about 'educating our masters'; it is more painful to think, and talk, about educating our successors.

I believe that there is, for most teachers, a natural progression from an initial interest that is centred on the younger pupils in a school, through a later interest in those in their late teens, to an ultimate concern about how to help colleagues to develop their potential by providing a better management structure in which the skills and expertise of one's successors can be nurtured in the interest of the next generation of children. An increased interest in working with sixth-form pupils does not therefore necessarily imply an absence of concern about pupils as persons or an overriding concern about an academic subject. There are, as we have seen, powerful pressures within the staff group to push sixth-form tutors into this role—pressures emanating from those who seek to build up and maintain the old grammar-school 'standards' without much regard to the changing nature of the sixth-form intake. Within the sub-group of sixth-form tutors there will be a need to respond to these pressures from other colleagues in order to preserve what is known and, by comparison with its alternative, predictable. But the persons who make up this sub-group, within the boundary of the sixth form or upper school for which they have responsibility, are persons who have caring concerns for young people, and—however alien some of those young people may sometimes appear to be—can see in them parts of their own earlier selves with which they can sympathetically identify, even perhaps in moments of anger and bewilderment. The difficulty of handling these complex feelings about young people then reproduces within the sub-group of tutors the same kind of polarization that exists in the staff group as a whole, with the result that a strong dichotomy between 'pupil-centred' and 'subject-centred' attitudes is set up in that part of the system. It then becomes a very vital part of the task of leadership in that sub-section of the staff group to work towards some understanding of these processes and thus to reduce the dichotomy. For it is through working on the meaning of the polarization that people become able to reduce its effects upon their own personal and professional relationships with pupils.

Examination of experience in the staff group

It must by now be apparent that the Nailsea staff, in working with me in the way they did, had to examine the effects of polarization and the real meaning of ambivalence at many different levels in the system. With the growing sanction to bring out in staff meetings feelings that might formerly have been suppressed, the real educational problems with which people were having to grapple came more clearly into focus. To their own surprise, perhaps, the increasing freedom to acknowledge weakness, uncertainty and bewilderment created a climate in which leadership skills could grow and flourish. For in these situations it became more and more clear that leadership was not being exercised only by the designated leader or chairman in a particular meeting.

Many members of the staff from the most junior to the most senior offered leadership to their colleagues by opening up for investigation important areas of feeling and thought, often at considerable risk to themselves as persons. Nor was it only I, in my role as consultant, who made interpretative comments during staff meetings. The members of the standing committee in particular became increasingly able to do this, not because they arrived at staff meetings armed with prepared comments but because the work they did together during their weekly meetings made them more sensitive to the feelings of their colleagues and to the ideas with which those colleagues were struggling in the larger meetings. It seemed that as the most senior people learned to listen more attentively, they found themselves both intellectually and emotionally in touch with the deeper undercurrents in the staff discussions. Certain people—both in this top-management group and in the rest of the staff group—became less competitive in discussion than they had formerly been; and as the style and content of their contributions changed, quieter and more reserved colleagues found voices where before they had remained silent.

When I look back over the events of the spring and summer of 1970 certain meetings stand out as turning points in the development of a kind of joint capability within the staff group of relating questions about the inner feelings of persons in the sentient system to questions about the outward behaviour, in professional roles, of those same persons as colleagues in the task system. Three meetings in particular during that year appear to me in retrospect to have been crucial: the standing committee meeting of 30 January, the senior staff meeting of 19 May and the full staff meeting of 18 June. Each of these marked a new stage in the progress towards making available for public discussion matters which would, at an earlier stage in the school's history, have been considered private and therefore accessible only to personal friends.

Scrutinizing more closely the three occasions I have selected, I find that they show a gradual enlarging of the areas of human concern that can be encompassed in this way. The first of those three meetings, within the small-group boundary of the standing committee, marked a turning point, or sudden development, of a new kind of awareness in the area of inter-personal relationships; the second, within the wider boundary of the fairly large senior staff meeting, marked a turning point in the examination of inter-group relationships; and the third, in the very large group to which all the teaching staff belonged, and at least two of the non-teaching staff as well, marked a new stage of understanding in the area of the relationships between the institution and the outside world.

Significantly, I believe, each of these meetings took place soon after a full staff meeting devoted to open discussion of some aspect of my own gradual move towards the writing and publication of this report. The earliest of these was the meeting of January 1970, at which my internal report to the staff, distributed just before Christmas, was discussed. During that meeting the problem of differentiating between the role and the person was somewhat dramatically highlighted, when I was suddenly taken to task by a part-time teacher in the modern-languages department for allowing my feelings to show in meetings. She told me, with a directness and severity that I found unnerving, yet at the same time strangely reassuring, that she did not think I behaved as a consultant should, that I did not maintain the calmness she felt ought to be part of consultant behaviour, and that in getting 'worked up' (as indeed I had done earlier in that meeting when I felt that people were trying to evade the real task we were there to tackle) I stirred up too much emotional heat in the group. Following this confrontation, the staff began to recognize that I, like any of them, had to come to terms with the person I was, and use, as best I could, my own feelings about a situation as indicators that might help me to understand it better. Thus their struggle to relate themselves to me in my role as consultant could not be separated from the problem of relating themselves to me as a person, any more than their pupils could entirely separate them as the persons *they* were from them in their roles as teachers in that school. Both the staff and I had to acknowledge that another consultant, even if he or she had striven to behave consistently within the same role as I had tried to take, would have brought different personal characteristics to bear on the task. This problem of distinguishing between the role and the person without denying the effect of each upon the other was to recur in many ways during the coming months, when roles in the staff group and the characteristics of different persons in the same roles came under scrutiny.

It was less than a week after that meeting that the first significant turning point was reached in the standing committee of 30 January, when the members of the committee found themselves recognizing, with a considerable sense of shock, that their deliberations with colleagues over curricular matters were making unexpected demands on their capacity to work with the strong feelings exposed by those colleagues, as persons under stress in maintaining their roles in a difficult task. This recognition produced a sudden and dramatic fusion of the thinking and feeling sides of the task of consultation, which must, later, have influenced the way in which the members of the committee were able to help their colleagues to examine more critically the extent to which the staff structure was still forcing a separation between the handling of children as persons and the recognition of those children as learners.

In the senior staff meeting of 19 May there was a second turning point when the place of the house system in the total organization was discussed. The actual question before the senior staff at that time was not whether houses should continue to be part of the middle-school structure but only whether they should continue to be linked with the lower-school tutorial system. The surprise was that it became possible, even in that early meeting, for questions to be raised about the justification of the house system itself, and that although the house heads were anxious to defend the system, they did not appear to be as threatened in their own roles as might have been expected. This preliminary exploration of some of the issues paved the way for the subsequent discussions, first between the lower-school and middle-school tutorial staff groups later in that same term, then, many months later, between the standing committee and the house heads, and later still in the summer of 1971 in the senior staff group in the context of future reorganization and of the allocation of posts of special responsibility. These developments made it clear that already by the spring of 1970 the senior staff meeting had begun to provide a framework within which those in middle-management roles, whether technically in the curricular system or technically in the pastoral system, could share with each other and with the top-management group the responsibility for projecting their thinking forward into the future, recognizing that their own roles, if they remained in the school, might change radically as a result of this forward thinking, since it concerned broad questions of policy as distinct from immediate questions of implementation.

In the full staff meeting of 18 June 1970, which I now identify as a third turning point, the problem of determining how much of what had hitherto been private could increasingly be made public was explored in another context—that of assessment. In this context 'public' began to mean something more than in the earlier discussion about the house system and the still earlier encounters between the standing committee and certain individual colleagues: for it now involved the boundary between staff and parents, where before it had involved only the internal boundaries between staff groups and between individual staff members.

This was the meeting on assessment, in which problems of trust and distrust between parents and teachers were opened up, along with acknowledgements that the difficulty about arriving at acceptable assessment scales that could be used generally throughout the school and by all staff was closely linked with the wish to preserve the good aspects of a teacher's relationship with pupils by claiming for it a kind of privacy that might be at variance with the teacher's responsibility towards the parents of those pupils.

This progression corresponded with the gradual shift in the staff group's thinking about my written accounts, real or projected, of the Nailsea experience. In the January meeting, preceding the standing committee's first painful awakening to the stresses of top-management responsibility, the shift was towards an examination of their reactions to my first written communication to themselves as a staff group. In the May meeting, preceding the senior-staff group's discussion about role relationships between the lower and middle-school tutorial staff groups, the shift was towards consideration of the possibility that I might publish two articles about the implications for other schools of this school's experience. And in the June meeting, preceding the full staff meeting on the subject of assessment and the communication of information to parents, the shift was towards consideration of the more alarming, because less controllable, presentation of a course of six lectures to Bristol students, each lecture to be followed by a forty-five-minute discussion period.

In fact, in that year, I neither wrote the articles nor gave the lectures. But the opening up of discussion with the staff group about the two possibilities released them, it appeared, to open up new areas of difficult, even painful discussion among themselves. For it was around this time that the house heads were publicly challenged about the nature of their authority in the middle school, that Mike Burnham was publicly challenged about the nature of his authority in the upper school and that Denys John was publicly challenged about the nature of his authority in the school as a whole. And it was during this period that Denys John began to change the style of documentation for staff meetings and to develop a programme of phased discussions that were to lead up to known dates on which decisions about major policy matters would have to be made.

Consultation, documentation and decision making

Readers of this book may from time to time have wondered whether the reorganization of the management structure at Nailsea was in the direction of a strengthening or of a weakening of the 'hierarchy'. Now the word 'hierarchy' is very often used as though it were a descriptive term applicable only to those at the 'top'. But in fact the word means a 'graded organization'. We can therefore speak of a hierarchy of responsibilities that includes every single person in a school staff group; and we must recognize that every sub-section itself implies some hierarchical ordering of responsibilities. Even within the standing committee there were three identifiable orders of responsibility: namely the first-order responsibility of the headmaster, who was ultimately answerable to the outside world for what happened in his institution, the second-order responsibility of the deputy head and the senior mistress, who—notwithstanding all the uncertainties about their respective roles—could and did exercise authority on behalf of the headmaster over the school as a whole, and the third-order responsibilities of the heads of the three main sections of the school, who between them had authority over the lower, middle and upper schools but not over the whole school.

Part of the problem of growth for a large institution is that people are reluctant to acknowledge that such hierarchical divisions are present, or if not present, are needed, in every important sub-section as well as in the management system as a whole. The difficulty seems to arise from the error of perceiving each identifiable sub-group as separate from the rest rather than as interrelated with the rest. The standing committee's separateness from the rest, as a bounded group with the responsibilities of top management, had to be reconciled with its inclusion in the larger 'senior-staff group' that also included within *its* boundary the two dozen or so colleagues in middle-management roles. And the senior-staff group in its turn had to be recognized as both a separate consultative body within the organization and as an integral part of the full staff group (see Figure 57).

The strength of the resistance to the notion of 'hierarchy' as a necessary aspect of efficient organization was illustrated by Denys John himself on the occasion referred to in Chapter VI when, in introducing Dawn Castell into the already established Fourth Year Curriculum study group in the autumn of 1968, he assured her that there was 'no hierarchy' in that group. It was illustrated in my hearing again, about a year later, in a meeting of the house heads with Clive Vanloo, when consideration was being given to a suggestion that had come from one of the house tutors, that they might learn more about what went on in one another's house groups if they instituted a practice of inter-house visiting, perhaps by rotating tutors between the houses in some assemblies or on some lunch occasions. Peter Chapman remarked that it was difficult to find times when tutors could talk about educational matters, adding rather sadly and also with a touch of exasperation that on those occasions when 'the hierarchy' came to have lunch in one of the houses the conversation, inevitably perhaps, was just social. Later in this discussion Clive Vanloo was assured categorically by Graeme Osborn that he was 'not in the hierarchy'. It was clear from the discussion that all four house heads were thinking of the hierarchy as including Denys John, Robin Thomas and Joan Bradbury, as probably not including the three section heads, and as almost certainly excluding themselves. What was not clear was whether Graeme Osborn, in telling Clive Vanloo that he was not part of it, was offering him a friendly gesture implying solidarity between him and the house heads or a hurtful rebuff implying their rejection of him in his leadership role.

Consultation, participation, discussion about educational matters: all these imply situations in which some people talk and others listen, in which some ask questions and others attempt to answer them (or are expected to do so), in which some throw out challenges or appeals and others respond or fail to respond, in which some offer leads and others follow or turn the other way. Many people assume that ideas are unlikely to be generated during a

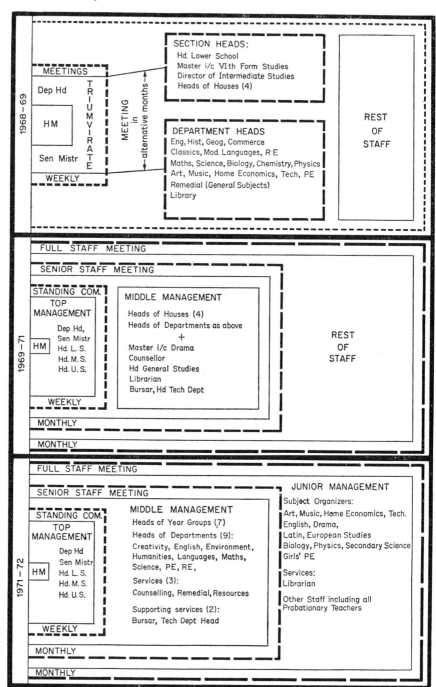

FIG. 57. Successive modifications of management and consultative structure.

large meeting unless someone writes a paper as a focus for discussion. Others believe that the important writing is done after a meeting when the ideas that have been generated are recorded, analysed and interpreted. In the earlier months of this three-year study the staff, more often than not, were provided either with a speculative or theoretical paper written by Denys John or with tabulated proposals, very often concerned with curriculum organization or time-tabling, drawn up sometimes by himself and sometimes by Robin Thomas and Joan Bradbury. In the later months, the staff were more likely to find themselves offered the more challenging task of responding to a broad theme, such as 'the tutorial function' or 'the role of the school counsellor' or 'lower-school organization' or 'assessment and relations with parents'. The effect of introducing this more open kind of discussion was that the old style of pre-meeting manifesto based on the head's ideas gave way to a new style of post-meeting summary, based on the verbal contributions of the staff during their meetings.

The staff experienced this change on one occasion quite suddenly and, perhaps for many of them, unexpectedly. In March 1970, following the January and February meetings on curriculum development when twenty-eight people had talked with the standing committee, Denys John issued to all his colleagues a document that must have been perceived by them to be radically different in tone and content from those he had circulated from time to time in the past. This document took the form of a collated summary of the suggestions yielded by those meetings, each item linked with the initials of the staff member who had been responsible for it, some being accompanied by the head's own comment or interpretation. To the seventeen separate items drawn from the meetings of the standing committee, he added two that were based on discussions he had had, outside the standing-committee meetings, with Tina Bateman and Margaret Fisher, who had put before him some of the problems of leadership and teamwork that they predicted might arise for them in the complex overlapping areas of humanities, religious education and counselling. The inclusion of these two additional items must have implied, both to the two persons concerned and to the rest of the staff that although Denys John as headmaster could not (and would not wish to) refuse to be accessible to individual staff members who were anxious about any particular aspect of a developing situation, he could not, as chairman of the standing committee, go into collusion with attempts to create 'private' conversations about staff-wide problems unless it was understood that the content of such conversations must be part of the available data for the public discussions in the senior-staff and full-staff meetings during the period of consultation.

The sequel to this new way of following up staff discussions was the evolution of a new way of preparing for them. In the summer term of that year the staff were given a framework in which the phases of consultation were clearly related, first to specific problems that needed to be examined by all staff, secondly to the differentiation between the standing-committee, senior-staff and full-staff meetings, and thirdly to the dates upon which any particular decisions would have to be made. The phasing of discussion on three different problems—namely, 'lower-school organization', 'third-year curriculum and time allocation', and 'assessments and objectives'—over the fifteen weeks of that summer term is shown in Figure 58, which has been reproduced from Denys John's own circular distributed to all staff at the beginning of the term. The special full staff meeting of 1 June, arranged unexpectedly to discuss my proposed lecture course, has been added to the diagram, but no other alteration has been made.

Did this schedule of phased discussions turn out to be an answer to all the problems of consultation? By no means. The special meeting to discuss the third-year curriculum, which took place on 7 July, affords an illustration of the inevitable gap between intention and actuality—a meeting that I described in the previous chapter as being focused on a curious 'exchange of boasts and confessions' about the use of time. In fact the standing committee, despite the forecast that decisions would be reached by 25 June, were still trying to find some way of providing an additional five hours for the options that were to start in Year III instead of in Year IV as they had formerly done; and when Denys John postponed his decisions he posted a notice in the staff common-room to make this known. A schedule, clearly, is not infallible. It is at best a forecast of the kind of sequence that may prove helpful in controlling the boundaries of debate and in regulating the relations between the sentient and task systems so that the need to preserve known advantages or comfortable situations does not militate against necessary change. The schedule does not protect the headmaster, or any of his colleagues, from the unpredictable difficulties that may interfere with the process. Nor should it insulate the staff group against unexpected creative ideas that may necessitate a modification of the schedule.

Sub-group discussion and plenary discussion in general staff meetings

One of the constraints upon creativeness in the general staff discussions was the sheer size of the full staff group, which, by 1970, numbered seventy-five, including the ten part-time staff who were, of course, entitled to attend staff meetings. The discussions about the possible substitution of sectional staff meetings, based on the tutorial teams in the lower, middle and upper schools, had exposed the fears of being over-identified with one particular age group of pupils in the school, and this particular solution to the problem of size was not reconsidered. But the need to find ways of tackling the difficulties of exchanging useful information and ideas in the large group was now being openly acknowledged. Sometimes this acknowledgement would take the form of accusatory remarks—surprise that colleagues within the same staff group should be unable to enter into a face-to-face relationship or deal

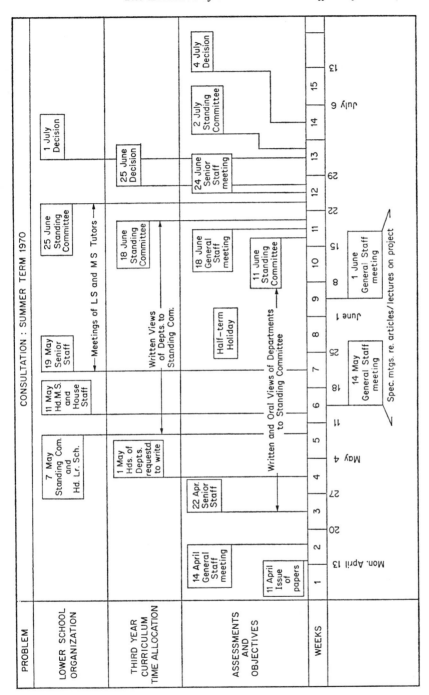

FIG. 58. Schedule of staff meetings in relation to consultation and decision making.

openly with one another, impatience with adults who, although accustomed to exercising authority in the classroom, could be so inarticulate, or even totally silent, with their peers, indignant denial that there could be anything to fear in a group of people whom one knew and worked with every day. At other times there would be a far greater acceptance of the reality that even a group of known colleagues could be intimidating, that experience of communicating effectively with children in a classroom was no guarantee of ability to communicate, in a meeting, with fellow teachers in the staff room. Sometimes it appeared that it was some of those in middle-management roles who wished to deny the difficulties and that the most senior and the most junior members of the staff group could most easily find a meeting ground in a willingness to tolerate their own insecurity and inadequacy in face of the difficulties.

There was one staff meeting in particular, during the spring of 1970, that revealed a great deal of anxiety about risking experience and opinion in the public arena of a full staff meeting. This was a meeting devoted to the subject of tutorial work—an area of teaching that was clearly felt to be so personal that any exploration of real experiences would make tutors feel exposed and vulnerable. The anxiety showed itself in the first few minutes when someone broke the silence by announcing that John Phillips, although unable to attend the meeting, had left a list of the tutorial functions that he considered to be the most important. This list—read out to the meeting—recalled vividly to me the written manifesto which Denys John had offered to the section heads about ten months earlier, and which had aroused from them a veiled but unmistakable hostility. The use of John Phillips as a kind of absent leader also recalled another senior staff meeting of that period—the department heads' meeting at which the absent Lewis Smith had been used, and indeed had offered himself, in much the same way, when 'the role of a department head' had been the theme for discussion. It seemed that, faced with the need to scrutinize their own roles in public, the staff were very liable to resist any kind of laying down of a law by the head; yet, when he refrained from laying down any law, they looked round for a substitute who might offer to do so in his place. The particular difficulty of probing into the area of tutorial work turned out to be linked with fears lest some colleagues, in their other roles as subject teachers, particularly if they were involved with English or religious education, might be encroaching on the work of tutors. There was also anxiety about the developing programme of H.R. work, which, because it required the splitting of tutor groups, was proving divisive, giving rise to assumptions that most members of staff were 'good' at one aspect of tutorial work and 'bad' at another, and that the H.R. tutor was perhaps being perceived, by children and by colleagues, and possibly also by parents, as compensating for a tutor's weakness in handling problems of human relationships as they might be arising in his own tutor group.

Eventually, out of the exploration of these problems, a creative idea emerged. In the autumn of 1970, one of the new members of staff suggested to Denys John the new form of staff meeting described in Chapter IV, which came into effect almost immediately. The proposal was that the first hour or so of the full staff meeting should be spent in small groups which would contain members from a cross-section of departments and sections and from all levels of responsibility, and that the groups should then come together into a plenary session for the last half-hour of the meeting and work as a total group. This suggestion provided a much more acceptable alternative to the earlier notion of having separate meetings of the lower, middle and upper-school tutorial staff groups, since it did not threaten people with loss of the already tenuous sense of belonging to the whole school and therefore to a corporate body of staff.

The staff now had the opportunity, in its monthly general meetings, to explore important problems of policy, as well as immediate problems of implementing agreed policies, in groups that were small enough to offer support so that people felt more prepared to risk exposing their ideas and sharing bad experiences as well as good ones. But the new-style staff meeting went further than this. It also provided a work pattern in which the problems of bringing back, not the content necessarily, but the resultant learning into the large and increasingly complex staff group, including both its full-time and its part-time members, could really be examined. For people could now test out their ideas both in the intimate setting of a small but diverse group of colleagues and in the public arena of the full staff group, where 'colleagues' had so often appeared to be 'strangers'. It also raised a number of questions about role definition, group cohesion and commitment to a new set of relationships, questions that could be used as pointers to comparable problems arising every day in the management of learning situations in classroom, laboratory, workshop and gymnasium.

Unexpectedly the standing committee found themselves having to examine again in this new context how the role of the head differed from and related to the roles of his five most senior colleagues, for it was these five who had to take on the responsibility for accepting in the small groups a role that was consistent with their task as members of top management. And immediately new questions presented themselves. Were the members of the committee to be 'leaders', 'consultants' or just 'ordinary members' of the groups? Should there be six groups or only five? If the headmaster did not actually take a group himself, should he move round from one to another to 'get a feel of the discussions'? And if he did this what effect would his presence or absence have on the groups and on the members of the standing committee as they tried to work out their own roles in relation to the task of the groups? Should each standing-committee member remain with the same group throughout the school year, or should they rotate? Ought the groups them-selves to be reshuffled at intervals or perhaps for every meeting in the interest of variety of experience, or ought they to persist with the same membership so that some identity could be established that would assist their work at the task?

Surprisingly, yet in another way predictably, there was pressure from the staff for movement, variety and impermanence. This pressure was surprising because so many had experienced the difficulties of communicating effectively with colleagues who were not well known to them; it was, nevertheless, predictable in face of the evidence (shared by many members) that commitment to task-centred working groups over a long period could prove exacting and even painful. The standing committee—again surprisingly at one level and predictably at another—found themselves very ready at first to collude with those who wanted to keep the groups fluid, thus both depriving themselves of the opportunity to work through authority problems with comparable cross-sections of the staff group, and protecting themselves from the need to test their own leadership skills beyond the known limits of their competence.

Even Denys John with the experience of the HR staff study group behind him and knowing that his role as headmaster would inevitably affect his leadership of any one small group in the situation, nevertheless chose to take one of the groups himself in the first meeting. In the later meetings, when he relinquished this role, he decided to go in and out of his colleagues' groups rather than accept the much greater strain of staying out of them during that first hour. Yet had he stayed out—as on an earlier occasion he had been able to stay out of the special meeting of the lower and middle-school tutorial teams chaired by Robin Thomas—he would probably have freed himself to work more creatively in the follow-up session with the whole staff group, and would have freed the other five members of the top-management group to carry a greater authority in working with the sub-groups during the preceding hour.

Again, my own experience in this situation, as in so many others, illuminated for me the nature of a headmaster's dilemma in making these decisions. For when I attended one of these new-style staff meetings I too found myself uncertain what I ought to do during that first hour when the staff were dispersed and working in five different places with five different leaders or co-ordinators. Like Denys John, I decided to 'visit' groups. In the time available I visited three, the third for only the last few minutes of its time. I scarcely knew whether it was joining a group or leaving it that made me more anxious, since the first felt like intruding on privacy and the second felt like expressing rejection or boredom, however much I really wanted to remain.

Examining the situation in the standing committee the following week, we learned that the arrival of either Denys John or myself in a group produced an immediately inhibiting effect upon the members, as sensed by the five standing-committee members who had been leading or interpreting the discussions. Yet neither of us had been aware of any particular change in the atmosphere as we moved in on a group and sat down to listen to its deliberations. Nor had we any means of knowing, except at second hand through the reports of the standing-committee members, how the quality or content of the discussion before the entrance of either of us had differed from what happened while either of us was present. As for any discomfiture, nervousness or sense of being intruders that he or I might have felt, this had evidently passed unnoticed by the members, just as their sudden inhibitedness had passed unnoticed by us. There was a further problem for Denys John in deciding whether or not he would continue the 'visiting' or 'sitting-in' pattern in later meetings. For a decision to visit groups could be interpreted either as 'the head taking an interest' or 'the head keeping tabs on us', even perhaps as 'the head interfering'; conversely, however, a decision *not* to visit them could be interpreted either as indifference or as trust.

Having decided to delegate responsibility for the small-group sessions entirely to the other five members of the standing committee, Denys John then had to face the assembled staff group without any knowledge of what had been going on during the previous hour and a quarter. The natural defence against the discomfort of this situation, for himself and for the large staff group, was to build in a reporting session, which in fact he did, at the urgent written request of one of the younger men on the staff. But the reporting back—undertaken, appropriately, by the standing committee members—quickly reduced the time available for discussion from forty-five minutes to about twenty-five, since it was difficult in practice for anyone to give a coherent account in less than four minutes of a discussion that had only just ended, leaving no time for any considered preparation of a more condensed report. Thus the standing committee found themselves forced into a sort of collective monologue, which was time-consuming and repetitive, however competent the individual reporting might be, and which forced the rest of the staff into the roles of audience, with consequent frustration on all sides.

The removal of this defence, in the meeting of November 1971, a meeting devoted to problems of staff-pupil relationships within the school, left the staff feeling exposed and unprotected. The standing committee was taken to task for having 'abdicated' from the responsibility of reporting back to the meeting; some argument followed about the value or futility of such reporting; and again, as on the two earlier occasions to which I referred above, there was resort to an absent leader, this time Pip Ridgwell, who had been unable to attend the meeting but had furnished his group with a written statement giving his views about the present troubles the school was experiencing. Nevertheless, it required only a quiet but provocative question from Denys John—'Are we evading the real topic?' and an acknowledgement from Pat Richardson (who had initiated the protest at the beginning) that they had now wasted ten minutes, for the real discussion to get under way. As it turned out, the removal of the ritual reporting did, after the initial resistance, free the staff to open up some of their real anxieties about how they were operating as the adults responsible for the work and general climate of feeling in the school. Repeatedly it seemed that these anxieties were focused on the fear that they could not match their concern for the children and young people in their care with the skill needed to stimulate them to effective work and learning.

It was hard for Denys John to close a meeting in which so much frustration and inadequacy was being expressed. And in fact there was a burst of discussion at the very end of the time available which made it very difficult for him to close it, as he suddenly found himself under attack for interpreting the questions about 'sanctions' as references to the need to punish children. Yet to close it on all this uncertainty—knowing that it would be another month before he could hold another full staff meeting—must itself have been an indication to the staff of his own belief that the staff had strengths as well as the weaknesses they had been acknowledging, and that there was leadership available to them in the intervening days and weeks if they could find ways of mobilizing it, not only in the section heads and in the year-group and department heads, but within teaching and tutorial teams. For the evidence that even some of the youngest members of staff could offer such leadership had been there in the meeting for all to see.

The oldness and newness of a school

Sometimes one hears in one context the formulation of an idea that quite suddenly illuminates another. A few months ago, by chance, listening to a radio talk by Hans Keller about the music of Beethoven, I heard him say: 'We cannot understand the newness of Beethoven's mind except in the context of the oldness of his creative memory.' A week or so later, in another radio talk, he illustrated over and over again his belief that at the very moment when Beethoven was exhibiting one characteristic he was also exhibiting the opposite. If we transfer these insights to the field of education, we find they are just as applicable in helping us to understand schools as in helping us to listen more sensitively to music. For a school, too, must reconcile creatively its newness and its oldness, and its staff have to learn to recognize in one another not only the obvious and familiar behaviour that everyone has learned to expect but also the less obvious, often unseen or unheard dual of that behaviour. We have to try to acknowledge the latent radicalism of the 'conservative' teacher and the latent conservatism of the 'radical' teacher, and so avoid the mutual stereotyping that is so destructive of personality and therefore so impoverishing to the work of the institution.

The tension between nostalgia for the past and hope for the future could at times produce an effect almost like a collision. For the wish to return to a past that had been, in fantasy, trouble-free, was inevitably accompanied by a scarcely acknowledged wish to punish those who offended against that image—a wish that might express itself in a rather desperate search for certainty about what 'sanctions' were available to staff when they found themselves baffled by the defiant or merely casual attitudes of pupils, or in futile longings for assurance that seventy-five colleagues working in the same school could be relied on to agree about standards and to be entirely consistent in the demands they made on pupils. But almost in the same breath could come a challenge that they ought rather to be examining self-critically their own deficiencies in setting up learning situations for these bored, indifferent or rebellious pupils and that they should be devising ways of engaging these pupils in work that they might find satisfying.

There was some evidence that at least one member of the staff, apart from Denys John himself, feared that the reorganization of the departments might prove to be only 'another aspirin', and that fundamental rethinking had yet to be started in the area of curriculum change. Yet this same member of the staff, despite the at times despairing talk about declining standards of behaviour, felt that real progress in understanding had been made on the caring side of the school's work, if only, perhaps, because far more attention was being given to the personal needs of those very pupils who gave the staff most trouble.

Because the sharing of a caring concern for children and young people brings into play the parent or potential parent in every man or woman, the members of a staff group can risk more exposure to one another in the pursuit of a more effective organization for caring. But the professional training in a subject or group of subjects that every student has to undergo before he can take on the role of a teacher, places him in a situation of rivalry with many of his colleagues and is thus a divisive agent in the staff group. Real exposure of 'teaching' problems is therefore more difficult to tolerate than exposure of problems that can be described as 'tutorial'. Paradoxically, the area in which both the teacher and the pupil are presumed to perceive one another most clearly as persons, may after all prove less difficult to talk about in public than the area in which those same persons as learners and as promoters of learning have to confront and evaluate one another. For the ability to handle in one's own classes the day-to-day consequences of curriculum development is still perceived as the real test of professional competence, as though it were not indissolubly bound up with the other, more elusive, kind of tutorial competence, where personal awareness of children as children is more easily acknowledged to be of primary importance.

Experienced teachers are being judged in both roles by their pupils, by the students who come into the school for limited periods to carry out their assigned school practice, by young probationary teachers who join their departments or houses or year groups, by parents who build up images of them from the slender evidence of children's conversations about what goes on in their classes and tutor groups and from the other kind of evidence afforded by their own discussions with them during parents' evening or in special interviews at times of crucial decision-making or at times of crisis.

The school is constantly under pressure, from outside as well as from inside, to review its own methods of evaluating its own work.

The stability of a staff group is never certain. Every school of any size or importance experiences annually the fluctuating intake and output of students in training, the inward flow of new colleagues and the inevitable loss of old colleagues. In addition there may be the temporary withdrawal of experienced staff on secondment to the universities to pursue further studies in education, and the consequent necessity to assimilate their new ideas, often critical of school values and practices formerly taken for granted. Every school must

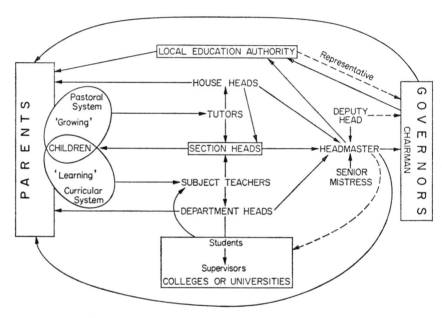

FIG. 59. Patterns of accountability.

therefore accept a three-fold responsibility to work at the task of reconciling the old and the new, first in its own internal arrangements for the planning and implementation of policy (which has really been the main theme of this book), secondly in its relations with the colleges and departments of education that carry responsibility for the initial training of teachers, and thirdly in its relations with other educational institutions through the experienced teachers it exports, either to pursue advanced studies or to take up responsible posts in other parts of the educational system.

In this chapter I have been examining some of the ways in which the Nailsea staff refined and modified their own procedures for consultation and decision making during a period when the old and the new influences on policy were often in considerable conflict. In the final chapter I shall consider from a slightly different perspective how these various influences were impinging on the school's self image and try to draw some conclusions about the nature of a staff group's interaction with students in training, with new members of staff, with governors and with the pupils on whose behalf the endless pursuit of understanding goes on (see Figure 59).

CHAPTER XII

Teachers, Governors, Parents and Pupils in a Changing Society

Reorganization and the search for a new image

When the school system of a whole region is in a state of reorganization, every school in that region has to come to terms with its own position in the developing design. Some lead the way; others follow. The former may be perceived as pace-makers, the latter as lagging behind. In looking at a cluster of schools in different phases of change within a changing regional pattern, we may employ the analogy of a family in which there are many children, each of whose life stories is influenced in various elusive ways by the accident of his or her position in the family. What is it like to be the elder brother in a family of schools in a region that is gradually going comprehensive in its secondary sector?

Nailsea school, although not the first secondary school in the region to 'go comprehensive', was a close second, and throughout the period of this study the only one that had started life as a grammar school. The recurrent anxiety about the school's image in the neighbourhood, as I was sensing it during the latter phase of my work, was related, I believe, to both these facts —to the appearance of competing rivals in the field and to the loss of the old grammar-school image and the long-drawn-out search for a new image to take its place.

The growing preoccupation with arguments for and against house and year-group systems sprang both from the internal evidence about the divisive effects of the house system and from the need to look outwards in order to keep abreast of developments in other schools that were going through comparable experiences of redefining their roles in the community. For the institutions with which Nailsea could now be compared were coming nearer every year, as new comprehensive schools came into existence in the neighbouring areas of the county. Indeed they were coming so near that they were actually taking children who would formerly have been Nailsea pupils and teachers who had been on the Nailsea staff. Much of the depression about the changing image of the school must have been springing from the fear that it might be comparing unfavourably with these new neighbours, and from the sense of loss as the talent and experience of people who had found new strengths at Nailsea began, inevitably, to drain away to other schools where such expertise was needed. When a school has been first, or nearly first, in the field, it is hard for it to find itself becoming one of a crowd.

Yet this periodic loss from the institution of the very strength that it has built up is part of the life of any vital staff group. For it is not only educated adolescents and young adults that the school exports into the environment, but also teachers who have themselves been growing and learning from their experience within the school.

There were some at Nailsea who feared that the prolonged examination of role relationships and authority structures within the staff group might have been setting up a task that was in conflict with the primary task of educating children. The danger that it could have become this is without doubt a real one. And of course I cannot be certain that it did not, for some people if not for others. The criterion, as I see it, is whether or not the self-examination is being pursued within the context of working towards greater understanding of the needs of the pupils and towards increased skill and sensitivity in handling complex relationships with pupils, parents and prospective employers. We have seen that this process of self scrutiny was by no means comfortable or easy. Yet even a process that is initially threatening may imperceptibly become self-indulgent if its purpose in the working institution is forgotten. Similarly, it would be possible for a school to become, by gradual unnoticed stages, a laboratory for the further training or self-education of teachers instead of an institution geared to the growth needs of children. Indeed the American term 'lab. school' contains this suggestion. The problem is centred on the paradox that the teacher, however experienced he may be, can learn more about his craft only by modifying his practice in accordance with ideas that are as yet untested—or untested in relation to his own skills. And since he cannot do this in isolation, he must seek clarification of his own relationships with his colleagues, on whose co-operation any experimental venture will depend. He must therefore at least attempt to work at both levels—with pupils and with colleagues. And it may be that the work with colleagues must come first.

In fact schools, like hospitals, have always had to accept as their secondary task—or, as some people would prefer to say, as a related task—part reponssibility for the training of future teachers. All the signs are that the schools will find themselves, in the very near future, having to accept a larger share of this responsibility. Unless they accept also the obligation to foster and develop the leadership skills of teachers already in employment, they may find this difficult to discharge. The recent research studies into the whole problem of school practice, carried out by Edith Cope in the University of Bristol and described in two reports to the D.E.S.[1], have revealed strikingly how complex and ambiguous can be the perceptions that students, practising

---

[1] Cope, E., *School Experience in Teacher Education*, University of Bristol 1971 and *A Study of a School Supervised Practice*, University of Bristol 1971.

teachers and college supervisers may have of one another's contribution to the school-practice experience. Surprisingly, class teachers in the samples chosen seemed to have less confidence in their own capacity to help students in training than the students themselves had in this. This suggests that the management systems within the schools may have been failing somehow to give opportunities to teachers, as they gain experience in their work with children, to exercise leadership in the staff group and to take part in the planning and organization of new ventures.

The school in the eyes of students in training

I have been concerned in this book with problems about staff participation in the organization of change and therefore, by implication, with the further professional development of teachers whose initial training was already behind them. For the processes by which persons become more effective teachers and the processes by which schools become more effective institutions are inseparable from one another. If the person can be only as effective as the institution will allow him to be, so the institution can be only as effective as the persons within it enable it to be.

And so it is in the school itself that the problems about staff consultation and the problems about teacher training begin to intersect. Before actually accepting a post as a probationary teacher in a school, the man or woman entering the teaching profession will already have been playing a part, as a student in training, in one or more schools. And the school he or she joins will in all probability have been host to a long succession of students.

Exposure is always bound to hurt. And because teachers cannot be trained without the schools and training institutions being mutually exposed, some conflict is inevitably present between those who teach the children and those who train the teachers. And when things go wrong, each is liable to hold the other responsible. Much of the present dissatisfaction about the content and structure of teacher education, like the dissatisfaction about what goes on in some schools, is centred on the problem of the clash between 'traditionalism' or 'conservatism' on the one side and 'progressivism' or 'radicalism' on the other. We read in the press from time to time about the bizarre and often frightening behaviour of head teachers who deal with their own fear of the new trends, particularly where attitudes to dress and hair style, drug-taking and sexual behaviour are concerned, by taking repressive action against the young. We also hear, less directly and much less dramatically, about head teachers who, recognizing that these are inevitably present in a society that is changing so rapidly that the real *values* of young people are almost as difficult for adults to understand as their confusions, take steps to share with staff and pupils the problem of exploring difficult and disturbing areas. The evidence about the values of the schools, like the evidence about the values of young people, is conflicting. But because the bad things in the schools are more spectacular, and because teaching can be a frightening and soul-destroying business, many young teachers see only the disturbing evidence, and fear that the 'system', particularly as it operates in relation to thirteen, fourteen and fifteen-year-olds, will defeat them, along with their pupils, the moment they enter it.

Much of this feeling of despair and anger has found its way into novels, films and television programmes about schools, teachers and pupils. Such material, with its admixture of fiction and documentary, can have an important role in awakening the conscience of the nation. Inevitably, however, it can also exert upon those teachers who are honestly struggling with the problems an impact that is felt as destructive. The propaganda that is aimed at improving the climate of the school thus increases the polarization and the consequent bitterness and distrust within the staff group. But it rarely does so in such a way as to enable this distrust to be examined so that some possibility of replacing mutual suspicion with the beginnings of mutual trust can be created.

Exposure to students—with their youth, their intolerance, their idealism, their creativeness—can be more threatening to a group of teachers than the exposure to experienced teachers who have left the schools; for such people, having moved into positions in colleges, university departments, local authorities or the inspectorate, may be suspected by those who remain in the schools of having escaped into these more comfortable situations from classroom stresses to which they have proved unequal. The strain that students put on teachers is, in fact, too often underestimated. From outside it may be tempting to see their presence in a school only as an additional teaching force to lighten the classroom load.

The part played by students and by their supervisors in the life of the Nailsea staff group does not fall within the scope of this book. Yet inevitably the presence of the students impinged on my own experience of working with the staff and cannot therefore be ignored in this final chapter. Students were present at Nailsea in large numbers every year, six of them, out of a total annual intake of about thirty, coming in for the whole of the spring term from the university school of education of which I myself was a member. In the 1969–70 session Denys John built in for all the students a regular fortnightly meeting in his room so that they could discuss with him their experiences in the school and their impressions of it as an institution in which to work. On occasions when he could not lead this discussion because of commitments outside the school Joan Bradbury would deputize for him. During that spring term of 1970 I attended three of these meetings, initially so that I could be available to the students to discuss with them, in the head's presence, their perception of my work with the staff group and indeed to offer them some explanations about the way in which the project had begun so that they should not be too much in the dark as the term went on. And so the first of these three meetings began with this topic.

T.S.T.M.—12

As Denys John and I tried to clarify for them the nature of my working relationship with the staff I had an increasing sense of being regarded by them in a protective, almost possessive way. It appeared to me that they wanted to preserve their relationship with me, and through me, with the headmaster, so that all the difficulties they themselves were experiencing as students in the school could be put outside the door of his room. Before long it became evident that what they really wanted to discuss was not so much my project within the school system as a whole, but rather the impact upon the staff group of the humanities project within the school and in particular the nature of the hostility and anxiety that it aroused from time to time.

In the second of the three meetings, the six Bristol University students were joined by a Bath University student, whose practice periods were organized in a different pattern; and by the third meeting this group of seven had been augmented by four students from a college of education who had already had a period of school practice in other schools. The student group thus had experience, in miniature as it were, of something comparable to what the staff group experienced every autumn with the influx of new colleagues, including some straight from college or university and some from posts in other schools. The interaction between the old and new members in the two situations was, it appeared, not dissimilar. For both sub-groups (the students and the new staff) were obsessed with the need to question the values of the school and to understand their own conflicting feelings about what they experienced in joining it. This took the form, both with the students and with the new staff, of enlarging on the difficulties of knowing what was expected of them as teachers in this school because of the lack of uniformity in the demands made by the established staff, both upon children and upon one another. It was as if people coming into the school to take roles in it wanted to maintain that this was the first institution they had ever entered in which people were not in complete agreement about objectives, standards and priorities. Yet their problems in joining this institution could not in essence have been different from problems they must all have encountered over and over again in joining other educational institutions, whether as pupils, as students in training or as experienced teachers.

In all three of the meetings between the students and Denys John or Joan Bradbury (or both), it soon became obvious that the real need was to talk about their relations with the school staff rather than simply about their relations with pupils. But it was difficult for them to know what sanction there was to bring into the head's room experience of this kind without feeling that they might be betraying confidences or in some obscure way informing on staff. The other side of this dilemma, for Denys John and Joan Bradbury, was to know how to free the discussion without becoming receptacles for unwanted information about their colleagues. Thus what was perhaps being tested, on both sides, was the extent to which discussion between the headmaster and his staff about painful and controversial issues was open and honest enough to enable him to contain within himself both the cooperative and mutually appreciative feelings between staff and students and the inevitable tensions between them. It seemed difficult for the students to use this situation as a forum for opening up questions about maintaining the balance between their different roles as teachers without—consciously or unconsciously—seeking to split the head and the senior mistress apart from the rest of the staff, by speaking of their difficulties in working with teachers who held such diverse views of what teaching should be like and what it was really for. This splitting took the form mainly of complaints that pupils did not work as hard as they had expected them to do, and of surprised references to the informality in the upper school or—as they perceived it in some pupils —casualness in their approach to staff members. In fact, comments like these were by no means new to Denys John or to Joan Bradbury, since they had been voiced, as we have seen, by staff members themselves in full staff meet-ings and in tutors' meetings long before these particular students had arrived in the school. Indeed, Joan Bradbury told the students this, and urged them to talk with sixth-form tutors about the problem, about which, she indicated, many staff were as concerned as were the students.

It was not until the four college students joined the student group that the other side of this ambivalence towards the school and its pupils became evident in what the university students said about their experiences. The college students seemed to be even more critical in their comments on pupil behaviour than the university students had been. It might have been the least tolerant members of the middle-aged establishment speaking. Suddenly the university students began to defend their Nailsea pupils, arguing that the casual manners and relative lack of academic fervour among some of the sixth-formers, about which they themselves had been complaining only a fortnight before, seemed a fair price to pay for the friendliness and good-will they were also experiencing in their dealings with them and hence for the good working relationships that could be established. It is perhaps significant that, even when they began to defend their pupils, they did not refer to any of the evidence that some pupils did work hard and even accepted quite conventional standards of social behaviour. Or—if any such references were made—it is equally significant that I did not hear them clearly enough to recall them when I wrote my own record of that meeting later in the day.

Listening to the fairly sharp exchanges between the sub-groups, ranged on opposite sides of the head's long table, with Joan Bradbury at one end of it and myself somewhere near the other end, I had the feeling that the university students' head start of half a term over their colleagues from the college was now pushing them into an emotional identification with the school, whereas the college students, coming that much later into the situation and finding the university group installed, as it were, still felt more identified with the schools in which they had done their earlier practice. Thus the university students were more accepting of the social norms they found at Nailsea, whereas the college students seemed to be under some pressure to perceive Nailsea as too 'liberal' in comparison with the other schools in which they had practised.

It seemed to me as I thought about this situation that all the students, at different stages of their progress through the term, needed to handle their own initial difficulties in joining the staff group and in identifying their roles within it by projecting some of their own anxieties about the whole business of teaching into the experienced Nailsea staff. For if they could persuade themselves that even experienced teachers—under the leadership of an experienced head—might at times feel unequal to the demands of running a comprehensive school in the early seventies, they could avoid the pain of examining where they themselves might be falling down in their roles as students trying to learn something about the practice of education.

Because the school reflected in itself the changes taking place in the whole system of secondary education, the students—while still apprentices to the profession—were having to grapple within themselves with the nagging question: were they seeing the decay of what had once been a good system, or the beginnings of what would, a few years thence, be a much better system? Ought they to be lamenting the gradual disappearance of the former country grammar school that had catered for a selected intake or applauding the growth of the future neighbourhood school that was to cater for an increasingly comprehensive intake? Were they expecting too much of the staff who were struggling to adjust their demands to this changing intake of pupils, even at the sixth-form level, or too little of themselves as the future colleagues of teachers in similarly challenging situations?

Behind this, moreover, there were powerfully ambivalent feelings towards the pupils themselves. I sensed in these discussions a kind of oscillation between admiration and envy of the young people—so like their own former selves—whom they were now encountering or at least seeing around the school if they were not actually teaching them. It was as though they wanted at one moment to say: 'Why were we, in our sixth-form days, so conforming?' and then, at another moment, to say: 'How boorish some of these sixth-formers are and how poor intellectually compared with what we were at their age!' This wish to idealize (or denigrate) their own pupil behaviour, as sixth-formers of a former decade, clearly contained within it a good deal of envy of a generation for whom school was, it seemed, less threatening than it had been for them. It almost seemed to me, as I listened in amazement to their somewhat righteous indignation, that they were expressing on behalf of staff members twice their age the envious feelings of the middle-aged when they contemplate the relative freedom of the young in the 1970s. If, as I felt, they were coping with some of their own anxieties by projecting them into the staff group, they were also, it appeared, introjecting from the staff group a good deal of this resentment of the middle-aged against the young.

The impact of new colleagues upon an established staff group

Between these student discussions with Denys John and Joan Bradbury in the head's room in the middle of that spring term of 1970 and a discussion between some of the new members of staff and myself in the sixth-form block earlier in that same term there were some interesting parallels. My meeting with the new staff had been arranged at their request so that they could discuss with me their difficulties, as newcomers to the school in the preceding term, in understanding the nature of my work with the staff and indeed in identifying themselves at all with the staff group about which I had written in my internal report of December.

Of the fifteen new staff members, nine came. Eight of these nine were women, and only one—Margaret Fisher—held senior office in the school. The only other senior person among the newcomers was David Sellick who did not come to the meeting. He was reported, about half-way through that meeting, as having wondered whether he 'ought' to come, evidently because the others, apart from Margaret Fisher, had no opportunity of working with me in smaller staff meetings (as he and she had in the senior staff meeting), being relatively junior colleagues, quite a number of them in their probationary year. His decision to stay out of the meeting, and Margaret Fisher's slight hesitation, expressed unconsciously, as it seemed, in her late arrival at it, suggested that there was a general uncertainty about where the boundary between 'experienced' and 'inexperienced' should be drawn, particularly within the group of new staff who were all equally inexperienced in the particular ways of this school. It seemed that the problem of joining a staff group was difficult to disentangle from the problem of being a probationary or relatively inexperienced teacher still coping with the task of joining the teaching profession.

Although the ostensible purpose of their meeting with me was to clarify the nature of my role in the school, the first real question about it that was asked—by Janet Roberts, who had convened the meeting—seemed to have more to do with the problem of their own identity, as a group of new staff members, in the staff group as a whole. As the discussion of my report got under way, it began to turn into something different. Increasingly I felt that I was being invited to respond to a rather seductive approach by shifting the focus of the discussion from their feelings about my report and about my behaviour in staff meetings to their feelings about their colleagues and about the ethos of the school. Gradually I began to feel that I was being offered a new role, as leader of this group of enlightened people who, if they could capture me and seduce me into doing with them the work that the head was having to do with the whole staff group, they (the newcomers) and I might together be able to solve not just their problems in joining the staff group but the difficulties that even the established staff were experiencing in this time of change and uncertainty.

These were the same new members of staff who in the autumn term, had presented their own anxieties so forcibly to Denys John that he had come to a standing committee meeting with a great deal of uncertainty about the effectiveness of his own leadership in the staff group. Now, face to face with these same people, I was being offered a picture of timid, inarticulate young members of staff who did not dare offer opinions, either in full staff meetings or in their subject departments, and who were overwhelmed by the difficulties of joining such an institution. Yet my own image of many of these newcomers, on the evidence of the contributions I had heard them make to staff discussions, was quite a different one. If the adult *envy* of the young was being projected by the staff group into the students, it seemed on the evidence—both of Denys John's experience in the autumn term and of mine in the spring term—that the adult *fear* of the young was being projected into the new staff. This fear that one might not be able to control pupils had as its counterpart the fear that one might not be able to communicate with colleagues about the problems. In fact both these fears were shared by established members of staff as, conversely, the skills attributed to the established staff were also present in the new staff. Both among the new staff and among the old staff there were some who took an active part in discussions and others who remained silent.

The students in training and the new members of staff appeared to share a need to perceive this school as somewhat uncertain about its objectives, implying that other schools they had known had been magically free from such uncertainties. Those who belonged to the school and had been part of its development for varying lengths of time must have had difficulty in separating the fantasies, both about Nailsea and about other schools, from the facts; for the newcomers, whether temporary or permanent, whether in training or already trained, were echoing strongly their own need to know whether Nailsea was improving or deteriorating. To tolerate the reality that development might contain elements of both kinds of change was evidently very difficult, particularly when parents sought for reassurances where none could be given or for simple answers to complex questions to which the answers were not yet known.

The school and its governing body

The anxieties of the staff about the opinions of the outside world found an unusual outlet during the summer of 1971, when serious consideration was given, over a period of some weeks, to the possibility of devising a way of involving the school governors in staff meetings, not merely at a social level, or with the notion of limiting them to observer status, but with a view to finding some way of working with them more directly so that governors could have more knowledge about the kinds of problems the staff were trying to solve. Although by Christmas no action had been taken to put this idea into effect, the suggestion did not seem, at the time, to be merely fanciful. Was it a natural sequel to the earlier series of meetings between the standing committee and individual colleagues? And if so, what comparable problems of preserving task boundaries while recognizing their permeability did the suggestion highlight?

In any school, the incorporation of governors in staff meetings would demand a great deal of hard thinking on both sides about what the roles of the governors might be in relation to the task of a staff meeting and how the headmaster, as chairman of the staff meeting, would relate his own role to the task, once the new dimension was introduced. It was, indeed, an indication of the complexity of such a proposal that the first reaction of some members of the staff, both in a small group and in the plenary session, was to take flight into the counter-suggestion that it might be more important to bring in the parents rather than the governors. It did not really take long, however, for everyone present to recognize that to invite 'parents' in general, who after all were over 2000 in number, would either be a completely safe, because unreal, invitation, or might lead to such haphazard and chaotic breaking of boundaries that the staff would no longer be able to conduct any serious business at all.

During the small-group phase of this meeting, one member of the standing committee had reminded his group, at a moment when it seemed that governors and parents were being perceived as alternative contenders for this new role, that part of the function of a governing body was to represent the parents of the school's pupils, since the people in the surrounding community who were most directly affected by the policies and actions of the school were the parents. The notion of inviting all sixteen governors to use this representative function through direct contact with the staff during some of their processes of policy-making seemed therefore to be, potentially, a very sophisticated proposal.

It soon became clear that if such a plan was to be carried through in a sophisticated way, time for thought, both in the staff group and in the governing body, would be needed to clarify how the task and the roles were to be defined, in terms of the different kinds of experience that would be relevant to such joint work, and in terms of the two inter-related phases of the new kind of staff meeting. Would the chairman of the governors, like the headmaster, tolerate the deprivation of not taking part in the small-group discussions? What criteria would he use in deciding with the other governors how they should be distributed between the groups? How would he and they decide between the greater personal involvement with the work of a specific group that would be likely to follow if each remained with the same group on every occasion and the possible advantages or detachment that might go with a roving commission? Would the governors, in talking through such issues, be able to face the conflicts **within** their own group, thus perhaps mirroring to some extent the problems of working with conflict that staff themselves had had to face?

The argument that I have tried to develop in the course of this book has now almost come full circle. I began by considering the school as an open system, an institution that could survive only by carrying out its function of taking in children from the environment, providing an educational programme for them and sending them out into the environment after so many years as more mature and informed persons than they had been on entry. I reported in Chapter III on the way in which the negotiations between myself, the head-master, the staff and the governors were conducted during the six months before my work with the school actually began. At that time, and later when my internal report to the staff was to be distributed to them and to the governors, there must have been considerable fear on the side of the school that the effects of such an undertaking as I envisaged might be to discredit the staff with the governors and, at the same time, a hope that if things became too uncomfortable the governors might step in and protect them by demanding that I be asked to withdraw.

By the summer of 1971—three years after my first approach to the school—the staff had evidence that the governors, in identifying themselves with a long-term task of this kind, had not found it necessary to take sides either with me against the staff or with the staff against me, even though many of them, in the special meeting that followed the issue of the 1969 report, had had challenging questions to ask me both about my motives for taking the role I did and about the evidence on which I was basing my conclusions.

By 1971, it seemed, the staff were able at least to contemplate exposing even more to the governors, at the very time when the effects of recent changes upon the image of the school in the neighbourhood were causing concern and uneasiness. What, then, is the role of a governing body of a school? Since they are neither the employers nor the clients of the school, the governors, as a group, must accept a lonely yet intensely involved role in relation to the institution. They have the power to hamper the school in new ventures; yet when they enter the school they enter it as visitors, normally by invitation. They must, it seems, be all things to all people. They are expected to be equally sympathetic to children, parents, teachers and pros-pective employers, and indeed to any people who happen to live in the school's immediate neighbourhood. They do not claim to have professional expertise in education; yet they may include in their number persons who do have and practise such expertise in other schools or in colleges or univer-sities. Their responsibility looks clear enough as it is spelled out in govern-ment circulars; yet it is in fact a very difficult one to define in operational terms.

In times of change and uncertainty, when the political balance of the employing body may be changing and when the social class structure of the school population may also be changing, the governing body may find that its major task is to offer to the headmaster and his staff, and indeed perhaps to a succession of heads and staff members, the stability of a containing framework within which change, innovation and adaptation, as well as the preservation of what continues to be valid and necessary, can go on. Yet, because individual governors do not stay on the governing body indefinitely, the burden of this task inevitably falls upon the chairman, who may have to hold a balance between conflicting views about what the tasks of the school should be, and, in order to support the head in what he is trying to do, may have to contain within himself the tensions and anxieties present in the neighbourhood about the new directions the school is taking. In the last resort—because the governors must make the well-being of the school's pupils their primary concern, rather than the preservation of the staff— they may have to recommend the dismissal of a teacher; and this decision, along with the conflicts surrounding it, will ultimately have to be taken by the chairman.

I am saying, then, that the governors have always to steer a difficult course between an over-zealous interference and a passive lack of concern. Active interest in the affairs of the school demands the capacity to enquire and take notice of evidence. But the staff, as the professional body responsible for carrying out the task of educating children, must feel that they have the trust of the governors to carry out that task to the best of their ability. To take responsibility as a governor, particularly when the person in that role is also a teacher in another educational institution, or a parent whose children are in the school, or an employer who might one day employ some of the school's pupils, requires a skill and sensitivity that can easily be underestimated. For the governors, who often seem to belong to an outdated concept of school administration, and who are generally perceived as fringe members of the institution, can in fact be very close to what we may call the heart-beat of the school.

New insights in relating to adolescents in a changing school culture

I cannot end this book without asking the question that any reader of it is likely to ask, and that the governors, in sanctioning the work we did, must often have asked themselves. Have we, in this network of roles and relation-ships, lost sight of the children for whom the whole system exists? I do not think so. For it is the needs of the children that have been at the centre of everything that has been discussed. I did not go into classrooms or workshops or laboratories, except on two occasions when I attended open days; and I attended these as a visitor and therefore primarily in a social role. During the first term of my work with the school I went to the meetings of the school council, and on one occasion talked with the headmaster and with the boy and girl presidents, for a few minutes, about the problems of making a school-wide council mean something to all its members, from the youngest who were still children to the oldest who were near-adult. Much later I attended a school operatic performance and a school concert. And on a few occasions, probably not more than three, I had lunch in the school dining-room and talked with children who happened to be sitting at the same table as myself. These were not occasions on which I could make any attempt to gather evidence about the extent to which the quality of staff-pupil relation-ships in the school was being affected, beneficially or adversely, by the work the staff were doing in the area of their own role relationships. Nor were such encounters meant to provide such evidence.

Yet I would not wish to imply that I had no evidence of any kind about the way in which teachers in this school related themselves to children. In an indirect way I felt that I had a great deal of evidence. Although I frequently heard people expressing anxiety about problems of control and although from time to time I would become aware of the name of a particular pupil who was causing trouble, I never heard flippant, destructive or despairing talk about any boy or girl in the school. There seemed to me, in fact, to be a marked absence of the kind of common-room gossip, hostile to children or merely contemptuous of them, which has pervaded some of the horror stories, comic or tragi-comic, published in various forms about secondary schools in recent years. What I did hear was serious, informed discussion about what needed to be done to help individual pupils or groups of pupils who were causing concern or anger or both. Such discussions might be between a tutor (or house head) and a section head, between all the tutors or house heads in a particular section, between the members of the standing committee.

On one occasion I attended a special meeting about one particular boy in the middle school whose problems of adjustment were causing concern both to fellow-pupils and to staff. This meeting was convened by the school counsellor, chaired (at her request) by the middle-school head, and attended by all those who had any teaching contact with the boy. At this meeting the boy's tutor, the head of his house and a number of people who taught him, including his P.E. teacher, pooled their experience and discussed in a highly sophisticated way the available evidence that might help them, in their various roles, to help the boy. This kind of recognition that problems required thought and concern, whether they were centred on individuals, on particular groups in the school or on the school as an institution within a local community, seemed to me to provide the kind of evidence we all needed. For they showed, repeatedly, that learning was more likely to be promoted if conflicts were exposed so that the reasons for the conflicts could be examined than if they were denied or concealed or superficially patched up. Four examples of this kind of insight may be appropriate ones with which to approach the end of this book, since the kind of authority problem they highlight must be familiar to all teachers.

The first was a case of bullying in the middle school; the second was the series of events that led to the abolition of uniform for upper-school pupils; the third was a case of incipient 'gang warfare' between a group of fourth-year boys and another group from a neighbouring village; and the fourth was a case of drug trafficking that involved a small handful of boys in the middle and upper schools and was at the time briefly reported in the local press.

The bullying centred on a knifing incident—not serious in its physical consequences but frightening in its implications. A third-year boy had been cornered in one of the house rooms after school by two other members of his tutor group. They had begun by teasing him in a fairly harmless way, dancing round him, one of them flourishing a pen-knife. Eventually the cornered boy, in trying to duck between his assailants to reach the door, received a slight jab in the arm from the pen-knife. Naturally enough the parents of the victim of this bullying with its unexpected (and probably accidental) climax, demanded that the boy be protected from further molestation of this kind by being transferred to another tutor group.

The impressive thing about this incident, as it was subsequently described to me, was that the tutor concerned made a quick decision to have the whole matter discussed in a fifty-minute tutorial meeting of the tutor group. In the course of this discussion two very significant things happened. Several of those who had been present when the knifing took place began to acknowledge spontaneously that they, as well as the two who had actually been doing the teasing, had been to blame, since they had all stood round and allowed the situation to become dangerous, perhaps letting the two attackers do something on their behalf. Furthermore, the victim himself, who had frequently been a target for mild bullying in that group, began dimly to recognize that he too, perhaps, had to ask himself some questions. Why was he so ready to accept this role of the boy who invited attack, partially seeking victimization? Why was it that, although he was quite a big boy physically, he had been so easily terrorized by the antics of the other two, who were in fact rather thin little boys and not at first sight at all physically intimidating?

Meanwhile, the head of the middle school was discussing with the parents of the victim the whole episode and the history of which it was a part, and trying to help them to perceive more clearly that a flight from that tutor group, in which already the children were being helped towards some valuable new insights about the nature of bullying as a group phenomenon, might merely lead to an escalation of the problem rather than help the boy himself to take his own step to move out of the role of ready victim into a more mature relationship with the other members of his group. In at least one other tutor group, during a period devoted to H.R. work, the incident was discussed in such a way that these children too were able to explore the idea that all of them had a personal responsibility towards one another as members of the group to exert influence to check the violence that could so easily spring up within it. In that other group one child said: 'We let bullying go on in our group too.' And the H.R. tutor to that group was the headmaster.

The events in the upper school, preceding and following the decision to abolish school uniform for sixth formers, have already been referred to earlier in this book, mainly in the context of the rising anxieties among the staff about the narrowness of the margin between liberalism and abdication. But they also had a very positive side. For the very fact that this testing out was going on, and the very fact that the sixth-form pupils, on their own initiative, were able to discuss the matter with the head of their section and subsequently, by setting up a delegation through the channels of their own sixth-form forum, to negotiate with the headmaster about it, was a sign of growth in the institution as a whole—a sign that there could be a confrontation between pupils and staff that was challenging yet not merely destructive. The outcome of the confrontation could thus be perceived as an agreement rather than a defeat of one side by the other, an agreement that placed on the pupils' shoulders part of the responsibility for whatever results might issue from the agreement as time went on.

My third example takes us outside the boundary of the school, both physically and sociologically, into a near-by roadway where a potentially dangerous situation was developing during one lunch hour between a group of fourth-year boys and another group of boys from outside the school. At about 1.30 a telephone call was put through to the deputy head, the headmaster being at that moment engaged with a visitor and due to leave within the next half-hour for a meeting in London. The caller—a local inhabitant—asked the deputy head whether he was aware that some Nailsea boys had gathered in a lane outside the school grounds and were preparing to engage in a gang fight with another group, said to be on their way to the scene from a neighbouring village; the Nailsea boys, he was told, were armed with improvised weapons. The deputy head, accompanied by the head of the middle school and a number of the male teaching staff, went to the scene and got the boys back inside the school. The other 'gang' was nowhere to be seen. The head of the middle school then called a meeting of all the fourth-year boys and, in the presence of the deputy head, talked to them about the possible consequences of what the boys out in the road had been doing. Between the appearance of the masters on the scene and the assembly in the school hall the weapons had vanished. The head of the middle school appealed to the assembled pupils, saying he hoped that anyone who knew where the weapons were would have enough courage to bring them in or ensure that they were put in his room within the next hour. In the meeting itself it was impossible to guess whether there would be any response whatever to this appeal. The boys maintained poker faces. But ten minutes later, a group of them, including some of those who were considered to be among the most difficult members of the fourth year, presented themselves in the middle-school head's room, admitted that they knew where the weapons were and undertook to go and fetch them. Twelve of the weapons were in fact turned in without protest, less than half an hour after the meeting in the school hall. By the time the headmaster left for London the incident was over. The appeal to reason and common sense in the presence of the whole of the age group concerned had succeeded where resort to punishment might well have failed, as indeed the mounting of an adult-directed search for the weapons—contemplated but rejected—might also have failed. The boys themselves, given the chance to make restitution, did so, at least in part. No-one could be certain, of course, that all the weapons had been handed over. The identity of the other 'gang' was never known to the staff. But the incident must undoubtedly have produced some learning about the nature both of the responsibility of adults towards the young and of the responsibility of young people towards each other.

Bullying, if handled sensitively, can be contained within the group and even be followed by valuable learning about inter-personal relationships. A demonstration of sixth-form power, if the staff recognize that the power exists, can be contained within the institution and may promote new insights into the problems of handling negotiations on behalf of others. Even gang warfare between members of one institution and a group from outside that institution may, if the adults can both control the outbreak and appeal, afterwards, to the law-abiding parts of the delinquent group, be halted before too much harm is done. But the first appearance in a school of drug-trafficking is doubly threatening because it brings the persons concerned into the region of criminality, and because it seems to involve a whole neighbourhood and mark the school as a target (or a source) of a deadly kind of infection.

When it was discovered that drugs had been brought into the school and passed to two boys in the middle school by an intermediary in the upper school, the headmaster had to make decisions about how to ensure that the disease could be halted, without the boys concerned being expelled and so pushed out beyond reach of any help the school might be able to give them. This time the school governors and the police, as well as all the parents, had to be notified immediately, both of the incident and of the measures that would be taken to guard against the possibility of any repetition. In many secondary schools expulsion of those involved, if they were over the age of fifteen, would have been regarded as inevitable. These boys were not expelled; nor was the threat of expulsion used in the circular letter to parents, although there was a warning that any pupil found in possession of drugs would immediately be suspended. When this was announced by the head in the senior staff meeting, which by chance was taking place on the very day the crisis broke, it was immediately obvious that even the threat of suspension was perceived by some staff members as inappropriate and unduly harsh, and that the headmaster was bound to find himself at the centre of conflicting pressures, both in the staff group and in the governing body, and no doubt also in his own mind. But again, what was impressive about the handling of the affair, as I perceived it, was that anxiety about the reputation of the school could be contained alongside a sense of responsibility towards the boys who had been involved, rather than allowed to erupt into a demand for punishment that would have ruled out any possibility of working at the problem with those who most needed help.

We have looked at a good many triangular situations in the course of this book, in the context of relationships between persons, in the context of relationships between groups within an institution and in the context of relationships between institutions. And we cannot think seriously about the task of management in a school without being aware, in many different situations, of the interacting roles of teachers, parents and governors, each with a strong sentient system that can very easily militate against that genuine cooperation that is needed to ensure that children get the education to which they all have the right. We are perhaps accustomed to thinking about dyadic (or two-fold) relationships, such as those between teachers and pupils, between subject teachers and tutors, between students and supervisors, between teachers and governors. But in fact it is often the triadic (or three-fold) relationships that are more crucial in the study of the quality of life and work in an institution. A teacher, in relating to pupils, must also be answerable to parents. A student, in relating to his college supervisor, must also be answerable to the school staff. A parent, in relating to teachers, must also be answerable to his children. A child, in relating to his tutor, must also be answerable to his subject teachers. A headmaster, in relating to the governing body of a school, must also be answerable to the parents. A governor, in relating to parents, must also be answerable to the staff of the school. And so we could go on, adding innumerable examples to this list.

In the last resort the staff of a school must be answerable to the pupils who leave them to enter the adult world. For once a pupil has left the school it is he who must assess it—not his parents who may or may not have tried to understand what school has meant to him, not the governors who have watched the policies of the school on his behalf, not the teachers who have taught him, tutored him and assessed him over the years. It is the pupil himself who must judge, as the years go on, the extent to which the school enabled him, when he was a boy, to grow up and discover himself. And the people who are least likely ever to know how his memories of it change over succeeding years are those who staffed the school while he was one of its pupils.

Epilogue

This book has been about the experiences of one school, perhaps of many schools. In a sense it can never be finished, since with every day or week that I continue to work at it, new events cry out to be recorded, new ideas are being discussed and new contingencies are arising that have to be met. For any member of staff who might say desperately to the headmaster: 'Don't change anything else!' there could be another who says: 'But we haven't really changed anything yet!' For any outsider who might say: 'That school is deteriorating', there could be another who says: 'I should like my children to go there'.

I am often asked whether Nailsea is a good school, and how I compare it with other schools. To the first question I can only reply: I do not know what 'good' means to one questioner as compared with another; but I do know that it is a school that has filled my thoughts and sustained my interest and concern for three and a half years. To the second question I can only reply: I do not know how it compares with other schools, since it is the only school that I have studied and worked with in this way. Such questions must be answered by every reader for himself, for every reader will bring to his study of the situations described here the shadows or the concrete realities of the schools he has known or heard of or read about; and in making judgements about the school that inhabits these pages, he will also be making judgements about those other schools.

KEY TO NAMES AND NUMBERS USED IN TEXT OR IN DIAGRAMS

1. Alphabetical list of names

Name	Number in diagrams	Role to which originally appointed	Date of appointment (Sept. unless otherwise stated)	Subsequent promotion or change of role	Date of promotion or change of role	Date of departure
FULL-TIME TEACHING STAFF						
Armitage, Dr P. T.	71	Head of Science	1968			1970
Atkinson, Dr W. P.	12	Head of Modern Languages	1961	Head of Languages Depart.	1971	
Bateman, Mrs J. E.	80	German (part-time 1964–9)	1969	Year Group Head	1971	
Bradbury, Mrs J. A.	13	German; Mistress i/c Girls' Welfare	1961	Senior Mistress	1962	
Burnham, M. W.	19	Head of English	1962	Master i/c Sixth Form Studies	1966	
				Head of Upper School Apr.	1969	
Castell, Miss D. C.	72	Mathematics	1968	Deputy to House Head	1970	
Chapman, Miss P. D.	58	House Head	1966	Year Group Head	1971	
Chapman, P. N.	37	Head of Physics Apr.	1964	House Head	1966	
Clarke, R. H.	59	Head of Remedial Education Apr.		Year Group Head	1971	
Ferguson, Mrs A. E.	46	Head of Home Economics Apr.	1966			
Fisher, Miss M. C.	81	Counsellor	1965			Died 1971
Frost, J. A.	48	Head of Music	1965	Year Group Head	1971	1970 (Dec.)

No.	Name	Subject	Year	Additional Position	Year	
74	Glover, Mrs A.	Art (part-time 1966–8)	1968			
75	Grist, R. B.	Head of Mathematics	1968			
6	Harbinson, J. A.	Head of Physical Education	1960	Head of Lower School	1963	1969
76	Jarratt, R. J.	General Subjects and Remedial	1968			
1	John, D. W.	Headmaster	1959			
62	Johnson, D.	Head of Physics Jan.	1967			1970
49	King, Mrs C. M.	History (part-time 1964–5)	1965			1969
24	London, Miss G. M.	Head of Biology	1963	Deputy to Head Upper School	1966	
				Organizer of Biology and Rural Science	1971	
21	Lloyd, G.	Head of Chemistry	1962			1970
65	Miller, R.	Head of Physical Education	1967			1970
50	Morris, G. R. J.	English	1965	Head of Library	1967	
				Head of Sixth Form General Studies	1969	
				Year Group Head	1971	
86	Moth, Miss S.	English	1969			
42	Osborn, P. G.	Head of Religious Education	1964	House Head	1966	
				Head of Humanities Dept.	1971	
52	Phillips, J. B.	Chemistry and Physics	1965	Deputy to House Head	1966	1971
				Head of Dep't of Creativity	1971	
27	Purvis, T.	Head of Art	1963	Deputy to Head Lower School	1967	
66	Redfern, Mrs S. M.	Mathematics	1967	Deputy to Head Upper School	1969	
29	Richardson, Mrs P. E.	French	1963	Organizer of European Studies	1971	1971
8	Ridgwell, C. A.	Technical Subjects	1960	Head of Technical Education	1963	
				Year Group Head	1971	
88	Roberts, Mrs J. M.	Science	1969	Organizer of Secondary Science Courses	1971	

Name	Number in diagrams	Role to which originally appointed	Date of appointment (Sept. unless otherwise stated)	Subsequent promotion or change of role	Date of promotion or change of role	Date of departure
Routley, C. W.	9	Latin	1960	Head of Classics	1964	
				Head of Resources	1971	
Sellick, M. D. L.	90	Head of Religious Education	1969			
Silk, D. I.	102	Music (part-time 1967–70)	1970			
Smith, L. S.	54	English	1965	Head of English	1967	1971
Smith, Mrs M. D.	77	Biology (Rural Studies)	1968	Deputy to Head Lower School	1969	
Sollars, Miss R. J.	34	Head of History Apr.	1964	Year Group Head	1971	1971
Thackeray, Miss P. J.	43	English	1964			1970
Thomas, W. R.	3	History	1959	Head of History and Religious Education	1963	1964 (Apr.)
Thomas, W. R. (returned)		Deputy Head Jan.	1968			
Tucker, Miss E. M.	78	Girls' Physical Education	1968			
Vanloo, C.	68	Director of Intermediate Studies	1967	Head Middle School Apr.	1969	
Vincent, B. G. C.	44	Biology	1964			1971
Walker, Miss C. M.	11	Mathematics	1960	House Head	1966	1971
Weyman, Mrs V. A.	91	Geography	1969	Assistant to Head of Dep't of Environment	1971	
White, G. A.	45	Head of Geography Jan.	1965	Head of Department of Environment	1971	
Williams, D. M.	56	Drama	1965	Deputy to House Head	1966	
PART-TIME TEACHING STAFF						
Bateman, Mrs J. E.	P17	German	1965	To full-time (80)	1969	

Name		Subject			To full-time	
Glover, Mrs A.	P22	Art		1966	To full-time (74)	1968
John, Mrs A. A.	P3	French		1962	To full-time (49)	1965
King, Mrs C. M.	P14	History		1964	To full-time (102)	1970
Silk, D. I.	P24	Music		1967		
NON-TEACHING STAFF						
Hawker, Mrs E.	S1	Secretary		1959	School Bursar Nov.	1966
Smith W. J.	T1	Head Technician	Nov.	1967	Head of Technical Services	1969

2. Initials coded against numbers used in diagrams.

No.	Initials	Year of appointment
1	DWJ	1959 (Nos. 1–4)
3	WRT	
6	JAH	
8	CAR	1960 (Nos. 5–11)
9	CWR	
11	CMW	
12	WPA	1961 (Nos. 12–18)
13	JAB	
19	MWB	1962 (Nos. 19–21)
21	GL	
24	GML	
27	TP	1963 (Nos. 22–34)
29	PER	
34	RJS	
35	SEB	
36	ATC	
37	PNC	
38	PJG	
40	HMJ	
42	PGO	1964 (Nos. 35–46)
43	PJT	
44	BGCV	
45	GAW	
46	AEF	
47	VCC	
48	JAF	
49	CMK	
50	GRJM	
52	JBP	
53	DAR	
54	LSS	1965 (Nos. 47–59)
55	PST	
56	DMW	
57	ERW	
58	PDC	
59	RHC	
62	DJ	1966 (Nos. 60–63)

No.	Initials	Year of appointment
65	RM	
66	SMR	1967 (Nos. 64–70)
67	HT	
68	CV	
71	PTA	
72	DCC	
73	BD	
74	AG (from part-time)	
75	RBG	1968 (Nos. 71–79)
76	RJJ	
77	MDS	
78	EMT	
79	MV	
80	JEB (from part-time)	
81	MCF	
86	SM	
88	JMR	1969 (Nos. 80–92)
90	MDLS	
91	VAW	
102	DIS (from part-time)	1970 (Nos. 93–105)

PART-TIME TEACHING STAFF

P3	AAJ	1962
P24	DIS (later 102)	1967

NON-TEACHING STAFF

S1	EH	1959
T1	WJS	1967

NOTE: Numbers in brackets indicate number of appointments in a particular year.

APPENDIX II

NUMBERS OF PUPILS IN SECTIONS AND HOUSES: 1965–71
(Number of tutors given in brackets)

Year	Lower School — Years I & II	Middle School					Upper School — Years VI, VII & VIII	Totals
		Year III	Year IV	Year V				
65–6	186 (7)	118 (4)	134 (5)	86 (4)			171 (12)	695
		House System: Years III & IV						
		B	G	R	Y			
66–7	297 (10)	67 (2)	63 (2)	28 (1)	63 (2)	114 (5)	164 (11)	796
		House System: Years III, IV & V						
		B	G	R	Y			
67–8	373 (13)	96 (3)	91 (4)	56 (2)	99 (3)		207 (13)	922
68–9	374 (13)	89 (3)	136 (5)	85 (3)	102 (3)		207 (13)	993
69–70	366 (13)	135 (4)	132 (4)	148 (5)	130 (4)		207 (13)	1118
70–71	414 (10)	146 (4)	159 (5)	153 (5)	161 (5)		224 (13)	1257

Bibliography

Bazalgette, J. L. (1971), *Freedom, Authority and the Young Adult*, Pitmans.

Bion, W. R. (1961), *Experiences in Groups*, Tavistock Publications.

Bion, W. R. (1962), *Learning from Experience*, Heinemann.

Bion, W. R. (1963), *Elements of Psycho-Analysis*, Heinemann.

Bion, W. R. (1965), *Transformations*, Heinemann.

Bion, W. R. (1970), *Attention and Interpretation*, Tavistock Publications.

Gosling, R., Miller, D. H., Turquet, P. M. and Woodhouse, D. L. (1967), *The Use of Small Groups in Training*, Codicote Press.

Grainger, A. J. (1970), *The Bullring: A Classroom Experiment in Moral Education*, Pergamon Press.

Guntrip, H. (1961), *Personality Structure and Human Interaction*, Hogarth Press.

Guntrip, H. (1971), *Psychoanalytic Theory, Therapy and the Self*, Hogarth Press.

Jaques, E. (1951), *The Changing Culture of a Factory*, Tavistock Publications.

Jaques, E. (1970), *Work, Creativity and Social Justice*, Heinemann.

Klein, M. (1963), 'Our Adult World and its Roots in Infancy', in *Our Adult World and Other Essays*, Heinemann.

Lacey, C. (1970), *Hightown Grammar. The School as a Social System*, Manchester University Press.

Miller, E. J. (1959), 'Technology, Territory and Time: The Internal differentiation of complex production systems', *Human Relations*, 12: 243–72.

Miller, E. J. and Rice, A. K. (1967), *Systems of Organization*, Tavistock Publications.

Palmer, B. W. M., 'Thinking about Thought': an Introduction to theories published by W. R. Bion since 'Experiences in Groups' based on a paper presented at the Forum on Behavioural Studies, 28 June 1971, Grubb Institute of Behavioural Studies.

Phenix, P. H. (1964), *Realms of Meaning*, McGraw Hill.

Rice, A. K. (1963), *The Enterprise and its Environment*, Tavistock Publications.

Rice, A. K. (1965), *Learning for Leadership: Inter-personal and Inter-group Relations*, Tavistock Publications.

Rice, A. K. (1970), *The Modern University: A Model Organization*, Tavistock Publications.

Rice, A. K. (1969), 'Individual, Group and Intergroup Processes', *Human Relations*, 22: 6: 565–84.

Richardson, E. (1967), *The Environment of Learning*, Nelson. Reprinted, Weybright and Talley, 1968. Reprinted, Heinemann, 1973.

Richardson, E. (1967), *Group Study for Teachers*, Routledge and Kegan Paul.

Richardson, E. (1967), 'Projects, Pupils and Teachers: reflections on a school-practice term', *The New Era*, 48: 8: 159–66.

Richardson, E. (1969), 'The staff group and its problems of authority and shared responsibility', *The New Era*, 50: 10: 241–8.

Sofer, C. (1961), *The Organization from within*, Tavistock Publications.

Sofer, C. and Hutton, G. (1958), *New Ways in Management Training*, Tavistock Publications.

Turquet, P. M. (1974), 'Threats to Identity in the Large Group: A study in the Phenomenology of the Individual's Experience in Groups', in Miller, E. J. (ed.), *Task and Organization* (in press).

Index

361